THE FAMILY
Handyman®

DIY
PROJECTS
UNDER
$200

Editorial and Production Team
Vern Johnson, Peggy McDermott, Rick Muscoplat,
Marcia Roepke, Mary Schwender

Photography and Illustrations
Ron Chamberlain, Tom Fenenga, Bruce Kieffer, Mike Krivit,
Don Mannes, Ramon Moreno, Shawn Nielsen, Doug Oudekerk,
Frank Rohrbach III, Eugene Thompson, Bill Zuehlke

Text, photography and illustrations for *DIY Projects Under
$200* are based on articles previously published in *The Family
Handyman* magazine (2915 Commers Dr., Suite 700, Eagan, MN
55121, familyhandyman.com). For information on advertising in
The Family Handyman magazine, call (646) 293-6150.

ISBN: 978-1-62145-283-6

The Family Handyman
Editor in Chief   Ken Collier
Project Editor   Eric Smith
Design & Layout   Diana Boger, Teresa Marrone
Senior Editors   Travis Larson, Gary Wentz
Associate Editor   Jeff Gorton
Administrative Manager   Alice Garrett
Senior Copy Editor   Donna Bierbach
VP, Group Publisher   Russell S. Ellis

Published by Home Service Publications, Inc.,
a subsidiary of The Reader's Digest Association, Inc.

PRINTED IN CHINA

1 2 3 4 5 6 7 8 9 10

A Note to Our Readers
All do-it-yourself activities involve a degree of risk. Skills,
materials, tools and site conditions vary widely. Although the
editors have made every effort to ensure accuracy, the reader
remains responsible for the selection and use of tools, materials
and methods. Always obey local codes and laws, follow
manufacturer instructions and observe safety precautions.

Contents

1 KITCHEN & BATH

2 STORAGE & ORGANIZING

3 GARAGE UPGRADES

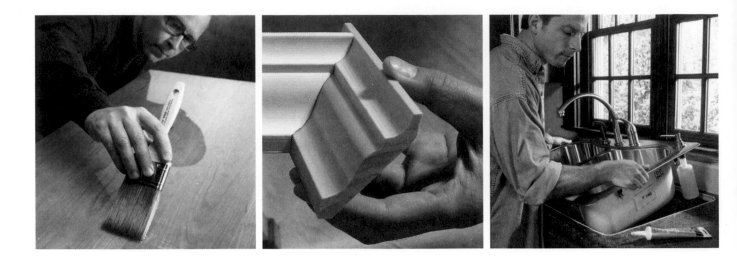

4 WOODWORKING & CARPENTRY

5 PAINTING & FINISHING

6 ELECTRICAL & PLUMBING

7 YARD & GARDEN

8 WORKSHOP PROJECTS

Chapter One

KITCHEN & BATH

Weekend bath remodel

Transform your bathroom with a larger mirror and better lighting

You don't have to gut a bathroom to make the room feel fresh, bright and inviting and improve the storage. If your sink, tile and shower are still in good shape, then handsome light fixtures, a stylish mirror and a new medicine cabinet may be all you need to revitalize the space. These upgrades will cost only a fraction of a total redo, and you can install them yourself in one weekend.

In this article, we'll show you how to remove a medicine cabinet and overhead lights and replace them with a big mirror and wall lights (sconces) on each side. You'll get two big benefits: The larger

mirror will make your bathroom seem larger, and the two sconces will be much more effective than one light over the mirror. They give you an even light, without deep shadows, much like the "makeup lights" used by actors and models.

The drawback of this project is that

you'll have to find a place for the items that were stored in the medicine cabinet. We installed a small glass shelf for the everyday items, and a shallow cabinet on the other side of the room for infrequently used items.

This project doesn't require special carpentry skills or tools, but you should have basic wiring experience. Of course, any time you open a wall, you may find unexpected pipes, electrical cables or framing. If you can't work around them, hire a pro to propose a solution. And before getting started, apply for an electrical permit so that an inspector will check your work. Talk to your inspector about the timing of the inspection. Typically it will occur after the wiring is done but before the wall is repaired, and possibly again after the fixtures are installed.

Select your mirror

Mirrors come in many sizes, so before you run off to the store, map your wall (Photo 1). The goal is to select a mirror size that'll not only look good but also leave ample room for the light sconces. Use a stud finder to locate all the framing within the wall and then measure the distances from the center of the sink to neighboring walls or other cabinets.

Measure from a centerline over the sink and then mark all the framing and clearances on a drawing. Next, mark the distances from the neighboring studs to the centerline. That'll help you position the new electrical boxes in the open stud spaces.

When you shop for a mirror, your goal is to pick the widest one that'll fit in the space above the sink, while making sure the light fixtures fit into the open stud spaces, not on top of a stud. We show one of many mirror-mounting systems, which vary widely. Most mirrors come with the hardware and instructions for simple installation.

Select your light fixtures

Choosing your sconces calls for some thought. Avoid colored globes because they'll cast less light and affect skin tones. We recommend white frosted glass to lessen the glare of the bulbs. If good makeup lighting is important, select fixtures that are rated for 100-watt bulbs. Then replace the existing light switch with a dimmer switch so you can set the lighting intensity to fit your needs (and mood!).

Remove the old medicine cabinet and light

Before you tear into the wall, plug the sink drain to keep fasteners and debris from going down. Pull the old medicine cabinet free of the wall by removing the screws that hold the cabinet sides to the framing (Photo 2). Those screws should be obvious when you open the door. Sometimes you'll need to cut through caulk between the drywall and the cabinet frame with a utility knife. Then turn off the circuit breaker that powers the existing light and remove the light fixture.

Fixtures vary, but most have a finished cover that's held on with thumbnuts. Remove the thumbnuts to access the mounting bracket screws that hold it to the wall (Photo 3). Once you have access to the wiring, check it with a noncontact voltage tester to make sure the power is off. Then disconnect the wire connectors and work the wires through the bracket as you pull the fixture mount

1 **Mark out the wall. Determine stud locations, then make a sketch of the wall, marking the sink center and studs. Use the stud locations to plan the size of your mirror; the lights should fall between, not on, the studs.**

2 **Remove the medicine cabinet. Back out the screws inside the cabinet, tape the doors closed and lift the cabinet out of the wall.**

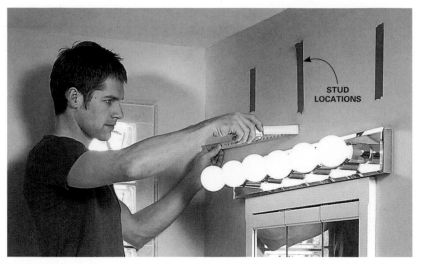

3 **Remove the light bar. Remove the cover, disconnect the wires, and then unscrew the mounting plate from the wall. Make sure the power is off.**

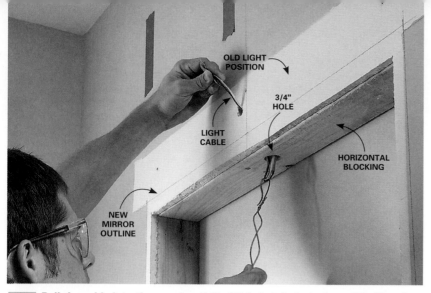

4 **Pull the cable into the opening.** Drill a 3/4-in. hole in the horizontal blocking, then fish the cable into the wall opening using a coat hanger or stiff wire. Install 2x4 backing for new drywall (see Photo 6).

OLD LIGHT POSITION

3/4" HOLE

LIGHT CABLE

HORIZONTAL BLOCKING

NEW MIRROR OUTLINE

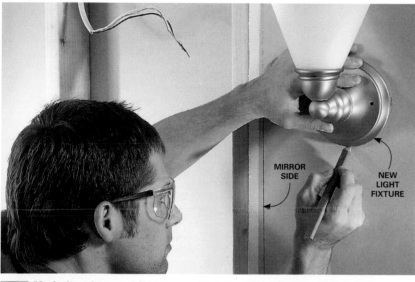

5 **Mark the mirror and first fixture.** First, draw the edges of the mirror, making them level and at a pleasing height. Trace around the base of the first sconce.

MIRROR SIDE

NEW LIGHT FIXTURE

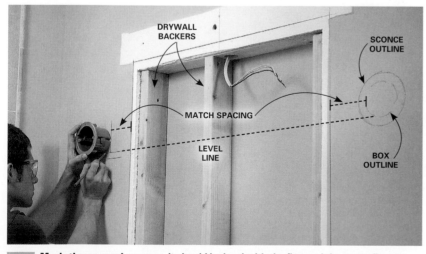

6 **Mark the second sconce.** It should be level with the first and the same distance from the mirror edge. Trace the outline of a remodeling box inside the sconce outline and cut out the box hole.

DRYWALL BACKERS

SCONCE OUTLINE

MATCH SPACING

LEVEL LINE

BOX OUTLINE

free of the wall. If there's a cable clamp at the back of the fixture, loosen that first.

Mark the new mirror and sconce locations

With the old cabinet removed, mark the new mirror location (Photo 5). Use a level to mark the center of the sink above the opening. Center the mirror in place and ask family members to vote on the best height. (Some mirrors come with instructions that include recommended heights or even templates to help with placement.) After the position is decided, outline the mirror on the wall. Use those marks to help position one of the sconces. Then trace around the base 65 to 75 in. from the floor (Photo 5). Or simply hold the sconce up and adjust it up and down until you find a pleasing position.

Center a remodeling box in the circle and trace around it. Then position the box on the other side to match the first (Photo 6), leveling across to mark the bottom and measuring from the mirror edges to mark one side. If this position falls over a stud, readjust both boxes. Draw the second remodeling box hole and cut out both openings with a drywall saw. Push the boxes into the holes as far as you can and mark the shoulders that surround the flip-out clamps (Photo 7). Pull out the boxes and cut out those areas as well, testing and recutting as necessary until they'll slip into the holes. You want them to fit tightly for maximum sconce support. Then set the boxes aside for now.

Wire the boxes

Let the cable hang while you nail in the drywall backing (Photo 6), then nail a round junction box to the center framing and feed the existing power cable into the box. Drill 1/2-in. holes through the middle of the framing and run the new cables through the sconce holes. Wherever

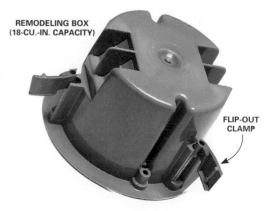

REMODELING BOX (18-CU.-IN. CAPACITY)

FLIP-OUT CLAMP

Getting power to the sconce lights

In most cases, you can use the same cable that fed the overhead light to supply power to the new sconces. But the cable is rarely long enough to reach either sconce directly. That's why we suggest running the existing cable to a new junction box positioned close to the old light but hidden behind the mirror. From there you can feed two new cables to both new sconce boxes.

The existing cable to the light fixture usually leads from the wall switch up into and across the ceiling and then down through the framing above the old light. To find out if that's your situation, drill a 3/4-in. hole through the 2x4 at the top of the medicine cabinet recess and try to pull the cable into the opening (Photo 4). If there's enough cable to reach a new junction box, you can proceed as we show in the photos. However, according to the electrical code, the box must remain "accessible." If the box is behind the mirror, you have to fasten the mirror in such a way that you can easily remove it.

There are three alternatives for handling the junction box:

1. If the cable comes from an accessible attic above, pull the wire up into that space and mount a covered junction box in the attic.

2. If the cable comes from above and is too short or the space above is inaccessible, install a new junction box at the old fixture location and cover it with a decorative cover plate painted to match the wall.

3. If the cable comes through the wall studs to the old fixture, pull it back and run it to the nearest sconce box. Then run a second cable from that box to the sconce box on the opposite side.

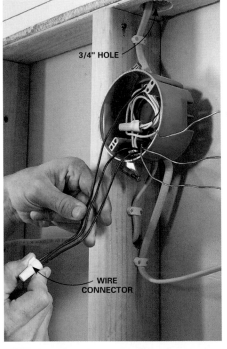

DECORATIVE COVER PLATE

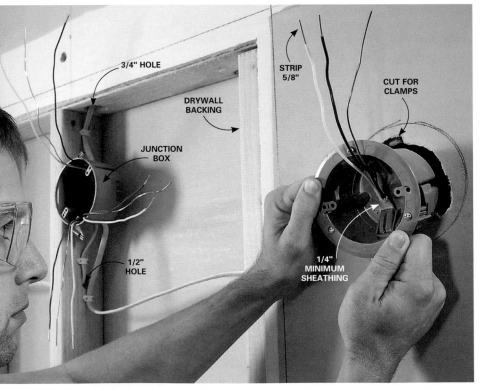

3/4" HOLE

DRYWALL BACKING

JUNCTION BOX

1/2" HOLE

STRIP 5/8"

CUT FOR CLAMPS

1/4" MINIMUM SHEATHING

3/4" HOLE

WIRE CONNECTOR

7 **Install and wire the boxes.** Nail the junction box and run the existing cable to it. Then run cable to the remodeling boxes used for the sconces and tighten them in place.

8 **Connect the wires.** Connect the new cable to the existing cable, black to black, white to white, and ground to ground. Screw a connector onto the exposed wires and tuck the wires into the boxes.

cables run into a box, strip off 8 in. of sheathing and strip 5/8 in. of the insulation from the ends of the wires (Photo 7). Then slip the cables through the clamps at the back of the boxes until at least 1/4 in. of sheathing penetrates the boxes.

Join the black (hots), white (neutrals), and bare or green ground wires as we show. In the sconce boxes, protect the ends of the wires with wire connectors and fold the wires into the boxes. Now you can hang drywall in the hole, tape the joints and sand and repaint the wall (Photo 9). Finally, mount the lights following the manufacturer's instructions (Photo 10).

Hang the mirror

Mirrors have a variety of mounting systems. The manufacturers supply directions and often even a template to help position the wall fasteners accurately. Work off your centerline and make sure the mirror is level (or plumb). We highly recommend that you discard the plastic drywall anchors that come with some units and replace them with screw-in anchors for a safer, stronger mounting system. You'll find these anchors at any home center or hardware store.

9 **Patch the drywall.** After the inspector has approved the wiring, patch the drywall, tape the seams and sand the joints. Repaint the entire wall.

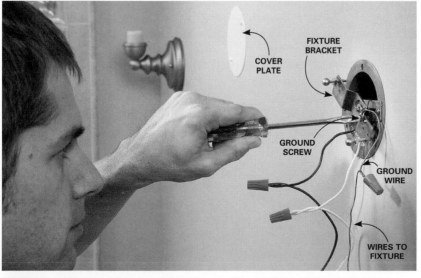

COVER PLATE

FIXTURE BRACKET

GROUND SCREW

GROUND WIRE

WIRES TO FIXTURE

10 **Mount the light fixtures.** Attach the mounting bracket to the box and attach the ground wire to the grounding screw. Then connect the wires as shown and mount the fixture.

MOUNTING SCREW

11 **Hang the mirror.** Hang the mirror using wall anchors. You must be able to easily remove the mirror to access the cover plate.

Mosaic tile backsplash

Nothing packs more style per square inch than mosaic tile. So if your kitchen's got the blahs, give it a quick infusion of pizzazz with a tile backsplash. Because the small tiles are mounted on 12 x 12-in. sheets, installation is fast. You can install the tile on Saturday and then grout it on Sunday morning.

Professionals charge about $20 per sq. ft. for installing the tile (plus materials), so you'll save $20 for every sheet you install yourself. The sheets cost $5 to more than $20 per sq. ft. at home centers and tile stores.

The total cost for this backsplash was about $200. The sheets of tile shown cost $10 apiece plus adhesive and grout. For an 8-ft. backsplash, you could save about $45 by using a less expensive tile.

Shown here are slate tiles, which sometimes crumble when you cut them. Other types of mosaic tile, especially ceramic tiles, are easier to cut.

Here you'll learn how to install the tile sheets. You'll need basic tile tools, available at home centers and tile stores, including

METALLIC   GLASS

Mosaic tile sheets make it easy to achieve a great backsplash. Layout is a cinch— you can simply cut the mesh backing on the sheets to fit the tile along counters and cabinets. In fact, the hardest part of this or any other tiling project may be choosing the look—the tiles come in a variety of shapes and materials, and many sheets have glass or metallic tiles built in for accents. To add to your options, strips of 4 x 12-in. tiles are available for borders. So, you can match the existing look of your kitchen—or try something new!

VENT HOOD

TAPE

GAP BETWEEN TAPE AND WALL

LEDGER BOARD

1 Mark a centerline between the upper cabinets so the tiles will be centered under the vent hood. Screw a ledger board to the wall to support the tile.

3/16" TROWEL

CENTERLINE

OUTLET EXTENDER

MASTIC

2 Spread a thin layer of mastic adhesive on the wall, starting at the centerline. Spread just enough adhesive for two or three sheets at a time so the adhesive doesn't dry before you set the tile.

a 3/16-in. trowel and a grout float. You'll also need mastic adhesive, grout and grout sealer. You can rent a wet saw to cut the tiles.

Prepare the walls

Before installing the tile, clean up any grease splatters on the wall (mastic won't adhere to grease). Wipe the stains with a sponge dipped in a mixture of water and mild dishwashing liquid. If you have a lot of stains or they won't come off, wipe on a paint deglosser with a lint-free cloth or abrasive pad so the mastic will adhere. Deglosser is available at paint stores and home centers.

Then mask off the countertops and any upper cabinets that will have tile installed along the side. Leave a 1/4-in. gap between the wall and the tape for the tile (Photo 1). Cover the countertops with newspaper or a drop cloth.

Turn off power to the outlets in the wall and remove the cover plates. Make sure the power is off with a noncontact voltage detector (sold at home centers). Place outlet extenders (sold at home centers) in the outlet boxes. The National Electrical Code requires extenders when the boxes are more than 1/4 in. behind the wall surface. It's easier to put in extenders now and cut tile to

fit around them than to add them later if the tile opening isn't big enough. Set the extenders in place as a guide for placing the tile. You'll remove them later for grouting.

On the wall that backs your range, measure down from the top of the countertop backsplash a distance that's equal to three or four full rows of tile (to avoid cutting the tile) and make a mark. Screw a scrap piece of wood (the ledger board) to the wall at the mark between the cabinets.

The area between the range and the vent hood is usually the largest space on the wall—and certainly the most seen by the cooks in the house—so it'll serve as your starting point for installing the tile. Make a centerline on the wall halfway between the cabinets and under the vent hood (Photo 1). Measure from the centerline to the cabinets. If you'll have to cut tile to fit, move the centerline slightly so you'll only have to cut the mesh backing (at least on one side).

Install and seal the tile

Using a 3/16-in. trowel, scoop some mastic adhesive out of the tub and put it on the wall (no technique involved here!). Spread the mastic along the centerline, cutting in along the ledger board,

3 Tap the tile into the mastic with a wood scrap and a rubber mallet. Stand back, look at the tiles and straighten any crooked ones.

4 Cut tile sheets to the nearest full row to fit around outlets, then fill the gaps with tiles cut on a wet saw.

vent hood and upper cabinets (Photo 2). Then use broad strokes to fill in the middle. Hold the trowel at a 45-degree angle to the wall to spread the mastic thin—you should be able to see the layout lines where the points of the trowel touch the wall. Have a water bucket and sponge on hand to keep the trowel clean. Whenever the mastic starts to harden on the trowel, wipe it off with the wet sponge.

Place plastic tile spacers on the ledger board and countertop. This leaves a gap so the tiles don't sit directly on the countertop (you'll caulk the gap later).

Align the first tile sheet with the centerline, directly over the spacers. Press it onto the wall with your hand. If the sheet slides around and mastic comes through the joint lines, you're applying the mastic too thick (remove the sheet, scrape off some mastic and retrowel). Scrape out any mastic in the joints with a utility knife.

Eyeball a 1/16-in. joint between sheets of tile (you don't need spacers). After every two or three installed sheets, tap them into the mastic with a board and rubber mallet (Photo 3).

If tiles fall off the sheets, dab a little mastic on the back

and stick them right back in place. The sheets aren't perfectly square, so you may need to move individual tiles to keep joints lined up. Move the tiles with your fingers or by sticking a utility knife blade in the joint and turning the blade. If an entire sheet is crooked, place a grout float over the tile and move the sheet. You'll have about 20 minutes after installing the tile to fine-tune it.

If you're lucky, you can fit the tile sheets under upper cabinets and around outlets by cutting the mesh backing with a utility knife. If not, you'll have to cut the tile with a wet saw. Nippers and grinders cause the slate tiles to shatter or crumble, although you can use these tools on ceramic tile.

Slice the backing to the nearest full row of tile, install the sheet around the outlet or next to the cabinet, then cut tiles with a wet saw to fill the gaps (Photo 4). Cut the tiles while they're attached to the sheet. Individual tiles are too small to cut (the blade can send them flying!).

Let the tile sit for at least 30 minutes, then apply a grout sealer if you're using natural stone (like slate) or unglazed quarry tile. The sealer keeps the grout from sticking to the tile (it's not

5 Force grout into the joints with a float. Scrape off excess grout by moving the float diagonally across the tile.

DULL SIDE

6 Rake the grout out of the joints at inside corners and along the bottom with a utility knife so you can fill them with caulk. Keep the dull side of the blade along the countertop.

needed for nonporous tiles such as ceramic). Pour the sealer on a sponge, then wipe on just enough to dampen the tiles.

Grout and clean the tile

Wait 24 hours after installing the tile to add the grout. Use a premium grout that has a consistent color and resists stain. Since the backsplash will be subject to splatters and stains from cooking and food prep, spend the extra money for a premium grout. You can find it at home centers or tile stores. Use unsanded grout for tile with gaps of 1/8 in. or less, and sanded grout if the gaps are more than 1/8 in.

Mix the grout with water until it reaches mashed potato consistency, then put some on the wall with a grout float. Work the grout into the joints by moving the float diagonally over the tiles (Photo 5). Hold the grout float at a 45-degree angle to the tile. Scrape off excess grout with the float after the joints are filled.

Ten minutes after grouting, wipe the grout off the surface of the tiles with a damp sponge. If the grout pulls out of the joints, wait another 10 minutes for it to harden. Continually rinse the

sponge in a bucket of water and wipe the tiles until they're clean.

These slate tiles have a lot of crevices that retain grout. While most of the grout comes off the tiles with the wet sponge, some won't. Most pro installers leave some grout in slate and other rough-surface tile—it's just part of the deal with some types of natural stone. But if you want the tile completely clean, remove the grout from individual tiles with a toothbrush.

After cleaning the wall, use a utility knife to rake the grout out of the joints along the bottom of the backsplash and in the inside corners (Photo 6). These expansion joints allow the wall to move without cracking the grout.

Two hours after grouting, wipe the haze off the tiles with microfiber cloths. Then caulk the expansion joints with latex caulk. Use a colored caulk that closely matches the grout (available at tile stores).

After seven days, sponge on a grout sealer to protect the grout against stains.

That's it! Now every time your family and friends gather in your kitchen, they'll be impressed with your custom backsplash.

Kitchen cabinet rollouts

Base cabinets have the least convenient storage space in the entire kitchen. Rollouts solve that problem. They make organizing and accessing your cabinet contents back-friendly and frustration free.

If you're stuck with cabinets without rollouts, don't despair. Here you'll learn how to retrofit nearly any base cabinet with rollouts that'll work as well as or better than any factory-built units.

It's really very easy. Once you take measurements, you can build the rollout drawer (Photos 2 – 6), its "carrier" (Photos 7 – 9), and attach the drawer slides (Photos 6 and 7), all in your shop. Mounting the unit in the cabinet is simple (Photos 10 – 12).

You'll also learn how to construct a special rollout for recycling or trash (Photos 14 – 15).

The project will go faster if you have a table saw and miter saw to cut out all the pieces. A circular saw and cutting guide will work too; it'll just take a little longer. You can build a pair of rollouts in a Saturday morning.

What wood products to buy

These rollout drawers are made entirely of 1/2-in. Baltic birch plywood. Baltic birch is favored by cabinetmakers because it's "void free," meaning that the thin veneers of the plywood core are solid wood. Therefore sanded edges will look smooth and

attractive. If your local home center doesn't stock Baltic birch, find it at any hardwood specialty store.

If you choose, you can make the sides of the rollout drawers from any 1x4 solid wood that matches your cabinets and then finish to match (use plywood for the bases). But if you use 3/4-in. material for the sides, subtract 3 in. from the opening to size the rollout (not 2-1/2 in., as described in Photo 2 and Figure A).

The drawer carriers (Figure A) are made from pine 1x4s for the sides (Photo 7) and 1/4-in. MDF (medium-density fiberboard) for the bottoms (Photo 9). The MDF keeps the drawer bottom spaced properly while you shim and attach it to the cabinet sides. It can be removed and reused for other carriers after installation. If MDF isn't available, substitute any other 1/4-in. hardboard or plywood.

Side-mounted slides are the best choice among drawer slide options. Their ball-bearing mechanisms and precise fit make for smooth-operating drawers that hold 90 lbs. or more. Shown here are 22-in. full-extension side-mount drawer slides that have a 90-lb. weight rating. That means they'll be sturdy enough even for a drawer full of canned goods. Full-extension slides allow the rollout to extend completely past the cabinet front so you can access all the contents. You can find slides at any home center or well-stocked hardware store.

Measure carefully before you build

Nearly all standard base cabinets are 23-1/4 in. deep from the inside of the face frame (Photo 1) to the back of the cabinet. So in most cases, 22-in.-long rollout drawer and carrier sides will clear with room to spare. Check your cabinets to make sure that 22-in. rollouts will work. If you have shallower cabinets, subtract whatever is necessary when you build your rollouts and their carriers (see Figure A).

Then measure the cabinet width. The drawer has to clear the narrowest part of the opening (Photo 1). When taking this measurement, include hinges that protrude into the opening, the edge of the door attached to the hinges, and even the doors that won't open completely because they hit nearby appliances or other cabinets. Plan on making the drawer front and rear parts 2-1/2 in. shorter than the opening (Figure A).

Shown here are drawers with 3-1/2-in.-high sides, but you can customize your own. Plan on higher sides for lightweight plastic storage

1 Open the cabinet doors to their widest point and measure the narrowest part of the cabinet opening (usually at the hinges).

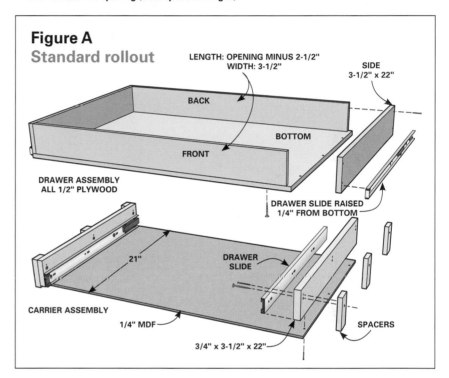

Figure A
Standard rollout

LENGTH: OPENING MINUS 2-1/2"
WIDTH: 3-1/2"

BACK

SIDE
3-1/2" x 22"

BOTTOM

FRONT

DRAWER ASSEMBLY
ALL 1/2" PLYWOOD

DRAWER SLIDE RAISED
1/4" FROM BOTTOM

DRAWER
SLIDE

21"

CARRIER ASSEMBLY

1/4" MDF

3/4" x 3-1/2" x 22"

SPACERS

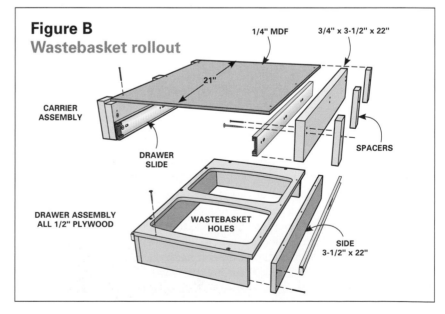

Figure B
Wastebasket rollout

1/4" MDF

3/4" x 3-1/2" x 22"

21"

CARRIER
ASSEMBLY

DRAWER
SLIDE

SPACERS

DRAWER ASSEMBLY
ALL 1/2" PLYWOOD

WASTEBASKET
HOLES

SIDE
3-1/2" x 22"

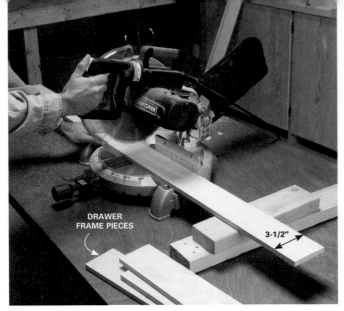

2 Rip 1/2-in. plywood down to 3-1/2 in. wide and cut two 22-in. lengths (drawer sides) and two more to the measured width minus 2-1/2 in. (drawer front and back; Figure A).

DRAWER FRAME PIECES

3-1/2"

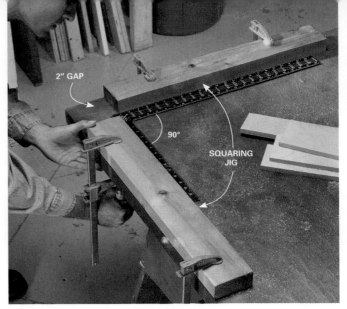

3 Clamp or screw two straight 24-in. 2x4s to the corner of a flat surface to use as a squaring jig. Use a carpenter's square to ensure squareness. Leave a 2-in. gap at the corner.

2" GAP

90°

SQUARING JIG

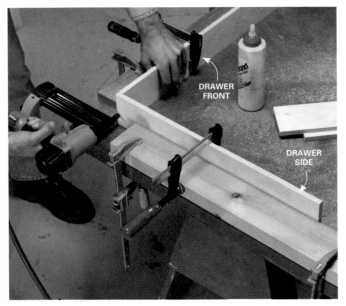

4 Spread wood glue on the ends and clamp a drawer side and front in place, then pin the corner together with three 1-1/4-in. brads. Repeat for the other three corners.

DRAWER FRONT

DRAWER SIDE

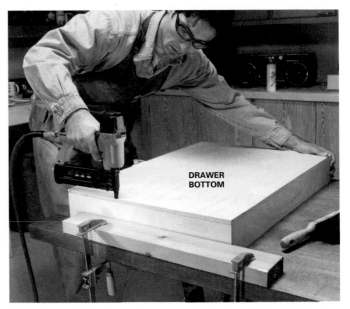

5 Cut a 1/2-in. plywood bottom to size. Apply a thin bead of glue to the bottom edges, and nail one edge of the plywood flush with a side, spacing nails every 4 in. Then push the frame against the jig to square it and nail the other three edges.

DRAWER BOTTOM

containers or other tall or tippy items, and lower sides for stable, heavier items like small appliances.

Drawer slides aren't as confusing as they may seem

At first glance, drawer slides are pretty hard to figure out, but after you install one set, you'll be an expert. They're sold in pairs and each of the pairs has two parts. The "drawer part" attaches to the rollout while the "cabinet part" attaches to the carrier. To separate them for mounting, slide them out to full length and then push, pull or depress a plastic release to separate the two parts. The cabinet part, which always encloses the drawer part, is the larger of the two, and the mounting screw hole locations will

be shown in the directions. (Screws are included with the drawer slides.) The oversized holes allow for some adjustment, but if you follow the instructions, you shouldn't have to fuss with fine-tuning later. When mounting the slides, you should make sure to hold them flush with the front of the rollout drawer and carrier sides (Photos 6 and 7). The front of the drawer part usually has a bent metal stop that faces the front of the drawer.

Assembling parts and finishing the rollouts

It's important to build the rollout drawers perfectly square for them to operate properly. Photos 3 and 4 show a simple squaring jig that you can clamp to a corner of any workbench to help. Use the jig to

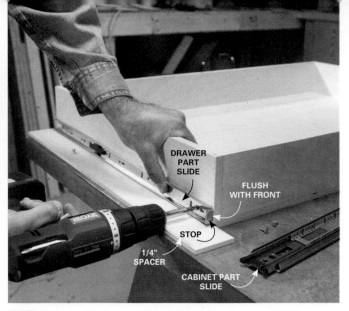

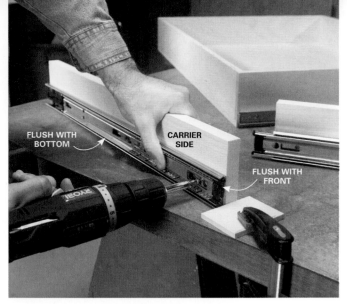

6 Separate the drawer slides and space the drawer part 1/4 in. up from the bottom. Hold it flush to the front and screw it to the rollout side.

7 Mount the carrier part of the drawer slide flush with the bottom and front of the carrier sides.

Labels on image 3: DRAWER PART SLIDE, FLUSH WITH FRONT, STOP, 1/4" SPACER, CABINET PART SLIDE

Labels on image 4: FLUSH WITH BOTTOM, CARRIER SIDE, FLUSH WITH FRONT

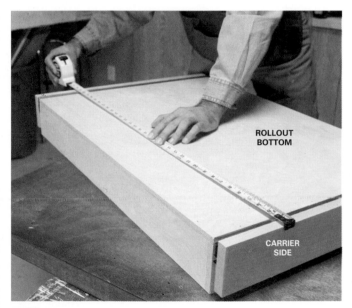

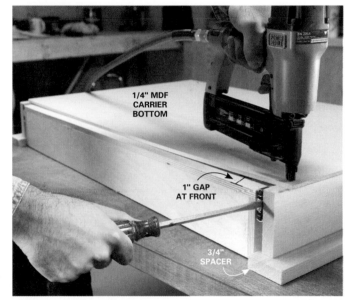

8 Slide the drawer and carrier sides together and measure the carrier width. Cut 1/4-in. MDF to that width and 1 in. less than the carrier depth (usually 21 in.).

9 Rest the carrier assembly on 3/4-in.-thick spacers, pull the carrier sides slightly away from the drawer, then nail on the carrier bottom (no glue).

Labels on image 1: ROLLOUT BOTTOM, CARRIER SIDE

Labels on image 2: 1/4" MDF CARRIER BOTTOM, 1" GAP AT FRONT, 3/4" SPACER

nail the frame together, but even more important, to hold the frame square when you nail on the bottom panel. If it hangs over the sides even a little, the drawer slides won't work smoothly.

Use 1-1/4-in. brads for all of the assembly. Glue the drawer parts together but not the bottom of the carrier. It only serves as a temporary spacer for mounting. (After mounting the carrier and drawer, you can remove it if it catches items on underlying drawers or even reuse it for other carriers.) If you'd like to finish the rollout for a richer look and easier cleaning, sand the edges with 120-grit paper and apply a couple of coats of water-based polyurethane before mounting the slides.

To figure the spacer thickness, rest the lower carrier on the bottom of the shelf, push it against one side of the cabinet and measure the gap on the other (Photo 10). Rip spacers to half

that measurement and cut six of them to 3-1/2 in. long. Slip the spacers between both sides of the carrier to check the fit. They should slide in snugly but not tightly. Recut new spacers if needed. In out-of-square cabinets, you may have to custom-cut spacers for each of the three pairs of spacers, so check each of the three spacer positions. It's easiest to tack the spacers to the rollouts to hold them in place before predrilling 1/8-in. holes and running the screws through the rollout frames and spacers and into the cabinet sides (Photo 11).

Slip the rollout into its carrier and check for smooth operation. If you followed the process, it should work perfectly. If it binds, it's probably because the spacers are too wide or narrow. Pull out the carrier, remove the spacers and start the spacer process all over again.

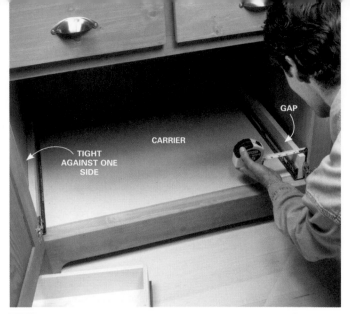

10 Remove the drawer, tip the carrier into the cabinet and push the carrier against one side. Measure the gap and rip six 3-1/2-in.-long spacers to half of the thickness.

11 Nail the spacers to the center and each end of the carrier sides (not into the cabinet; see inset photo). Then predrill and screw the carrier sides to the cabinet in the center of each shim. Slide the drawer back into place.

12 Cut plywood spacers to temporarily support the upper rollout and set them onto the carrier below. Rest the second carrier on the spacers and install it as shown in Photo 11.

13 Build an upside-down version of the carrier and rollouts for the wastebasket drawer (Figure B). Center and trace around the rim of the wastebasket(s). Use a compass to mark the opening 1/2 in. smaller.

The best way to level and fasten the upper rollout is to support it on temporary plywood spacers (Photo 12). The photo shows pieces of plywood cut 7 in. high. In reality, the exact height is up to you. If, for example, you want to store tall boxes of cereal on the bottom rollout and shorter items on the top, space the top rollout higher. You can even build and install three or more rollouts in one cabinet for mega storage of short items like cans, cutlery or beverages. (Those now-obsolete shelves you're replacing with rollouts are good stock to use for your spacers.) Again, pin the spacers in place with a brad or two to hold them while you're predrilling and screwing the carriers to the cabinet sides. Be sure to select screw lengths that won't penetrate exposed cabinet sides! In most cases, 1-5/8-in. screws are the best choice. Strive for 1/2-in. penetration into the cabinet sides. Countersink the heads as far as necessary to get the proper penetration.

Building wastebasket rollouts

Wastebasket rollouts are just upside-down versions of standard rollouts. That is, the carrier is mounted on the top rather than the bottom of the rollout and the slides are positioned at the bottom edge of the carrier sides. That lets the wastebasket lip clear the MDF. Follow Figure B on p. 17 for the details.

This wastebasket rollout is built inside an 18-in.-wide cabinet, so it fits two plastic containers back to back. If you only have

14 Drill 1/2-in. starting holes and cut the openings with a jigsaw.

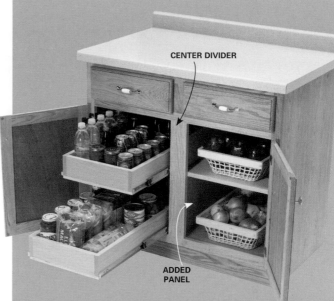

CENTER DIVIDER

ADDED PANEL

Building rollouts in cabinets with center dividers

Many two-door cabinets have a center divider (photo above), which calls for a slightly different strategy. You can still build rollouts, but they'll be narrower versions on each side of the divider. (Check to be sure they won't be so narrow that they're impractical.) The key is to install a 3/4-in. plywood, particleboard or MDF panel between the center divider and the cabinet back to support the carriers.

Cut the panel to fit loosely between the divider and the cabinet back and high enough to support the top rollout position. Center the panel on the back side and middle of the divider and screw it into place with 1-in. angle brackets (they're completely out of sight). Use a carpenter's square to position the panel perfectly centered and vertical on the cabinet back and anchor it there, again using angle brackets. Measure, build and install the rollouts as shown here.

15 Mount the wastebasket carrier and drawer as shown in Photos 10 and 11.

ROLLOUT

1" ANGLE BRACKET

ADDED PANEL

a 15-in. cabinet to work with, you may be limited to one container mounted sideways. Buy your containers ahead of time to fit your opening.

With some wastebasket rollouts, you may need to knock the MDF free from the carriers after mounting so the wastebasket lips will clear. That's OK; it won't affect operation.

It may not always work to center rollout assemblies in all openings with equal spacers on each side. That's especially true with narrow single cabinets that only have one pair of hinges. It's best to test things before permanent mounting. But if you make a mistake, it's a simple matter to unscrew the assembly, adjust the shims and remount everything.

If you're tired of digging through cans and boxes to find a jar of tomato sauce hidden at the back of the cabinet, these rollout bins are the perfect solution. You can size them to fit inside any lower cabinet and customize them to suit the items you want to store.

Here you'll learn exactly how to build them. The bins are simply plywood boxes with adjustable shelves—very easy to build. Sizing the boxes and mounting them on drawer slides can be tricky, but the techniques shown here make those steps nearly foolproof.

Money, time and tools

All the materials for these three rollouts cost just under $100. You could buy and install a manufactured system, but expect to spend three times that amount, or more.

You don't need advanced cabinet-building skills or tools to make your own rollouts—the joinery and assembly are simple. But a table saw or track saw is almost mandatory for fast, accurate, good-looking results. A pneumatic brad nailer will make the job faster and easier, although you can hand-nail or screw the parts together. Ordinarily, the side-mount drawer slides are tricky to install, but this project makes even that step foolproof, so don't let that part intimidate you. You'll be surprised how fast you can build yourself a few rollouts. Put in a full day and you'll be loading them with groceries that evening.

Sizing your rollouts

Everything you need for this project is available at home centers (see the Materials list, p. 24). You'll have to guess at the quantity of rollouts at this point so you can buy the proper number of drawer slides. One sheet of plywood will provide enough material for at least four rollouts. You can roughly figure one rollout for every foot of open base cabinet space you have. You can always return

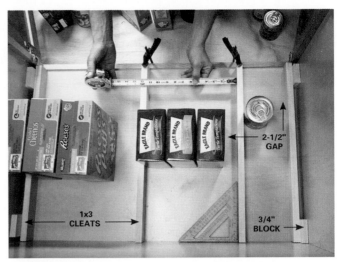

1 Plan rollout widths by laying out the cleats along with the items you want to store. Space the end cleats with 3/4-in. blocks.

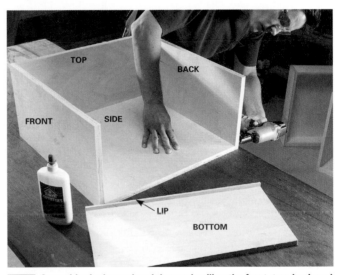

2 Assemble the boxes by gluing and nailing the front, top, back and bottom to the side panel and to each other. Nail the lip to the bottom shelf before assembling.

Get more storage space— without remodeling

Lower cabinets offer the biggest storage spaces in most kitchens. But according to kitchen designers, the back half of this space is usually wasted—it's packed with long-forgotten junk or left unused because stored items are out of view and hard to reach. Rollout bins let you see and use the whole space.

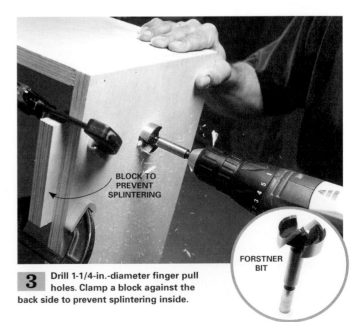

3 Drill 1-1/4-in.-diameter finger pull holes. Clamp a block against the back side to prevent splintering inside.

Figure A:
Typical rollout

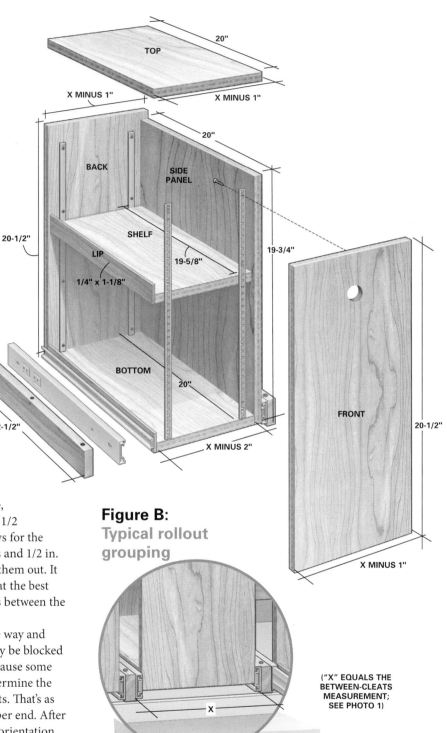

Materials list

ITEM	QTY.
1x3 the width of the cabinet (hold-down rail)	1
1x3 (drawer slide cleats)	2'
1/4-in. x 1-1/8-in. mullion (base and shelf front lips)	8'
2' shelf standards with clips	4
90-lb.-rated full-extension side-mount drawer slides	1 pair
1-1/2-in. pneumatic air nailer brads	
Wood glue	
Small box of 3-in. screws	
1-1/4-in. Forstner drill bit (for drilling finger pulls)	

any uncut lumber or hardware you don't use.

To determine the width of your rollouts, gather the items you want to store. Cut the 1x3 cleats to length and space them from each side of the cabinet with 3/4-in. blocks (Photo 1). That space allows the rollouts to clear the doors and hinges later. Then start arranging the items you want to store, separating them with the cleats. Leave at least 2-1/2 in. between your items and the cleats. This allows for the clearance of wood thicknesses and drawer slides and 1/2 in. extra to make it easy to load the items and take them out. It takes a bit of rearranging and thought to arrive at the best sizes. If your base cabinets have vertical dividers between the doors, give each opening its own rollouts.

You'll probably have some rollouts facing one way and some the other. That's because rollout access may be blocked by neighboring cabinets at inside corners or because some cabinet doors don't swing all the way open. Determine the access direction while you assemble your rollouts. That's as simple as drilling the finger pull hole at the proper end. After the boxes are assembled, they'll work for either orientation.

Choosing the materials

Choose any 3/4-in. veneered interior plywood for your rollouts. Avoid construction plywood; it won't be as flat and may warp later. If you'd like your rollouts to match your cabinets, choose whatever type of wood does the job. The plywood end grain is sanded on these, but if you'd like a more polished look, buy iron-on edge banding to match the wood type and iron it on after assembling the boxes.

Buy nice, straight, knot-free 1x3s for the cleats—the wood type doesn't matter. Select 22-in. European side-mount

Figure B:
Typical rollout grouping

("X" EQUALS THE BETWEEN-CLEATS MEASUREMENT; SEE PHOTO 1)

drawer slides rated to support 90 lbs. They'll come with their own screws and installation directions that show you how they work.

Cutting the parts

Most base cabinets are 22-1/2 in. deep and have a 21-in.-high opening (measured inside the face frame, not the cabinet interior). If your cabinets match these measurements, use the height and width dimensions shown in Figure A for all of the side panels. Also use Figure A for the lengths of each top, bottom, front and back panel and shelves. If your cabinets have shorter openings or are shallower, subtract those differences from the Figure A measurements to cut your parts. Calculate the rollout widths based on your layout work inside the cabinet (Photo 1). Subtract 1 in. from the distances between the cleats to get the width for each rollout's top, front and back panel. That'll leave the 1-in. clearance needed for the drawer slides. Subtract 2 in. to establish the width for each bottom panel and the adjustable shelves. That'll leave an additional 1-in. clearance for the thickness of the 3/4-in. side panel and the 1/4-in.-thick lip in the front.

Be especially careful when you lay out the cleats, measure openings and cut the rollout parts. European side-mount drawer slides leave very little room for error. It's best to use a table saw for all of the cuts and to double-check widths and lengths so the boxes will fit together perfectly and engage and operate smoothly in the slides.

Assemble the rollout boxes

Glue and nail the lip on each bottom panel (and shelf) before assembling the rollouts. A thin bead of wood glue on each edge is all you need. Then hold the edges of each panel flush while you pin them together with 1-1/2-in. brads spaced about every 4 in. (Photo 2). Next, drill the 1-1/4-in.-diameter finger pull hole. A Forstner bit will make the neatest hole, but a sharp spade bit will work, provided you use a block on the back side to prevent splintering (Photo 3). The hole defines each rollout's open side.

Cut the 24-in.-long shelf standards down to 18 in. with a hacksaw. Look at the embossed shelf numbers to determine which end is the top and cut from that end. Nail the standards in place with the brads provided (Photo 4).

This is the best time to apply the finish of your choice to the rollouts. Lightly sand everything with 220-grit sandpaper and add the finish. These boxes have two coats of water-based polyurethane to protect the wood against dirty fingers and marks from cans.

Install the drawer slides and cleats

Rip the 1x3s down to 2 in. and then screw on the drawer slides (Photo 5). It's easiest to remove the drawer part of the slide to access the anchor holes. Hold the slides flush with the top and front of each cleat while you punch little starter holes with a scratch awl, and then send in the screws. Drive just one screw at a time so you can adjust the placement as you add screws. You'll need right and left sides for the end cleats. Then remove the drawer side slides and lay the cleats in the cabinet.

Begin with one of the end cleats and press it against the temporary 3/4-in. blocks while you drill three 1/8-in. pilot holes.

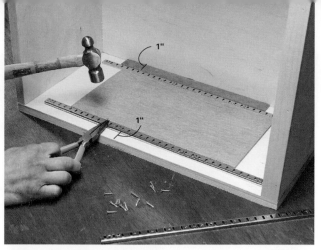

4 Nail shelf standards to the inside of the front and back of each box. Use spacers to position them.

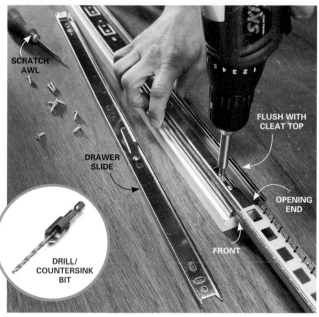

5 Screw the drawer slides to the cleats. Position each slide flush with the front and top of the cleat.

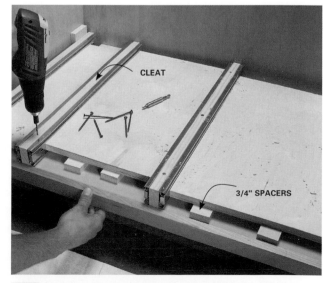

6 Predrill and screw the cleats to the cabinet. Use plywood scraps the same width as the boxes for perfect spacing.

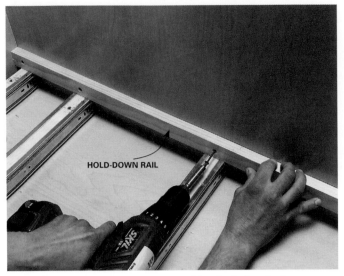

HOLD-DOWN RAIL

7 Screw the hold-down rail to the cabinet back directly above the cleats with 1-5/8-in. screws.

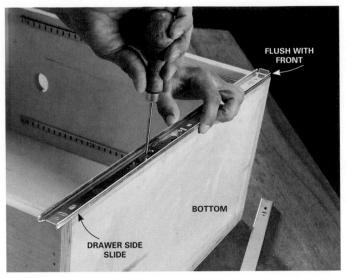

FLUSH WITH FRONT

BOTTOM

DRAWER SIDE SLIDE

8 Release the drawer slides from the cleat slides and screw them to the side of each box flush with the bottom and the front.

A combination drill/countersink bit works great for this. Then screw the cleat to the cabinet floor with 3-in. screws (Photo 6). Space the next cleat with a leftover scrap from the first rollout top, front or back. That way the spacing between the drawer slides will be perfectly sized for smoothly operating rollouts. Hold the spacer up from the cabinet floor with 3/4-in. blocks so it'll be centered on the drawer slides. Hold the cleat snug, but not tight, against the spacer while you drill and then screw it to the cabinet floor. Repeat that step with the rest of the cleats. Skip the 3/4-in. blocks on the last cleat and just use the rollout spacer. Screw a 1x3 "hold-down" rail to the back side of the cabinet (Photo 7). It'll help hold the rollout cleats in place when you pull out heavily loaded rollouts.

Finally, disengage the drawer side slides and screw them to the bottom of each rollout flush with the bottom and front (Photo 8). Finish up by inserting each rollout, then load them up!

9 Slip the box-mounted slides into the cleat slides and push the box all the way in to fully engage the slides.

Rollouts turn wasted space deep inside cabinets into accessible storage space.

Manufactured kitchen rollouts

Rollouts are one of the easiest and most satisfying upgrades you can make to your kitchen. They bring everything that's tucked out of sight in the back of cabinets right to your fingertips—you actually gain usable storage space.

If you don't want to pull out the tools to build your own rollouts, you can shop for moderately priced yet sturdy ones online or at home centers. You simply mount them to the existing shelves in your cabinets with four screws.

The biggest mistake is ordering the wrong size. When you measure the opening in the front of the cabinet, be sure to account for the door, hinges and other obstructions.

This two-level rollout fits around the drainpipes under a sink.

Customize your cabinets

If you have a short cabinet flanked by two taller cabinets, you can add this combination shelf/wine glass rack/plate rack.

Cut the shelf to length, then add mounting strips on each end. Cut four 9-in. sections of wine glass molding from a 3-ft. length, then glue and nail them to the bottom of the pine shelf. Wine glass molding is available from woodworking stores and online. Cut curved brackets from each end of a 1x6 maple board and cut the center 1 in. wide to serve as shelf edging (Photo 1). Finally, install the unit by driving screws through the mounting strips and into the cabinets on each side.

To display your plates and keep them accessible and chip-free, build and install this plate rack (Photo 2).

To create the two plate rack "ladders," measure the cabinet, then build each ladder so the finished height equals the height of the inside of the cabinet. The finished width should be equal to the width of the face frame opening. Drill 3/8-in. holes, 3/8 in. deep in 3/4-in. x 3/4-in. square dowels and space them every 1-1/2 in. Cut the dowels to length, add a drop of glue in each hole, insert the dowels, then use elastic cords or clamps to hold things together until the glue dries.

A drill press comes in handy, but you can also get good results using a cordless drill, a steady hand and a 3/8-in. drill bit with masking tape wrapped around it as a depth guide for the holes in the rails.

1 Build a shelf to fit snugly between adjacent cabinets. Use a jigsaw to create curved brackets, nail wine glass molding to the bottom of the shelf, then install the entire unit as one piece.

WINE GLASS MOLDING

CURVED BRACKETS

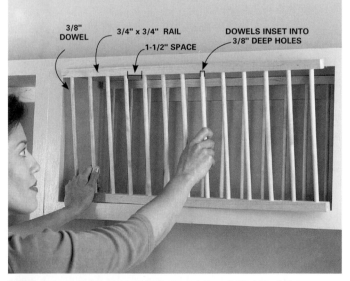

3/8" DOWEL
3/4" x 3/4" RAIL
1-1/2" SPACE
DOWELS INSET INTO 3/8" DEEP HOLES

2 Cut, assemble and install the two plate rack "ladders." Use short screws to secure the ladders in the cabinet opening. Set the rear ladder 4 in. away from the back of the cabinet and the front ladder snug against the back of the face frame.

Bathroom cabinet

In many bathrooms, a picture or a small shelf hangs above the toilet. But you can make better use of that space by building an attractive cabinet that offers about three times as much storage as a typical medicine cabinet.

The following pages will show you how to build it. The simple joinery and store-bought doors make this a great project for the woodworking novice. Assembling the crown and base is a bit tricky, but the how-to photos will show you how to do that.

The total materials bill for this cabinet was $150. You'll need a miter saw to cut the trim. A table saw and a brad nailer will save time, but you can make all the cuts with a circular saw and drive the nails by hand if you prefer.

The height and width of your cabinet may differ slightly from these measurements, depending on the bifold doors available at your home center. So choose your doors first and then alter the lengths of the sides and the top, bottom and middle shelves if

necessary. Bifold closet doors are sold as a pair, usually joined by hinges. Each of these doors measured 11-15/16 in. wide, and they were cut to length.

The easy-to-install hinges are available online or at woodworking stores. All the other tools and materials, including the cabinet doors, are available at home centers. You may not find the exact crown and base moldings used here, but most home centers carry a similar profile. Any 2-1/4-in. crown molding is appropriate for this project. "Base cap" molding was used for the base. For a more contemporary look, you could skip the crown and base altogether, since they're purely decorative.

Build a basic box

Cut the plywood parts to size. The dimensions are given in the Cutting list (p. 29). To make the short end cuts, use the homemade guide shown in Photo 3 and described on p. 30.

Figure A
Bathroom cabinet

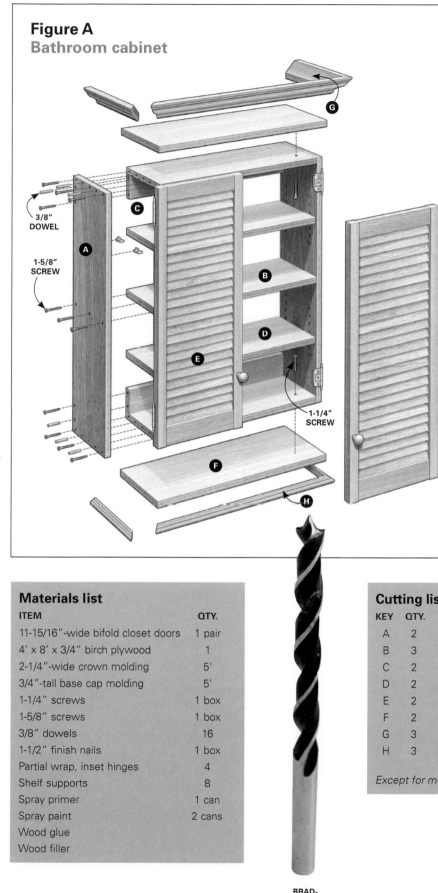

3/8" DOWEL

1-5/8" SCREW

1-1/4" SCREW

Assemble the cabinet box with glue and screws, followed by wood dowels for extra strength (Photo 1). You can buy long dowels and cut them into short pieces, but dowels precut and fluted for woodworking are easier to work with. This assembly method is quick and easy and gives strong results. But because the method requires lots of wood filler to hide the fasteners, it's for painted work only. If you want to use stain and a clear finish, biscuits or pocket screws are a better choice.

Drill 1/8-in. pilot and countersink holes for the screws using a drill bit that does both at once. Attach the top, bottom and cleats to one side, then add the other side. Mark the middle shelf position on the sides, slip it into place and screw it (there's no need for glue).

Before you drill the dowel holes, make sure the box is square by taking diagonal measurements; equal measurements means the box is square. If necessary, screw a strip of plywood diagonally across the back of the box to hold it square. For clean, splinter-free holes, drill the dowel holes with a 3/8-in. brad-point bit, making the holes 1/8 in. deeper than the length of the dowels. That way, you can sink the dowels below the surface of the plywood and fill the holes with wood filler. With the box completed, drill holes for the adjustable shelf supports (Photo 2) using a brad-point drill bit. Most shelf supports require a 1/4-in. hole.

BRAD-POINT BIT

Materials list

ITEM	QTY.
11-15/16"-wide bifold closet doors	1 pair
4' x 8' x 3/4" birch plywood	1
2-1/4"-wide crown molding	5'
3/4"-tall base cap molding	5'
1-1/4" screws	1 box
1-5/8" screws	1 box
3/8" dowels	16
1-1/2" finish nails	1 box
Partial wrap, inset hinges	4
Shelf supports	8
Spray primer	1 can
Spray paint	2 cans
Wood glue	
Wood filler	

Cutting list

KEY	QTY.	SIZE & DESCRIPTION
A	2	8" x 32-5/8" sides
B	3	8" x 22-1/2" top, bottom and middle shelf
C	2	3" x 22-1/2" top and bottom cleats
D	2	8" x 22-1/4" adjustable shelves
E	2	11-15/16" x 32-3/8" doors
F	2	9" x 24" crown and base frames
G	3	2-1/4"-wide crown molding (cut to fit)
H	3	3/4"-tall base molding (cut to fit)

Except for moldings, all parts are 3/4-in. plywood.

Cut and hang the doors

Cut the doors using a saw guide (Photo 3). To make a guide, screw a straight 1x3 to a 14 x 18-in. scrap of 3/4-in. plywood. Then run your saw along the 1x3 to cut off the excess plywood and create a guide that steers your saw perfectly straight and indicates the exact path of the cut. Simply mark the doors, align the guide with the marks, clamp it in place and cut.

Screw the hinges to the doors 3 in. from the ends (Photo 4). The fronts and backs of louvered doors look similar, so check twice before you drill. Stand the doors against the cabinet, setting them on spacers to create a 1/8-in. gap at the bottom. The gap between the doors should also be about 1/8 in. Clamp each door into position and screw the hinges into place (Photo 5). If the doors don't align perfectly because the box is slightly out of square, don't worry; you can square the box when you hang it. The hinges also adjust up or down 1/16 in.

Add the crown and base

Measure the top of the cabinet (including the doors) and cut the plywood crown and base frames to that size. Set your miter saw to 45 degrees and cut the crown molding with it upside down and leaning against the fence (Photo 6). Also miter a "tester" section of molding to help you position the sidepieces when you nail them into place. To avoid splitting, predrill nail holes. With the sides in place, add the front piece of crown molding. Cut it slightly long and then "shave" one end with your miter saw until it fits perfectly. Add the molding to the base frame the same way. Screw both the crown and the base to the cabinet (Photo 8).

Store-bought closet doors make it fast and simple

Building cabinet doors is a tricky, time-consuming job. But you can avoid all that fussy work by buying closet doors and cutting them to fit the cabinet.

A quick finish

Brushing paint onto louvered doors is slow, fussy work, but you can avoid that hassle by using spray primer and paint. First, remove the doors and hinges. Cover the dowels, nails and screw heads with wood filler and sand the filler smooth. Also fill any voids in the plywood's edges. Sand the cabinet box, crown, base and doors with 120-grit sandpaper. Spray all the parts with a white stain-blocking primer. When the primer dries, sand it lightly with a fine sanding sponge. Finally, spray on at least two coats of spray paint. High-gloss paint will accentuate even tiny surface flaws, so consider using satin or matte.

To hang the cabinet, locate studs and drive two 3-in. screws through the top cleat. Then rehang the doors. Close the doors to check their fit. Nudge the bottom of the cabinet left or right to square it and align the doors. Then drive screws through the bottom cleat.

DOWEL

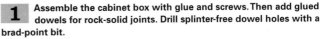

1 Assemble the cabinet box with glue and screws. Then add glued dowels for rock-solid joints. Drill splinter-free dowel holes with a brad-point bit.

DEPTH MARKER

2 Drill shelf support holes using a scrap of pegboard to position the holes. Wrap masking tape around the drill bit so you don't drill all the way through.

3 Cut the doors using a homemade saw guide to ensure a straight cut. Lay the door face down so any splintering takes place on the back of the door.

SAW GUIDE

CLOSET DOOR

4 Mount the hinges on the doors. A self-centering drill bit positions the screw holes for perfectly placed hinges.

SELF-CENTERING BIT

5 Position the doors carefully and clamp them to the cabinet. Then screw the hinges to the cabinet from inside for a foolproof, exact fit.

6 Cut the crown molding with it upside down and leaning against the fence. Clamp a block to the fence so you can hold the molding firmly against it.

HOLD-DOWN BLOCK

7 Nail the crown to the frame. Nail the mitered corners only if necessary. If they fit tight and are perfectly aligned, let the glue alone hold them together.

8 Center the crown on the cabinet and fasten it with screws driven from the inside. Then center the cabinet on the base and attach it the same way.

CROWN

BASE

Add a kitchen outlet

Additional outlets above the counter can be surprisingly easy if you have base cabinets. Just drop the wire down through the wall, pull it into the cabinet, then fish it through adjoining cabinets to the new outlet. Use flexible conduit and keep it as high and far back as possible.

CONDUIT

INSIDE BACK OF CABINET

Add a second medicine cabinet

Here's a way to add more storage and bump up the sophistication of your bathroom. Mount matching medicine cabinets and add shelves between them. To support these shelves, we drilled holes in the sides of the cabinets and inserted adjustable shelf pegs. The shelves are simply boards finished to match the cabinets. This makes the most of the wall space above your toilet and sink. You could also mount something similar over a double sink setup. The cabinets can be surface mounted or recessed. The shelves give the unit a nice finished quality.

Add a vanity drawer top tray

Drawers are often too deep for small bathroom stuff like razors, medicine and cosmetics. That means wasted space. These handy sliding trays reduce that waste and increase drawer real estate by 50 percent.

- To size the tray, measure the drawer: Subtract 1/16 in. from the width of the drawer space and divide the length in half. Cut a piece of 1/8-in. hardboard this size.
- You can make the tray any depth you like. If the opening in the vanity is taller than the height of the drawer, your tray can protrude above the drawer sides.
- Finish the tray with a couple of coats of polyurethane or spray lacquer.
- Stored items tend to slide around in the trays, so add shelf liner (available at home centers and discount stores).

Figure A

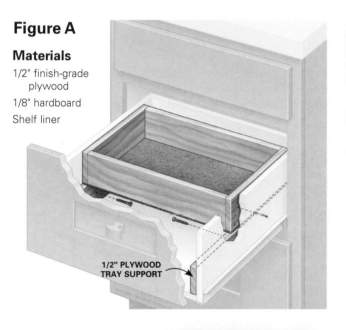

Materials

1/2" finish-grade plywood
1/8" hardboard
Shelf liner

1/2" PLYWOOD TRAY SUPPORT

TRAY SUPPORTS

1 Add tray supports. Fasten strips of plywood to the drawer to support the tray. You only need two screws per support.

Pullout towel rack

Pullout towel racks are typically meant for kitchens, but they're also perfect for cramped bathrooms. They keep damp hand towels and washcloths off the counter so they can dry out of the way. You can find pullout towel racks at discount stores and online retailers.

SHELF LINER

2 Line the trays. Cut shelf liner to fit the trays. Liner helps stored items stay put when you slide the tray.

Organize your kitchen

For me, kitchen time is wasted time. I want to get the job done, get out and get on with life. So I designed these projects to give you efficiency, easy access and effortless organization. If you're like me, you'll appreciate the time savings. If you're not like me—if you actually enjoy your kitchen—you'll love the projects even more because cooking will be more convenient.

—Gary Wentz, Senior Editor, *The Family Handyman*

WHAT IT TAKES

TIME: 1 to 4 hours, depending on the project

COST: $10 to $50 if you have to buy all the materials. If you have some wood scraps lying around, most of these projects will cost less than $10.

SKILL LEVEL: Beginner to intermediate

TOOLS: Drill, sander, table saw

Perfect place for lids

You can mount a drawer for pot lids under your pot shelf—or under any other cabinet shelf. Before you remove the shelf, put some pencil marks on it to indicate the width of the cabinet opening at its narrowest point (usually at the hinges). Your drawer front and slides can't extend beyond those marks (or you'll spend hours building a drawer that won't open). Then remove the shelf. If it's made from particleboard, I recommend that you replace it with 3/4-in. plywood and transfer the marks to the new shelf. If you can build a simple drawer box, the rest will be easy.

Hidden cutting board

The secret to this project is "rare earth" magnets. The ones I used are just 5/32 in. in diameter and 1/8 in. tall. Browse online to find lots of shapes and sizes. Implant magnets at the corners of your cutting board and add more if needed.

Make the metal plate under the cabinet larger than the cutting board so the board will be easy to put away. Glue the sheet metal to plywood with spray adhesive. Drill holes near the corners and screw it to the underside of a cabinet.

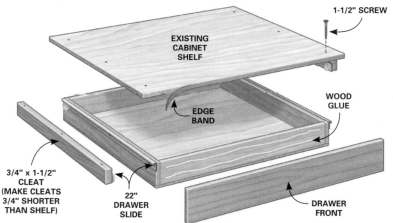

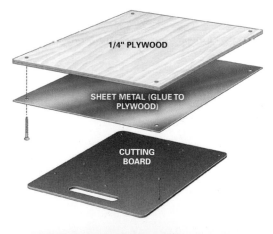

Building notes

- All the wood projects shown here are finished with Minwax Wipe-On Poly.
- Unless otherwise noted, all the materials for these projects are available at home centers.
- Several of these projects require joining 1/2-in.-thick wood parts. You can do that with a brad nailer, but if your aim is a smidgen off, you'll blow a nail out the side of the part. Trim-head screws are safer. Their thin shanks won't split thin wood (as long as you drill pilot holes), and their small heads are easy to hide with filler (or ignore).

TRIM-HEAD SCREWS

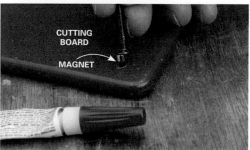

Magnetize your cutting board. Drill holes sized for the magnets and drop in a dab of super glue. Insert the magnets with a nail head. Slide the nail sideways to release the magnet.

Drawer in a drawer

Deep drawers often contain a jumbled pile of interlocking utensils. My solution is a sliding tray that creates two shallower spaces. Make it 1/8 in. narrower than the drawer box, about half the length and any depth you want (mine is 1-3/4 in. deep). When you position the holes for the adjustable shelf supports, don't rely on measurements and arithmetic. Instead, position the tray inside the drawer box at least 1/8 in. lower than the cabinet opening and make a mark on the tray. My shelf supports fit tightly into the holes, but yours may require a little super glue.

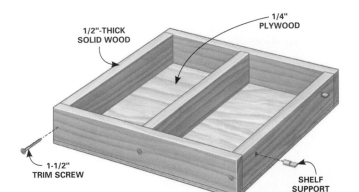

1/2"-THICK SOLID WOOD

1/4" PLYWOOD

1-1/2" TRIM SCREW

SHELF SUPPORT

SHELF SUPPORT

Add a divider for upright storage

I don't know why the pan or tray you need is always the one at the bottom of the pile. But I do know the solution: Store large, flat stuff on edge rather than stacked up. That way, you can slide out whichever pan you need. Cut 3/4-in. plywood to match the depth of the cabinet, but make it at least an inch taller than the opening so you can fasten it to the face frame as shown. Drill shelf support holes that match the existing holes inside the cabinet. Finally, cut the old shelf to fit the new space.

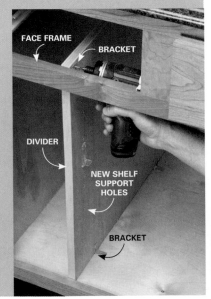

FACE FRAME

BRACKET

DIVIDER

NEW SHELF SUPPORT HOLES

BRACKET

Fasten the divider with brackets. Screw two brackets to the cabinet floor; one to the face frame and one to the back wall of the cabinet (not shown).

Rollout storage panel

If you know how to mount a slab of plywood on drawer slides, you can take advantage of all the nifty shelves, hooks and holders sold at home centers. It's easy as long as you remember two critical things: First, make sure the drawer slides are parallel (see photo below). Second, make your cleats thick enough so that the slides will clear the cabinet door hinges. (I glued 1/2-in. plywood to 3/4-in. plywood to make my cleats.)

To install the panel in the cabinet, reassemble the slides. Hold the whole assembly against the cabinet wall and slide the panel out about 4 in. Drive screws through the cleats at the rear, then slide the panel out completely and drive screws at the front.

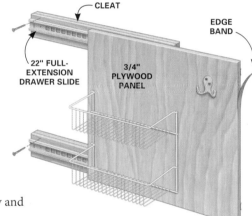

CLEAT

EDGE BAND

22" FULL-EXTENSION DRAWER SLIDE

3/4" PLYWOOD PANEL

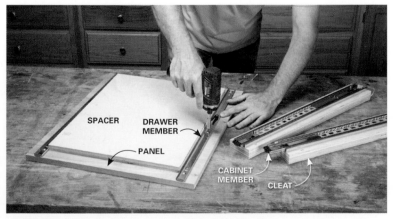

Mount the slides. They have to be absolutely parallel for smooth operation, so place a plywood spacer between the drawer members as you screw them to the panel. Screw the cabinet members to cleats.

SPACER

DRAWER MEMBER

PANEL

CABINET MEMBER

CLEAT

Convenient cutting board

The slickest way to store a cutting board for instant access is shown on p. 35. But that only works for cutting boards less than 10-1/2 in. wide. For larger boards, mount a rack on a cabinet door. I used a sheet of 1/4-in.-thick acrylic plastic, but plywood would also work. You can cut acrylic with a table saw or circular saw as long as you cut slowly. Knock off the sharp edges with sandpaper. I also rounded the lower corners with a belt sander. For spacers, I used No. 14-8 crimp sleeves (in the electrical aisle at home centers). But any type of tube or even blocks of wood would work.

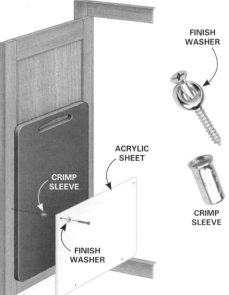

FINISH WASHER

ACRYLIC SHEET

CRIMP SLEEVE

CRIMP SLEEVE

FINISH WASHER

Drop-down tablet tray

This tray will keep your tablet off the countertop. As it swings down, it also swings forward, so the tablet isn't hidden under the cabinet.

The mechanism is simple; just make and position the arms exactly as shown here and it will work smoothly. I cut the aluminum parts and rounded the corners with a grinder. When closed, the tray is held up by small cabinet door magnets. I clipped the plastic ears off the magnets and glued the magnets into place with epoxy. The liner in the tray is a foam placemat cut to fit. Don't worry, small magnets won't harm your tablet; it actually contains magnets.

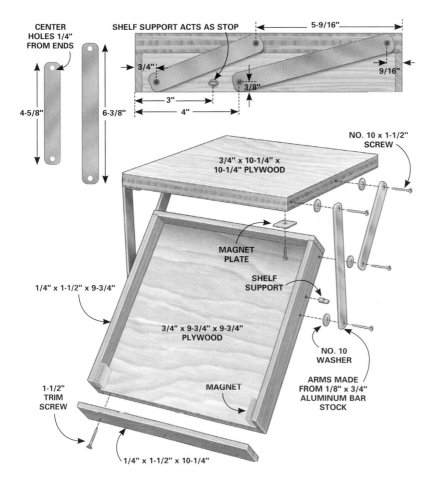

CENTER HOLES 1/4" FROM ENDS

SHELF SUPPORT ACTS AS STOP

5-9/16"

3/4"

9/16"

3/8"

3"

4"

4-5/8"

6-3/8"

NO. 10 x 1-1/2" SCREW

3/4" x 10-1/4" x 10-1/4" PLYWOOD

1/4" x 1-1/2" x 9-3/4"

MAGNET PLATE

SHELF SUPPORT

3/4" x 9-3/4" x 9-3/4" PLYWOOD

NO. 10 WASHER

1-1/2" TRIM SCREW

MAGNET

ARMS MADE FROM 1/8" x 3/4" ALUMINUM BAR STOCK

1/4" x 1-1/2" x 10-1/4"

Instant knife rack

You can size this knife rack to suit any cabinet door and any number of knives. To build it, you just need a table saw and wood scraps. Run the scraps across the saw on edge to cut kerfs. Adjust the blade height to suit the width of the knife blades. You have to remove the saw's blade guard for these cuts, so be extra careful. Also cut a thin strip to act as an end cap. Glue and clamp the kerfed scraps together and sand the knife rack until the joints are flush. To mount it, use two 1-1/4-in. screws and finish washers.

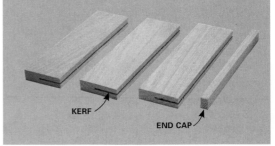

KERF

END CAP

Flip-down paper tray

This tray is perfect for pens and paper. When closed, it's mostly hidden by the cabinet face frame. To install the tray, screw on the hinges first. Then open the cabinet door above and clamp the tray to the underside of the cabinet while you screw the hinges to the cabinet.

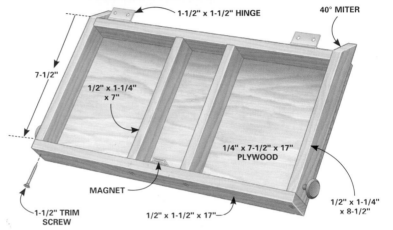

1-1/2" x 1-1/2" HINGE

40° MITER

7-1/2"

1/2" x 1-1/4" x 7"

1/4" x 7-1/2" x 17" PLYWOOD

MAGNET

1-1/2" TRIM SCREW

1/2" x 1-1/2" x 17"

1/2" x 1-1/4" x 8-1/2"

Add a shelf

Most cabinets come with only one or two shelves, leaving a lot of wasted space. So I added one (and sometimes two) shelves to most of my cabinets. All it takes is 3/4-in. plywood and a bag of shelf supports. The supports come in two diameters, so take an existing one to the store to make sure you get the right size.

A new look for old tubs and showers

Over time, the metal on tub and shower controls and spouts can become tarnished and dull-looking despite all efforts to clean and polish it. An easy way to solve the problem is to simply install new trim.

Almost any tub spout and showerhead can be replaced by unscrewing the old one and screwing on a replacement. The handle and trim for the tub/shower controls can also usually be replaced without redoing any plumbing by using a universal replacement kit (available for most brands at home centers and plumbing supply stores). If you're unsure what kind of replacement to buy, just take the old handle and trim (or snap a photo) to a plumbing supply store to find a matching replacement.

Turn off the water supply, then remove the handle and trim (Photo 1). Most shower handles have a removable cap covering a screw that holds the handle on; otherwise, look for a setscrew under the handle.

Tub spouts unscrew (Photo 2), or pull off if they have a setscrew underneath. You may need to use two hands or even a wrench to unscrew them if the spout was caulked. Replace the spout with one that's threaded or attached in the same way, or buy a universal-type replacement spout that comes with adapters to fit any configuration.

Clean old caulk and dirt off the wall before installing the new controls and spouts. Attach the new handle and trim in the reverse order that you took them off (Photo 3). Caulk the wall under the rim of the escutcheon plate with acrylic caulk before you tighten it down, when it's roughly 1/4 in. away from the wall. Leave a 1-in. gap at the bottom, then wipe off excess caulk after the plate is tightened down.

ESCUTCHEON

COVER

1 Pry the cover off the shower handle, then remove the screw under the cover and slide the handle and escutcheon off.

UNSCREW

2 Remove the tub spout by turning it counterclockwise or by unscrewing a setscrew and pulling it off.

H

C

THREADED FITTING

3 Fasten the trim ring with the "H" mark on the left, then screw on the rest of the faucet.

Replacement trim kit

SHOWERHEAD

HANDLE

TUB SPOUT

ESCUTCHEON

OVERFLOW COVER

Decorative backsplash rack

Backsplash racks offer easy access and stylish storage. Most versions take just a few minutes to install. Type "backsplash rack" into any online search engine to find a range of styles and add-ons. Backsplash racks have a few disadvantages, though. All your kitchen utensils have to look good, since they're on display. And if you ever decide to remove the rack, you'll be left with screw holes in the backsplash; not a big problem with drywall, but ugly and unfixable in tile.

Organize your knives

Store your kitchen cutlery in style with this handsome knife block. It's fast, easy and fun to build, and includes a 6-in.-wide storage box for a knife sharpener. To build one, you only need a 3/4-in. x 8-in. x 4-ft. hardwood board and a 6-in. x 6-1/2-in. piece of 1/4-in. hardwood plywood to match.

Begin by cutting off a 10-in. length of the board and setting it aside. Rip the remaining 38-in. board to 6 in. wide and cut five evenly spaced saw kerfs 5/8 in. deep along one face. Crosscut the slotted board into four 9-in. pieces and glue them into a block, being careful not to slop glue into the saw kerfs (you can clean them out with a knife before the glue dries). Saw a 15-degree angle on one end and screw the plywood piece under the angled end of the block. Cut the 6-1/2-in. x 3-in. lid from the leftover board, and slice the remaining piece into 1/4-in.-thick pieces for the sides and end of the box. Glue them around the plywood floor. Cut a rabbet on three sides of the lid so it fits snugly on the box, and drill a 5/8-in. hole for a finger pull. Then just add a finish and you're set for years of happy carving!

5/8" DEEP

9"

6"

15°

6-1/2"

CUT TO FIT

1/4" PLYWOOD

6"

15°

3-1/2"

6-1/2"

CUT RABBET TO FIT

Chapter Two

STORAGE & ORGANIZING

Throw & go bins

Storage for a family on the move

Shelves and cabinets are great places to store kid stuff, but when you're in a hurry (and kids always are), it's nice to just throw and go. That's why we built these bins. They're great for sports gear but handle all kinds of miscellaneous garage clutter.

We loosely based the design on a row of old bins at a country store. It was worth the little bit of extra effort to build something that brings back good memories yet serves a practical purpose in the present.

WHAT IT TAKES

COST: $150

TIME: One day to build, plus painting

SKILL: Beginner to intermediate

TOOLS: Table saw or circular saw, drill, jigsaw or handsaw

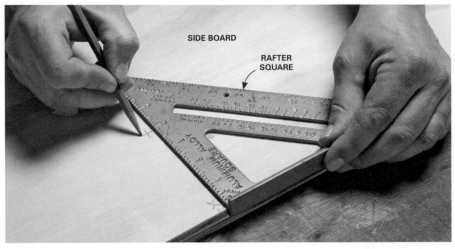

1 Lay out the side profiles. After measuring and marking the location of the bin fronts, use a square to mark the recessed portion of the front.

2 Connect the dots. Use a straightedge to connect the dots. You only need to lay out one side board. Once it's cut, that board will act as a pattern for the rest.

3 Cut two at a time. Clamp two sides down and cut them both at the same time. That way, if you make any small cutting errors, the pair of sides will still match up. Make most of the cut with a circular saw, and then finish it off with a jigsaw.

Cut the parts

Cut the sides, top and bottom from 3/4-in. plywood using a table saw or circular saw. Use "BC" plywood, which is good enough for paint, or buy birch veneer plywood if you plan to use stain.

This project requires a full sheet of plywood plus a 2 x 4-ft. section. Many home centers carry 4 x 4-ft., and some even stock 2 x 4-ft., so you don't have to buy two full sheets. However, they charge a premium for smaller sheets, and you won't save more than a few bucks. You can buy two full sheets and use the leftover on other projects. The same goes for the 1/4-in. plywood—you only need a 4 x 4-ft. sheet, but a 4 x 8-ft. is a better value.

The fronts of the bins get the most abuse, so build them from a solid 1x6 pine board. Solid wood holds up better than a plywood edge. You can rip down the two center boards when you're cutting up the other parts, but hold off on cutting them to length until the top and bottom boards are in place. That way you can cut them exactly to size.

Mark the side profile

This part of the process seems a little tricky, but it's really quite simple if you follow these directions. Hook a tape measure on the bottom front of one of the side boards. Measure up and mark the edge of the board at: 0, 4 in., 15-1/2 in., 19-1/2 in., 31 in. and 35 in. Now go back and measure over 4 in. at the following locations: the bottom, 15-1/2 in., 31 in. and the top (Photo 1). These marks represent the indented portion of the side. Start at the end of the board, and connect the dots (Photo 2). It's just that easy.

Cut and sand the sides

Clamp two side boards down to your work surface. Arrange them so the best sides of the plywood will be on the outside of the bins. Use a circular saw to make most of each cut. (Sometimes it's necessary to hold the blade guard up when you start a cut at an angle.) Finish the cuts with a jigsaw (Photo 3). A handsaw will work fine if you don't own a jigsaw.

Sand the edges with 80-grit sandpaper while the sides are still clamped together (Photo 4). Use one of the two cut side

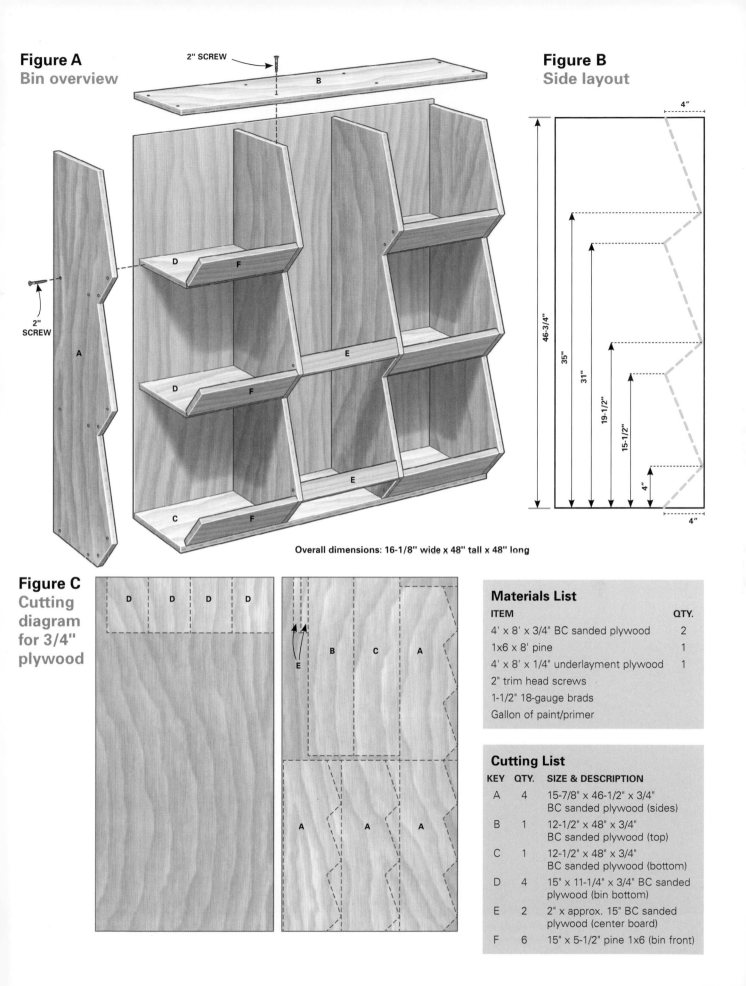

Figure A
Bin overview

2" SCREW

B

2" SCREW

A

D   F

D   F

E

D   F

C   F

E

Overall dimensions: 16-1/8" wide x 48" tall x 48" long

Figure B
Side layout

4"

46-3/4"

35"

31"

19-1/2"

15-1/2"

4"

4"

Figure C
Cutting diagram for 3/4" plywood

D   D   D   D

E

B   C   A

A   A   A

Materials List

ITEM	QTY.
4' x 8' x 3/4" BC sanded plywood	2
1x6 x 8' pine	1
4' x 8' x 1/4" underlayment plywood	1
2" trim head screws	
1-1/2" 18-gauge brads	
Gallon of paint/primer	

Cutting List

KEY	QTY.	SIZE & DESCRIPTION
A	4	15-7/8" x 46-1/2" x 3/4" BC sanded plywood (sides)
B	1	12-1/2" x 48" x 3/4" BC sanded plywood (top)
C	1	12-1/2" x 48" x 3/4" BC sanded plywood (bottom)
D	4	15" x 11-1/4" x 3/4" BC sanded plywood (bin bottom)
E	2	2" x approx. 15" BC sanded plywood (center board)
F	6	15" x 5-1/2" pine 1x6 (bin front)

boards to mark one of the other uncut side boards, and repeat the process.

If you've already chosen a color for your project, now would be a good time to sand and finish all the parts. That way, you'll only have to touch up the fastener holes after assembly. Some of the plywood edges may have voids, which can be filled with wood putty or patching compound.

Assemble the bins

Lay out two of the sides back to back with the good side of the plywood facing down. Using a straightedge, mark lines between the notches to serve as a reference line for the bottoms of the bins. The bottom of the whole unit will serve as the bottom of the lowest bins, so fasten the bottom on the second lowest bin first. Align the board above the reference line.

Fasten the bottoms and the fronts with three 1-1/2-in. brads. Once it's all put together, go back and reinforce it all with two 2-in. trim head screws in each side of every board.

Once the bottoms are in place, come back and install the 1x6 fronts (Photo 5). Align them flush with the outside edge of the plywood. You'll notice a small gap between the bin bottom and the front. This makes assembly easier, especially if your

4 **Sand two at a time.** Smooth out the cuts before you unclamp the sides. Make sure to keep each pair together when you assemble the bins.

side cuts weren't perfect. It won't be noticeable when it's up against the wall. Once the first bank of bins is done, assemble second one.

Finish it up

Fasten the top and bottom flush with the outside edges of the bins. Again, drive three brads into each side board and then go back and secure them with a couple of trim head screws.

Use the 1/4-in. plywood back to square up the project. Start with the two factory-cut sides of the plywood, and start fastening it to either the top or bottom, making sure it's perfectly flush with the edge. Then fasten one side, working away from the previously fastened top or bottom, straightening and nailing as you go. Install one screw through the back into each bin bottom for a little extra support. Before you finish the other two sides, set up the project and check that things are square.

Measure between the two banks of bins, and cut your center boards to that size. Pin them in with brads and secure them with a screw. The center boards can be located anywhere you want depending on the type of items you're going to store.

If your project is going to be sitting on concrete, you may want to install a couple of strips of treated lumber on the bottom. Rip 5/8-in. strips of treated lumber and tack them onto the perimeter of the bottom.

You can screw the project to the wall if you know your kids will be using it as a ladder, but it's pretty stable as it is. All that's left is to go tell the family that there are no more excuses for throwing stuff on the floor.

18-GAUGE BRAD NAILER

5 **Assemble the bins.** Build the bin sections before you install the top and bottom. If you have a brad nailer, make assembly easier by tacking all the parts together before you drive in the screws.

Laundry room ironing center

To keep your ironing gear handy but out from underfoot, make this simple ironing center in a couple of hours. All you need is a 10-ft. 1x8, a 2-ft. piece of 1x6 for the shelves and a pair of hooks to hang your ironing board.

Cut the back, sides, shelves and top. Align the sides and measure from the bottom 2 in., 14-3/4 in. and 27-1/2 in. to mark the bottom of the shelves (Photo 1). Before assembling the unit, cut a 1 x 1-in. dog ear at the bottom of the sides for a decorative touch.

Working on one side at a time, glue and nail the side to the back. Apply glue and drive three 1-5/8-in. nails into each shelf, attach the other side and nail those shelves into place to secure them. Clamps are helpful to hold the unit together while you're driving nails. Center the top piece, leaving a 2-in. overhang on both sides, and glue and nail it into place (Photo 2). Paint or stain the unit and then drill pilot holes into the top face of each side of the unit and screw in the hooks to hold your ironing board. Mount the shelf on drywall using screw-in wall anchors.

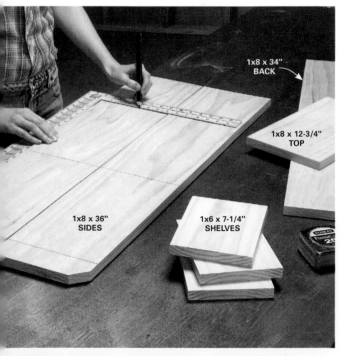

1x8 x 34" BACK

1x8 x 12-3/4" TOP

1x8 x 36" SIDES

1x6 x 7-1/4" SHELVES

1 Place the sides next to each other and mark the shelf positions. For easier finishing, sand all the parts before marking and assembly.

TOP

2 Glue and nail the back and shelves between the sides, then add the top. After painting or staining, screw on hooks for the ironing board.

Hide-the-mess lockers

Build simple boxes and add store-bought doors

My daughter, Kellie, recently bought a nice little house with a nice big coat closet by the front door. The problem is, since the garage is in the back, everyone, including the dog, uses the back door.

I designed and built these hide-the-mess lockers with people like Kellie in mind. Each locker is big enough to stash a coat, backpack, boots, hats, and odds and ends that normally wind up on the floor. Since they're modular and space efficient, you can build one for each member of the family—including the dog (leashes, toys, food, you name it). Now everyone has a personal place for stashing stuff—and the responsibility for keeping it organized.

The louvered door is made from one of a pair of closet bifold doors, which you can buy at almost any home center. Since the doors come in pairs and you can get two locker "boxes" from each sheet of plywood, you'll make the best use of materials by building them in twos. Here's how to do it.

Meet the pro

Spike Carlsen is a carpenter, author and former editor at *The Family Handyman*. You can find his books in stores and at online booksellers. Find out more at spikecarlsen.com.

Money, materials and tools

My total materials cost was just under $100 per locker. Since I was planning to paint the lockers, I used inexpensive "AC" plywood. If you plan to stain your lockers, and use hardwood plywood such as oak or birch and hardwood doors, you'll spend about $150 per locker. On a row of lockers, only the outer sides of the end lockers show, so you can use inexpensive plywood for the inner parts and more expensive material for the outer parts. Expect to spend at least a day buying materials, rounding up tools and building a pair of lockers. Set aside another day for finishing.

A table saw is handy for cutting up plywood, but a circular saw with a guide will provide the same results. You'll also need a miter saw to cut the screen molding. A finish nailer will help you work faster, but hand-nailing will work too as long as you drill holes to prevent splitting.

1 Build a simple box. Cut the plywood parts and assemble them with trim-head screws. Make sure the box opening is 1/4 in. taller and wider than the door itself.

2 Square it up. Take diagonal corner-to-corner measurements, then adjust the box until the measurements are equal and the box is square. Install the back, using one edge of the back to straighten the box side as you fasten it. Check once again for squareness, then secure the other edges of the back.

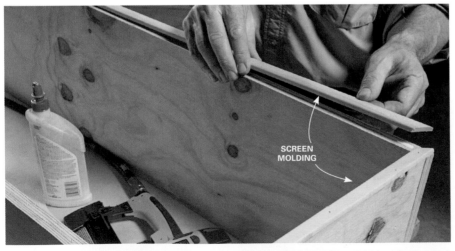

3 Cover the plywood edges. Install screen molding over the front edges of the box. Apply wood glue lightly and use just enough nails to "clamp" the molding in place while the glue dries.

Buy the doors first

There are a variety of bifold doors available. If you need more ventilation, use full louvered doors; if ventilation isn't an issue, use solid doors. The doors you buy may not be exactly the same size as mine, so you may have to alter the dimensions of the boxes you build. Here are two key points to keep in mind as you plan your project:

■ You want a 1/8-in. gap surrounding the door. So to determine the size of the box opening, add 1/4 in. to the height and width of the door. Since my bifold doors measured 14-3/4 x 78-3/4 in., I made the opening 15 x 79 in.

■ To determine the depth of the shelves, subtract the door thickness from the width of the sides (including the 1/4-in. screen molding). My doors were 1-1/8 in. thick, so I made the shelves 10-7/8 in. deep (12 minus 1-1/8 equals 10-7/8 in.). When the doors are closed, they'll rest against the shelves inside and flush with the screen molding outside.

Get building!

Use a table saw or straight-cutting guide to cut the plywood sides (A) and top and bottom (B). The Cutting list on p. 52 gives the parts dimensions for my lockers. If you plan to paint or stain the lockers, it's a good idea to prefinish the insides of parts. Once the lockers are assembled, brushing a finish onto the insides is slow and difficult.

Assemble the boxes with 2-in. trim-head screws (Photo 1). Trim-head screws have smaller heads than standard screws and are easier to hide with filler. Cut the 1/4-in. plywood back (C) to size. Make certain the box is square by taking diagonal measurements (they should be equal; see Photo 2), and then secure the back using 1-in. nails. Use the edges of the back as a guide to straighten the edges of the box as you nail the back into place.

Cut 1/4 x 3/4-in. screen molding and use glue and 1-in. finish nails or brads to secure it to the exposed front edges of the plywood (Photo 3). Cut the shelf front and back (D), sides (E) and slats (F) to length, then assemble the three slatted shelf units (Photo 4). With the locker box standing upright, position the shelves and hold them temporarily in place with clamps or a couple of screws. Adjust the shelf spacing based on the height of the locker's user and the stuff that will go inside. Once you have a suitable arrangement, lay the locker on its back and screw the shelves into place (Photo 5). The shelves are easy to reposition in the future as needs change.

Add the hardware and finish, and then install

Remove the hinges that hold the bifold doors to each other. Determine which way you want the door to swing, then mount the hinges onto the door accordingly. (Note: You'll need to buy another set of hinges if you're building two lockers.) Remember, you want the louvers to point downward on the outside! With the locker on its back, position the door and secure the hinges to the plywood side (Photo 6). Install door handles and magnetic catches to hold them closed.

Remove the doors (but don't finish them yet!) and install the locker boxes. Your lockers can stand against baseboard, leaving a small gap between the backs of the lockers and the wall. Or—if you remove the baseboard—they can stand tight against the wall. Either way, installing them is a lot like installing cabinets: Fasten all the boxes together by driving 1-1/4-in. screws through the side of one locker into the next. Then screw the entire assembly to wall studs.

Install the unfinished doors to make sure they all fit properly, then remove them again. This may seem like a waste of time, but there's a good reason for it: Your locker boxes may have shifted a little during installation, and the doors may not fit properly. If a door or two need some edge sanding, you want to do that before finishing.

When you've checked the fit of all the doors, remove them one last time for finishing. Whether you're using paint or a natural finish, louvered doors are a real pain. If your plans include a clear coat, consider polyurethane or lacquer in spray cans: You'll get better results in far less time, though you'll spend an extra $5 to $10 per door. After finishing, install the doors and load up those lockers!

4 **Build slatted shelves.** Plywood shelves would work fine, but slatted shelves allow better ventilation so wet clothes and shoes can dry. Space the slats with a pair of wood scraps.

5 **Install the shelves.** Stand your locker up and position the shelves to suit the stuff that will go in it. Mark the shelf locations, lay the locker on its back and screw the shelves into place. Make sure the shelves are inset far enough to allow for the door.

6 **Mount the hinges.** Remove the hinges from the doors (they'll be pointed the wrong way) and reinstall them on the door based on the direction you want it to swing. Prop up the door alongside the box and align the door so there will be a 1/8-in. gap at the top and bottom of the box. Then screw the hinges to the box.

Figure A
Locker construction

Overall Dimensions:
16-1/2" wide x 81" tall x 12-1/4" deep

Materials list (for two lockers)

Because bifold doors are sold in pairs, and one sheet of 3/4-in. plywood yields two lockers, you can make the best use of materials by building an even number of lockers.

ITEM	QTY.
30" bifold door pack (2 doors)	1
3/4" x 4' x 8' plywood	1
1/4" x 4' x 8' plywood	1
1/4" x 3/4" x 8' screen molding	5
3/4" x 1-1/2" x 8' solid wood	9

2" trim-head screws, 1-1/4" screws, 1" nails, 1-1/2" nails, wood glue, no-mortise hinges, door handles and magnetic catches.

Cutting list (for one locker)

These locker parts suit a door measuring 14-3/4 x 78-3/4 in. Verify the exact size of your doors before building.

KEY	QTY.	SIZE & DESCRIPTION
A	2	11-3/4" x 80-7/8" sides (3/4" plywood)
B	2	11-3/4" x 15" top/bottom (3/4" plywood)
C	1	16-1/2" x 80-1/2" back (1/4" plywood)
D	2	3/4" x 1-1/2" x 15" shelf front/back (solid wood)
E	2	3/4" x 1-1/2" x 9-3/8" shelf sides (solid wood)
F	6	3/4" x 1-1/2" x 15" shelf slats (solid wood)

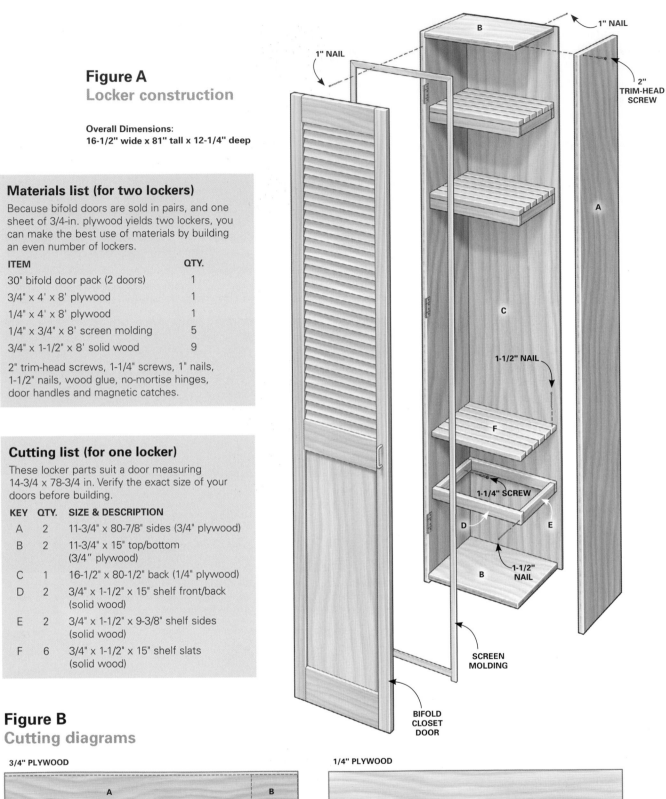

Figure B
Cutting diagrams

3/4" PLYWOOD

1/4" PLYWOOD

Shoe ladder

1 Clamp the 1x3 support to a piece of scrap wood as you drill the holes to prevent the wood from splintering.

6-3/4"
1-3/8" 3-1/2" 3/4" HOLE 5/8"
5-1/8"

Without constant vigilance, shoes tend to pile up into a mess next to entry doors. Untangle the mess with a simple, attractive shoe ladder that keeps everything from boots to slippers organized and off the floor.

Cut and drill the dowel supports (Photo 1), then screw them to 1x4s (Photo 2). Cut the 1x4s to fit your shoes and the available space—an average pair of adult shoes needs 10 in. of space. Nail or glue the dowels into the dowel supports, leaving 2 in. (or more) extending beyond the supports at the end to hang sandals or slippers.

Apply finish before you mount the shoe ladder to the wall. Screw the shoe ladder to studs or use heavy-duty toggle-bolt–style anchors to hold it in place.

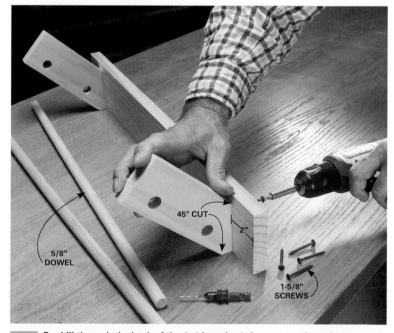

45° CUT
2"
5/8" DOWEL
1-5/8" SCREWS

2 Predrill through the back of the 1x4 into the 1x3 supports, then glue and screw the pieces together.

Storage cabinet

Thiis handsome cabinet is actually made from two inexpensive, unfinished cabinets purchased from a home center. The two cabinets are joined together with oak plywood and strips of solid oak, turning them into a new, larger cabinet. Use it to store books, small appliances, games and more. Assembly is amazingly fast and easy when you use a brad nailer and glue. Materials cost about $175.

First, screw the face frames of the two cabinets together. Drill pilot holes and drive screws through the lower face frame into the upper. Then lay them on one side and hold a straightedge across the fronts of the face frames to be sure they form a straight, flat surface. Slip a strip of cardboard between the two cabinet boxes to get the face frames aligned.

Next, add spacer strips that match the thickness of the protruding edge of the face frames. Cut strips just a hair thicker than 1/4 in. from a 2x4. Cutting thin strips on a table saw can be tricky, even dangerous, so use extra caution.

Fasten the strips with plenty of glue and a few brad nails. Then add the side panel (Photo 1). Make sure the front edge of the panel is perfectly flush with the face frames, and remember that the panel overhangs the lower cabinet by 1 in. Follow the same steps on the other side.

Lay the unit on its back and check that the doors are centered on the cabinets and in line with each other before

1 **Cover the sides.** Screw two cabinets together and glue spacer strips to the sides. Then glue on the side panels. Tack the panel into place, positioning nails where they'll be hidden by the legs or rails later.

2 **Add the legs and rails.** Attach one of the front legs, then dry-fit the rails and the other leg. When they all fit right, glue and tack them in place. Follow the same dry-fit routine for the side rails and the back legs.

3 **Top it off.** Glue the two layers of the top together. To attach the top, drive screws from inside the cabinet, through the fillers and into the top.

you add the legs and rails. The doors on these cabinets were a mess—we had to slip paper spacers behind one of the hinges and completely reinstall another.

Now you're ready to glue and nail on the legs and rails (Photo 2). Glue front leg parts (L, M and N) together, then add them to the cabinet. The top rail (T) is too thin to nail to the face frame, so just nail it to the center stile (S) and clamp it in place until the glue sets. Then remove the doors, finish-sand the whole chest and add the top, which is just two layers of plywood edge-banded and glued together (Photo 3).

Materials list

ITEM	QTY.
12" x 15" x 30" cabinet	1
12" x 30" x 30" cabinet	1
3/4" x 4' x 8' oak plywood	1
1x6 oak	30'

Edge band, knobs, wood glue, 2" screws, Minwax Early American stain, Minwax Wipe-On Poly

Cutting list

KEY	QTY.	SIZE & DESCRIPTION
A	1	12" x 30" x 15" cabinet
B	1	12" x 30" x 30" cabinet
C	1	3/4" x 13-3/4" x 35" top*
D	1	3/4" x 13-1/8" x 33-3/4" sub top*
E	2	3/4" x 3" x 28-1/4" fillers*
F	4	1-1/2" x 45" spacers (thickness varies)
G	2	3/4" x 12" x 46" side panels*
H	4	3/4" x 1-1/2" x 9-1/4" side rails
J	2	3/4" x 1-3/4" x 49" back legs
K	2	3/4" x 1-3/4" x 3" back leg blocks
L	2	3/4" x 1" x 3" front leg blocks
M	2	3/4" x 1" x 49" front leg sides
N	2	3/4" x 1-3/4" x 49" front legs
P	1	3/4" x 1-1/2" x 30" rail backer*
Q	1	3/4" x 1-1/2" x 29-1/2" bottom rail
R	1	3/4" x 5/8" x 29-1/2" middle rail
S	1	3/4" x 7/8" x 14-3/8" stile
T	1	3/4" x 1/4" x 29-1/2" top rail

*Plywood parts

Figure A
Storage cabinet

Overall dimensions:
50-1/2" tall x 35" wide x 13-3/4" deep

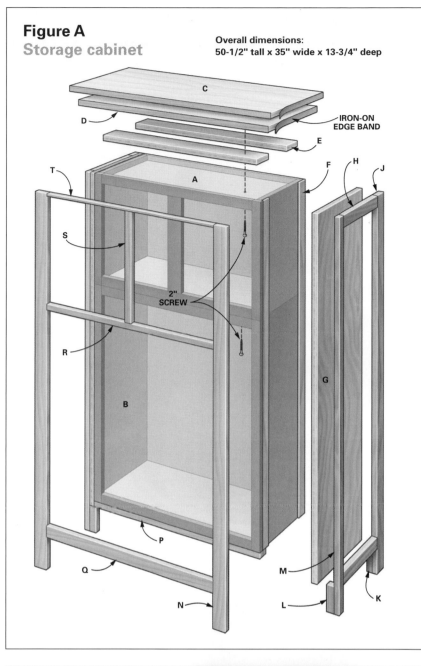

IRON-ON EDGE BAND

2" SCREW

Cheap trick: Edge banding

EDGE BAND

Every cheapskate should learn how to use iron-on edge band. It's the easiest way to cover plywood edges, and it makes inexpensive plywood look like solid wood. The top on this chest, for example, used less than $20 worth of plywood. Solid wood would have cost more than twice as much.

Leaning tower of shelves

This stylish but sturdy shelf unit will neatly hold your stuff

This shelf unit may look lightweight and easy to topple. But don't be fooled. It's a real workhorse. The 33-1/2-in. x 82-3/4-in. tower features five unique, tray-like shelves of different depths to hold a wide variety of items up to 13-1/4 in. tall. Despite its 10-degree lean, the unit is surprisingly sturdy, and its open design won't overpower a room.

Whether you choose to make this piece more functional, as in this office setting, or place it in a family room to showcase treasures, the basic construction is the same. Select the type of wood and stain or paint to dress it up (or down) to fit the look of any room.

All the materials can be purchased at home centers or lumberyards. The only special tools you'll need are a power miter saw for crisp angle cuts and a brad nailer for quick assembly and almost invisible joints. And you'll have to rustle up an old clothes iron for applying oak edge-banding. Once you've gathered all the material, you can build the shelf unit in one afternoon.

Buying the wood

This unit was built with red oak and oak veneer plywood and finished with two coats of red oak stain. The beauty of this project is that any wood species will work. If you plan to paint it, select alder or aspen for the solid parts and birch for the plywood.

One note when buying boards: Use a tape measure to check the "standard" dimensions of 1x3s and 1x4s. They sometimes vary in width and thickness. Also check the two full-length 1x4s you plan to use as the uprights to be sure they're straight, without warps or twists. And always examine the ends, edges and surface for blemishes or rough areas that won't easily sand out.

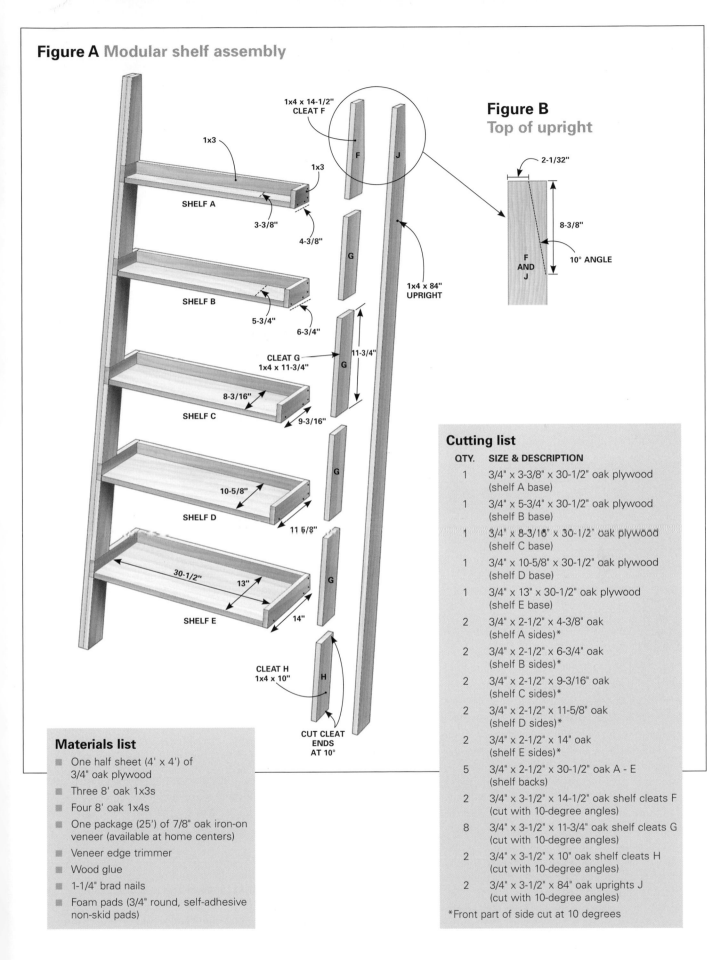

Figure A Modular shelf assembly

1x4 x 14-1/2"
CLEAT F

1x3

1x3

SHELF A

3-3/8"

4-3/8"

F

J

SHELF B

5-3/4"

6-3/4"

G

CLEAT G
1x4 x 11-3/4"

11-3/4"

G

8-3/16"

9-3/16"

SHELF C

G

10-5/8"

11 5/8"

SHELF D

G

30-1/2"   13"

14"

SHELF E

CLEAT H
1x4 x 10"

H

CUT CLEAT
ENDS
AT 10°

1x4 x 84"
UPRIGHT

Figure B
Top of upright

2-1/32"

8-3/8"

F
AND
J

10° ANGLE

Materials list

- One half sheet (4' x 4') of 3/4" oak plywood
- Three 8' oak 1x3s
- Four 8' oak 1x4s
- One package (25') of 7/8" oak iron-on veneer (available at home centers)
- Veneer edge trimmer
- Wood glue
- 1-1/4" brad nails
- Foam pads (3/4" round, self-adhesive non-skid pads)

Cutting list

QTY.	SIZE & DESCRIPTION
1	3/4" x 3-3/8" x 30-1/2" oak plywood (shelf A base)
1	3/4" x 5-3/4" x 30-1/2" oak plywood (shelf B base)
1	3/4" x 8-3/16" x 30-1/2" oak plywood (shelf C base)
1	3/4" x 10-5/8" x 30-1/2" oak plywood (shelf D base)
1	3/4" x 13" x 30-1/2" oak plywood (shelf E base)
2	3/4" x 2-1/2" x 4-3/8" oak (shelf A sides)*
2	3/4" x 2-1/2" x 6-3/4" oak (shelf B sides)*
2	3/4" x 2-1/2" x 9-3/16" oak (shelf C sides)*
2	3/4" x 2-1/2" x 11-5/8" oak (shelf D sides)*
2	3/4" x 2-1/2" x 14" oak (shelf E sides)*
5	3/4" x 2-1/2" x 30-1/2" oak A - E (shelf backs)
2	3/4" x 3-1/2" x 14-1/2" oak shelf cleats F (cut with 10-degree angles)
8	3/4" x 3-1/2" x 11-3/4" oak shelf cleats G (cut with 10-degree angles)
2	3/4" x 3-1/2" x 10" oak shelf cleats H (cut with 10-degree angles)
2	3/4" x 3-1/2" x 84" oak uprights J (cut with 10-degree angles)

*Front part of side cut at 10 degrees

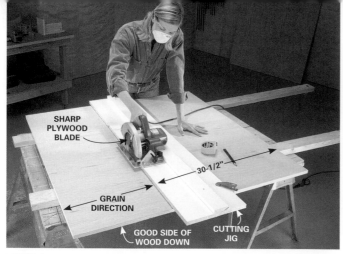

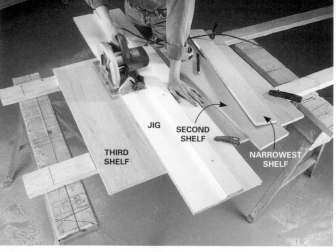

1 Cut 3/4-in. shelf plywood to width first, using a circular saw and a homemade jig for exact cuts. Use a sharp plywood blade and cut with the best side of the wood facing down to minimize splintering.

2 Cut the individual shelves, beginning with the narrowest, using the jig for perfectly straight cuts.

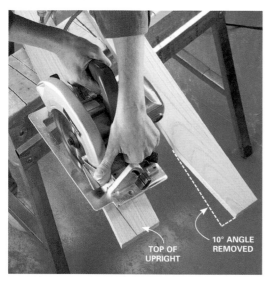

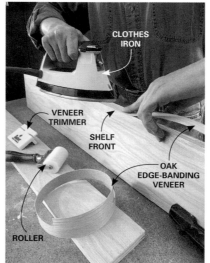

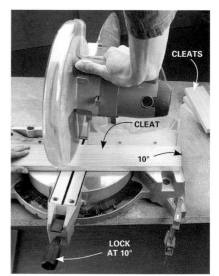

3 Cut both shelf uprights to length with a miter saw. Clamp to sawhorses. Mark the 10-degree angle at the top (dimensions in Figure B), then cut with a circular saw.

4 Iron edge-banding veneer to the front edge of all five shelves. Roll the entire surface to ensure a solid bond, and trim the edges.

5 To maintain accuracy, lock the miter box at 10 degrees, then cut all angled pieces—uprights, cleats and one end of shelf sides—without changing the table.

Cut plywood shelves first

Lay a couple of 2x4s across sawhorses (Photo 1) to cut the half sheet of 3/4-in. plywood cleanly and without pinching the saw blade. Since all five shelves are 30-1/2 in. wide, cut this width first, making sure the grain will run the long way across the shelves. Remember to wear safety glasses, earplugs and a dust mask. Make a homemade jig to fit your circular saw and clamp it to the plywood.

Next, cut all five shelf depths, starting with the smallest shelf (3-3/8 in.) first. Cut smallest to largest so you'll have enough wood to clamp the jig. Important: Make sure you account for the width of your saw blade when you cut each shelf.

Now mark and cut the top of all four 1x4 uprights (the end that rests against the wall), according to Photo 3 and the two dimensions provided in Figure B. Use a sharp blade in your circular saw to prevent splintering.

Select the best front of each plywood shelf, clamp it to the bench on edge and sand it smooth with 150-grit paper on a

sanding block. Then preheat a clothes iron to the "cotton" setting and run it over the top of the edge-banding veneer, making sure the veneer extends beyond all edges (Photo 4). Roll it smooth immediately after heating. Let each shelf edge cool for a couple of minutes before trimming and sanding the edges.

Cut the uprights and shelf frame next

Now set up the miter saw, which you use to make all the 90-degree straight cuts first (five shelf backs and 10 shelf sides; see Cutting list). Important: Remember that one end of each shelf side has a 10-degree cut, so first cut them square at their exact length, then cut the angle carefully so the long edge of each piece remains the same.

Next, rotate the miter saw table to the 10-degree mark and cut all the angle pieces. First cut the bottom of both uprights so each upright rests flat against the floor and wall (see Figure A). Then trim the top of the upright to match the bottom, being careful to maintain the 84-in. total length. Next, cut the cleats based on the

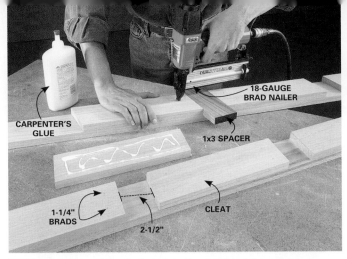

6 Glue and nail the shelf cleats to the uprights using a 1x3 spacer. Hold each cleat tight to the spacer.

- CARPENTER'S GLUE
- 18-GAUGE BRAD NAILER
- 1x3 SPACER
- 1-1/4" BRADS
- 2-1/2"
- CLEAT

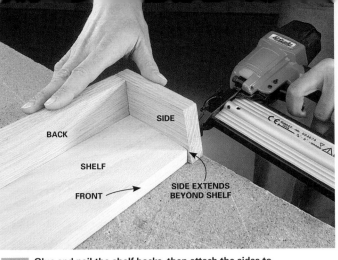

7 Glue and nail the shelf backs, then attach the sides to the plywood shelves. Position the sides to overlap the shelf base as shown.

- BACK
- SIDE
- SHELF
- FRONT
- SIDE EXTENDS BEYOND SHELF

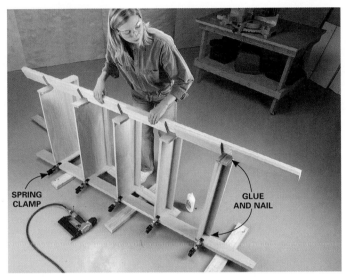

8 Clamp the shelves into one upright. Spread glue in the shelf notches of the other upright, position it flush with the front of the shelves and nail. Flip the unit over and attach the other upright.

- SPRING CLAMP
- GLUE AND NAIL

9 Set the shelf unit against a straight wall, check for squareness and apply three bar clamps until the glue dries.

- BAR CLAMP
- 1/2" GAP
- NON-SKID FOAM PAD

Cutting list dimensions, which are measured edge to edge (Photo 5 and Figure A). Leave the top cleats long and cut them to exact fit during assembly. Then, to speed finishing, use an orbital sander with 150-grit sandpaper to smooth all pieces before assembly.

Assemble uprights first, then the shelves

To begin assembly, lay out both uprights and all cleats to ensure that the angles are correct so the shelves will be level when the unit is against the wall. Then glue and nail the first cleat flush with the base of each upright (using five or six 1-1/4-in. brads) on each cleat. Work your way upward using 1x3 spacers (Photo 6). Make sure the spacer is the exact same width as the shelf sides! Set these aside to dry.

For shelf assembly, first glue and nail on the shelf backs. Next, apply the sides with glue and nails (Photo 7).

For final assembly, lay one upright on 2x4s, then clamp on the shelves as shown in Photo 8. Apply the glue, position the second upright on top flush with the front edge of the shelves, then sink four 1-1/4-in. brads into each shelf from the upright side. Carefully turn the unit over and repeat the process to attach the second upright. Work quickly so the glue doesn't set. Lift the ladder shelf and place it upright against a straight wall. Check it with a framing square and flex it if necessary to square it up and to make sure that the uprights rest flat against the floor and wall (assuming your floor is level). Attach three bar clamps as shown in Photo 9 while the glue dries.

The shelf is highly stable as designed, but once you've stained or painted it, you can add self-adhesive foam gripping pads to the bottom of the uprights. And if you don't feel secure having it on a slippery floor, the unit's width is perfect for screwing the top of the uprights into wall studs.

Coat hooks for DIYers

Distinctive hooks, DIY style

Looking for a present for a DIYer (or yourself)? Here's a gallery of creative coat hook ideas to spark your imagination.

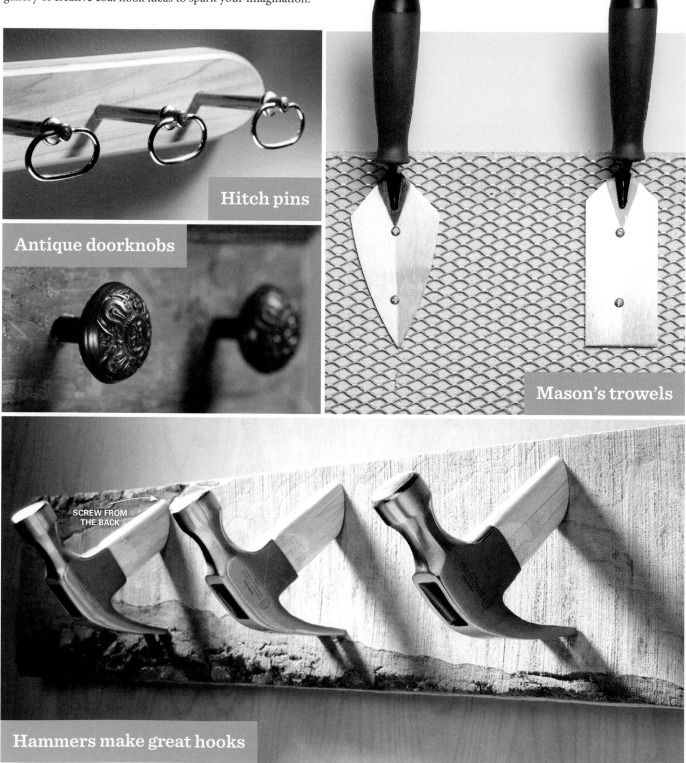

Hitch pins

Antique doorknobs

Mason's trowels

SCREW FROM THE BACK

Hammers make great hooks

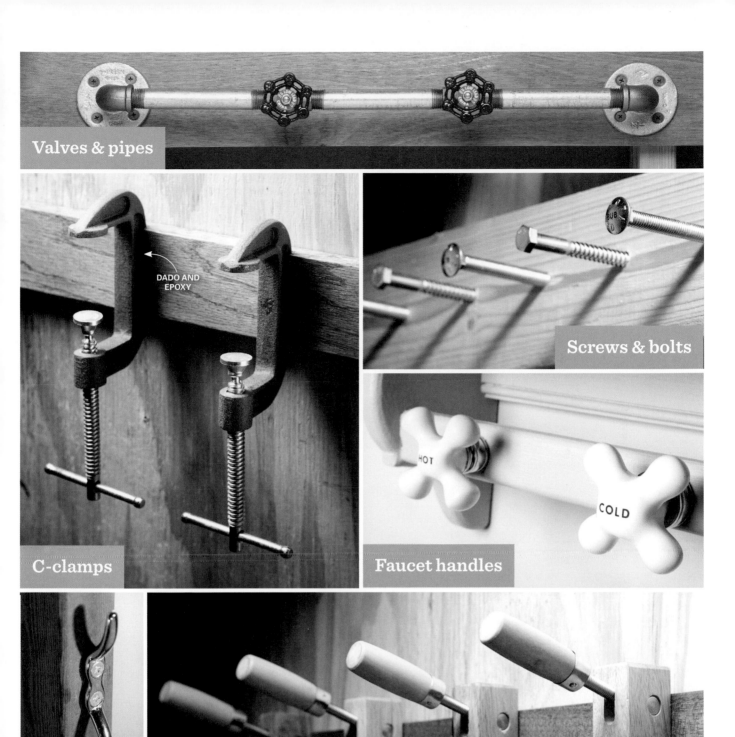

Valves & pipes

C-clamps

DADO AND EPOXY

Screws & bolts

Faucet handles

HOT

COLD

Cleats

Hand screw clamps

THREADED ROD IN ANGLED HOLE

Traditional coat & mitten rack

This coat rack is easy to build with butt joints connected by screws that get hidden with wooden screw-hole buttons and wood plugs. It mounts easily to the wall with screws driven through the hidden hanging strip on the back. The five large Shaker pegs are great for holding hats, umbrellas and coats, and the hinged-hatch door at the top keeps the clutter of gloves and scarves from view.

Maple is an ideal wood for Shaker-style pieces, but any hardwood will do. All you need for this project is wood, hardware and varnish.

Cutting the pieces

First transfer the pattern measurements in Figure A, p. 63 (using a compass), and then cut the sides (A) with a jigsaw. Next cut the top (D) to length and rip the shelf (B) to the width given in the Cutting list, p. 63. Cut the hanging strip (F) and the peg strip (C) to the same length as the shelf (B). Now drill the 3/8-in. counterbore holes for the screw-hole buttons (with your spade bit) 3/16 in.

deep into the outsides of parts A (as shown in Figure A, and Photo 2). Also drill the 3/8-in. counterbore holes in the top. These holes must be 3/8 in. deep.

Mark and drill the 1/2-in. holes for the Shaker pegs in the peg strip. Drill the holes for the Shaker pegs perfectly perpendicular to the peg strip to ensure they all project evenly when glued in place.

Note: Be sure this project is screwed to the wall studs. Drill two holes into the hanging strip at stud locations and use 2-1/2-in. or longer wood screws.

Figure A
Coat & mitten rack details

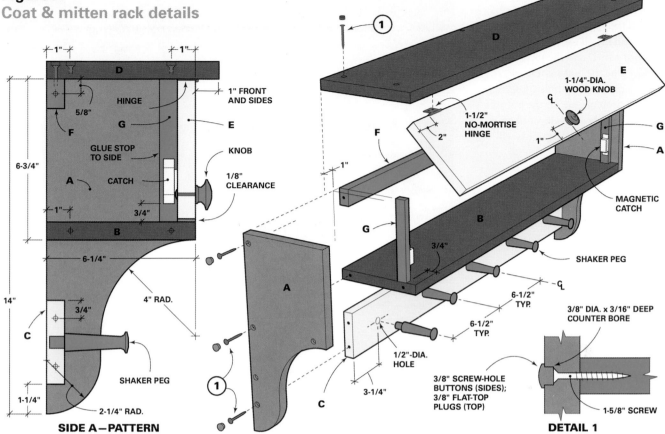

1" FRONT AND SIDES

HINGE

5/8"

GLUE STOP TO SIDE

KNOB

CATCH

1/8" CLEARANCE

6-3/4"

A

B

6-1/4"

4" RAD.

14"

3/4"

C

SHAKER PEG

1-1/4"

2-1/4" RAD.

SIDE A—PATTERN

D

E

F

G

1

3/4"

A

C

3-1/4"

1/2"-DIA. HOLE

1-1/4"-DIA. WOOD KNOB

1-1/2" NO-MORTISE HINGE

2"

1"

MAGNETIC CATCH

SHAKER PEG

6-1/2" TYP.

6-1/2" TYP.

3/8" DIA. x 3/16" DEEP COUNTER BORE

3/8" SCREW-HOLE BUTTONS (SIDES); 3/8" FLAT-TOP PLUGS (TOP)

1-5/8" SCREW

DETAIL 1

Cutting list

KEY	PCS.	SIZE & DESCRIPTION
A	2	3/4" x 6-1/4" x 14" maple sides
B	1	3/4" x 6-1/4" x 32-1/2" maple shelf
C	1	3/4" x 3-1/2" x 32-1/2" maple peg strip
D	1	3/4" x 7-1/4" x 36" maple top
E	1	3/4" x 5-13/16" x 32-5/16" maple hatch
F	1	3/4" x 1-1/4" x 32-1/2" maple hanging strip
G	2	3/4" x 1/2" x 6" maple hatch stop

Materials list

ITEM	QTY.
1-1/2" no-mortise hinges	1 pair
1-1/4" beech knob	1
Narrow magnetic catch	2
3-3/8"-long Shaker pegs	5
3/8" screw-hole buttons	10
3/8" plugs	5
3/8" spade bit	1
1/2" spade bit	1
1-5/8" wood screws	15
Wood glue	1 pint
Wipe-on polyurethane	1 pint
150- and 220-grit sandpaper	

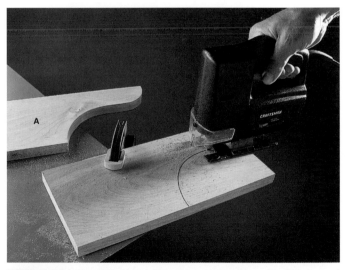

1 Cut the side pieces (A) using a jigsaw or band saw. Sand the curved edges smooth.

Assembly

Lay the pieces on your workbench, as shown in Photo 3. Align the hanging strip (F), the shelf (B), and the peg strip (C) as shown and clamp the sides (A) to these parts. Predrill the holes with a combination pilot hole/countersink bit using the center of the counterbore holes as a guide. Next, screw the sides to B, C and F. Fasten the top (D) to the sides in the same manner.

Glue and clamp the hatch stops to the insides of parts A, as shown in Figure A. To finish the assembly, cut the hatch (E) to size and install the hinges to the underside of part D and the top of the hatch. Now glue the buttons and pegs into their corresponding holes. Use only a small drop of glue for the buttons but be sure to apply a thin layer of glue completely around the plugs. This will swell the plugs for a tight fit.

Finishing

Lightly sand the entire piece after assembly with 220-grit sandpaper. Apply two coats of clear wipe-on polyurethane to all the surfaces (remove the hinges and knobs). Once the finish is dry, add two magnetic catches to the hatch-stop molding (G).

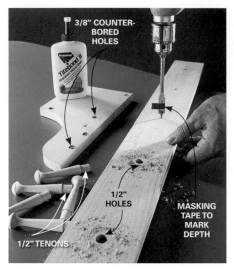

2 Drill the 1/2-in. holes 5/8 in. deep for the 3-3/8-in. Shaker pegs. Drill the 3/8-in. counterbore holes 3/16 in. deep for the screw-hole buttons in the sides (see Figure A, Detail 1).

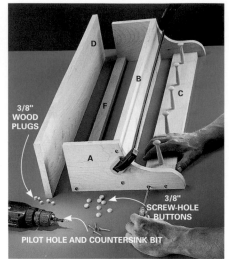

3 Assemble the shelf by clamping parts C, F and B to the sides. Drill pilot holes and screw the pieces together. The screws will be covered by the buttons and plugs.

Shoe-storage stool

Build this double-duty step stool from six pieces of 3/4-in. plywood.

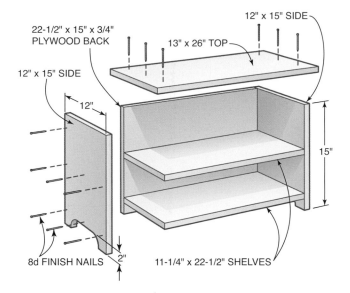

Build this handy stool in one hour and park it in your closet. You can also use it as a step to reach the high shelf. All you need is a 4 x 4-ft. sheet of 3/4-in. plywood, wood glue and a handful of 8d finish nails. Cut the plywood pieces according to the illustration.

Spread wood glue on the joints, then nail them together with 8d finish nails. First nail through the sides into the back. Then nail through the top into the sides and back. Finally, mark the location of the two shelves and nail through the sides into the shelves.

Mobile stacking totes

Stud stuffer

Make these stacking totes from 1/2-in. birch veneer plywood. The dimensions given here allow each tote to interlock snugly with the one above and below it. You can cut four totes from one full sheet of plywood—five from about a sheet and a third. Cut all the plywood parts to size, cut out the hand grips and sand all edges smooth. Then glue and assemble the totes with 4d finish nails. Leave them unfinished or apply paint or stain. Mount 2-in. casters on the bottom tote to make the stack mobile.

Transform a bare wall space into an attractive storage shelf. This shelf fits anywhere between studs (behind a door, for example) spaced 16-in. on center. Build the box as tall as you want. (It could be a broom closet!) Use 14-1/4-in.-wide, 1x4 boards screwed together at each corner with 1-5/8-in. drywall screws. Frame the box with trim that matches other trim in the room. Nail and glue on a 1/4-in.-thick plywood back. Cut out the hole in your wall. Screw or nail the box to the studs through the sides of the box. You can finish yours off with a 1x4 shelf.

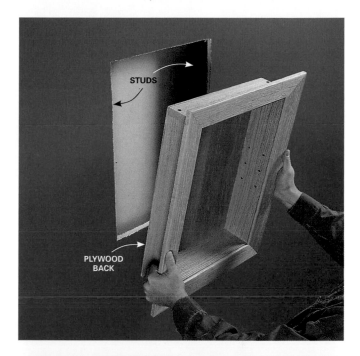

STUDS

PLYWOOD
BACK

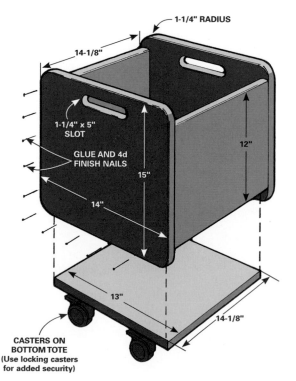

1-1/4" RADIUS

14-1/8"

1-1/4" x 5"
SLOT

GLUE AND 4d
FINISH NAILS

12"

15"

14"

13"

14-1/8"

CASTERS ON
BOTTOM TOTE
(Use locking casters
for added security)

NAIL HERE

3-tier basket stand

You've seen chests of drawers—well, here's a "chest of baskets." It can be used in nearly any room—but its small footprint makes it perfect for bathrooms with limited floor space. Use it for towels, hair dryers, extra toilet paper and anything else that fits.

The total materials bill for our pine stand, including the baskets, was about $50. We bought baskets at a craft store, but lots of other retailers like Pier 1, West Elm and IKEA also carry them. Make sure to buy your baskets first; you need to construct the stand based on their dimensions.

To keep the frame of the stand both lightweight and strong, we used biscuit joinery. It's a clever way to join wood, and a technique you can use with many other projects. See p. 68 for biscuit joiner tips.

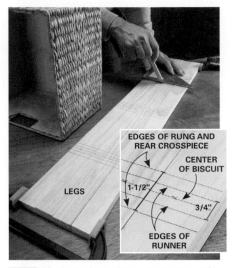

Image 1 labels: EDGES OF RUNG AND REAR CROSSPIECE, CENTER OF BISCUIT, LEGS, 1-1/2", 3/4", EDGES OF RUNNER

Image 3 labels: RUNG, LEG

1 **Mark the legs.** Clamp the legs together and mark them all at the same time. That way, all your marks will line up and you'll avoid mismatches.

2 **Cut the biscuit slots.** Cut slots in the ends of the rungs and sides of the legs. Assemble each ladder in a "dry run" to make sure they fit together correctly.

3 **Assemble the "ladders."** Join the rungs to the legs with glue and biscuits, then clamp the ladders together. Work fast! You have to assemble eight joints before the glue begins to set.

Biscuits make it easy—and strong

How to build it

You'll build the two "ladders" that form the sides of the stand, then glue and nail the crosspieces to join the two ladders.

To get started, cut all the parts to length (see Cutting list, p. 68). Mark the rung and crosspiece locations on the legs. Mark all four legs at the same time to ensure the framework is uniform and square (Photo 1).

As you mark the legs, keep picturing how your baskets will sit on the runners, especially if you're using baskets smaller or larger than ours; it will help you avoid mental errors. Use the biscuit joiner to cut slots in the edges of the legs and ends of the rungs (Photo 2). You'll need to clip the biscuits to suit the 1-1/2-in.-wide legs and rungs (see p. 68).

Apply glue to the biscuits and slots (Photo 3) and assemble each joint. Clamp the ladders together and set them aside until the glue dries.

Join the two ladders by gluing and nailing the crosspieces between them. Remember that the three front crosspieces that will support the baskets lie flat. Next, install the basket runners (Photo 4) even with the flat crosspieces that run across the front. Glue and nail the 3/4-in. plywood top to the stand, then apply cove molding to cover the edges (Photo 5).

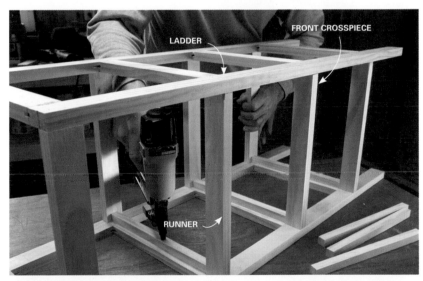

Image labels: LADDER, FRONT CROSSPIECE, RUNNER

4 **Connect the ladders.** Install the front and back crosspieces with glue and nails. Then add the runners that support the baskets.

Image labels: PLYWOOD TOP, COVE MOLDING

5 **Top it off.** Glue and nail the plywood top to the top of the stand, then apply cove molding to neaten up and hide the edges.

Figure A
Basket stand

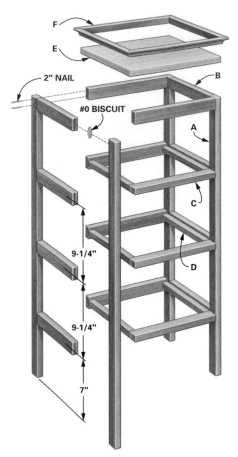

F
E
2" NAIL
#0 BISCUIT
A
B
C
D
9-1/4"
9-1/4"
7"

Overall Dimensions:
14-1/2" x 15-1/4" x 36-3/4"

Materials list

Here's what we used to make this basket stand: 30 ft. of 1x2, 6 ft. of 3/4-in. x 3/4-in. square dowel, 6 ft. of 3/4-in. cove molding, 3/4-in. plywood, 12 x 12 x 8-in. baskets, No. 0 biscuits, wood glue, 2-in. finish nails, cherry Danish oil finish.

Cutting list

KEY	PCS.	SIZE & DESCRIPTION
A	4	3/4" x 1-1/2" x 36" legs
B	8	3/4" x 1-1/2" x 10" rungs
C	8	3/4" x 1-1/2" x 12-1/4" crosspieces
D	6	3/4" x 3/4" x 10-3/4" runners
E	1	3/4" x 13" x 13-3/4" top
F	4	3/4" cove molding (cut to fit)

Using biscuit joiners

A biscuit joiner is a superb tool for joining wood where it would be difficult to use nails or screws. The joint is strong, invisible and easy to create. The compressed wood biscuits expand on contact with moisture in the glue. Since the biscuits are placed in slots that are wider than the biscuit, you can adjust the joint a little after butting the two pieces together. Biscuits come in three common sizes: No. 0, No. 10 and No. 20. Whether you're building this basket stand or some other biscuit project, here are some of our favorite biscuit tips:

Clip biscuits for narrow stock

The smallest common biscuits (No. 0) are almost 1-7/8 in. long. That's too long for the 1-1/2-in. wide parts on this basket stand. But there's an easy solution: Just clip about 1/4 in. off both ends of each biscuit. Your slots will still be too long and visible at inside corners, but a little filler and finish will hide them.

Number the joints

While you're marking the center lines of each biscuit slot, also number each joint. That will eliminate confusion and misalignments during assembly.

Make a glue injector

Spreading a neat, even bead of glue inside a biscuit slot isn't easy. You can buy special injectors online, or make your own using the cap from a marker and a fine-tooth saw.

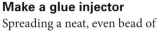

Always do a dry run

Biscuits grab fast. During glue-up, you don't have time to correct mistakes or dig up a longer set of clamps. So always test the whole assembly—including clamps— before you get out the glue. For complicated assemblies, give yourself more working time by using slow-setting wood glue. Titebond Extend is one brand.

Closet rod and shelf

This project will save you hours of ironing and organizing. Now you can hang up your shirts and jackets as soon as they're out of the dryer—no more wrinkled shirts at the bottom of the basket. You'll also gain an out-of-the-way upper shelf to store all sorts of odds and ends.

Just go to your home center and get standard closet rod brackets, a closet rod and a precut 12-in.-deep melamine shelf. Also pick up some drywall anchors, or if you have concrete, some plastic anchors and a corresponding masonry bit. Follow the instructions in Photos 1 and 2.

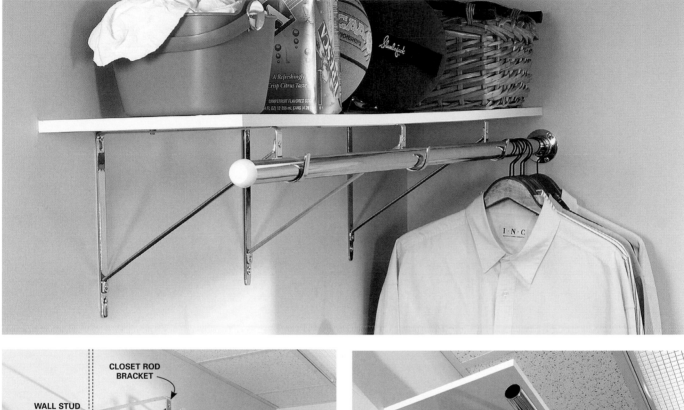

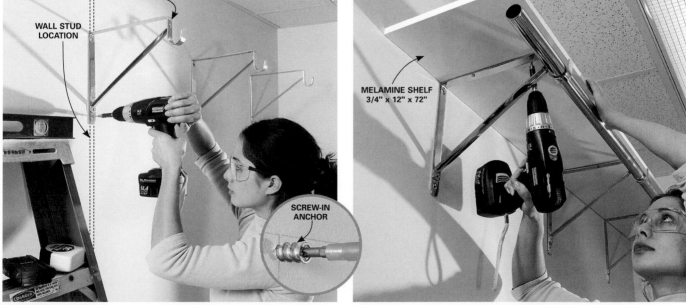

1 Draw a level line about 78 in. above the floor and locate the studs behind the drywall. Fasten at least two of your closet rod brackets into wall studs (4 ft. apart) and then center the middle bracket with two 2-in.-long screws into wall anchors (inset).

2 Fasten your 12-in.-deep melamine shelf onto the tops of the brackets with 1/2-in. screws. Next, insert your closet rod, drill 1/8-in. holes into the rod, and secure it to the brackets with No. 6 x 1/2-in. sheet metal screws.

Chapter Three

GARAGE UPGRADES

Super sturdy drawers

Super big, super tough, super easy

WHAT IT TAKES

(for four units)

COST: $460

TIME: 2 days

SKILL: Beginner to intermediate

TOOLS: Circular saw (table saw preferable), drill, 18-gauge brad nailer, router/round-over bit, clamp

Getting started

We'll focus on how to build one unit, but you can build as many as you like and arrange them whichever way works best. Refer to the Cutting diagram (p. 76), and cut all the plywood components except the back (C), drawer bottoms (D) and hardwood drawer fronts (L, M, N). Cut these parts to size as you need them in case one or more components get a little out of whack. Many home centers will help you cut your plywood so it's easier to haul home, but don't wear out your welcome and expect them to make all the cuts for you.

Cut and install the drawer supports

Lay the two sides (A) next to each other on your workbench. Position them so the surface with the most flaws faces up—this will be the inside and won't be visible once the drawers are installed. Also, determine which of the plywood edges have the fewest flaws and voids, and arrange the pieces so the best edges face toward the front. Measure up from the bottom on each side 14 in., 26 in. and 38 in., and make a pencil mark near the outside edge of each side. Use a straightedge, and draw a line between your marks and across the face of both sides at the same time. These will be the guidelines for the tops of the drawer supports (P).

Cut 18 in. off the 6-ft. pine 1x4, and set it aside to be used as the center brace (Q). Rip down what's left of the 1x4 into 1-in. strips to be used as the six drawer supports, and cut them to length (see Cutting list on p. 76).

Install the drawer supports with glue and 1-1/2-in. brads (Photo 1). The drawer supports should be 1/2 in. short on the front side to accommodate the thickness of the hardwood drawer fronts. Flip the sides over and install three 1-1/2-in. screws in each support. Countersink all the screws a bit on the outside of the entire carcass so the holes can be filled with wood filler before painting.

Assemble the carcass

Apply wood glue and tack on the top or bottom (B) to the sides with three or four brads. Even if you picked the straightest plywood available at the home center or lumberyard, it will

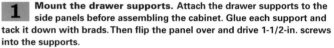

18-GAUGE BRAD NAILER WITH 1-1/2" BRADS

DRAWER SUPPORT

DRAWER SUPPORT GUIDELINE

1 **Mount the drawer supports. Attach the drawer supports to the** side panels before assembling the cabinet. Glue each support and tack it down with brads. Then flip the panel over and drive 1-1/2-in. screws into the supports.

STAY 1-1/2" FROM END

1-1/2" TRIM HEAD SCREWS

2 **Assemble the carcass. Fasten the sides to the top and bottom** with glue and brads, and then add screws. To avoid splitting the plywood, drill pilot holes for the screws and stay 1-1/2 in. from the ends.

3 **Add the back. Use the back to square up the cabinet. Fasten** the whole length of one side, and then align the other sides with the back as you go.

probably cup and curl a bit after it's cut up. So whenever you join two pieces of plywood, start on one end and straighten out the plywood as you go.

Secure each joint with three 1-1/2-in. screws before moving on to the next one. Whenever drilling close to the edge of plywood, avoid puckers and splits by predrilling 1/8-in. holes for the screws. And stay at least 1-1/2-in. from the end of the plywood that's being drilled into (Photo 2). If a screw is installed too close to the end, it will just split the plywood instead of burying into it.

Spread glue on the back edge of the carcass and fasten the back with 1-1/2-in. brads along one whole side first. Then use the back as a guide to square up the rest of the carcass (Photo 3). Finish attaching the back with screws every 16 in. or so.

The center brace keeps the plywood sides from bowing in or out. Measure the distance between the drawer runners at the back of the carcass. Cut the center brace that same length. Install the brace between the two middle runners 4 in. back from the front. Make sure the brace is flush or just a little lower than the drawer supports or the drawer will teeter back and forth on it. Hold it in place with a clamp and secure it with two 3-in. screws through each side (Photo 4). Install a brace at more than one drawer support location if your plywood is particularly unruly.

Assemble the drawers

Lay out each drawer so all the best edges face up. Then, just as you did with the carcass, assemble the drawers with glue, brads and screws. Cut the drawer bottoms after the sides (F, H, K) and fronts/backs (E, G, J) are assembled. That way you can cut the bottoms exactly to size. A perfectly square bottom will ensure your drawers are also square. Make sure the bottom is flush or a little short on the front side of the drawer; otherwise the hardwood drawer fronts won't sit flat on the front of the drawer (Photo 5).

Fasten the drawer fronts

Our home center carried three options of hardwood plywood: oak, birch and one labeled just "hardwood." We went with the generic hardwood, but if you do the same,

4 **Install the center brace.** The brace prevents the sides from bowing in or out. Clamp the brace in place, and then fasten it with 3-in. trim head screws.

3" SCREW   CENTER BRACE

DRAWER BOTTOM

GLUE

5 **Build the drawers.** Assemble the drawers just as you built the cabinets: Glue, nail and screw the sides, front and back. Then square up the box as you fasten the bottom.

make sure you get enough to finish your project because the grain and color will vary from one batch to the next.

The drawers may not sit perfectly flat until they are filled with stuff, so before you secure the hardwood drawer fronts, add some weight to the drawer you're working on and the one above it. And center each drawer in the opening before you secure the drawer front.

Start at the bottom, and cut the hardwood drawer fronts to size one at a

time. Cut them so there's a 1/8-in. gap between the bottom and the sides and the bottom of the drawer above it. Rest the drawer front on a couple of shims to achieve the gap at the bottom and eyeball the gaps on the side. Glue it and secure it with four brads, one in each corner (Photo 6). There's no need for screws; the handle bolts will sandwich everything together. If you're building several of these storage units and purchased a piece of hardwood plywood larger than 2 x 4 ft., you'll have the option to line up the grain on the drawer fronts the same way it came off the sheet. It's a small detail that can add a lot to the looks of your project.

Build and attach the handles

Rout the edges of the handle with a 1/4-in. round-over bit before cutting the handles (R) to length. Next, cut the dowels for the handle extensions (S) to length.

Build one simple jig to align the dowels on the handles, and to position the

handles on the drawer fronts. Cut a 3/4-in. piece of plywood the same width as the drawer fronts and rip it down to 4-3/8 in. Fasten a scrap of 3/4-in. material to the end of the jig. Measure in from each side and mark a line at 2-1/8 in., 3-1/8 in. and 4-3/8 in.

This jig is designed to center the top handle on the top drawer front and keep the others the same distance down from the top on all the other drawers. If you want all the handles centered, you'll have to build two more jigs or mark center lines on the other drawers.

HANDLE

Set the jig on your workbench and line up the handle with the two outside lines. Line up the dowels on the inside and middle lines on the jig and glue the dowels to the center of handles. No need for clamping—just keep pressure on them for 10 to 20 seconds. Then set them aside

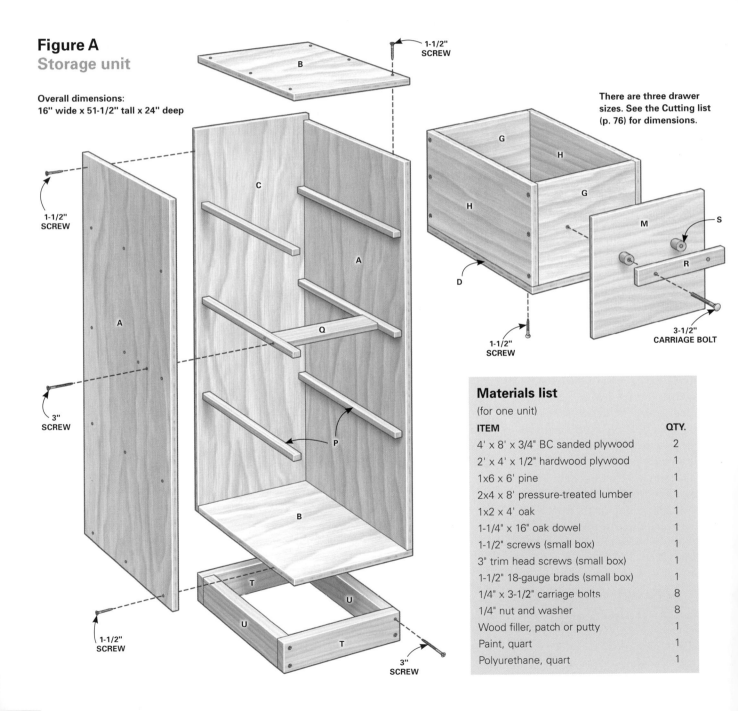

Figure A
Storage unit

Overall dimensions:
16" wide x 51-1/2" tall x 24" deep

1-1/2" SCREW

B

1-1/2" SCREW

C

A

3" SCREW

A

Q

P

B

T

U

U

T

1-1/2" SCREW

3" SCREW

There are three drawer sizes. See the Cutting list (p. 76) for dimensions.

G

H

G

H

D

M

S

R

1-1/2" SCREW

3-1/2" CARRIAGE BOLT

Materials list
(for one unit)

ITEM	QTY.
4' x 8' x 3/4" BC sanded plywood	2
2' x 4' x 1/2" hardwood plywood	1
1x6 x 6' pine	1
2x4 x 8' pressure-treated lumber	1
1x2 x 4' oak	1
1-1/4" x 16" oak dowel	1
1-1/2" screws (small box)	1
3" trim head screws (small box)	1
1-1/2" 18-gauge brads (small box)	1
1/4" x 3-1/2" carriage bolts	8
1/4" nut and washer	8
Wood filler, patch or putty	1
Paint, quart	1
Polyurethane, quart	1

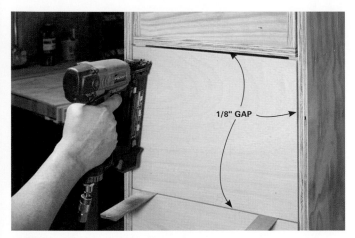

6 **Position the drawer fronts.** Slip the drawer boxes into the cabinet. Center the drawer fronts and shim under them to achieve 1/8-in. gaps. Secure the fronts to the drawer boxes with glue and one brad in each corner.

1/8" GAP

7 **Add the handles.** Build a simple jig and clamp it onto the drawer front. Hold the handle in place and drill holes for the carriage bolts.

DOWEL GUIDELINES
HANDLE GUIDELINE
3/4" SCRAP
JIG

for an hour or so to let the glue dry. The glue is just to keep the dowels in place until the handle bolts are installed.

Clamp the jig onto the top of the drawer front, and line up the handle with the guidelines. Drill a starter hole through each handle and the drawer front with a 1/8-in. drill bit before drilling the final holes with a 1/4-in. bit (Photo 7). The 1/8-in. bit probably won't be long enough to clear all the material, but it still helps make a cleaner hole when you drill through the second time.

Mark the bottom of each handle extension and the area near the hole on each drawer with the same number so you can install that same handle on the same drawer after you apply the finish.

Build and secure the base

If you're building only one unit, cut the base parts (T) and assemble them with glue and two 3-in. screws that are compatible with pressure-treated lumber. Secure the base to the bottom of the carcass with glue and 1-1/2-in. screws: three on the sides and two each on the front and back.

Finish the components

Patch all the screw holes, brad holes and voids on the carcass with wood filler or wood patch. Paint only the outside and front of the cabinet. Don't bother painting the insides, backs or sides that are going to be sandwiched together. Cover the hardwood drawer fronts and edges with two coats of polyurethane, or a similar coating of your choice. Avoid discoloration around the brad hole on the drawer fronts by filling them with matching putty between coats of poly. You can stain the oak handles with a medium-tinted stain to make them "pop" a little more before finishing them with two coats of poly.

Install the handles with the carriage bolts, washers and nuts. Seat the carriage bolts with a hammer so they don't spin while you turn the nut, and turn them tight.

Install multiple units

If you're building several units, build the base and then set each unit in place individually (Photo 8). Create a toe space by building the base 4 in. narrower than the units. This garage floor slants down toward the overhead door, so we had to rip down the base to make the whole thing level. You may just need a few shims to make yours level. Level each storage unit as you go and screw them to the base and to one another with 1-1/2-in.screws. Angle the screws a bit so they don't poke through when you screw the units together.

Rip down a couple of cleats and screw them to the sides for the middle shelf to sit on. Leave them a couple inches short of the front so you don't see them. Attach the lower shelf to the base before you install the middle shelf (Photo 9).

Once all the units are in place, attach the top(s) so the seams fall in the middle of one unit. Screw the whole thing to the wall studs last using one screw per unit. The front side of the base may need a few shims to make it sit flush against the wall.

Touch up the exposed screw holes and scuff marks with paint. Now all that's left is to file away all that clutter.

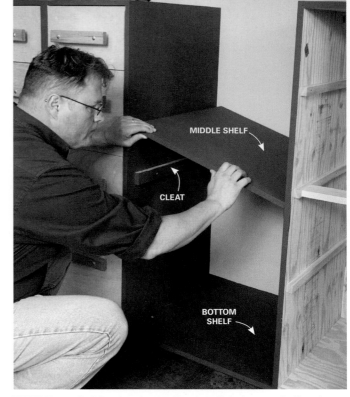

8 Set the carcass on the base. When installing multiple units, build, paint and lay down the base first, and then attach each unit to the base.

9 Hang shelving between units. Install the bottom shelf on the base. Install cleats to support other shelves.

Cutting list (for one unit)

KEY	QTY.	SIZE & DESCRIPTION

3/4" BC SANDED PLYWOOD

A	2	46-1/2" x 23-1/4" sides
B	2	16" x 23-1/4" top/bottom
C	1	48" x 16" back*
D	4	22-3/4" x 14-1/4" drawer bottoms*
E	2	12-3/4" x 12" bottom drawer front/back
F	2	22-3/4" x 12" bottom drawer sides
G	4	12-3/4" x 10" middle drawer front/back
H	4	22-3/4" x 10" middle drawer sides
J	2	12-3/4" x 7-1/4" top drawer front/back
K	2	22-3/4" x 7-1/4" top drawer sides

1/2" HARDWOOD PLYWOOD

L	1	14-1/4" x 13-7/8" bottom drawer front*
M	2	14-1/4" x 11-7/8" middle drawer fronts*
N	1	14-1/4" x 8-3/8" top drawer front*

CUT FROM 6' PINE 1x4

P	6	22-1/2" x 1" x 3/4" drawer supports
Q	1	12-1/2" x 3-1/2" x 3/4" center brace

CUT FROM 4' OAK 1x2

R	4	10" x 1-1/2" x 3/4" handles

CUT FROM 1' OAK 1-1/4" DOWEL

S	8	1" x 1-1/4" handle extensions

CUT FROM 8' PRESSURE-TREATED 2x4

T	2	16" x 1-1/2" x 3-1/2" base front/back
U	2	17" x 1-1/2" x 3-1/2" base sides

*Cut to fit

Figure B
Cutting diagram

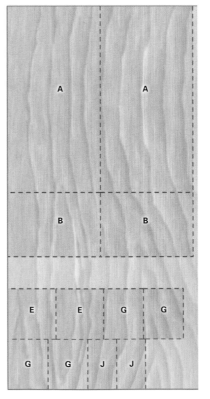

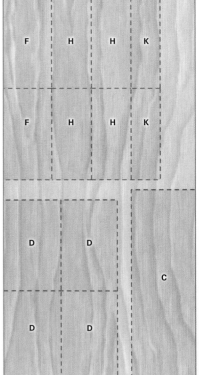

Stain or seal a concrete floor

Concrete stain gives concrete the mottled look of natural stone.

KEMIKO CONCRETE STAINS

Concrete stain

A stain isn't really a coating but a translucent decorative coloring that soaks into the concrete and creates a pigmented, marbled appearance that resembles natural stone. It typically requires two coats and is applied with a roller or sprayer and then immediately worked into the concrete with a nylon scrubbing brush. The stain itself doesn't protect the concrete, so after it dries, you rinse the surface and then apply one or two coats of urethane sealer to protect against moisture, chemicals and stains (see "urethane sealer" below). Depending on the traffic your floor gets, you may need to wax the sealer annually and touch up the stain and reseal the floor every two years.

Cost: 20¢ to 85¢ per sq. ft. for one coat (not including the price of the urethane topcoat). Available at home centers and online dealers.

Concrete sealers

S ealers are like floor paint, but tougher. After paints, they're the least expensive coating and they're very easy to apply with a brush or roller. They dry to a clear satin or semigloss finish depending on the product, and you can also get them tinted. There are water-based and solvent-based versions.

Concrete sealers come in clear and tinted versions.

QUIKRETE COMPANIES

URETHANE SEALER

Urethane sealer is significantly tougher than acrylic/latex sealer, but it doesn't bond well with bare concrete. It provides a clear, high-gloss finish that resists chemicals better than epoxy alone and is less likely to yellow in sunlight, which is why it's used as a seal coat over epoxy and concrete stain. However, urethane sealer is more expensive than acrylic sealer, and solvent-based versions require the use of a respirator during application.

Cost: 25¢ to 50¢ per sq. ft. for one coat depending on the product. Available at home centers and online.

ACRYLIC/LATEX SEALER

Like floor paint, acrylic/latex sealer is vulnerable to chemicals and isn't as tough as an epoxy, so it'll benefit from an annual protective waxing or reapplication every few years. Acrylic/latex sealer will stick better to a concrete floor than urethane sealer, which is why it's sometimes used as a primer for oil-based floor paint or epoxy.

Cost: 20¢ or less per sq. ft. for one coat; at home centers and online.

Install a retractable air hose reel

There's nothing like having compressed air handy for filling tires or running air-powered tools in the garage. But what a hassle it is to unfurl (and trip over) and stow an air hose all the time. However, you can reach up and pull the air hose down from the ceiling if you install a retractable air hose reel just like pros have in their shops. It's really very easy to do and quite affordable.

The whole job will only take an afternoon. You'll need to have copper soldering tools and the know-how to sweat copper joints.

Many home centers carry air line accessories. If yours doesn't, check out local tool suppliers or online sources. Hose reel prices range from $60 to more than $250. For the average DIYer, the 25-ft., $60 model will work just fine. Expect to pay about $99 for a 50-ft. model. The high-end models offer smoother operation and a sophisticated rewind mechanism that reduces the possibility of "hose whip." (Hose whip is a great way to take out a windshield—don't ask how we know!)

Find a location directly in front of the hood of your car or in the middle of your work area. Position the compressor in a permanent, out-of-the-way spot. Then measure the distance across the ceiling and down to the compressor, and also over to your workbench. Add about 15 percent for waste, and purchase that amount of 1/2-in. copper tubing. (Type L is fine.)

Materials list

- Hose reel ($60 to $250)
- Air filter/regulator/oiler (optional; $61)
- 1/2-in. copper tubing (run distance plus 15 percent for waste)
- 45-degree fittings
- Male pipe thread fitting(s) for hose reel
- Copper-tubing mounting straps
- Snubber hose ($10)
- Two quick-connect fittings
- One 2x8 x 6-ft. mounting plank
- Four 5/16-in. x 4-1/2-in. lag screws (plank to rafters)
- Four 5/16-in. 2-in. machine bolts, nuts, washers and lock washers (hose reel to plank)
- Pipe dope

1 Predrill the ceiling-mounting holes and hose reel–mounting holes in the 2x8. Bolt the hose reel to the 2x8.

2 Hold the assembly against the ceiling and lag-screw it into the rafters.

2x8 MOUNTING BLOCK

FLAME PROTECTOR

1/2" COPPER

45-DEGREE ELBOW

QUICK-CONNECT FITTINGS

AIR FILTER/PRESSURE REGULATOR/OILER

AIR COMPRESSOR

SNUBBER HOSE

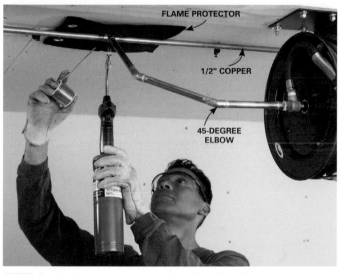

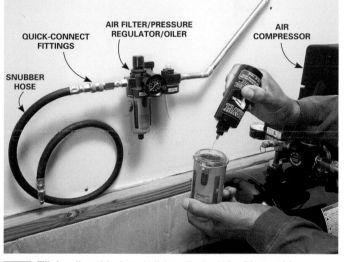

3 Sweat the connections near the ceiling. Use a flame protector between the fittings and the ceiling.

4 Fill the oiler with air tool oil. Install a "snubber" hose with a quick-connect fitting to connect the air compressor to the system.

Consider adding an optional filter/pressure regulator/oiler to your system. They're a little pricey, but the filter and oiler will keep your air tools in top condition. Use a snubber hose to connect and disconnect the compressor from the air line.

Buy whatever fittings you need to make the runs. Use 45-degree fittings at turns rather than 90-degree ells to reduce pressure drops. Buy solder-on male pipe thread adapters to connect to the air hose reel and the filter/oiler.

Start by measuring a 2x8 long enough to span two rafters. Trace the mounting holes from the hose reel onto the 2x8 plank and drill four 5/16-in. holes. If you have a finished ceiling, countersink the bolt heads on the back of the plank. Next, predrill two 5/16-in. holes at each end of the plank for the rafter mounting

bolts and matching holes in the rafters. Mount the hose reel to the plank with the nuts facing down. With a helper on the opposite side to hold the rather heavy assembly in place, mount the plank to the rafters using 5/16-in. x 4-1/2-in. lag screws.

Assemble the fittings and copper tubing from the hose reel up to the ceiling and sweat the parts for that portion of the run. After it cools, apply pipe dope to the threaded fitting and screw the section into the hose reel. Then assemble and sweat the rest of the copper tubing. Anchor the tubing to the framing every 4 ft. with mounting straps as you work your way toward the compressor.

Mount the air filter/regulator/oiler securely on the wall and attach a quick-connect fitting. Connect the assembly to your air compressor with a snubber hose.

Organize your garage in one morning

There are lots of ways to create more storage space in your garage, but you won't find another system that's as simple, inexpensive or versatile as this one. It begins with a layer of plywood fastened over drywall or bare studs. Then you just screw on a variety of hooks, hangers, shelves and baskets to suit your needs. That's it. The plywood base lets you quickly mount any kind of storage hardware in any spot—no searching for studs. And because you can place hardware wherever you want (not only at studs), you can arrange items close together to make the most of your wall space. As your needs change, you'll appreciate the versatility of this storage wall too; just unscrew shelves or hooks to rearrange the whole system.

Shown here are three types of storage supplies: wire shelves, wire baskets, and a variety of hooks, hangers and brackets (see p. 81). Selecting and arranging these items to suit your stuff can be the most time-consuming part of this project. To simplify that task, outline the dimensions of your plywood wall on the garage floor with masking tape. Then gather all the stuff you want to store and lay it out on your outline. Arrange and rearrange items

to make the most of your wall space. Then make a list of the hardware you need before you head off to the hardware store or home center.

Money, materials and planning

The total materials bill for the 6 x 16-ft. section of wall shown here was about $200. Everything you need is available at home centers. Shown is 3/4-in.-thick "BC" grade plywood, which has one side sanded smooth. You could save a few bucks by using 3/4-in. OSB "chip board" (oriented strand board) or MDF (medium-density fiberboard). But don't use particleboard; it doesn't hold screws well enough for this job. Aside from standard hand tools, all you need to complete this project is a drill to drive screws and a circular saw to cut plywood. You may also need a helper when handling plywood—full sheets are awkward and heavy.

This project doesn't require much planning; just decide how much of the wall you want to cover with plywood. You can cover an entire wall floor-to-ceiling or cover any section of a wall. In this garage, the lower 3 ft. of wall and upper 18 in. were left uncovered, since those high and low areas are best used for other

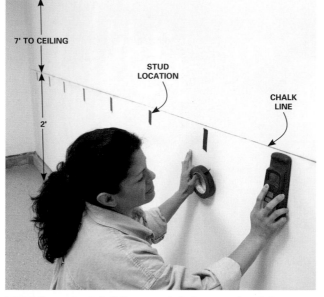

1 Snap a level chalk line to mark the bottom edge of the plywood. Locate studs and mark them with masking tape.

2 Screw temporary blocks to studs at the chalk line. Start a few screws in the plywood. Rest the plywood on the blocks and screw it to studs.

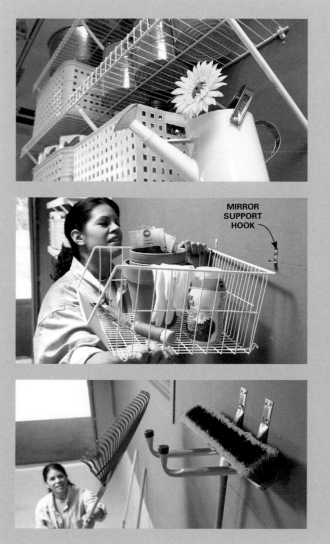

Storage supplies for every need

Wire closet shelves are sturdy and inexpensive, and they don't collect dust like solid shelving. They come in lengths up to 12 ft. and you can cut them to any length using a hacksaw or bolt cutters. Standard depths are 12, 16 and 20 in. You'll get more shelving for your money by cutting up long sections than by buying shorter sections. Brackets and support clips (Photo 4) are usually sold separately.

Wire or plastic baskets are perfect for items that won't stay put on shelves (like balls and other toys) and for bags of charcoal or fertilizer that tend to tip and spill. They're also convenient because they're mobile; hang them on hooks and you can lift them off to tote all your tools or toys to the garden or sandbox. You'll find baskets in a variety of shapes and sizes at home centers and discount stores. You can use just about any type of hook to hang baskets. Heavy-duty mirror supports fit these baskets perfectly.

Hooks, hangers and brackets handle all the odd items that don't fit on shelves or in baskets. Basic hooks are often labeled for a specific purpose, but you can use them in other ways. Big "ladder brackets," for example, can hold several long-handled tools. "Ceiling hooks" for bikes also work on walls. Don't write off the wall area below the plywood—it's prime space for items that don't protrude far from the wall. We drove hooks into studs to hang an extension ladder.

3 Set the upper course of plywood in place and screw it to studs. Stagger the vertical joints between the upper and lower courses.

VERTICAL JOINT

12" SCREW SPACING

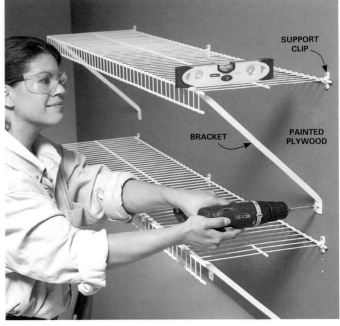

4 Fasten the back edge of shelves with plastic clips. Set a level on the shelf and install the end brackets. Then add center brackets every 2 ft.

SUPPORT CLIP

BRACKET

PAINTED PLYWOOD

types of storage. To make the most of the plywood, a course of full-width sheets was combined with a course of sheets cut in half. If your ceiling height is 9 ft. or less, a single 4-ft.-wide course of plywood may suit your needs.

Cover the wall with plywood

When you've determined the starting height of the plywood, measure up from the floor at one end of the wall and drive a nail. Then measure down to the nail from the ceiling and use that measurement to make a pencil mark at the other end of the wall. (Don't measure up from the floor, since garage floors often slope.) Hook your chalk line on the nail, stretch it to the pencil mark and snap a line (Photo 1).

Cut the first sheet of plywood to length so it ends at the center of a stud. Place the end you cut in the corner. That way the factory-cut edge will form a tight joint with the factory edge of the next sheet. Be sure to place the rough side of the plywood against the wall. Fasten the plywood with 10d finish nails or screws that are at least 2-1/4 in. long (Photo 2). Shown here are trim screws, which have small heads that are easy to cover with a dab of spackling compound. Drive screws or nails every 12 in. into each stud. If you add a second course of plywood above the first as shown (Photo 3), you'll have to cut the plywood to width. You can use a circular saw, but a table saw gives you faster, straighter cuts. Some home centers and lumberyards cut plywood for free or for a small charge.

With all the plywood in place, go ahead and mount the hardware, or take a few extra steps to dress up the wall first: You can add 3/4-in. cove molding along the lower edge of the plywood for a neater look and to cover up the chalk line and screw holes left by the support blocks. You can also frame

5 Acrylic photo frames make great label holders. Just slip in your labels and hot-glue the frames to wire baskets. Frames are sold at office supply and discount stores.

the window trim with doorstop molding to hide small gaps between the trim and the plywood. Caulk gaps between the sheets of plywood and fill screw holes. Finally, prime the plywood, lightly sand it with 100-grit sandpaper and paint it.

Handy hooks

When you're out shopping, you might find elaborate hangers designed to hold specific toys and tools. These specialty hooks are nice, but you don't have to spend $10 or more just to hang a bike or garden tools. With a little ingenuity, you can hang just about anything on simple screw-in hooks that typically cost a dollar or two. You can place hooks anywhere on your plywood wall. If you don't put them on the plywood, be sure to locate them at studs.

Drill a hole at a 45-degree angle and turn in a screw hook to hang a bicycle by the front wheel.

Hang ladders on hooks below the plywood for easy access.

Find extra space overhead

LIKELY TO GET CLOBBERED BY A FALLING BALL

Create extra storage space by screwing wire closet shelving to joists in your garage or basement. Wire shelving is see-through, so you can easily tell what's up there. Wire shelves are sold by the foot at home centers.

Install a garage door opener

What's missing, what matters in the instructions

Choosing a new opener

Garage door openers are available at home centers, starting at $140. When buying an opener, choose a 1/3 hp or 1/2 hp opener for a single garage door (1/3 hp can be hard to find at some home centers). Go with 1/2 hp for a double door and 3/4 hp for a door that has a wood or faux wood overlay (they can be heavy!). Openers have a set opening speed, so installing an opener with a higher horsepower won't open your door any faster.

Openers are available with a chain drive, screw drive or belt drive. Chain drives (a long chain pulls the door open and closed) are the least expensive, but they're loud. Screw drives (a long threaded rod drives a mechanism that opens and closes the door) are priced in the mid-range. They require the least maintenance, but they're not as quiet as belt drives. Belt drives (a rubber belt opens and closes the door) are the quietest, making them the best choice if you have living space above the garage. They're also the most expensive (about $50 more than a chain drive).

Make sure the door parts are working

If your garage door is opening slowly or making a lot of noise, the problem may not be your opener. So before you buy a new one, check for broken or wobbly rollers and brackets. But don't replace the bottom roller bracket yourself—the cable attached to it is under extreme tension. You'll need to call a pro.

If you're replacing the rollers, get nylon rollers. They operate more quietly than steel rollers and cost only a few bucks more.

Next, check the torsion spring (mounted on the header above the door opening) to see if it's broken. When one breaks, you'll see a gap in the coils (Photo 1). You'll need a pro to replace a broken spring.

Finally, check to make sure the door is balanced. Close the door and pull the emergency release cord (always close the door first so it can't come crashing down!). Lift the door about halfway up and let go (Photo 2). The door shouldn't move. If it

slides up or down, the torsion spring needs to be adjusted (or maybe even replaced).

Adjusting the torsion spring is dangerous, so don't attempt it yourself (you could get seriously hurt). Call a pro to adjust it.

Set the opener on a ladder for easier installation

Follow the manufacturer's instructions to assemble the opener and mount the rail to the header bracket above the door. Then set the opener on a ladder where you're going to install it. The ladder (usually an 8-footer) holds the opener in position while you measure for your lengths of angle iron (Photo 3). If necessary, put boards under the opener to raise it.

Have the door open when you install the opener (clamp locking pliers onto the roller track below a roller to keep the door

1 **Check for a broken spring.** If you have two garage doors and they get similar use, have the springs above both doors replaced when one breaks. The other one would probably break within a year.

2 **Check the door balance.** Open your door halfway and let go. If the door moves up or down on its own, the torsion spring is out of adjustment, which causes your opener to work harder and wear out faster.

RAIL

CENTER OF DOOR

3 **Position the opener.** Place the opener on a ladder and use scrap lumber to get it at the height you need. Align the opener's rail with the center of the garage door.

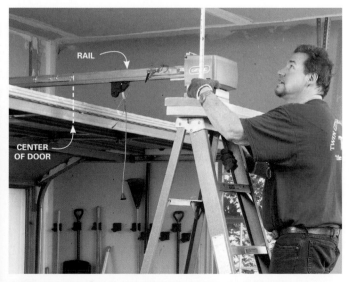

ANGLE BRACE

SLOTTED ANGLE IRON

4 **Hang the opener with angle iron.** Don't use the flimsy strap that comes with some openers. Solid mounting means less vibration and a longer life. If the opener is more than 6 in. from the ceiling, attach an angle brace to eliminate sway.

from closing). It's easier to align the opener with the center of the garage door when the door is open.

Buy heavy-duty angle iron

Garage door openers come with everything you need for installation. But the mounting straps that are included are often so flimsy that you can bend them with your hands, so buy slotted angle iron at a hardware store. Cut it to size with a hacksaw.

Angle iron provides a stronger installation and reduces vibration, which helps extend the opener's life span. In an unfinished garage, attach the angle iron directly to the face of a joist with 1-in. lag screws. For finished ceilings, attach angle iron along the bottom of a joist with 3-in. lag screws. Hang the opener using two more lengths of angle iron and nuts and bolts (Photo 4). Use lock washers or thread-locking adhesive to keep vibration from loosening the nuts.

Replace all the components

Don't be tempted to reuse the old photoelectric eyes and wall button (opener button). The new photo eyes and wall button are designed to work with your new opener.

If the wires that run from your opener to the photo eyes and to the wall button are exposed, replace them, too. Those wires have probably been in your garage for 10 years or more, and they may be nicked or worn. Newer openers are extremely sensitive and won't work if a wire is damaged. It only takes about 15 minutes to run the new wire, so it's time well-spent. If the wires are protected inside the wall, you don't need to run new wire.

Check the door's opening force

Your instructions probably don't cover checking the opening force. If your door encounters more than about 5 lbs. of resistance when it's opening, you want it to stop. This is an important safety feature. The "resistance" could be your finger caught in the track.

To check the opening force, rest your foot on the door handle near the floor and open the door using the remote control. When the door lifts against your foot, it should stop with very little pressure (Photo 5). If the door continues to open, adjust the force (see the next step).

Fine-tune the opening and closing force

The opener's instructions probably tell you to place a 2x4 on the floor under the center of the door, then close it. When the door contacts the wood, it should stop and then reverse. Proper closing force ensures that if something is in the door's path, the door won't crush it.

The locations of the opening and closing force adjustment screws vary. Our unit has two screws on the front. When adjusting the opening or closing force, turn the screw only about 1/8 in., then recheck the force (Photo 6).

Fix a reversing door

The most common problem with garage door openers is the door reversing when it's closing, even when there's nothing obvious obscuring the photoelectric eyes. If your closing force is adjusted correctly, then the problem is almost always the photoelectric eyes. The eyes are very sensitive—even cobwebs can interfere with them.

First make sure the eyes are still in alignment (something may have knocked them out of whack). Then make sure the eyes are clean and the path between them is clear. Finally, look for loose wires in the eyes and the opener.

REMOTE CONTROL

HANDLE

5 Check the opening force. Rest your foot on the door and open it with a remote control. The light pressure from your foot should cause the door to stop. If it doesn't, adjust the opening force.

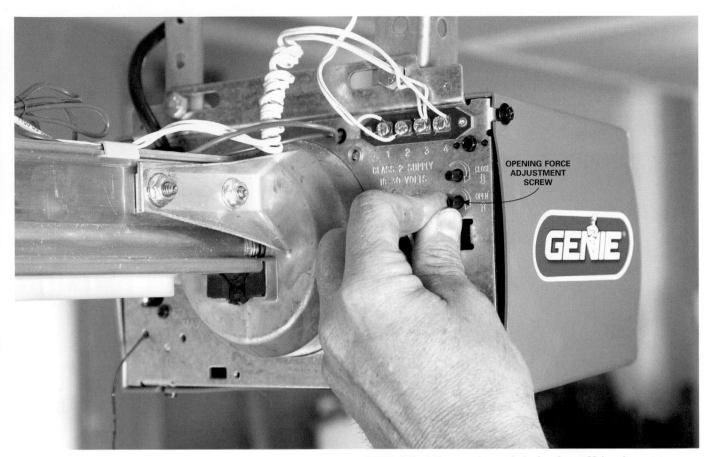

6 Adjust the opening and closing force. Make minor adjustments to the opening and closing force screws, then retest the force. A 1/8-in. turn is sometimes all you need.

If the door starts to open and then stops on its own, increase the opening force. Likewise, if it stops on its own while closing, increase the closing force. You might have to make several small adjustments to get the force exactly how it should be.

Use bulbs that handle vibration

Garage door openers vibrate, so you'll need special lightbulbs that can handle it. Look for "rough service" or "garage door" on the label (Photo 7).

Be sure to use the wattage specified in your manual. If you use a higher wattage, the heat could melt the plastic cover over the bulbs or even damage the circuit board inside the opener.

This is one place where LED or CFL bulbs aren't the best choice. CFLs aren't designed to handle the vibration. And since the lights are on only briefly, the energy saved with these bulbs would be negligible.

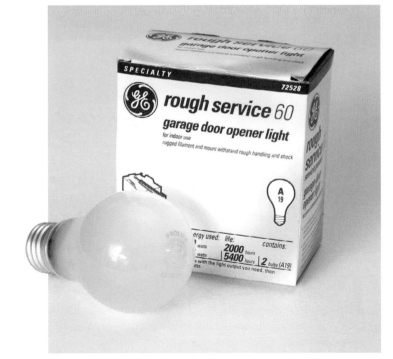

7 Install tough bulbs. Use "rough service" bulbs and don't exceed the wattage listed on the opener. Bulbs that are too hot can damage the opener.

Ultimate wall system in a (long) weekend

Flexible garage storage that you can build with just a circular saw and a drill

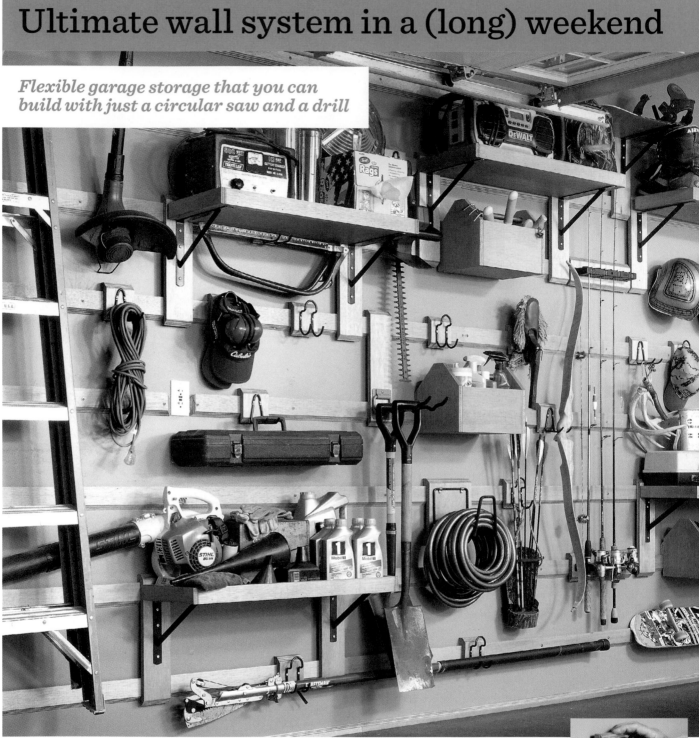

The problem with organizing garages is that there are so many different kinds of things to store that it's overwhelming trying to decide how to do it. But with this system, you don't have to worry about the ultimate positioning of all your hooks and shelves because you can rearrange them at will. And you don't have to plan ahead for future storage needs either. You can easily add on to the system just by assembling more hangers and rearranging the existing ones. Once the beveled strips are attached, you never have to locate a stud

or use drywall anchors to hang hooks or other hardware. Just screw them to an appropriate-size wood-cleat hanger and put them up wherever you want.

The system consists of beveled strips that are screwed to the wall studs, and custom-made wooden hangers that lock onto the strips. We built everything with utility plywood, which costs about $45 a sheet. You can cut enough strips from a 4 x 8-ft. sheet to cover a 12-ft.-long wall. And you can assemble enough hangers,

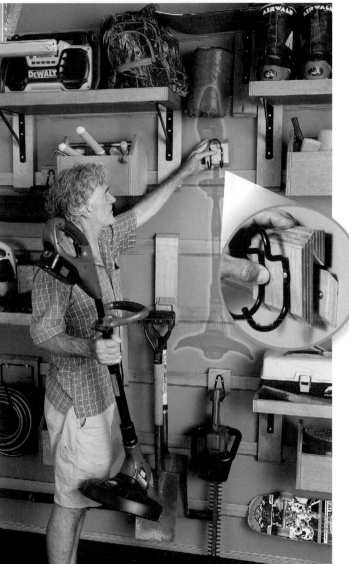

WHAT IT TAKES

TIME: 2 or 3 days. Expect to spend the weekend cutting and mounting the strips and building some hangers.

COST: $100 and up. Your cost will vary depending on how much wall you want to cover and how many accessories you build. The materials for the wall shown here cost $275.

SKILL LEVEL: Beginner to intermediate. If you have a few basic carpentry skills like measuring, leveling and using a circular saw, you'll have no trouble with this project.

TOOLS: Circular saw and a drill.

tool totes and other miscellaneous holders from another 4 x 8 sheet to get a good start on organizing your garage. See the Materials list on p. 91 for other items you may need. We used four sheets of plywood to build everything you see in the photo.

It would be a little quicker to cut the parts using a table saw and a miter saw, but you don't need these tools; we'll show you how to safely and accurately cut all the parts using just a circular saw. You'll be surprised at how quickly and easily you can cut the parts with the help of a few simple saw guides. But before

Reorganize in minutes!

Rearrange, reorganize, add on, make room for new stuff. It's as easy as lifting off the hangers and putting them somewhere else. There's nothing complicated about this storage system. The matching bevels and gravity hold the hangers securely until you want to move them. And you can build the whole system with just two power tools—a circular saw and a drill. What could be simpler!

Build a saw guide for perfect cuts

To make the saw guide, start by marking a line and cutting a 5-in.-wide strip from the edge of an uncut sheet of plywood (photo below). You could simply clamp this straightedge to the plywood as a saw guide, but then you would have to compensate for the distance from the guide to the saw blade every time. The photo below right shows how to build a guide that you can line up with the cutting mark, a technique that is quicker and more accurate.

Make another guide just like this one, except set the saw to cut 90 degrees when you cut off the excess 1/4-in. plywood. You can use the opposite edge of the same sheet of plywood for the straight edge. Use this guide for non-beveled cuts.

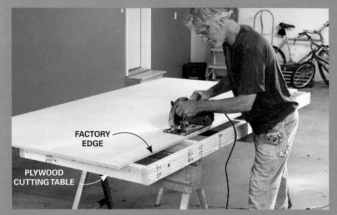

Make a straightedge. Saw off the factory edge of a sheet of plywood to use as a straightedge. It doesn't matter if you don't saw perfectly straight because you'll only use the factory edge. Draw arrows toward the factory edge to identify it.

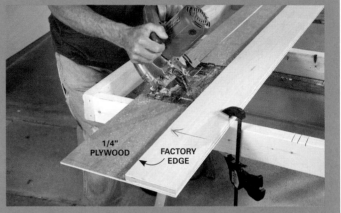
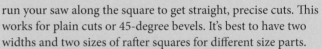

Build the guide. Attach a 12-in.-wide strip of 1/4-in. plywood to the straightedge with short screws. Make sure to face the factory edge of the straightedge toward the excess base material. Then, with the saw set to a 45-degree bevel, run the saw's bed along the straightedge to cut off the excess base. Make a second guide using the opposite edge of the 4 x 8 sheet of plywood, only set the saw to cut 90 degrees.

Build these simple guides for cutting the small parts

Both of these crosscut guides are simple: All you need to do is glue a 1-3/8-in.-wide strip of plywood or MDF to a wider strip. Set the workpiece on the guide, clamp on a rafter square and run your saw along the square to get straight, precise cuts. This works for plain cuts or 45-degree bevels. It's best to have two widths and two sizes of rafter squares for different size parts.

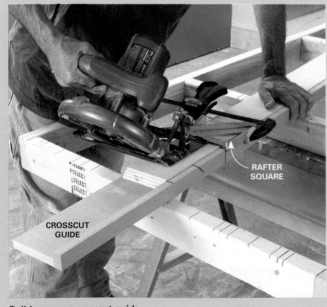

Build a narrow crosscut guide

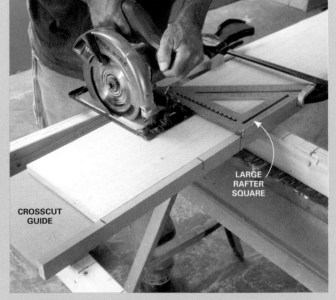

Build a wide crosscut guide

you start, make sure you have a sharp blade for your circular saw. To make clean, splinter-free cuts in plywood, buy a 40-tooth carbide blade. In addition to a circular saw and drill, you'll need a hammer, level, tape measure, pair of clamps, chalk line with dust-off chalk, and small and large rafter squares.

Screw the strips to the wall

Cut the strips from a sheet of plywood. Photo 1 shows how. You won't be able to cut the narrow beveled strips from the last 10 or 12 in. of the plywood sheet with this guide. Instead, use the remaining wide strip for the totes or other wider parts.

Next, to ensure that the strips are straight and level and that all the screws hit the center of the studs, make a grid of chalk lines. Start by drawing a level line to mark the bottom of the lowest strip (Photo 2). Then make marks every 12 in. above the line and connect the marks with chalk lines (Photo 3). Use special dust-off chalk—it's easily erasable.

Next, locate the center of a stud. Use a stud finder or knock on the wall until you feel and hear a solid spot. Then zero in on the center by probing with a nail (Photo 4). Do this above the lines, where the nail holes will be covered by the strips. Find both edges of the stud with the nail. Then mark the center. In most cases, studs are 16 in. apart, and you can measure from this first center mark to find the remaining studs. Whatever method you use, probe with a nail at each stud to make sure you hit solid wood. Make marks for the center of the studs at the top and bottom and connect the marks with chalk lines. With the grid done, it's easy to align and attach the strips (Photo 5).

Cut out the parts for the hangers

With the saw guides, it's fast and easy to make long, table saw–quality cuts in plywood. But what about all those small parts? One problem with cutting small parts freehand is that it's hard to keep the cuts square. Another is that the cutoff pieces tend to fall away just before the cut is finished, creating a little torn-off section. You can solve both these problems, and

1 **Cut beveled strips.** Start by positioning the beveled guide 1 in. from the edge and cutting a strip with a bevel on one edge. You can use this to make hangers. Then make a series of marks 2-1/2 in. apart on each end of the sheet. Line up the saw guide with the marks to cut the beveled strips.

2 **Mark a level line.** Measure up from the floor 9 in. and make a mark. Use a straight board and a level to draw a level line.

Materials list

Here's what we used. Adjust the quantities for your project.

ITEM	QTY.	ITEM	QTY.
2' x 4' x 3/4" MDF (crosscut guides)	1	1-1/4" construction screws (to attach cleats to hangers)	100
2' x 8' x 1/4" plywood or hardboard (saw guide base)	1	1-3/4" construction screws (optional—for cabinets)*	100
4' x 8' x 3/4" plywood	4	2-3/4" construction screws* (to attach cleats to wall)	175
No. 4 x 3/4" wood screws (to attach 1/4" plywood to straightedge for guide)	20	8-oz. bottle of wood glue	1
7/8" pan-head screws (to attach hardware to cleats)	100	3/4" copper tubing (optional)	
		Hooks and other hardware**	

* We used GRK No. 8 Cabinet Screws. Search "GRK" online to find a retailer or online source.

** We used the Everbilt Hook Assortment Pack, Flip-Up Tool Holder and Flip-Up Bike Holder, which are available at Home Depot.

make marks for repeatable cuts, by building two crosscut guides (p. 90). We bought a 2 x 4-ft. piece of MDF at the home center, but you can use any flat scraps of plywood.

Start by cutting two fence strips 1-3/8 in. wide by 3 or 4 ft. long. Then cut a 4-1/2-in.-wide strip and a 9-1/2-in.-wide strip for the base pieces. Use your straightedge saw guide to make these cuts. Glue and clamp the fence parts to the base pieces. Or you can glue and screw them. If you use screws, remove them after the glue sets.

The sidebar on p. 90 shows how to use the crosscut guides. When you make the first cut, mark the location of the square on the crosscut guide. To make several parts that are the same length, measure from the saw kerf in the work support and make a mark. Line up the end of the material with this mark and align the clamp with the clamp mark.

3 **Mark the cleat locations with chalk lines.** Measure up from the level line and make marks every 12 in. Do this on both ends. Then snap chalk lines between the marks. Use dust-off chalk, which won't leave permanent stains on the wall.

4 **Mark the center of the studs.** Locate a stud with a finder or the knuckle-knocking method. Then probe with a nail until you find both edges of the stud. Mark the center of the stud. Measure from this mark—most studs are 16 in. center-to-center—to find the remaining stud centers. Double-check by probing with a nail at each mark. Repeat this process at the uppermost chalk line and connect the marks with chalk lines.

5 **Screw the strips to the studs.** Line up the bottom of the strips with the lines and drive a screw into each stud. We used washer-head cabinet screws, but any type of screw will work.

Go crazy!

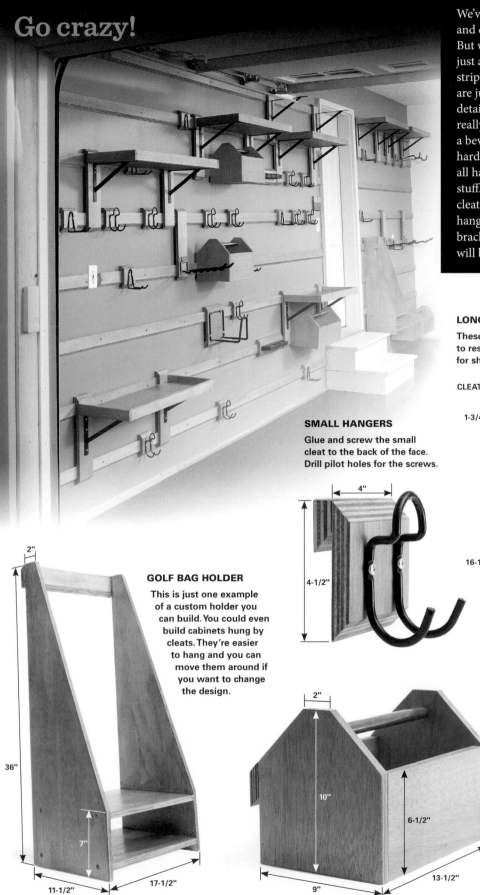

We've shown you how to mount the strips and cut out parts for the simple hangers. But with a little ingenuity, you can hang just about anything from these beveled strips. The golf bag holder and tote boxes are just a few ideas. We haven't included detailed plans because frankly, it doesn't really matter. Anything you can attach to a beveled cleat is fair game. Home centers, hardware stores and sporting goods stores all have hooks and brackets for hanging stuff. You just have to build a wooden cleat to screw them to. Have something to hang? Have fun inventing a new hanging bracket. When you're finished, your garage will be the envy of the neighborhood.

LONG HANGERS

These are like the small ones, only long enough to rest on the horizontal cleat below. Use these for shelf brackets and other longer hardware.

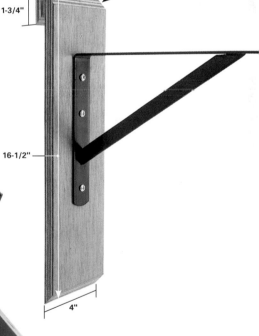

CLEAT
45° BEVEL
1-3/4"
16-1/2"
4"

SMALL HANGERS

Glue and screw the small cleat to the back of the face. Drill pilot holes for the screws.

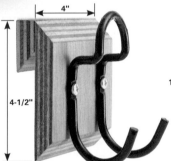

4"
4-1/2"

GOLF BAG HOLDER

This is just one example of a custom holder you can build. You could even build cabinets hung by cleats. They're easier to hang and you can move them around if you want to change the design.

2"
36"
7"
11-1/2"
17-1/2"

WOODEN TOTES

Build plywood boxes and attach cleats to the back. We drilled 7/8-in. holes, 1/2 in. deep in the ends with a Forstner bit to hold the 3/4-in. copper tubing handles.

2"
10"
6-1/2"
9"
13-1/2"

Chapter Four

WOODWORKING & CARPENTRY

Crowning touch

This three-piece crown molding technique vastly simplifies installation— and the result looks great!

Crown molding can be intimidating, because walls often aren't flat and nailing is difficult. Don't worry. This three-piece system solves those problems. Here you'll learn how to install trim on the walls and ceiling first, then add the crown. The three combined pieces look elegant and go up more easily than a single large piece. We'll also walk you through the tricky cuts at corners.

It's a weekend project

The built-up crown designs shown here take a bit longer to put up than single-piece crown, but the results will be better, especially if you have little trim experience. With any crown, corners are the most time consuming. If you have a simple four-corner room, you and a helper can probably install all the moldings in a day. A room with six or eight corners might take a full weekend. Painting or finishing will also add a day or two.

Our three-part pine crown cost about $3.50 per linear ft., or about $200 for a 12 x 15-ft. room. That's slightly less than the cost of single-piece crown molding of about the same size. Hardwood molding like oak or maple will cost 30 to 100 percent more, depending on where you live. If you don't have a vehicle that can haul long moldings home, ask about delivery charges when you compare prices.

What you need

Before you go shopping, make a quick sketch of the room and jot down the length of each wall. If possible, buy pieces that are long enough to completely span each wall. This will save you the trouble of "scarfing" pieces together (Photo 20). Inspect each piece before you buy. Look for splits at the ends and deep milling marks that will be hard to sand out. If you plan to use a light-colored stain (or no stain at all) select pieces of similar tone.

You could install crown using a miter box, handsaw and hammer. But we strongly recommend using a miter saw and brad nailer. These tools don't just make the work faster—they provide better results. A miter saw lets you shave paper-thin slices off moldings until the length is perfect.

Start with the long wall and work in one direction

A long piece of molding is clumsy to handle and hard to measure and cut accurately. Installing it first makes it easier because the first piece has square cuts at both ends—no coping.

Work to the right. With the first piece in place, add the piece to the right next and work around the room in that direction. That way, you'll make most of your 45-degree cuts with the miter saw set to the left (Photo 9). With the saw set to the left, the motor is out of the way. That makes the molding easier to hold and the cut mark easier to see.

Outside corners and spliced pieces last. Outside corners (Photo 16) are fussy no matter when you tackle them. But in most cases, installing them last lets you avoid ending up with a piece that's coped on both ends. If you have a wall that's too long for a single piece of molding, install a scarfed piece last to avoid a double cope (Photo 20).

1 Experiment with built-up molding combinations to make your decision easier. Nail or glue samples together and hold them against the ceiling.

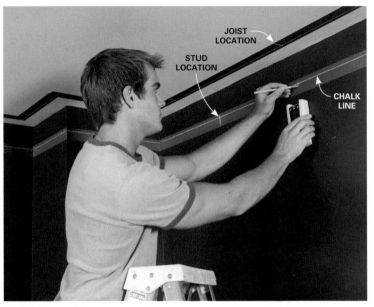

2 Run masking tape around the walls and ceiling so that about 1/2 in. of the tape will be covered by the rail trim. Mark the rail positions with a chalk line. Locate studs and ceiling joists.

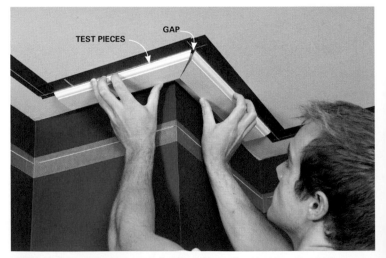

3 Find the right miter angle for the ceiling rails at inside and outside corners. Miter scraps to 45 degrees and hold them in place along the chalk lines. If there's a gap, adjust your saw's angle and cut again until they fit tight.

Figure A
Three-piece crown

The built-up crown we chose for this project combines standard crown molding with two pieces of base trim. The result is a large, dramatic crown that's easier to install and less expensive than single-piece crown molding of similar size.

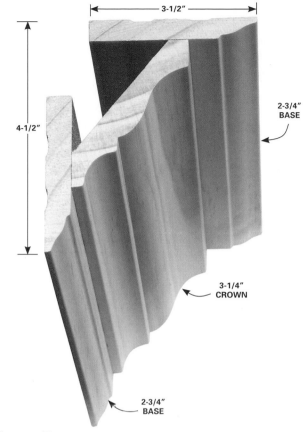

3-1/2"

4-1/2"

2-3/4"
BASE

3-1/4"
CROWN

2-3/4"
BASE

Figure B
Order of installation

At inside corners, a coped end fits over a square-cut end. In rectangular rooms, the last piece is often coped on both ends. In odd-shaped rooms like this one, you can usually avoid double-coped pieces. Outside corners are formed by two miter cuts.

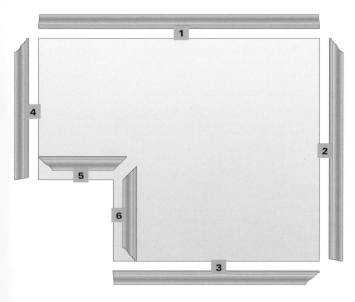

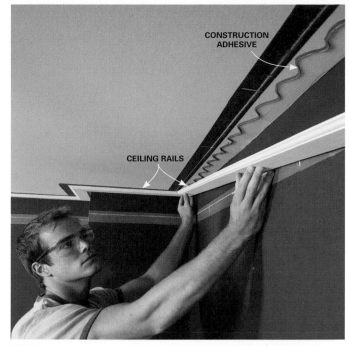

CONSTRUCTION ADHESIVE

CEILING RAILS

4 Glue the ceiling rails into place with construction adhesive. Nail the rails to joists wherever possible. Where you can't hit ceiling joists, drive nails into the drywall at a 45-degree angle. Angled nails will hold the rails in place until the adhesive sets.

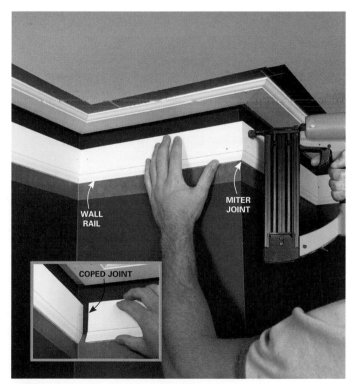

WALL RAIL

MITER JOINT

COPED JOINT

5 Nail the wall rails to studs with 2-in. brads. Cut coped ends for inside corners. Then miter outside corners using the same angle-finding technique shown in Photo 3.

Masking tape eliminates fussy touch-ups

You'll need chalk lines to position the rail trim, and marks at studs and ceiling joists so you know where to drive nails. Most carpenters would put these lines and marks right on the walls and ceilings and hide them with paint later. That means a lot of fussy painting along the new trim.

Here's an easier method: Stick bands of 2-in.-wide masking tape to the walls and ceiling. Masking tape can pull off paint, so use an easy-release tape. If you plan to paint the walls or ceiling, wait a couple of weeks before you apply the tape. (If your wall or ceiling is heavily textured, this method won't work because the tape won't stick well.) Snap chalk lines and mark framing locations on the tape (Photo 2). Install the trim over the tape and leave the tape in place to protect the walls and ceiling when you paint or finish the trim. When the finishing is done, cut and remove the exposed tape, leaving the covered tape in place permanently (Photo 21). Use a sharp knife blade and apply just enough pressure to slice through the tape.

Rail trim creates a foundation for the crown molding

Fastening crown molding directly to walls can be a headache, but well-fastened rail trim makes nailing the crown foolproof. Use construction adhesive on all rails—even where you can nail into studs and ceiling joists. That way, you can use just enough nails to hold the trim in place until the adhesive sets, and you'll have fewer nail holes to fill. Apply the adhesive lightly so the excess doesn't squeeze out and make a mess.

Miter the ceiling rails at both inside and outside corners. The corners of a room usually aren't perfectly square, so you'll have to use test pieces to find the exact angle for each corner (Photo 3). The crown molding tips and techniques shown in the rest of this article will help you install the wall rails. The wall rails are mitered at outside corners and coped at inside corners. Coping the wall rails is just like coping the crown (Photo 11) except that you stand the trim upright against the saw's fence when you make the 45-degree miter.

Customize your saw to miter the crown

Make square cuts with the crown lying flat on the miter saw's bed. To make miter cuts for copes and outside corners, you have to lean the crown molding—tilted at exactly the correct angle—against the saw's fence (Photo 11). Pencil lines on the bed or fence can help you position the crown right, but fence extensions and stop blocks make positioning fast and foolproof. If your fence doesn't already have holes that let you screw on extensions, you can drill holes. Or you can fasten the extensions with hot-melt glue and pry them off later. Besides providing a taller fence if needed, the extensions let you screw on stop blocks (Photo 10).

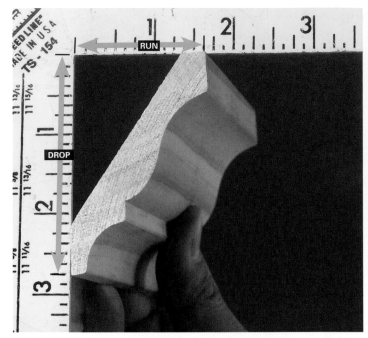

6 Measure the run and drop of the crown molding. Then nail two blocks together to make a marking gauge that duplicates the run and drop.

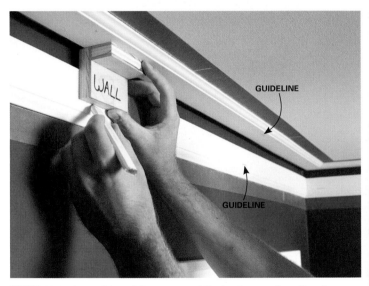

7 Mark the position of the crown molding's edges on the rails using your gauge. Place guidelines at all corners and every 2 ft. along walls. Use the marks to position the crown.

MARKING GAUGE

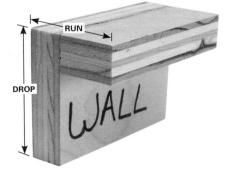

8 Measure accurately using a two-step technique. First measure from a corner and make a mark. Then measure from the other corner to the mark and add the two measurements.

9 Square-cut both ends of the first piece of crown and nail it into place. All the other pieces are cut square (or mitered) at one end and coped at the other.

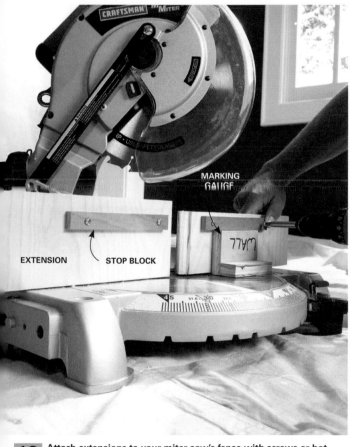

10 Attach extensions to your miter saw's fence with screws or hot glue. Then screw on stop blocks, using your marking gauge upside down to position them.

11 Cut crown molding at a 45-degree angle to prepare for coping. Place the molding upside down against the stop blocks. Before you cut, make sure the direction of the miter matches the slash mark.

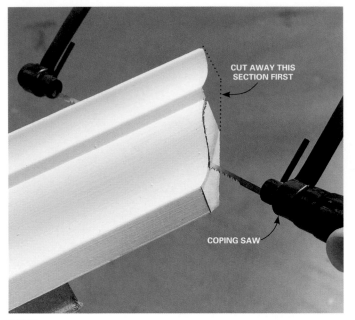

CUT AWAY THIS
SECTION FIRST

COPING SAW

12 Cut a cope by following the edge left by the miter cut. Hold the saw at an angle to undercut behind the face of the molding. With many moldings, you have to cut away one section to get at another.

Why cope?

You're probably wondering why you should go through the slow, fussy process of coping when you could just miter trim at inside corners. The answer is that wall corners are never quite square, and coped joints fit tight even when corners are badly out of square. Whether you're installing crown molding, chair rails or baseboard, coping is faster than finding the right miter angle through trial and error. If you really want to avoid coping, use corner blocks (available at most home centers and lumberyards). With these decorative blocks placed at inside and outside corners, you only need to make square cuts.

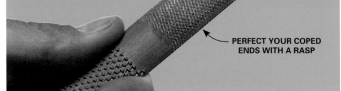

PERFECT YOUR COPED
ENDS WITH A RASP

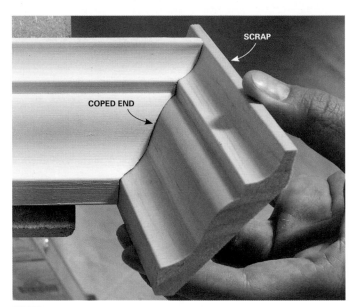

SCRAP

COPED END

13 Test-fit the coped end using a scrap. Perfect the cut with a rasp. If you need to remove lots of wood from the back side of the molding, use a sanding drum and drill.

COPED END

14 Push the coped end into place and check the fit. If the cope fits tightly but the piece is too long, shave the square-cut end on the miter saw.

Coping isn't as hard as it looks

Coping starts with a 45-degree cut on the miter saw, just as if you were going to make a miter joint at the inside corner.

This cut leaves an edge along the face of the trim that acts as a guideline for your coping saw. Cut along that edge and the resulting shape will fit against an adjoining piece of crown. Chances are your first attempt won't turn out perfectly, but after a couple of practice runs you'll be able to make good-looking inside corners. Here are some tips for smooth, successful coping:

- Every time you cut a miter (whether for coping or outside corners), you'll set the crown upside down against the saw's

fence. It's easy to get confused and cut the angle backward. To avoid mishaps, hold the molding up to the corner and draw a slash showing the direction of the cut (Photo 11).

- Clamp the molding to the work surface. Sawing is a lot easier with the molding locked into place.
- If the saw blade tends to slide to one side as you start a cut, make a small starter notch with a utility knife.
- Make sure the teeth in your coping saw point toward the handle. That way, the blade will cut smoothly on the pull stroke.
- Don't force the saw forward. Make even strokes, apply only light pressure and let the blade advance at its own pace.

BEND MIDDLE OUTWARD

15 "Spring" sections of crown into place. Jam the square-cut end into its corner. Then bend the middle outward as you guide the coped end into place. Let the crown straighten to force the coped joint tightly together.

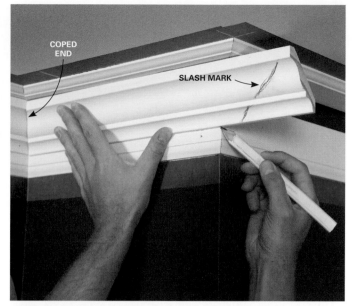

COPED END

SLASH MARK

16 Mark the length of outside corner pieces by coping one end and holding the piece in place. To get the angle right, use scraps of crown and the method shown in Photo 3. Draw a slash mark on the crown to indicate the direction of the miter cut.

17 Miter outside corners with the molding upside down. Cut the piece about 1/16 in. beyond the length mark and then shave off a bit if the piece is too long.

SCRAP

18 Check the length at outside corners using a test scrap. When the length is right on, set the piece aside. Then cope, miter and test-fit the other outside corner piece.

Shave pieces on the miter saw for a snug fit

Making a piece of crown fit between two inside corners is a combination of careful measuring and trial and error:

- Don't bend the tape measure into a corner and guesstimate the measurement. Instead, measure in from both corners and add the two measurements.
- Make a square cut on the end of the molding. Don't assume the factory cut is square.

- To prepare for coping, measure from the square end and mark the miter cut position on the bottom edge of the crown molding.
- Don't make your miter cut exactly at the mark. Instead, cut the piece about a nickel's thickness too long.
- "Spring" the molding into place (Photo 15). If it's too long, shave a hair off the square end and try again until it fits just right.

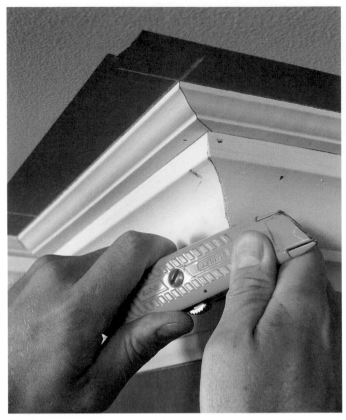

19 Erase small cracks in outside corner joints by rubbing with a utility knife handle. This crushes the wood fibers inward and closes minor gaps.

20 Join sections of crown on long walls using "scarf" joints. Set your miter saw to 22-1/2 degrees and make scarf cuts with the molding upside down just as you did for other miter cuts.

Four fussy spots

Outside corners. The joint at an outside corner is formed by two simple miter cuts, but making them fit takes several steps (Photos 16–18). Don't rush the process—outside corners are usually prominent and so are mistakes. If the crown will have a varnish finish, select two pieces with similar grain patterns.

Double copes. If your room doesn't have any outside corners or require scarf joints, you'll finish the job with a piece that's coped on both ends. This isn't as tough as you might think. The key is to start with a piece that's mitered to the right length. Miter both ends and hold the piece in place to check the fit. Then cope the ends as usual.

Scarf joints. On a wall that's too long for a single piece of molding, you'll have to "scarf" pieces together (Photo 20). The angled cuts of a scarf joint are less visible than square cuts. If you plan on a varnish finish, select pieces that have similar color and grain patterns. Cut and install the longer piece first so the shorter piece can overlap it at the joint. Glue the joint.

Odd-angle corners. Coped joints only work in square corners. If you have non-square inside corners—such as 45-degree corners in a window bay—you have to miter them. Find the correct angle for each corner using the method shown in Photo 3. Treat odd-angle outside corners just like square outside corners.

21 Remove the masking tape after finishing the crown. Run a sharp utility knife lightly along the rail to slice the tape.

Cutting board and serving tray

Slice, dice and serve in style on this easy, cutting-edge project. Here you'll learn a simple way to dry-fit the parts, scribe the arc and then glue the whole thing together. A 4-ft. steel ruler is used to scribe the arcs, but a yardstick or any thin board would also work. Be sure to use water-resistant wood glue and keep your tray out of the dishwasher or it might fall apart. And one more thing: Keep the boards as even as possible during glue-up to minimize sanding later.

Materials list

- Three 20-in. x 3-1/2-in. maple boards
- Two 23-1/2-in. x 1/2-in. x 3/4-in. walnut strips (handle strips)
- Two 5-in. x 1/2-in.-diameter dowels (handles)
- Four 3/4-in. x 3/4-in.-diameter dowels (for feet)

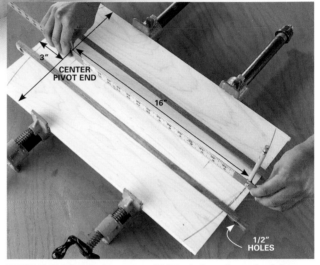

1 Drill 1/2-in. holes centered 3/4 in. in from the ends of the walnut strips. Then lightly clamp all five boards together so you can scribe the arcs on the ends.

2 Take the boards out of the clamp, saw and sand the arcs on each board, and then glue the assembly together, leaving the dowel handles unglued.

3 Unclamp, sand both sides and drill a 1/4-in.-deep, 3/4-in.-diameter hole at each underside corner. Glue in the feet and dowel handles, then wipe on a couple of coats of butcher block oil.

Craftsman bookcase

Veteran woodworker and Contributing Editor Dave Munkittrick helps a beginner re-create a classic

WHAT IT TAKES

Time: 12 hours.
This is a great weekend project. Our building time was about eight hours, plus a few hours more for final sanding and finishing.

Cost: $100
That includes wood, glue, screws and finishes. We used oak boards and plywood. If you choose another species, such as cherry or maple, expect to spend at least $40 more.

Skill level:
Beginning woodworker
This is a great project for anyone who's done some woodworking and is ready to tackle their first real furniture project.

Build it yourself and save $151,900!

This bookcase is inspired by a Gustav Stickley model that sold for $12 in 1910. One of the original Stickley models recently sold for $152,000, but you can build yours for about $100.

This is the perfect first-time furniture project—simple, useful and satisfying.

My neighbor, CT, asked me to help him build a bookcase he found in an old Stickley furniture catalog. I love Craftsman furniture and CT is a great neighbor. How could I refuse? We sat down to do a little research and figure out the details. CT wanted a slightly larger bookcase, so we stretched the width from 22 in. to 36.

I told CT we could build it in his garage with nothing more than a table saw, a drill and a pocket hole jig. If you don't own a pocket hole jig, you owe it to yourself to buy one. Pocket screws aren't as strong as most other types of joinery, but they are plenty strong for this bookcase, and you can't beat their speed and simplicity. CT agreed, especially when he found out that for $40 he could buy a complete pocket hole system. You'll also need at least four pipe clamps for this project.

Wood selection matters

At the home center, we took our time picking through the oak boards. We wanted straight, flat boards, of course, but we also looked closely at grain pattern. Novice woodworkers usually skip this tedious process, but they shouldn't. It has a big impact on the final look of the project. For the legs, we examined the end grain and chose boards with grain that ran diagonally across the ends (see Photo 4). This "rift sawn" wood has straight grain on both the face and the edge of the board. ("Plain sawn" boards typically have wilder grain on the face.) Straight grain will give the legs a look that suits the Stickley style. Also, glue joints disappear in straight grain wood, so the legs—which are made from sandwiched boards—look better. For that same reason, we chose boards with straight grain along the edges to form the bookcase top (see Photo 11).

Build a box and add face frames

After cutting the plywood box parts to size (see the Cutting List), we added the 3/8-in.-thick edging (J) to protect the bottom of the cabinet sides (A; Photo 1). We applied the same edging (H) to the plywood shelves (C). Then we drilled the pocket holes in the box top and bottom (B; Photo 2). After that, we drilled holes for

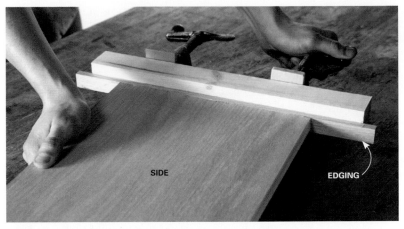

1 **Add edging to the sides. Cut the plywood box parts to size, then glue strips of wood to the bottom edges of the box sides.** This edging keeps the plywood veneer from chipping. Trim off the excess edging with a handsaw and sand it flush with the plywood. Take care not to sand through the thin veneer.

SIDE   EDGING

2 **Drill pocket holes. Pocket hole jigs are super easy to use: Place the jig where you want the holes; clamp and drill.** The stepped bit bores a pocket hole and a pilot hole at the same time. The holes on the ends are for attaching the top to the sides. The holes along the front and back are used to attach the box to the face frame.

JIG

POCKET HOLES

STEPPED BIT

3 **Assemble the box. Drive in the pocket screws with a drill.** To avoid stripping the screws in plywood and softwoods, switch to a screwdriver for the final tightening. Long clamps make assembly easier, but they aren't absolutely necessary.

Figure A
Bookcase

Overall Dimensions: 36" wide, 16" deep, 42" tall

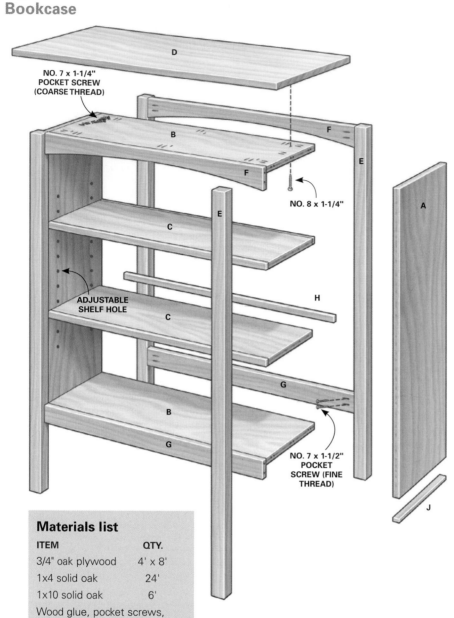

NO. 7 x 1-1/4"
POCKET SCREW
(COARSE THREAD)

NO. 8 x 1-1/4"

ADJUSTABLE
SHELF HOLE

NO. 7 x 1-1/2"
POCKET
SCREW (FINE
THREAD)

Materials list

ITEM	QTY.
3/4" oak plywood	4' x 8'
1x4 solid oak	24'
1x10 solid oak	6'

Wood glue, pocket screws, stain, polyurethane, adjustable shelf supports

Cutting list

MATERIAL	KEY	QTY.	DIMENSION	NOTES
3/4" Oak Plywood	A	2	10-1/2" x 32"	Sides
	B	2	10-1/2" x 29-3/4"	Top and bottom
	C	2	9-1/2" x 29-5/8"	Adjustable shelves
3/4" Oak	D	1	16" x 36"	Top
	E	4	1-1/2" x 1-1/2" x 41-1/4"	Legs (double up 3/4" stock)
	F	2	2-1/2" x 29"	Arched rails
	G	2	2" x 29"	Bottom rails
	H	4	1/2" x 29-5/8"	Edging for adjustable shelves
	J	2	3/8" x 10-1/2"	Bottom edge sides

adjustable shelf supports in the plywood sides and—finally—we assembled the box (Photo 3).

With the box assembled, we turned our attention to building two identical face frames. (Since the bookcase has no back, it needed two face frames.) Unlike a standard face frame, which has vertical stiles, our face frame has legs (E) made from two layers of 3/4-in.-thick boards. We glued up the leg blanks (Photo 4), ripped both blanks into two legs and sanded out the saw marks.

Like many other beginning woodworkers, CT figured that curves were complicated, so he was a little intimidated by the arched upper rails (F). But I showed him a neat trick for marking out a shallow arch (Photo 5). His curved cut (Photo 6) wasn't perfect, but a little sanding smoothed it out (Photo 7).

With the rails and legs complete, we were ready to drill pocket holes in the rails and assemble the face frames (Photo 8). It's easy to make mistakes during face frame assembly, so—before driving any screws—we clamped the frames together, then set them on the box to make sure everything was aligned correctly. We used similar caution when we finally attached the face frames to the box: We dry-fitted the face frames (Photo 9) before we glued and clamped them into place (Photo 10).

Top it off and finish up

CT figured that making the top (D) was a simple matter of edge-gluing two boards together (Photo 11). That's mostly true, but there are a few tricks that make it easier. First, always do a complete dry run by clamping up the boards without glue. That will alert you to any clamping or alignment problems before it's too late. Second, start with boards that are an inch or so longer than the final top. It's much easier to trim the boards later than to fuss with edge alignment during glue-up. Finally, to ensure that the tops of the boards meet flat and flush, use pocket screws on the underside of the top. A couple of pocket screws won't provide enough pressure to substitute for clamps, but they will hold the board flush while you crank on the clamps.

4 Glue up the leg blanks. Sandwich two 1x4s together and later cut the legs from this stock. Use scrap wood "cauls" to distribute clamping pressure evenly.

CAUL

LEG BLANK

ARCHED RAIL

5 Mark the arches. Make an "arch bow"—simply a 3/16-in.-thick strip of wood with slots cut into both ends. Hook a knotted string in one slot, tighten the string to bend the bow and tie off the other end.

6 Cut the arches. For a smooth cut, use a fine-tooth blade and move slowly, putting only light forward pressure on the saw. If your saw is variable speed, cut at full speed. If the saw has orbital action, switch it off.

7 Sand the arches. Smooth the arches with an orbital sander. Keep the sander moving so you don't sand too deep in one spot and create a wave in the curve.

8 Assemble the face frame. Clamp the face frame together and drive in pocket screws. Pocket screws rarely strip out in hardwood, so you can skip the screwdriver and use only a drill.

FACE FRAME

9 Dry-fit the face frames. Align the face frames, pocket-screw them to the box and check the fit. If your alignment is a bit off, you can drill new pocket holes and reattach the frames. If the fit is right, you're ready to remove the face frames and add glue.

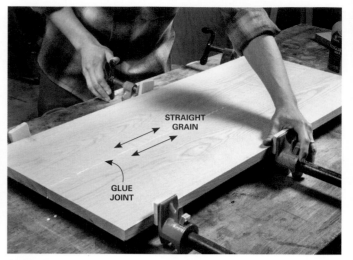

11 **Glue up the top.** Edge-glue the boards together to form the top. Choose boards that have straight grain lines along one edge and place those edges together. A glue joint with straight grain on both sides is almost invisible.

STRAIGHT GRAIN

GLUE JOINT

12 **Drill slotted screw holes.** Drill screw holes in the shelf box to fasten the bookcase top. Rock the bit back and forth to bore enlongated slots that will allow the top to swell with changes in humidity.

10 **Glue on the face frames.** Apply a light bead of glue over the box edges and screw on the face frames as before. There are no screws fastening the legs to the box sides, so you'll need to clamp them.

When the top was trimmed to size and sanded, CT drilled elongated holes (Photo 12) and screwed on the top (Photo 13). When I asked him to remove the top, he gave me a look that said, "What's the point of that?" I had two answers: Finishing is always easier when furniture is disassembled, and more important, both sides of the top need to be finished. Wood absorbs and releases moisture as humidity changes. Wood finishes slow that process. So wood with a finish on only one side will end up with differing moisture levels in the finished and unfinished sides. That leads to warping.

So we finished both sides of the top (and the rest of the bookcase) with a coat of stain followed by polyurethane. That's it. Not bad for a weekend of woodworking. I wonder how much CT's bookcase will be worth in a hundred years….

13 **Screw on the top from below.** Drive the screws snug, but not so tight that they won't allow for seasonal wood movement. Remove the top for sanding and finishing.

Super-simple DVD holder

This clever shelf holds DVDs, CDs or even small books. You can make yours with as many shelves as you like simply by changing the length of the trunk.

To get started, cut the trunk and shelves to length. Bevel one end of each shelf by tilting your miter saw or table saw blade to 5 degrees. Mark the notches in the shelves and trunk (Photos 1 and 2). Measuring from the top of the trunk, center the notches at 8-1/2, 11-1/2, 17-1/4, 20-1/4, 26-1/4 and 29 in. Cut the notches using a 5-degree guide block and a pull saw (available at home centers). Assemble the shelf (Photo 3). Screw metal straps to the back of the trunk, leaving one screw hole exposed so you can screw the DVD holder to the wall.

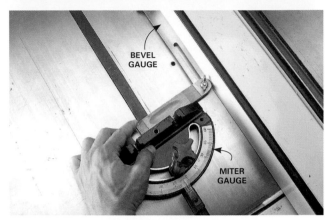

1 Set your bevel gauge at 5 degrees using the miter gauge and fence of your table saw.

2 Mark the notches on the edge of the trunk using the bevel gauge. Mark the face of the trunk with a square.

3 Test-fit each shelf and then glue it into place. If a shelf fits so tightly that it's hard to remove after test fitting, just leave it—no glue is needed.

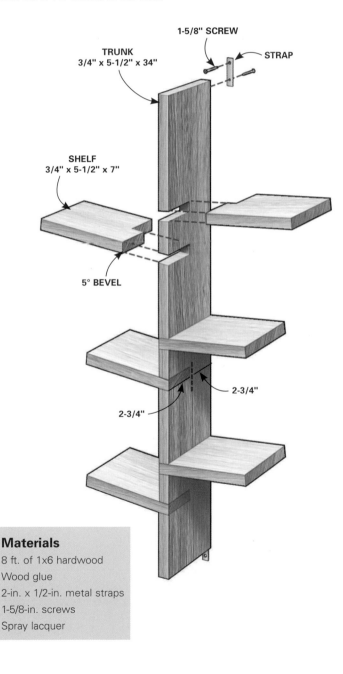

1-5/8" SCREW

TRUNK
3/4" x 5-1/2" x 34"

STRAP

SHELF
3/4" x 5-1/2" x 7"

5° BEVEL

2-3/4"

2-3/4"

Materials
8 ft. of 1x6 hardwood
Wood glue
2-in. x 1/2-in. metal straps
1-5/8-in. screws
Spray lacquer

Adirondack chair

Simple construction—maximum comfort.

Plop down in one of these solid wood chairs and you'll appreciate the comfort of this traditional design. You don't have to be an expert to build it either. All the parts can be cut with a circular saw and jigsaw, then assembled with a drill with a Phillips-tip bit, a few clamps and glue. Even if you're a novice, you'll be able to follow our plan drawing and clear step-by-step photos. And the Materials List and Cutting List will help you spend less time head-scratching and more time building.

We made our chair from yellow poplar. Poplar is lightweight, strong, inexpensive and easy to work with, plus it takes paint beautifully. If you have trouble finding it, almost any other wood will do: Alder, aspen, maple and white oak are excellent hardwood choices, and cedar, cypress, fir and pine are good softwood choices. Keep in mind that hardwood will be more durable, but softwood is certainly strong enough for this project.

Traditional Adirondack chairs are painted, but you can choose a clear

outdoor deck finish if you prefer. If you do opt for paint, check out the painting tips on p. 114 to help achieve a tough, long-lasting and good-looking painted finish.

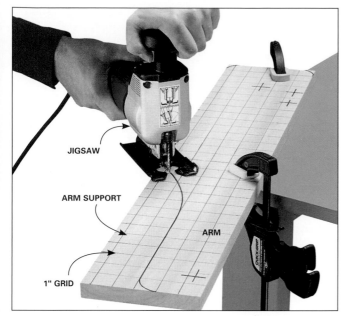

1 Draw full-size grids onto the arm and back leg pieces and follow the curves with a jigsaw.

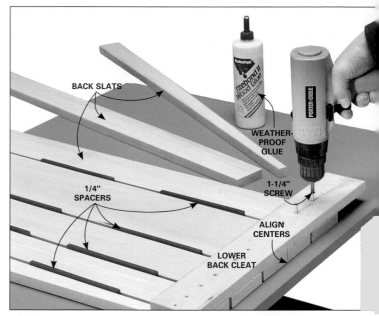

2 Slip 1/4-in. spacers between the back slats as you screw the horizontal back supports (G, L and N) to the slats. Predrill and countersink each hole and apply weatherproof glue to each joint.

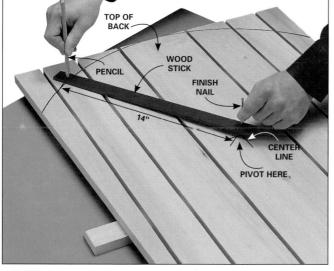

3 Make a compass from a scrap of wood by drilling a hole near each end. Put a nail in one end and use a pencil in the other hole to draw the 14-in. radius to form the curved top.

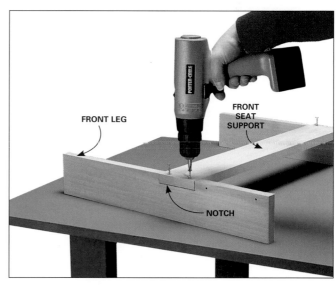

4 Cut and notch the front legs (E) with a jigsaw. Then glue and screw the front seat support into the notches.

Transfer the grid patterns

Enlarge the grids (Fig. A, p. 113) directly onto the board, or make a full-size pattern and transfer the shape to the board.

Once the shape is drawn, follow the lines with a jigsaw (Photo 1). Write "pattern" on the first leg and arm pieces and use them to make the others. If you're making more than one chair, now's the time to trace all the arm and leg pieces for each chair. The left arms and legs are mirror images of the right. Also, trim the small cutout piece of each arm (C) to make the arm support (K) for each side.

Cut the tapered back pieces

The two tapered back pieces are tricky to cut, and the safest way to do it is to cut them from a wider board. Draw the tapers shown in Figure A onto a 1x6 cut to length. Nail each end of the board to the tops of a sawhorse, placing the nails where they'll be out of the saw's path. Use a No. 4 finish nail on each end and hammer it in flush with the surface. Set the depth of your circular saw 1/8 in. deeper than the thickness of the board, and cut the taper from the wide end to the narrow end.

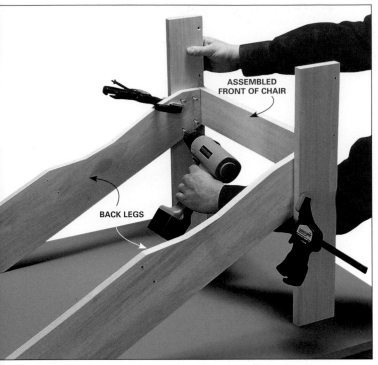

ASSEMBLED
FRONT OF CHAIR

BACK LEGS

5 Clamp the back legs (B) to the front assembly to accurately position them. Work on a flat workbench surface so the chair won't wobble. Apply glue, drill pilot holes and drive 1-1/4-in. deck screws.

WORK SMART

When you're building more than one chair, set up an assembly line and cut the building time per chair by 40 percent.

Materials list

ITEM	QTY.
1x6 x 10' poplar	1 piece
1x6 x 8' poplar	1 piece
1x6 x 12' poplar	1 piece
1x4 x 12' poplar	1 piece
1-5/8" galvanized deck screws	24
1-1/4" galvanized deck screws	68
Exterior oil primer	1 qt.*
White polyurethane gloss enamel	1 qt.*

*Enough paint to finish two chairs

Cutting list

KEY	PCS.	SIZE & DESCRIPTION
A	1	3/4" x 5-1/2" x 35" poplar (center back slat)
B	2	3/4" x 5-1/2" x 33" poplar (back legs)
C	2	3/4" x 5-1/2" x 29" poplar (arms)
D	1	3/4" x 3-1/2" x 23" poplar (front seat support)
E	2	3/4" x 3-1/2" x 21" poplar (front legs)
F	2	3/4" x 3-1/4" x 35" poplar (back slats)
G	1	3/4" x 3" x 20" poplar (lower back cleat)
H	4	3/4" x 2-1/2" x 35" poplar (back slats)
J	6	3/4" x 2-1/2" x 21-1/2" poplar (seat slats)
K	2	3/4" x 2-1/2" x 9" poplar (arm supports)‡
L	1	3/4" x 2" x 25-1/2" poplar (center back support)
M	1	3/4" x 2" x 21-1/2" poplar (back leg support)
N	1	3/4" x 2" x 21" poplar (upper back support)

‡Cut from pieces C

Next, draw a straight line on the remaining part to define the second piece and cut it. Note: Before you begin assembly, sand all the pieces and ease the edges with 100-grit sandpaper, followed by 150-grit.

Assemble the back first

Lay the back pieces face down on your workbench (Photo 2). Line up the bottoms and insert 1/4-in. spacers between the slats. Cut your 1/4-in. spacers from scrap boards or scrap 1/4-in. plywood. Screw each of the horizontal back supports G, L and N to the slats with 1-1/4-in. exterior deck screws. Predrill and countersink each screw hole.

You'll need to cut a bevel on the top side of the center horizontal back support (L). A table saw works best, but you could use the same circular saw method you used earlier to cut the tapered side back slats (H). Just set the bevel on your circular saw to 33 degrees, nail the 1x6 board to the sawhorses, mark the width and make the cut.

With a framing square, check that the back slats and horizontal supports are positioned 90 degrees to each other as you glue and screw the assembly (Photo 2). Once the back is fastened, turn the back assembly over, mark the top radius and trim it with a jigsaw (Photo 3).

Screw the chair frame together

Using your jigsaw, cut the notches on parts E as shown in Figure A. Glue and screw the front seat support (D) to the front legs (Photo 4). Next set the front assembly vertically on your workbench and glue and screw the back legs B to the front legs (Photo 5). Again, drill pilot and countersink holes for each screw. Then glue and screw the arm supports to the outer sides of the front legs (E).

Position the arms on the tops of the front legs and the arm supports (K). Make sure the arms hang 3 in. over the front leg and 1/4 in. over the inside edge of each leg. Before fastening the arms, make sure they're parallel (Photo 6).

Screw the back leg support (M) to each leg (see Figure A) and then set the back assembly into the frame and clamp it in place (Photo 7). Make sure the back of each arm projects 3/4 in. past the center back support (L). Glue and predrill each joint, screw the assembly together and then remove the clamps.

To finish the assembly, predrill and countersink holes in the ends of the seat slats. Position them approximately 1/4 in. apart and screw them to the back legs as shown. Use a power screwdriver where possible, and a hand screwdriver in tight places.

Figure A
Adirondack chair

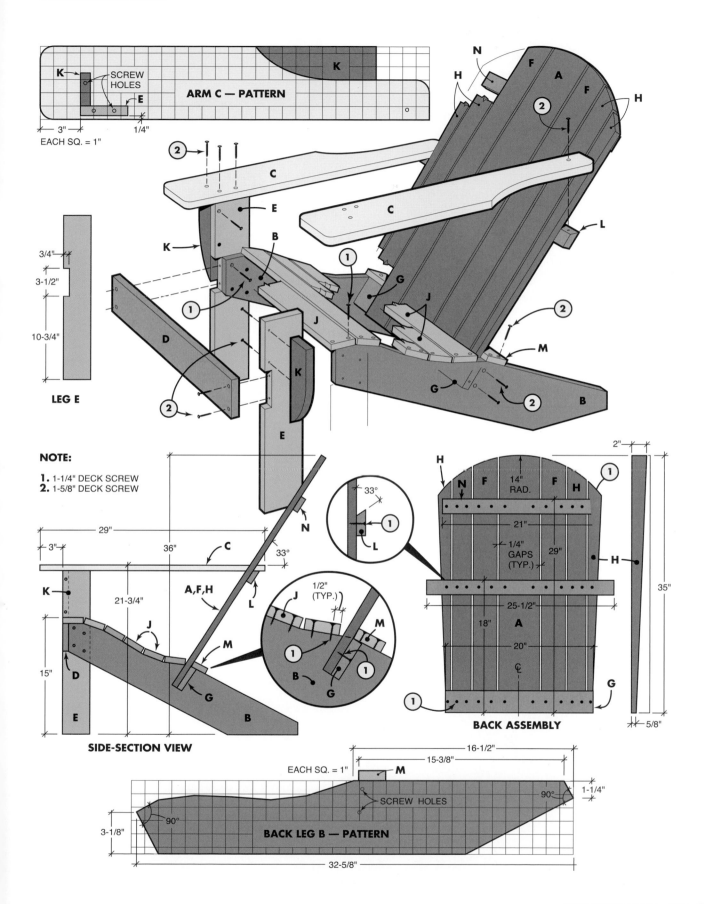

ARM C — PATTERN

K SCREW HOLES
E
3"   1/4"
EACH SQ. = 1"

LEG E
3/4"
3-1/2"
10-3/4"

NOTE:
1. 1-1/4" DECK SCREW
2. 1-5/8" DECK SCREW

29"
36"
3"
K
21-3/4"
D
J
15"
E   B
SIDE-SECTION VIEW

33°
A,F,H
L
M
G
N
C
33°

1/2" (TYP.)
J
M
B   G

BACK ASSEMBLY
H   N   F   14" RAD.   F   H
21"
1/4" GAPS (TYP.)
29"
25-1/2"
18"   A
20"
G

2"
H
35"
5/8"

EACH SQ. = 1"
16-1/2"
15-3/8"
M
SCREW HOLES
90°
1-1/4"
90°
3-1/8"
BACK LEG B — PATTERN
32-5/8"

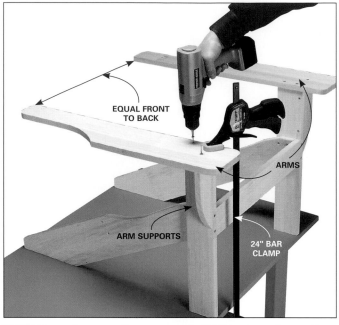

EQUAL FRONT TO BACK

ARMS

ARM SUPPORTS

24" BAR CLAMP

6 Glue and screw on the arm supports (K). Then glue and screw the arms to the front legs and arm supports. Use clamps to position the arms so they overhang the insides of the front legs by 1/4 in.

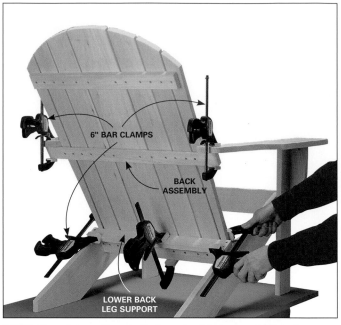

6" BAR CLAMPS

BACK ASSEMBLY

LOWER BACK LEG SUPPORT

7 Glue, clamp and screw the lower back leg support (M) to the back legs first. Then glue and clamp the back assembly, first to the back legs, then to the arm supports. Drill pilot and countersink holes for the screws.

Painting tips

You can use either a water-based or oil-based exterior primer and enamel topcoat.

Start applying the primer with the chair upside down. Use a 1-in.-wide sash brush for coating the edges of the seat slats, and then use a 3-in.-wide roller to apply primer to the flat surfaces and a 2-in. brush to smooth out the primer. Prime the back, then turn the chair over and prime the other surfaces in the same manner.

Let the primer dry overnight, then use a paint scraper to remove any runs and 120-grit sandpaper to lightly sand the entire surface. Apply the topcoat in the same order you applied the primer, then let the paint dry for at least three days before use.

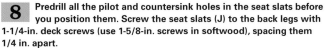

1/4" GAPS

SEAT SLATS

8 Predrill all the pilot and countersink holes in the seat slats before you position them. Screw the seat slats (J) to the back legs with 1-1/4-in. deck screws (use 1-5/8-in. screws in softwood), spacing them 1/4 in. apart.

Rustic shelf

Bring a bit of nature indoors with this simple branch-supported shelf. You'll have to find two forked branches about 1 in. in diameter, with one relatively straight side that will sit as flush to the wall as possible. We trimmed our branches from a crab apple, but you can use any smooth-barked tree. Our shelf is 12-in. melamine closet shelving with the ends painted white. Yours can be any wood you like, but keep the width to 12 in. or less.

To make square cuts on the branch ends, create a jig with scrap wood and a 2x4. Clamp the jig to your workbench. Then clamp each branch to the 2x4 and use the bottom edge of the jig to guide your cuts (Photo 1). Cut the branches above the crotch where the ends will be wide enough to support the shelf—one near the wall, the other close to the edge.

Clamp the shelf to the jig and trace around the branch. Drill pilot holes near the bottom of the marks at the front edge of the shelf so the screw tips won't poke through the branch (Photo 2). Bore countersink holes for the screw heads at the top of the shelf. Then hold the branches tight to the shelf while screwing them in. Hold the shelf level while you drill two holes through each branch into the drywall to mark the wall for drywall anchors. Screw your new shelf to the wall and fill it with your treasures.

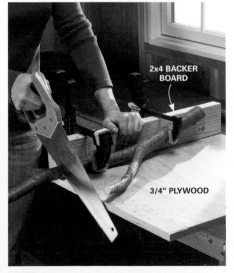

1 Build a simple jig to hold the branch steady. Cut the ends flush with the end of the jig.

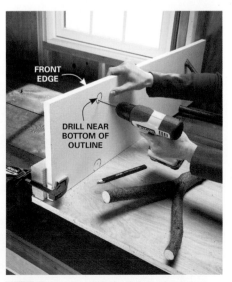

2 Trace around the branches where they touch the shelf bottom, then drill the holes and screw the shelf to the branches.

3 Drill pilot holes near the top and bottom of the branch into the drywall. Then sink drywall anchors and screw the shelf to the wall.

North woods bench

An inexpensive, easy-to-build classic

WHAT IT TAKES

TIME: Half day

COST: $12 to $20 (depending on the finish)

SKILL LEVEL: Beginner to intermediate

TOOLS: Tape measure, square, circular saw or jigsaw, drill, 1-in. hole saw

1 Cut the leg blanks. Set the saw to cut a 10-degree bevel. Mark the 1x12 and align the saw with the mark. Then use a large square to help guide the cut.

While visiting a cabin in the woods of northern Wisconsin, one of our editors saw the cute red stool shown below. Made by an anonymous carpenter, it was simplicity itself: pine boards, nailed together. And it had an interesting and ingenious design detail: a cloverleaf, clearly made with three overlapping drill holes. It was the kind of little bench that's perfect for the backyard, so we decided to make this modern version. A little longer and a little stronger than the original, but the same folk art detail. And since it's made from lumberyard pine, the price can't be beat. Here's how to make one.

This bench is simple enough to build with a few hand tools, but to speed things up, we chose to take advantage of the power tools in our shop. We used a miter saw to cut the stretchers to length and to cut the 10-degree angles on the ends of the center stretcher, and a circular saw for all the other cuts. If you don't own a miter saw, you can use a circular saw or jigsaw for all the cuts.

To make the holes for the clover shapes, you'll need a 1-in. hole saw mounted in a corded drill, or a powerful cordless drill.

We used No. 2 knotty pine to build this bench. You'll need one 6-ft. 1x12 and one 10-ft. 1x4. Select boards that are straight and flat, with solid, not loose, knots. We assembled the bench with countersunk 2-in. trim screws and then filled the holes with wood filler. If the bench is going outdoors, be sure to use corrosion-resistant screws.

2 Drill out the clover shape. Mark out a grid with lines spaced 1/2 in. apart. The centers of the holes are on four of the intersections. Drill all four holes halfway through the board. Then flip the board over and drill from the other side to complete the holes.

1" HOLE SAW

1/2"

1/2"

Cut out the parts

Using the Cutting List on p. 119 as a guide, cut the two legs and the top from the 1x12 (Photo 1). The legs require a 10-degree bevel on the top and bottom. Be careful to keep both bevels angled the same direction. Then cut the stretcher and aprons to length. The stretcher has a 10-degree angle on each end.

Next, mark the legs and aprons for drilling and cutting, using the dimensions in Figures B and C as a guide. Draw the grid layout as shown in Photo 2 to locate the holes. Use a nail or a punch to make starting holes for the hole saw at the correct intersections.

Drill the 1-in. holes halfway through the boards (Photo 2). Make sure the pilot bit on the hole saw goes through the board so you can use the hole to

3 Cut the leg angles. Mark the "V" in the center and the two outside angles on the legs. Then cut along the lines with a circular saw. Accurate cutting is easier if you clamp the leg to the workbench.

TRIM SCREW

APRON LOCATION

4 Screw the aprons to the legs. Drive trim screws through the legs into the stretcher. Then attach the outside aprons with trim screws.

guide the hole saw from the opposite side. Then flip the boards over to complete the holes.

Make the remaining cuts on the legs and aprons with a circular saw (Photo 3). Finish up by sanding the parts. We wrapped 80-grit sandpaper around a 1-in. dowel to sand the inside of the holes. Sand off the saw marks and round all the sharp edges slightly with sandpaper. If you plan to paint the bench, you can save time by painting the parts before assembly.

Build the bench

Start by marking the location of the stretcher on the legs. Arrange the legs so the bevels are oriented correctly, and screw through them into the stretcher. Next screw the two aprons to the legs (Photo 4).

The only thing left is to screw the top to the aprons. It'll be easier to place the screws accurately if you first mark the apron locations on the underside of the top and drill pilot holes for the screws (Photo 5). Stand the bench upright and align the top by looking underneath and lining up the apron marks. Then attach the top with six trim screws.

DRILL PILOT HOLE

5 Position the seat screws. Here's a goof-proof way to position the screws that fasten the seat to the bench frame. Center the frame on the seat and trace around the aprons. Then drill pilot holes through the seat to mark screw locations. Drive screws through the seat and into the aprons.

We finished this bench with old-fashioned milk paint. You can find milk paint online and at some paint stores. If the bench is going outdoors, rub some exterior glue on the bottom ends of the legs. That will prevent the end grain from soaking up moisture and rotting.

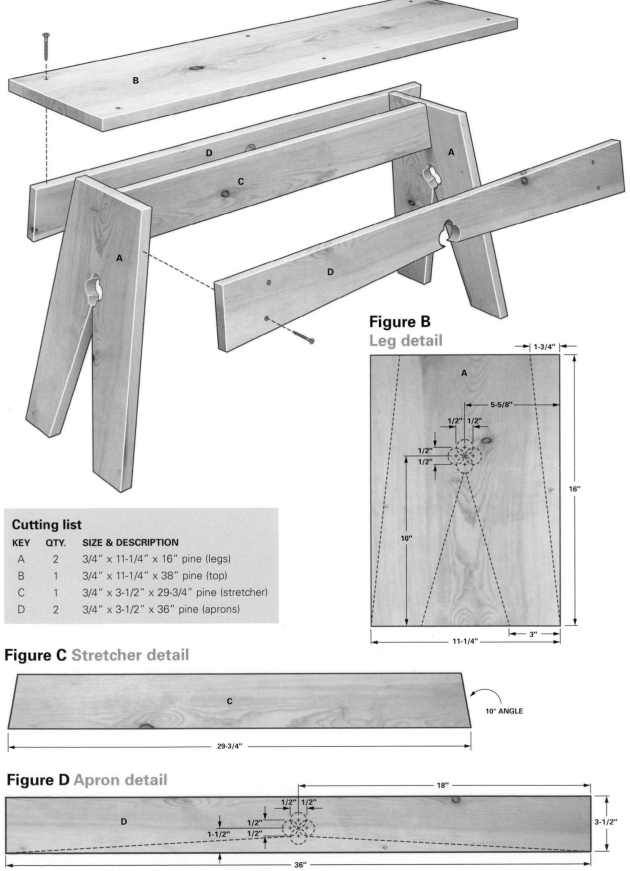

Figure A Exploded view

Overall dimensions: 38" long x 11-1/4" wide x 16-1/2" tall

B

D

C

A

A

D

Cutting list

KEY	QTY.	SIZE & DESCRIPTION
A	2	3/4" x 11-1/4" x 16" pine (legs)
B	1	3/4" x 11-1/4" x 38" pine (top)
C	1	3/4" x 3-1/2" x 29-3/4" pine (stretcher)
D	2	3/4" x 3-1/2" x 36" pine (aprons)

Figure B
Leg detail

1-3/4"

A

5-5/8"

1/2" 1/2"

1/2"

1/2"

16"

10"

11-1/4"

3"

Figure C Stretcher detail

C

10° ANGLE

29-3/4"

Figure D Apron detail

18"

1/2" 1/2"

1/2"

3-1/2"

1-1/2" 1/2"

36"

Chair rail

From ordinary to elegant in one weekend

The original purpose of chair rail was to protect walls from being damaged by chair backs. Today, this molding is a fast way to stylishly define a dining room, living room or entry hall, especially when used to separate wallpaper from paint, or between two different colors of paint.

This article will show you how to install chair rail, with tips to make the job go faster and easier and with less wasted material. Chair rail ranges in price from less than $1 per ft. for paint-grade pine to over $6 per ft. for large hardwood profiles. You can also make your own chair rail with standard trim or clear "1-by" material. The special-order cherry molding we used cost $5 per ft.

To cut the chair rail, you'll need a miter saw and a coping saw with extra blades (they break easily). A finish nailer isn't absolutely necessary but will give you faster, better results.

Make a sketch, then go shopping

Sketch out the floor plan of the room, noting the exact length of each section of wall. Add a foot to each length for waste to get the minimum size you need for each wall. Once you decide on a style, you'll need to do some juggling to make the standard lengths that the lumberyard sells fit the lengths that you need. The best way to keep track of what piece goes where and avoid wasting expensive wood is to make notes on the sketch. Here are some shopping tips:

- When possible, buy pieces long enough to span the entire wall; otherwise, you'll have to splice sections (Photo 7).
- If you plan to stain and varnish the trim, select pieces with similar grain pattern and color.
- Check each piece for flaws such as splits and tear-out.
- To avoid heavy sanding, select pieces that have a smooth surface. Watch out for deep "chatter marks" (a wavy surface left by the milling machine).
- Home centers only carry a few pine and oak chair rails. For a larger selection, ask about special-order profiles or visit a lumberyard that caters to professional contractors.
- Many types and combinations of moldings can be used as chair rail, even if they aren't called chair rail.

Also use your sketch to plan the location of coped cuts, so that you don't end up with pieces that have to be coped at both ends. If possible, locate coped pieces on walls where the non-coped end can be marked in place. That way you can shave the coped cut down, or even recut it if you have to, before you cut it to length. Even pros have to tweak their cuts, so leave yourself a little extra wood to work with.

Prepare the walls

Apply wallpaper or paint high enough (or low enough) for the chair rail to cover the edge. Chair rail is usually placed 36 in. above the floor but can be installed anywhere from 30 in. to 42 in. up, with wallpaper either above or below.

Lightly mark the bottom of the chair rail every 3 ft. around the perimeter of the room. Measure from the baseboard, the ceiling or the floor—whichever is most consistent. Find and mark all the studs (Photo 1).

Prefinish for a faster, neater job

For a job with sharp, crisp edges, stain and varnish (or paint) the chair rail before nailing it up (Photo 2). Before the first coat, sand all the chair rail lightly but thoroughly with 180-grit sandpaper. Test the finish on scrap pieces to make sure the color looks right. To match existing trim, you'll have to experiment on scraps of chair rail. Don't assume that stain colors will look the same on your chair rail as they do on store displays.

Cope corners for a perfect fit

Wall corners are almost never perfectly square, but coped joints cover this problem by fitting tightly against the adjoining piece even if the corner is a few degrees off.

Cut the piece for the first side of the corner at 90 degrees and nail it in place—but keep the nails a foot back from the corner

1 Locate studs and mark them with masking tape. If new wallpaper or paint is part of the project, complete those jobs before you install chair rail.

TIP: Split the difference

In older houses, where level floors and ceilings may be only a distant memory, perfectly level chair rail can actually look crooked. The best solution is to ignore the level and follow a compromise line halfway between level and the closest visual reference point—usually the baseboard. If in doubt, tack up a test piece or a piece of tape, then stand back and see if it looks right.

2 Prefinish the chair rail for less mess and smoother results. Apply the final coat after installing the chair rail and filling nail holes.

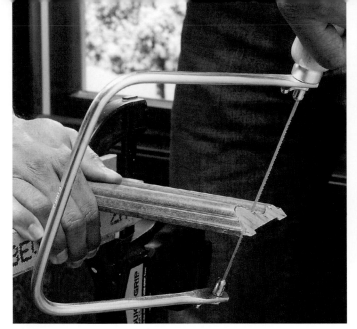

3 Cope inside corners by cutting along the profile left by a 45-degree miter cut. Hold the coping saw at an angle to "backcut" the chair rail.

4 Perfect the fit of coped ends with a file, rasp, utility knife or sandpaper. Don't try to shave off thin slices with a coping saw.

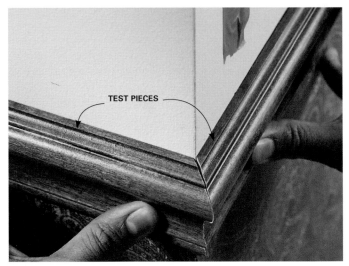

TEST PIECES

5 Close a gap with a shim. Slip the shim under the uncoped end to force it against the coped end. This only works if the gap is along the lower half of the joint.

6 Find the miter cut angle on outside corners by cutting and recutting test pieces until they form a tight corner.

for now. Cut the coped end of the next piece and tweak it until the joint is tight (Photos 3 and 4).

Here are some tips for making smooth, accurate cope cuts:

- Make sure the saw teeth point toward the handle. That way, the blade will cut smoothly on the pull stroke.
- Practice on scraps. You'll be surprised at how much your copes improve after a couple of practice cuts.
- Clamp the chair rail to a solid work surface. Cuts are smoother and easier if the molding can't shift or wiggle.
- Don't force the saw forward. Make smooth, even strokes, applying light forward pressure.

If the first wall isn't perfectly plumb, you may need to glue a thin shim under the bottom edge to tighten the joint (Photo 5). Don't cut off the shim in place—you may damage the wall. Instead, mark it, and then pull it out to cut it.

Once the coped joint looks right, hold it in place and mark the cut at the other end. Only one end should be coped. The other end will always be either an outside corner or a 90-degree cut.

Test outside corners for a tight fit

Outside corners often flare out slightly, so that the chair rail needs to be cut at more than 45 degrees. To get the exact angle, cut two scrap pieces at 46 degrees, then adjust the angle of the cut until the joint is tight (Photo 6). Both sides should be cut at the same angle.

Spread wood glue on one of the ends before nailing the pieces to the wall. Don't nail within 2 in. of the end unless you're using a brad nailer or predrilling, to avoid splitting the wood.

Dealing with dead ends

Create a "return" at an archway

To end chair rail at an archway or corner, form a return an inch from the corner. When you cut the return, leave the saw blade down until the blade stops spinning to avoid nicking the return as it falls away from the blade.

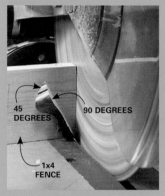

45 DEGREES 90 DEGREES

1x4 FENCE

1 Cut a return piece the width of the chair rail. Clamp a 1x4 to the fence so the saw blade won't mangle the return.

2 Push the return into place and hold it for a minute until the glue starts to set. Don't nail the return—it's too small.

Cut a "bevel" at thin window casing

Some types of chair rail are thicker than window and door casing. To solve this problem, bevel-cut the chair rail as shown below. Apply finish to the cut before you nail it up to avoid getting finish on the casing.

BEVEL CUT

Make the transition from thick chair rail to thin casing with a shallow 45-degree bevel cut.

7 Join sections of chair rail with a 30-degree "scarf" joint at a stud. For a strong joint, use glue in addition to nails.

8 Fill nail holes with colored putty. Blend different colors of putty to perfectly match the color of the wood. Then apply the final coat of clear finish.

Splice long runs

If your wall is too long for a single piece of chair rail, you can inconspicuously join two pieces by cutting the ends at 30 degrees and gluing them together (Photo 7).

Select two pieces with similar grain. Measure and cut the two pieces so that the splice occurs on a stud. Position the top piece so that all the edges line up, then nail it to the wall. Wipe away glue drips and touch up with filler and additional finish if necessary.

Fill nail holes

Before applying the final coat of finish, fill all nail holes. Use colored wood putty—either oil or water-based—to fill holes in natural woodwork (Photo 8). If you don't have the right shade, blend different colors with your fingers for a better match. Wipe away excess filler with a rag dipped in thinner for the oil-based putty, or water for the water-based product.

Use spackling paste for painted chair rail. Sand it flush, spot-prime the nail holes, then repaint.

Install a new interior door

anging a door correctly is one of the most satisfying jobs in the home improvement world, but it's often the most challenging. Unless it's installed correctly, your door can have uneven gaps along the jamb, or it can bind or not even latch.

Here you'll learn foolproof tips and techniques that'll give you great results every time. All you need are simple carpentry tools and some basic home improvement skills and tools to easily master the techniques. Allow about an hour and a half for your first door, and once you get the hang of it, your next door will go in twice as fast.

When you buy your door, pick up a package of wood shims and 4d, 6d and 8d finish nails. Also get a straight 7-ft. 2x4 and cut another 2x4 the width of your opening (Photo 1). Make sure that they are both straight as you sight down the edge. Since installing trim is part of the door installation, purchase some matching door trim and be sure you've got a miter saw to cut it. You'll also need to pick up a lockset for the door.

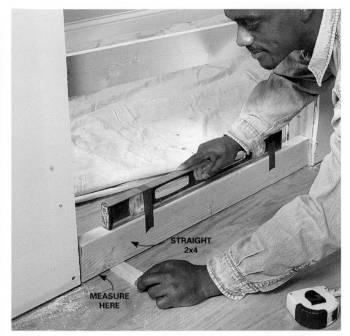

1 Check the floor for level and the jambs for plumb. Measure the exact amount the floor is off level. The opposite jamb must be cut by this much to level the door in the opening.

2 Mark and cut the jamb on the high side with your saw (remove any packaging strips at the bottom of the jambs). If you cut more than 1/4 in. from the jamb, you may need to trim the bottom of the door so it conforms to the floor slope.

3 Nail temporary cleats to the wall opposite the door opening to act as stops for the door frame. To ensure the jambs are centered in the wall, shim them away from the drywall slightly with a stack of three note cards as shown.

Check your rough opening carefully before starting

Here the focus is on installing standard prehung doors. These have a door jamb that's 4-9/16 in. wide and are made to fit into a 2x4 wall that's 4-1/2 in. thick. This gives just enough of a fudge factor to have the jamb a bit proud of (raised above) the wall surface on each side and to make up for any irregularities in the trimmer studs of the walls. Most openings will be about 82 in. high for standard doors, so that's what is shown here.

Before you order your door, check the width of your opening. It should be 2 to 2-1/2 in. wider than the door. This extra space gives you room to fit the jambs and the shims into the opening to hang the door. If your rough opening is 32 in., get a 30-in. prehung door. Also check the vertical sides of the rough opening to make sure they're reasonably plumb. Openings that have a trimmer stud out of plumb more than 3/8 in. from top to bottom will make it nearly impossible to install the door. It would be somewhat like trying to put a rectangle into a parallelogram. Small variations from plumb are quite common, however. Checking both sides and getting familiar with any problems with the opening will give you an idea of how much and where to shim the jambs later.

> **Tip:** If you're setting your door into adjoining rooms that'll be carpeted later, you can hold both jamb sides 3/8 in. above the floor and avoid having to trim your doors.

4 Push the door and frame into the opening. Open the door and shim the bottom edge of the open door to keep the frame tight against the stops on the other side.

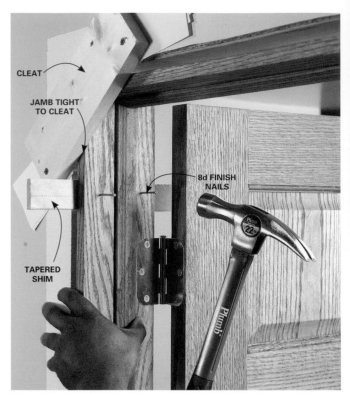

5 Center the frame in the opening. Slip a shim in from each side of the jamb (make sure the frame is pushed against the cleats) and nail the top sides of the door frame into the trimmer studs. The jamb should be perpendicular to your temporary cleats. Be careful not to twist the jamb as you nail it.

6 Shim the bottom of the door jamb up about 4 in. from the floor on the hinge side, making sure the hinge side is exactly plumb, and then nail it. Tape your level to a straight 2x4 as shown. Next, shim the center area of the jamb to straighten it and then nail it. Check the whole length with your straightedge.

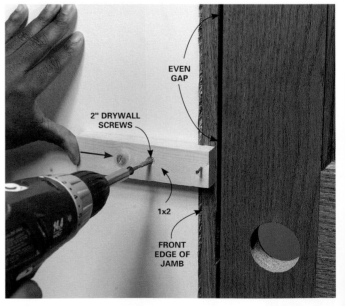

7 Tack a 4-in. 1x2 to the front edge of the jamb with a 4d finish nail. Set up an even 3/16-in. gap between the door and the strike-side jamb. Then screw the block to the studs to hold the jamb in this position.

Tip: Check the length of your prehung door jambs. They may be longer than you need. You may have to trim both sides to minimize the space under the door. In most cases, the door should clear the floor by 1/2 in.

8 Shim and nail the strike side near the strike plate and then near the floor.

Most installation problems occur because the floor isn't level under the doorway. If the floor slopes slightly and the jamb isn't trimmed to compensate, your latch won't line up. You must check the floor with an accurate level as shown in Photo 1.

How do you fit the jamb to floors of different heights?

Cut a 1-ft.-long strip of 1/4-in. plywood the same width as your door jamb. Drop it to the high side of the floor, tack it in place, set your scribe and mark the contour of the floor onto the plywood. Remove the plywood, cut the shape with a jigsaw and transfer the shape to the bottom of the jamb. Cut along your mark with a jigsaw. Do this for each side of the door. If your transition is more than 1/2 in., you may need to trim the bottom of the door as well.

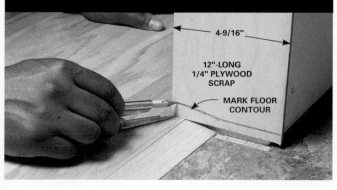

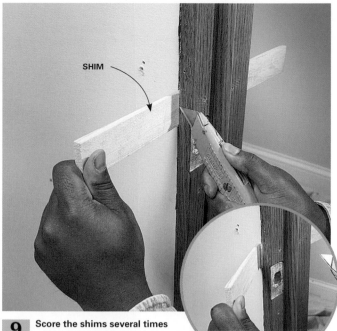

9 Score the shims several times with a sharp blade and then snap them off to make way for the trim.

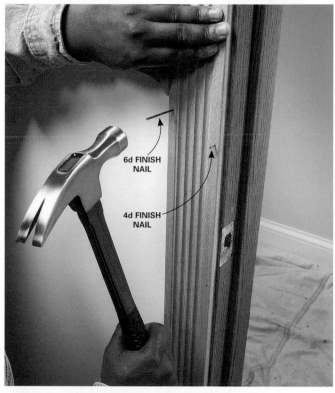

10 Nail the trim to the door frame with 4d finish nails. Nail the trim to the framing with 6d finish nails.

Tip: An accurate level is crucial for a good installation. Check it by laying it on a flat surface. Memorize the bubble's position. Then flip the level end for end and check the bubble. If the bubble doesn't settle in the exact spot, find an accurate level.

Replace your trim with a classic look

This Old World elegance is actually easier than standard trim

WHAT IT TAKES

TIME: 90 minutes per window or door.

SKILL LEVEL: Intermediate to advanced

COST: $35 per window and $40 per door for pine trim. Oak or maple trim would cost about twice as much.

TOOLS: A miter saw with at least a 40-tooth blade. A pneumatic trim nailer and compressor, and a table saw and router with a 1/4-in. round-over bit if you want to make a stool and fillet like the ones shown here.

This traditional trim style may look like it requires old-school carpentry skills, but the truth is, it's easier to install than contemporary trim. Modern trim—four pieces of casing that "picture frame" a door or window—requires wide miter cuts, which look sloppy if they're not perfect. Traditional trim is more forgiving. While it also requires miter cuts, they're shorter and less visible. And the most prominent joints are assembled with simple square cuts.

If you're nervous about installing the mitered crown molding that tops off the trim, check out "Make Your Own Moldings" on p. 131 where we show you how to make a simple router-shaped version that doesn't require any miters. We'll walk you through the steps and give you some tips and pointers for cutting and installing the moldings to create this classic trim style.

Getting started

The first step in any trim job is to prepare the jambs for trim. If you're replacing trim, pry it off and remove the nails from the jamb. Then scrape or sand the face of the jamb to smooth out any paint or finish that's built up. Finally, mark the reveal on the jambs to show where the edge of the trim goes (Photo 1, inset). A combination square set to 1/4 in. works great for marking the reveals. But you can also use a compass to scribe the marks, or simply measure and mark the reveals.

If possible, set up your miter saw in the room where you're installing the trim. Having the saw nearby will save you a ton of time. It's a good idea to rough-cut the casing and other moldings to length, allowing a few extra inches, and label them to make sure you have all the material you need and won't accidentally cut the wrong piece.

For tips on buying or making the moldings you'll need, see p. 131.

Mark, don't measure

With the moldings and other parts cut to rough length, and the reveals marked on the jambs, the fastest and most accurate method for marking the trim for cutting is to simply hold the molding in place and mark it (Photo 1). It's foolproof. You don't have to measure, do math or remember any numbers.

Install the window casings, stool and apron

The order of trim installation for windows varies a little depending on whether you're working on old double-hung windows or newer-style windows. On older double-hung windows, the stool rests on the angled sill and butts into the lower sash (check out Figure A if you're not sure what a stool is). You have to notch the new stool to fit, and nail it to the windowsill before you install the side casings. But on newer windows like the one shown here, the stool isn't notched and doesn't rest on the sill, so it's a little trickier to nail. An easy way to attach this type of stool is to install the side casings first, and then nail the stool to them (Photo 2).

The stool should protrude past the casings by about an inch (Photo 2). To find the length of the stool, make a mark 1 in.

1 Mark the side casing. Cut one end of the casing square. Line up the cut end with the pencil mark indicating the 1/4-in. reveal and mark the opposite end for cutting. Cut and install both side casings, keeping them aligned with the reveal marks.

2 Install the stool. Cut the stool so that it extends an inch past the casing on both ends. Then round the edges with a router or by sanding. Nail the stool to the side casings.

beyond the casing on both sides. Then hold the stool up and transfer the marks. After the stool material is cut to length, round the edges and ends. Or if you want a little fancier stool, rout the edges with a more decorative bit. You can even buy a special stool-shaping bit, but you may have to order it.

With the side casings and stool in place, the next step is to install the apron under the stool. Start by cutting a 45-degree miter on each end. Mark for the long point of the miters by resting the apron on the stool and making marks where the outside edges of the casings intersect the apron material. Snug the mitered apron against the bottom of the stool and nail it to the framing under the window. Then cut returns and glue them in (Photos 3 and 4).

Photo 3 shows how to use a sacrificial piece of wood behind the apron material. Any flat scrap of wood will work. This sacrificial backer board prevents the skinny piece of molding you're cutting off from getting caught by the blade and flung through the gap in the fence. Don't attach the sacrificial board to the saw. Just hold it in place along with the molding you're cutting. Then reposition it with each new cut so you're always making a fresh cut through the sacrificial board.

Build the head casing assembly

The final step for both the door and the window trim is building and installing the head casing assembly. It's made up of three parts: the fillet, a 1x6 and the cap molding. Traditionally this cap molding was solid, but since a solid molding this large is hard to come by, we substituted 2-1/4-in. crown molding. If you have a router and want to avoid using crown molding, check out Figure B on p. 131 for an attractive alternative.

Figure A
Window trim parts

Trim terminology can be confusing. Here's a labeled photo to show you the names of the parts we used.

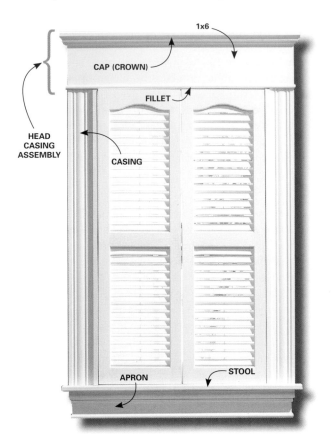

1x6
CAP (CROWN)
FILLET
HEAD CASING ASSEMBLY
CASING
APRON
STOOL

3 **Cut the mitered apron returns.** Set the miter saw to 45 degrees and cut a return from the apron molding. Use a sacrificial board to prevent the small cutoff from flying through the gap in the fence. Set the miter saw to the opposite angle to cut the other return from the opposite end of the molding.

MITERED RETURN

SACRIFICIAL BACKER

4 **Finish the apron.** Glue in the returns to complete the apron. Avoid nailing problems by letting the glue do the work. Just hold the return in place for 60 seconds while the glue grabs.

MITERED RETURN

APRON

Tips for choosing, buying and making traditional molding

Shopping for trim

We found the wide casing and base blocks at the home center, along with the fancy casing we used as an apron. We had to go to the local lumberyard for the 2-1/4-in. crown molding. If your local home center or lumberyard doesn't have what you want in stock, ask to see a molding book or chart that shows what styles are available to order. The Internet is also a good place to search for traditional moldings. Start with "molding and millwork."

Make your own moldings

You don't have to buy moldings. With a little ingenuity and a few standard router bits, you can make your own. Figure B shows an example of a cap molding for a head casing that we made by stacking two pieces of 3/4-in. oak. Shaping the edges of wood strips with a router and stacking them to make bigger moldings is a great technique for making your own moldings.

You can make moldings with a handheld router, but it's a lot easier and faster to mount your router in a router table. The Ryobi router table shown here works well, but there are plenty of other options. You can also make your own.

The photo at right shows how to use featherboards for safer and more accurate routing. You can make your own featherboards, or buy plastic ones like these.

The ends of the boards shown in Figure B are routed. This method eliminates the need for mitered returns, but it does expose end grain and means you have to cut the parts to length before you shape them. To rout the end of boards, use a shop-made push block like the one shown at the top of the page. It serves two functions. First, it allows you to hold the board square to the fence. And second, the push block prevents splintering by providing a backer behind the board you're routing.

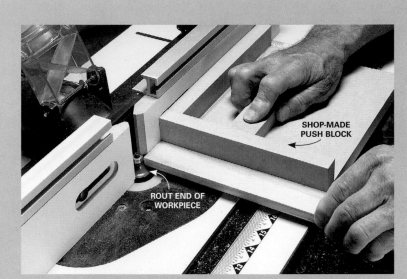

Build a simple push block to rout ends. Hold the board square to the fence and prevent tear-out with a shop-made push block like this.

SHOP-MADE PUSH BLOCK

ROUT END OF WORKPIECE

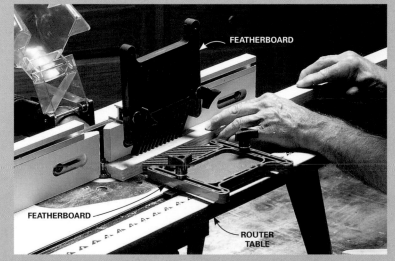

Hold the wood with featherboards. When you're making moldings with a router table, use featherboards to hold the wood tight to the fence and table. Set the featherboards to apply light pressure.

FEATHERBOARD

FEATHERBOARD

ROUTER TABLE

Figure B
Router-shaped cap molding

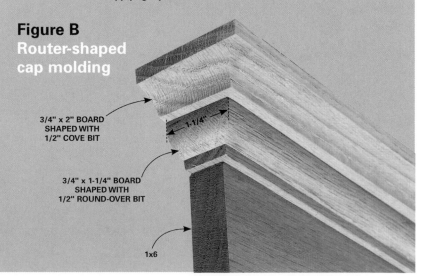

3/4" x 2" BOARD SHAPED WITH 1/2" COVE BIT

1-1/4"

3/4" x 1-1/4" BOARD SHAPED WITH 1/2" ROUND-OVER BIT

1x6

5 Mark the crown molding for the end return. Hold a piece of crown molding against the 1x6 you'll be using for the head casing and mark it for cutting.

2-1/4" CROWN MOLDING

6 Build a crown-molding jig. Build a simple jig to hold the crown molding at the correct angle while you cut it. Position the molding upside down and set the saw to 45 degrees. Avoid cutting all the way through the jig.

CROWN MOLDING CUTTING JIG

Figure C
Crown molding cutting jig

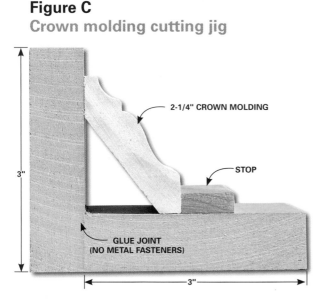

2-1/4" CROWN MOLDING

STOP

3"

GLUE JOINT
(NO METAL FASTENERS)

3"

This jig holds the crown molding at the correct angle in the miter saw, so it's easy to make accurate miters every time. Glue two strips of scrap wood together at a right angle. Then set the crown molding upside down in the jig and mark the position of the stop. Glue the stop to the bottom and you're ready to cut some moldings.

Start by setting the 1x6 on top of the side casings and marking it at the outside edge of each casing. Cut the 1x6 to length. Then cut the fillet 3/4 in. longer than the 1x6. Round over the edges and ends of the fillet to make a bullnose shape using a router and 1/4-in. round-over bit. Nail the fillet to the bottom of the 1x6.

Finish the head casing by wrapping the front and sides of the 1x6 with crown molding. Photos 5 – 8 show how. Make a jig (Photo 6 and Figure C) to hold the crown molding at the correct angle while you cut it. Remember to set the crown molding upside down in the jig. Mark and cut the short pieces of crown molding (Photos 5 and 6). Then cut a miter on one end of the long front piece and hold it in place on the 1x6 to mark the opposite end for the miter (Photo 7). Cut the second miter on the front piece.

Check the fit by holding the short mitered ends in place against the front crown molding. If the miters are tight and everything fits, complete the head casing by nailing the crown molding to the 1x6 (Photo 8). Complete the window trim by nailing the head casing assembly to the framing above the window (Photo 9).

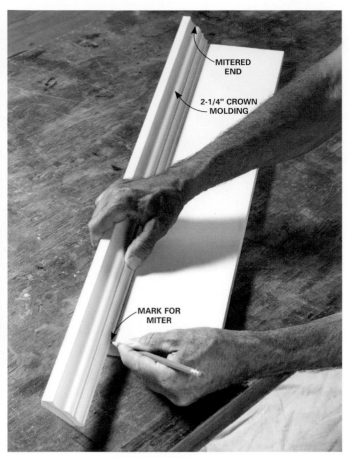

7 Mark the front crown molding. Cut a miter on one end of the front crown molding. Line up the cut with one end of the head casing and mark the opposite end for cutting. Set the molding in your jig and cut the opposite miter.

8 Attach the molding to the head casing. Nail the crown molding to the 1x6. Then glue and nail in the end returns. Nail the fillet to the bottom of the 1x6 to complete the head casing assembly.

9 Finish the window trim. Set the head casing on the side casings, making sure the fillet overhangs evenly on both ends. Then nail it to the wall framing.

Doors are similar

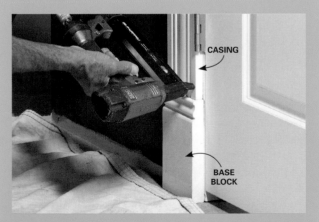

Door trim starts with a base block at the bottom

Trimming a door is just like trimming a window, except you start out with base blocks at the floor, as shown above. The base blocks should be about 3/8 in. wider than the casings. Trim them if necessary. The height of the base blocks should be about 1 in. greater than the height of the baseboard you're planning to install.

Bookcase built by two

Build it in a day with your favorite young woodworker

Here's a simple project that gives you a chance to pass some of your woodworking skills on to the next generation. Any kid will love spending the day with you assembling this bookcase. And by the end of the day, your helper will have hands-on experience with several power tools, plus an attractive bookcase to show off.

The bookcase parts are all standard dimensional lumber that you can find at any home center. The total cost of the knotty pine and other supplies we used was about $40. We joined the shelves and legs with biscuits. If you don't own a biscuit joiner but still want to build this project, you can simply nail or screw the parts together and fill the holes. We used a table saw to cut the 1-1/2-in. square legs from 2x4s and a router with a 45-degree chamfer bit to bevel the edge of the top. If you don't have a table saw or router, you can just use stock 2x2s for the legs and leave the edge of the top square.

Getting started

Use the Cutting List on p. 137 as a guide for cutting all the parts. The next step is to mark the shelf positions on the shelf sides. It's important to keep track of the orientation of the parts. For reference, we placed a piece of masking tape on the top of each side, and on the top side of each shelf. Use a framing square to draw lines indicating the bottom of each shelf (Photo 1).

No need to mark the location of biscuits on the shelves and sides. Instead make marks on the scrap of wood used as a fence. Draw marks to indicate the outside edges of the 1x8 shelves and sides, and mark 1 3/4 in. in from each edge to indicate the center of the biscuits. To use the fence, line up the outside marks with the edges of the part you're cutting slots in. And then line up the center mark on the biscuit-joining tool with the marks for the center of the biscuits (Photos 3 and 4).

To mark the legs and sides for biscuits, set the legs in position and make pairs of marks that line up with each other on the legs and sides (Photo 2). Put a piece of masking tape on the top of each 2x2 leg, and keep this facing up when you cut the biscuit slots. Photo 7 shows how to bevel the legs.

Cut slots for the biscuits

Biscuit joiners have a flip-down fence that can be used to position the slots, but instead we're showing a method that allows you to reference the slots from the base of the biscuit joiner. Photos 3 – 6 show the techniques.

Older kids and teens won't have any trouble mastering the biscuit joiner. With a little coaching, they'll be cutting slots like a pro. What's trickiest about cutting the slots is keeping track of the orientation of the parts. Just remember to keep the masking tape facing up, with one exception: The slots on the 1x8 top should be cut with the tape side down.

1 **Mark both sides at once.** Lay the bookcase sides together to mark the shelf locations. The layout marks have to be perfect, so closely supervise this step.

2 **Mark the biscuit slots.** Make pairs of corresponding marks on the legs and sides. Later you'll center the biscuit joiner on the marks to cut slots that align.

Four biscuit joiner techniques

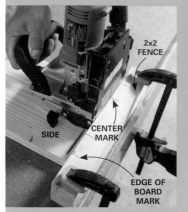

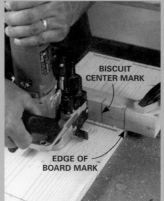

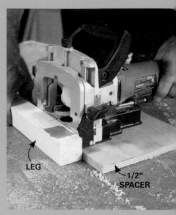

3 Slot the end of the side. Clamp the fence to the work surface and butt the end of the shelf to it. Then center the biscuit joiner on the mark and cut the slot. Repeat for the second slot.

4 Cut slots for the shelves. Line up the 2x2 jig with the edge of board mark and clamp it. Center the biscuit joiner on the center mark on the fence and cut the slot. Repeat for the second slot.

5 Cut slots for the legs. Line up the center of the biscuit joiner with the marks on the edge of the side and cut the slots. Make sure both the shelf side and the biscuit joiner are tight to the work surface when you cut the slot.

6 Position the slot with a spacer. Place a scrap of 1/2-in. plywood or particleboard on the work surface. Butt the leg against it and rest the biscuit joiner on the spacer while you cut the slots. The 1/2-in. spacer will automatically position the slots.

Glue the bookcase together

Here's where a helper really comes in handy. You have to work fast to spread the glue in the biscuit slots and onto the biscuits (Photo 8), and then assemble the parts before the glue starts to swell the biscuits (Photo 9).

Start by arranging all the parts on your work surface. Use a flux brush to spread the glue in the slots, and onto the biscuits after they are installed. Any small brush will work, though. When you have everything assembled, install clamps to hold the sides tight to the shelves while the glue dries. Check by using a framing square or by measuring diagonally from opposite corners to make sure the bookcase is square. Adjust it if needed. Then tighten the clamps. This is a good time to take a break while you let the glue dry for about an hour.

Build the top

To minimize potential cupping, we decided to make the top by gluing two pieces of 1x6 together rather than using a solid board. Choose a straight piece of 1x6 with a sharp, clean edge. Cut the pieces long and trim the top to length after you glue the two parts together. Cut biscuit slots in the sides of the two 1x6s to help hold them in alignment while installing the clamps. Glue and clamp the two 1x6s. Then let the glue set up about 30 minutes before routing the edge (Photo 10).

Add the legs, top and back

The legs are held to the sides of the bookcase with biscuits. When attached, the legs should protrude 1/2 in. past the outside, and overlap the shelves by 1/4 in. Glue in the biscuits, spread a line of glue along the edge of the side, and clamp the legs to the sides (Photo 11). Let the glue set for about 30 minutes.

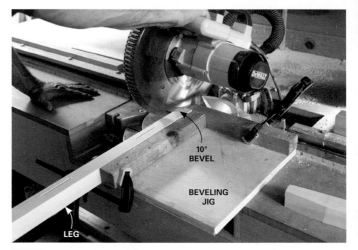

7 Bevel the legs with a simple jig. Screw two scraps to a small square of plywood to form a cradle for the legs. Clamp the jig to the miter saw fence, and cut a 10-degree bevel on the bottom of each leg.

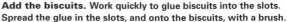

8 Add the biscuits. Work quickly to glue biscuits into the slots. Spread the glue in the slots, and onto the biscuits, with a brush.

Figure A Exploded view

Overall dimensions:
39-3/4" tall x 26-1/2" wide x 11" deep

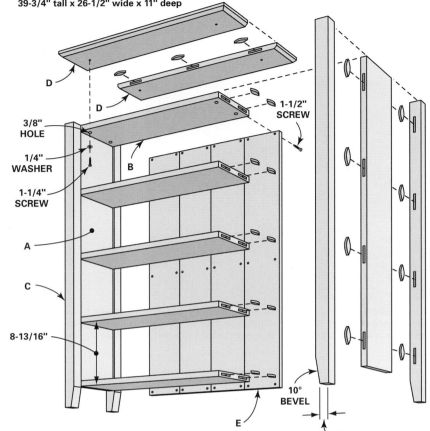

D

D

D

3/8" HOLE

1/4" WASHER

1-1/4" SCREW

B

A

C

8-13/16"

1-1/2" SCREW

1-1/2" SCREW

E

10° BEVEL

1"

Materials list

ITEM	QTY.
1x8 x 8' No. 2 pine boards	2
1x6 x 8' No. 2 pine board	1
1x6 x 10' No. 2 pine board	1
2x4 x 8' pine (rip to 2x2s for legs)	1
No. 20 wood biscuits	39
1-1/2" wood screws	24
1-1/4" drywall or wood screws	4
1/4" flat washers	4
Bottle of wood glue	1

Cutting list

KEY	QTY.	SIZE & DESCRIPTION
A	2	3/4" x 7-1/4" x 36" pine sides
B	5	3/4" x 7-1/4" x 22-1/2" pine shelves, top and bottom
C	4	1-1/2" x 1-1/2" x 39" pine legs
D	2	3/4" x 5-1/2" x 28" pine top (trim to 26-1/2" after joining)
E	4	3/4" x 5-1/2" x 36" pine back

9 **Assemble the shelves quickly.** Biscuits start to swell and lock in place soon after the glue is applied, so it's important to get the shelves assembled quickly.

BISCUIT

10 **Beveling the edge is a job for dad.** Use a router and a 45-degree chamfering bit to bevel the front and sides of the top. Your helper can hold the top to keep it from shifting on the Bench Cookies (sold at woodworking stores).

TOP

45° BEVEL

BENCH COOKIE

Drill four 3/8-in. holes at the corners of the bookcase top. The holes are oversized to allow the top to expand and contract. Attach the top with four 1-1/4-in. screws and 1/4-in. washers.

Complete the bookcase by screwing the four 1x6s to the back of the unit (Photo 12). Drill 1/8-in. pilot holes for the screws to avoid splitting.

A little final sanding and the bookcase will be ready for finish. Wipe-on poly or oil finish are both good options.

1-1/4"
SCREW

LEG

BEVEL
SIDE

11 Insert the biscuits and clamp the legs. Spread the glue and insert the biscuits. Then glue on the legs. Clamp them and wait for the glue to dry before moving on to install the top and back.

12 Screw on the back boards. Drill pilot holes to prevent splitting. Then screw the boards to the back of the bookcase. With a little coaching, young helpers will be driving screws like a pro.

Sturdy stepstool

Here's a great gift idea that will draw raves. The joints are accurately made in seconds with a plate jointer, but don't tell your admirers. You'll also need a miter saw to crosscut the boards and a jigsaw to cut the half-circles in the risers. The lumber you'll need:

- One 8-ft. 1x8 clear hardwood board (actual width is 7-1/4 in. and actual thickness is 3/4 in.). Oak is a good choice because it's readily available at home centers.
- One 3-ft. 1x3 hardwood board (actual width is 2-1/2 in. and actual thickness is 3/4 in.).

Cut the 8-ft. board into:
- Two 22-in. riser boards
- One 14-in. step board
- Two 11-in. riser boards
- One 14-in. seat board

You'll use 94 in. of the 96-in. board, so make practice cuts on a scrap board first to check the angle and length of cut. Don't cut the 3-ft. 1x3 board until you've dry-assembled the step, seat and risers and measured for a perfect fit.

To create two risers, join the 11-in. boards to the 22-in. boards with No. 20 biscuits and glue. Let dry 30 minutes, then lay the step and seat across and mark for two No. 20 biscuits at each joint. Dry-assemble the step, seat and risers with biscuits, then cut and snugly fit the crosspieces. Mark the riser-to-crosspiece joint and cut slots for No. 0 biscuits. Glue and firmly clamp the step,

seat and crosspieces to the risers. Check for square and let dry 30 minutes, then cut out the 4-1/2-in.-diameter arc on the bottom of the risers to create the legs. Finish-sand and apply your favorite finish. This project is designed for use on hard-surface flooring only—not carpeting.

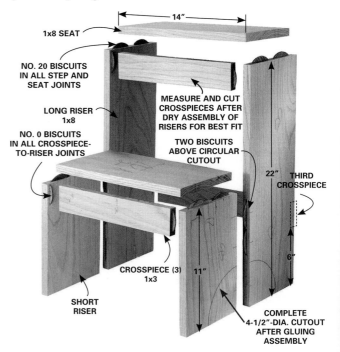

14"

1x8 SEAT

NO. 20 BISCUITS
IN ALL STEP AND
SEAT JOINTS

LONG RISER
1x8

NO. 0 BISCUITS
IN ALL CROSSPIECE-
TO-RISER JOINTS

MEASURE AND CUT
CROSSPIECES AFTER
DRY ASSEMBLY OF
RISERS FOR BEST FIT

TWO BISCUITS
ABOVE CIRCULAR
CUTOUT

22"   THIRD
CROSSPIECE

6"

CROSSPIECE (3)
1x3

11"

SHORT
RISER

COMPLETE
4-1/2"-DIA. CUTOUT
AFTER GLUING
ASSEMBLY

Stair-step plant stand

1 Dry-fit the first two layers (without glue or nails) using a square to get the spacing right, and make sure everything fits well.

2 Then glue and nail the boards at each intersection.

If you love to display potted plants, this simple plant stand is for you. Build it from boards that are cut into just two lengths, stacked into squares and nailed together. You'll only need seven 8-ft.-long 1x2s, exterior wood glue and a few dozen galvanized 4d finish nails. We used cedar for its looks and its longevity outside, but any wood will do. Cut the 1x2s into sixteen 20-in. pieces and twenty-seven 10-3/4-in. pieces.

Don't fret over the assembly; it's really very simple. Just follow the photos for the proper positioning of the two lengths and the number of layers. Adjust the gap spacing with scrap 1x2s, and make sure everything is square as you stack up each layer. When it looks good, nail the pieces together using one nail and a dab of glue at every intersection. Keep the nails 3/4 in. away from the ends of the boards to prevent splitting. When your plant stand is complete, sand all the outside edges and apply an exterior stain or preservative. Then start moving in the blooms.

Chapter Five

PAINTING & FINISHING

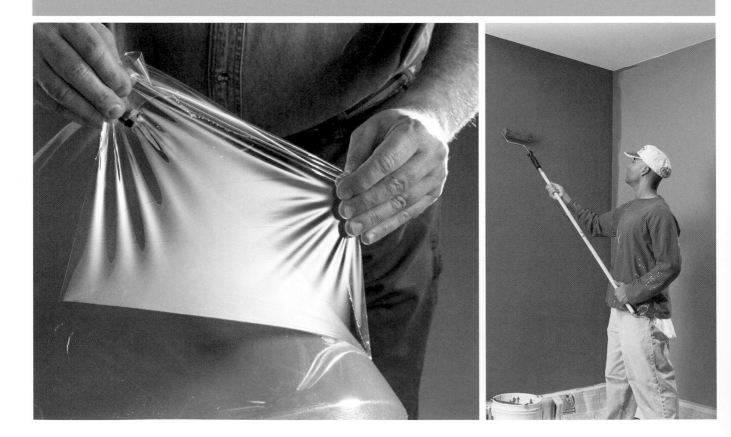

Finish a tabletop

Finishing a tabletop is tricky. On a big table especially, coating the entire surface before the finish becomes too sticky is the ultimate test of speed and skill. And your work has to be perfect. More than any other furniture surface, a tabletop reflects light and shows off every little flaw.

But that doesn't mean you can't do it. These tips will make the tough parts easier and help you achieve a perfect finish.

1. Wet the floor

A floor dampened with a mop or spray bottle has two benefits: It prevents you from kicking up dust as you walk around. And it raises the humidity, so polyurethane dries slower and remains workable longer.

2. Declare war on dust

Airborne dust is the wood finisher's nemesis. It settles on wet coatings and creates ugly pimples in the dried finish. You can sand them out, but it's better to minimize that labor by minimizing dust sources. Clean up the work area and change out of the dusty clothes you wore while sanding.

3. Limit air movement

If you're using water-based finishes, control airborne dust by turning off forced-air heating or cooling, and by closing windows and doors. This doesn't apply to oil-based finishes; ventilation is required to remove harmful fumes.

4. Tent the work area

Open rafters and trusses are an endless source of falling dust. So if you're working under an open ceiling, hang plastic sheeting above. Keep the plastic at least 12 in. from light fixtures or remove the bulbs. Sometimes, adding plastic "walls" is a lot easier than cleaning up the entire area. If you're using oil-based finishes, hang the sheets about a foot from the floor to allow for ventilation.

5. Prop up the tabletop

Set the top on screws so you can easily finish the edges.

6. Work fast

Depending on the conditions, oil-based poly may become too sticky to work with after just five to ten minutes. Water-based poly dries even faster. So have all your supplies lined up and ready to go before you start. And once you've started, there's no time for coffee or bathroom breaks.

7. Do a final sanding by hand

A random orbital sander is perfect for most of the sanding. But do a five-minute final sanding by hand using the same grit. Hand-sanding with the grain removes swirls and torn wood fibers left by the orbital action of the sander.

8. Remove the legs

A disassembled table is much easier to move and the legs are easier to finish. On a typical table, removing each leg is as simple as unscrewing a nut.

9. Sand every square inch the same

Any vaiation in sanding steps can show up in the final finish. If, for example, you run out of 80-grit sanding discs halfway through the initial sanding, you might be tempted to switch to 100-grit. But don't. Even after sanding with higher grits, stain may look different in differently treated areas.

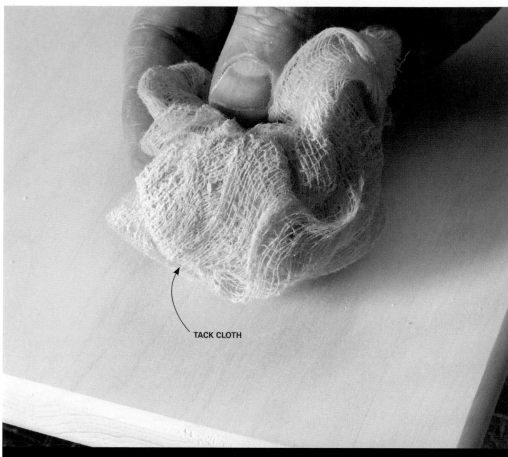

TACK CLOTH

10. Avoid blotches

Most common wood species— pine, birch, maple and cherry— absorb stain unevenly. For a more consistent finish, apply a prestain conditioner.

11. Vac and tack

A vacuum with a brush attachment will remove 99 percent of the sanding dust. But that's not enough. This photo shows how much dust is left over. After vacuuming, wipe with a tack cloth (available at home centers) if you plan to use oil-based stain or coatings. If you're using water-based finishes, use a lint-free rag dampened with mineral spirits.

12. Prevent regrets

The very best way to avoid wood finishers' remorse is to test your finishes on wood scraps of the same species as your masterpiece. Sand the scraps in exactly the same way you sand the table: Sanding lighter or harder or using different grits will change the look of any finish you apply.

13. Start with high-gloss poly

A few coats of semigloss or satin poly-urethane looks like a sheet of dull plastic over the wood. So build up coats of gloss poly first. Then, if you want less sheen, dull the finish by wet sanding (Tip 27) or wiping on a couple coats of satin or semigloss.

14. Inspect your sanding work

Stain will highlight any flaws in your sanding job (swirls or cross-grain scratches). Then you'll have to resand—and sanding stained wood is a real pain. To find flaws before you stain, use low-angle light (see Tip 16). Wiping on mineral spirits also helps to reveal problems.

15. Don't oversand

Most professionals we talked to stop at 150-grit on coarse-grain woods like oak or walnut and 180-grit on fine-grain woods like cherry or maple. But that doesn't apply to end grain. End grain shows sanding scratches more than face grain, so you may have to sand to 220- or even 320-grit.

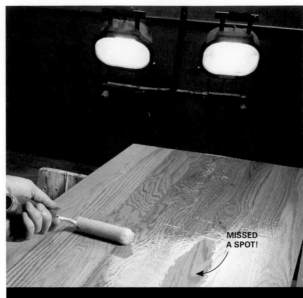

MISSED A SPOT!

16. Customize your lighting

Overhead lighting is great for most shop work, but it's bad for finishing. Try this instead: Turn off the overhead lights and position a bright light 4 to 5 ft. off the floor. The low-angle glare will highlight every flaw.

17. Skip grits when sanding

You don't have to use every available grit as you progress from coarse to fine. Instead, you can jump from 80-grit to 120- to 180-, skipping 100- and 150-grit.

18. Seal end grain

The end grain of wood soaks up finishes and often turns much darker than the face grain. Check for this on your test block (see Tip 12). If you get an ugly result, pretreat the end grain with a dose of finish that will limit absorption (wood conditioner, sanding sealer, shellac or polyurethane thinned 50 percent). Apply the treatment with an artist's brush and be careful not to slop onto the face grain.

19. Go with polyurethane

There are lots of clear finishes. But for a combination of usability and durability, you can't beat polyurethane. Oil-based poly, which dries slower than water-based, is best for beginners because it allows more working time. The other important difference is clarity: Water-based poly is absolutely colorless, while oil-based has an amber tone, which can be good or bad depending on the look you want.

20. Roll on oil-based poly

Coating a big surface with a brush—before the poly becomes gooey—requires speed and skill. Rolling, on the other hand, is faster, easier and almost goof-proof.

Rolled-on poly looks terrible at first, but the bubbles disappear in minutes, leaving a smoother surface than most of us can achieve with a brush. Beware of ridges formed by the edges of the roller and humps where you start and stop. You can minimize both of those flaws by applying lighter coats. We experimented with several kinds of rollers and got the best results with microfiber mini rollers. We also tried rolling on water-based poly; don't do it.

MICROFIBER ROLLER

GRAIN FILLER

21. Fill the grain

The deep grain lines in woods like oak or walnut will telegraph through the clear finish, no matter how many coats you apply. And that's fine; it's part of the character of coarse-grain woods. But if a perfectly smooth surface is the look you want, use a grain filler. You'll find several products online or at wood-working stores. With most, you wipe on the filler, squeegee off the excess with a plastic putty knife and then sand after it's dry for a smooth-as-glass surface.

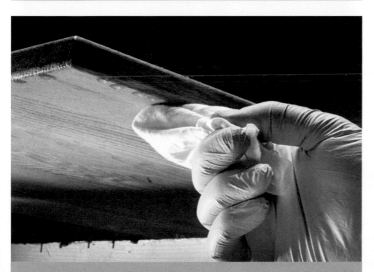

22. Wipe away drips

After the table is completely coated, wrap a rag around your finger and wipe off any drips along the underside.

23. Keep an eye on edges

Regardless of how you apply poly, you'll likely end up with some runs on the edges. So constantly check the edges as you work and be ready to smooth out runs with a brush.

24. Sand between coats

A quick hand-sanding between coats flattens out flaws before the next coat. Polyurethane tends to gum up sandpaper, so use paper or pads that resist clogging (320-grit). On shaped edges, use synthetic steel wool, such as Scotch-Brite pads, labeled "very fine."

25. Coat the underside

Wood absorbs moisture from the air, shrinking and swelling with changes in humidity. Polyurethane (or any coating) slows that absorption. So if you coat only the topside, the unfinished underside will shrink or swell at a different rate. That means a warped table. But one coat on the underside will stabilize the tabletop.

26. Apply at least three coats

With a thicker layer of protection, damage to the underlying wood is less likely—so your tabletop will look better longer, and reviving the finish will be easier. Some finishers apply four or even five coats.

27. Wet-sand before final coats

Load a sanding block with 600-grit wet/dry paper, dribble on some soapy water and rub the finish smooth. Then wipe the table dry, look for flaws and rub some more. Don't stop until you achieve perfection. Smooth shaped edges with synthetic steel wool.

28. Clean off the white stuff

As the table dries after wet-sanding, a white residue will appear. Be sure to clean it off completely. Residue left in the grain lines of coarse-grain wood will be trapped under the final coat and haunt you forever.

29. Don't sand through

If you sand through the polyurethane and remove some stain, you can touch up with more stain. But the repair won't be perfect, so take pains to avoid that mistake. Sand very lightly after the first coat, just enough to remove the dust whiskers. After the second coat, you can sand a little harder to flatten larger flaws. Always be careful around the edges of the table; that's where it's easiest to sand through.

SPRAY POLY

30. Spray the legs

Table legs—especially shaped legs—are almost impossible to coat smoothly with a brush. So instead, hang them from the ceiling with wire and spray them.

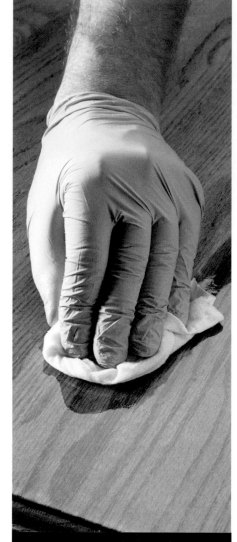

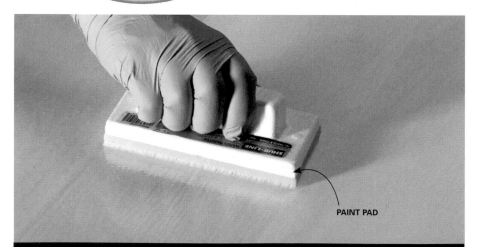

PAINT PAD

31. Pluck out problems

Tweezers are an essential emergency tool. If a fly, brush bristle or lint ends up in the finish, you can surgically remove it.

33. Wipe on the final coats

Wet-sanding leaves the surface perfectly smooth but dull. To restore the shine, apply two coats of wipe-on polyurethane (available in gloss, semigloss and satin). Wiping results in a very thin, fast-drying coat, so flaws like dust nubs or sags are less likely.

32. Apply water-based poly with a pad

Water-based poly dries faster than oil, so it's even harder to brush over a big surface. The solution is a paint pad, which applies poly fast and smooth. Just dip the pad into a pan of poly and drag the pad across the surface. Be sure to smooth out any ridges pushed up by the edges of the pad.

34. Never use wax or polish

All you need for routine cleaning and care of your table is a damp cloth. When normal wear eventually dulls the finish, you can renew it in just a few minutes with another coat of wipe-on poly. But if you've ever used furniture wax or polish, a fresh coat of poly may not stick.

Protect outdoor furniture

If you'd like to preserve the natural wood appearance of your wood entry door or your outdoor furniture, take a lesson from boat builders. Boat builders and restorers use multiple coats of epoxy and spar varnish to protect wood—instead of spar varnish alone—because the combination is much stronger than either finish is separately. Epoxy creates a tough, flexible moisture barrier; spar varnish adds depth and UV protection, which keeps the epoxy from yellowing and eventually disintegrating.

The epoxy, a special type for clear-coating wood, is sold at woodworking suppliers, hobby shops and marine supply stores, or go online. It's expensive—the 2 quarts used here cost $70—but when fully cured, the finish is very tough and will last for years.

To begin, sand and clean the wood, then stain it if desired. Mix the epoxy resin and hardener thoroughly in a disposable container. A batch will start to harden in about 30 minutes, faster if it's hot out, so just mix a small quantity the first time to see how far you get. Apply the epoxy with an inexpensive natural-bristle brush (Photo 1). You'll need a new brush for each coat. When the epoxy in the container starts to stiffen and feel warm, discard the container and the brush and mix a new batch.

Allow the epoxy finish to harden overnight, then sand thoroughly and apply another coat. The manufacturer recommends three coats.

Sand the final coat of epoxy after it has cured for at least 24 hours (Photo 2), then vacuum the surface and wipe it with a damp rag. Topcoat the epoxy with a minimum of three coats of exterior spar varnish (Photo 3). Add coats of varnish every few years to keep the finish looking fresh.

TIP: Two-part epoxy
Mix the resin and hardener thoroughly in a clean, disposable container, in the proportions specified by the manufacturer.

NATURAL-BRISTLE BRUSH

EPOXY

1 Spread the epoxy, then lightly drag the brush back through to even it out and eliminate bubbles. Work quickly and allow the thick epoxy to flatten without brushing it too much.

UNSANDED EPOXY

2 Sand each coat with 120-grit sandpaper to flatten out any ridges and flaws, then clean and resand with 220-grit to create a smooth, scratch-free surface for the varnish.

GLOSSY SPAR VARNISH

3 Apply three coats of oil-based spar varnish with a high-quality china-bristle brush, brushing with the grain. Sand the varnish between coats.

Paint a panel door

Paneled doors are the ultimate painting challenge. A large area broken up by shaped surfaces is just plain tough to cover before the paint becomes sticky and unworkable. And since doors are a prominent feature, ugly mistakes like brush marks or drips are noticeable. Even though I had painted dozens of them over the years, I still felt a twinge of anxiety whenever I saw "paint door" on my to-do list. So I set out to find easier ways to get better results. I tried different tools, used different paints and watched professional painters. Here's what I learned.

Gary Wentz is a Senior Editor at The Family Handyman.

WHAT IT TAKES

TIME: 3 to 5 hours per door

COST: $15 to $40 per door

SKILL LEVEL: Beginner to advanced

TOOLS: High-quality brush and rollers, powerful lighting, shop vacuum, sanding supplies, possibly a random-orbit sander

1 **Remove all the hardware.** Slice through paint buildup around hinges and latches. Otherwise, you might splinter surrounding wood as you remove hardware.

HARD RUBBER SANDING BLOCK

2 **Sand it smooth.** On flat areas, level out old runs and brush marks with a hard sanding block. For the shaped profiles, you'll need a combination of sanding pads, sponges and scraps of sandpaper.

3 **Remove the sanding dust.** A vacuum with a brush attachment removes most of the dust. Wipe off the rest with a damp rag.

Before you start

The actual work involved in painting a door typically amounts to three to five hours, depending on the condition of the door and how fussy you are. But add in the drying time and it's a full-day project. So if you're painting a door you can't live without—like a bathroom or exterior door—get started first thing in the morning so it can be back in service by day's end.

While you're picking a paint color, also think about sheen: With a flat finish, scuff marks and handprints are hard to wipe away. High gloss is easy to clean but accentuates every little flaw, so your prep and paint job have to be perfect. Satin and semigloss are good compromise choices. Also check the operation of the door. If it rubs against the jamb or drags on the carpet, now's the time to sand or plane the edges. If you have several doors that need painting, start with the least prominent one. It's better to make learning mistakes on the inside of a closet door than on your entry door.

Prep tips

Pros often paint doors in place. But from prep to painting, you'll get better results if you remove the door. Working in your garage, shop or basement, you can control lighting and drying conditions better. And laying the door flat minimizes runs in the paint job. Here's what to do after you remove the door:

- Clean the door with a household cleaner. Almost any cleaner will do, as long as it cuts grease. Areas around doorknobs are especially prone to greasy buildup.
- Remove all the door hardware to get a neater paint job and save time. If you're dealing with more than one door, avoid hardware mix-ups by labeling plastic bags that will hold the hardware for each door.
- Fill dents and holes with a sandable filler. You'll probably have to fill deep dents twice to compensate for shrinkage.

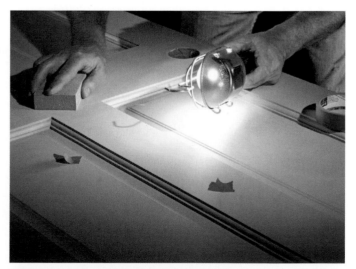

4 **Sand after priming.** Sand out any imperfections in the prime coat. Shine a light across the surface at a low angle to accentuate imperfections. If you find any spots that need an extra dab of filler, mark them with tabs of masking tape.

- Remove old paint from the hardware. Start with a product intended to remove paint splatter. You can use paint strippers, but they may also remove clear coatings from the hardware or damage some types of finishes.

Sanding tips

If your door is in good shape, all it needs is a light sanding with sandpaper or a sanding sponge (180 or 220 grit). That will roughen the surface a little and allow the primer to adhere better. But most likely, you'll also need to smooth out chipped paint and imperfections from previous paint jobs. This is usually the most time-consuming, tedious part of the project. Here are some tips for faster, better results:

- Paint often sticks to sandpaper, clogging the grit and making it useless. So be sure to check the label and buy sandpaper intended for paint. You may still get some clogging, but you'll get less. This goes for sponges and other abrasives too.
- Start with 120 or 150 grit. You can switch to coarser paper (such as 80 grit) on problem areas, but be sure to follow up with finer grit to smooth out the sanding scratches.
- On flat areas, a hard sanding block will smooth the surface much better than sponges or other soft-backed abrasives (Photo 2).
- Try a finishing or random-orbit sander on flat areas. It might save you tons of time. Then again, the sandpaper may clog immediately from heat buildup. It depends on the type and age of the paint.
- Buy a collection of sanding sponges and pads for the shaped areas. Through trial and error, you'll find that some work better than others on your profiles.
- Inspect your work with low-angle lighting (see Photo 4).

> **CAUTION: If your home was built before 1979, check the paint for lead before you sand. For more information, go to hud.gov/offices/lead.**

5 **Paint the edges and wipe off the slop.** Brush or roll paint onto all four edges. Immediately wipe any paint that slops onto the face of the door with a rag or foam brush. You don't have to completely remove the paint, but you do have to flatten it to prevent ridges (see photo below left).

6 **Brush around the panels.** Work the paint into the corners and grooves, then drag the brush over the paint to smooth it. Wipe away any slop around the panel as shown in Photo 5.

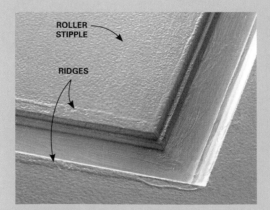

ROLLER STIPPLE

RIDGES

The wrong paint. Some paints show brush marks, ridges and roller stipple no matter how skillful or careful you are. Others go on smoothly and then level out beautifully, even if you're not a master painter.

Water-based alkyd is best

If you want a smooth finish, choose a paint designed for that. Some paints, even good-quality paints, just aren't formulated for smoothness. Smooth paints are usually labeled "enamel" or "door and trim." But the label alone doesn't tell you enough; some brands of "enamel" are much better than others. Advice from the store staff, and the price, are the best indicators. Super-smooth paints often cost $25 to $30 per quart! But I'm happy to spend an extra 10 bucks per door for first-class results.

Among the paints I've used, one category stands out for smoothness: water-based alkyds. These paints dry slowly for extra working time and level out almost as well as traditional oil-based alkyds. After applying them with a high-quality roller, I was able to skip the brush-out step shown in Photos 7 and 9 and still got perfect results. Cleanup is as easy as with any other water-based paint. The disadvantages of water-based alkyds are a very long wait before recoating (16 to 24 hours) and a high price tag.

My favorite painting tricks

Over the years, I've spent a lot of time observing and interrogating pro painters. Here are three pro tips that I've used over and over again:

Make the door flippable. Drive one screw into one end and two into the other. That lets you coat both sides of the door without waiting for the first side to dry. Drill pilot holes and drive 5/16 x 5-in. lag screws about halfway in. Smaller screws can bend and let the door drop just as you're finishing the final coat. (I learned this the hard way.)

Wet the floor. Two benefits for the price of one: A wet floor prevents you from kicking up dust that will create dust nubs in your finish. Better yet, it raises the humidity, which extends the time you have to smooth out the paint and gives the paint more time to level out. In my informal experiments, raising the humidity doubled the working time of the paint. (I also discovered that slick floors get even slicker when wet, which can lead to Three Stooges–style paint accidents. Be careful.)

Keep a pair of tweezers handy. Pluck out paintbrush bristles or rescue stuck insects without messing up the paint. This works great with other finishes too. For marital harmony, don't return the tweezers to the medicine cabinet. Buy a new pair (another lesson learned the hard way).

Tips for a perfect workspace

After the messy job of sanding is done, set the door aside and prep your workspace. For priming and painting, you want a work zone that's well lit and clean. Sawdust on your workbench will end up on brushes; airborne dust will create whiskers on the paint. The conditions in your work area should allow paint to dry slowly. Slower drying means more time for you to smooth the paint before it becomes gummy and more time for the paint to level itself. Here's how to prep your space:

- Clean everything. Vacuum work surfaces and sweep the floor.
- Minimize air movement for less airborne dust and slower drying. Close doors and windows. Turn off forced-air heating or cooling.
- Don't rely on overhead lighting; you may even want to turn it off. Instead, position a work light 4 to 5 ft. above the floor. This low-angle light will accentuate any drips or ridges.
- Have all your tools and supplies ready, including a pail of water to dunk your paint tools in as soon as you're done.
- If you're working in the garage, unplug the garage door opener so it can't be opened while you work. An opening door raises dust.

Priming tips

You can "spot-prime" a door, coating only patched dents or areas you sanded through to bare wood. But priming the whole door is best; the new paint will stick better and you'll get a more uniform finish. Here are some tips for this critical step:

- Your choice of primer is just as important as your choice of paint. At the paint store, ask for a primer that's compatible with your paint, levels out well and sands smoothly.
- Have the primer tinted, based on the color of your paint.
- Apply the primer with just as much care as the paint and following the same steps (see Photos 5 – 9). Also check out the painting tips in the next section.
- For an ultra-smooth paint job, apply two coats of primer. With a thick build of primer, you can sand the prime coat glassy-smooth, without sanding through to the old paint.
- Lightly sand the primer with 220-grit, inspecting as you go (Photo 4). A couple of quick passes is all it takes. If you're not in a rush to get the door back in service, let the primer dry overnight before sanding. The longer it dries, the better it will sand.

Painting tips

Painting a door is a race against time. You have to lay down the paint and smooth it out before it becomes too sticky to work with, or so stiff that brush marks won't level out and disappear. Keep moving. Don't stop to answer the phone or get coffee. Minutes count. In warm, dry conditions, even seconds matter.

- Consider a paint additive to slow down drying and improve leveling. Your paint dealer can recommend one that's compatible with your paint.
- Start with a dust-free door; wipe it down with a damp rag just before painting.

7 **Roll, then brush the panels.** Coat the panels quickly with a roller. Then smooth the paint with a brush. Be careful not to touch the profiles surrounding the panel.

8 **Roll the rails and stiles.** Roll the door in sections, coating no more than one-quarter of the door at a time. Then brush out the paint. Be careful not to slop paint over the edges around the panels.

- Spend the money to get a quality brush for a smoother finish. Pro painters disagree about the size and type to use. I prefer a 2-in. sash brush.
- Don't use cheap roller sleeves or you'll get fibers in the finish. I use a mini roller and get good results with microfiber, mohair and FlockFoam sleeves. Foam sleeves also leave a smooth finish, but they hold very little paint, which slows you down.
- Paint all four edges of the door first (Photo 5). Here's why: when painting edges, some paint inevitably slops onto the faces of the door. It's better to have that happen before the faces are painted.
- Brush on a light coat. A heavy coat of paint covers better and sometimes levels out better, but runs are more likely and brush marks are deeper. So start out lightly, then lay it on a little thicker as your brush skills improve.
- Roll on the paint where you can. Rollers lay on paint much faster than a brush, giving you a few more precious minutes to work the paint before it begins to stiffen.

- Brush out rolled paint. Brushed paint usually levels out better than rolled paint, and any brush marks are less noticeable than roller stipple. But you might be able to skip the brush-out step altogether. With top-quality enamel and roller sleeves, roller results can be super smooth. This depends in part on drying conditions, so try it on a closet door or a primed scrap of wood first.
- Plan to apply at least two coats and lightly sand between coats with 220-grit to remove any dust nubs.

The ultimate smooth finish

Even the most skilled painter can't match the perfection of a sprayed-on finish. There are two types of sprayers: "airless" and "HVLP" (high-volume, low-pressure). Both can apply a flawless coat in minutes, but HVLP is more forgiving; it produces a finer spray, which reduces your chances of blasting on too much paint and creating runs. Many HVLP sprayers won't spray acrylic/latex paint. For a model that will, expect to spend $100 to $150, well worth it if you have a house full of doors to paint. Aside from finish quality, a sprayer will also save you hours of brushwork if you have several doors to paint.

9 **Brush with the grain.** Brush across the joints where door parts meet. Then drag your brush in a straight line along the intersection. That way, any visible brush marks will look more like a wood grain pattern and less like sloppy brushwork.

Spray-texture a ceiling

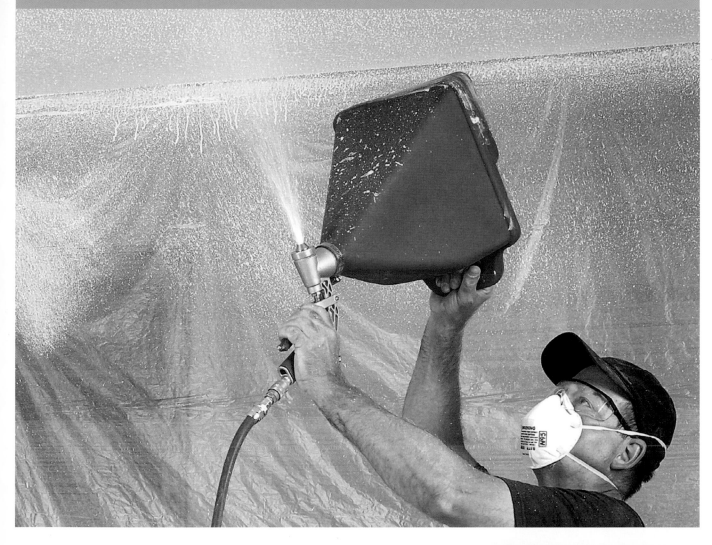

I f your spray-textured ceiling is just dingy or stained, you can renew it with a coat each of sealer and paint. But if the texture is falling off or missing in spots, you'll have to reapply texture to fix the problem. For small areas, say less than a foot in diameter, you could try using an aerosol can of repair texture. But the patch is bound to stick out like a sore thumb. For the best results, you're better off respraying the entire ceiling. It's a messy job, but it's not hard to do. In fact, after you spray one room, you'll probably want to keep going. You can spray-texture unsightly plaster or smooth drywall ceilings too. As with most jobs, the key is in the prep work, which is the time-consuming part too. Once the room is masked off, the

ceiling prepped and the texture mixed, it'll only take you about 15 minutes to spray the ceiling.

If any of the paper drywall tape is loose or the drywall is soft or damaged, you'll have to repair and sand these areas first. In addition to the putty knives and drywall joint compound for the repairs, you'll need a wide putty or taping knife for scraping, a roll of 1-1/2-in. or wider masking tape, enough painter's plastic to cover the walls, a gallon or two of primer/sealer, a bag of spray texture (enough to cover 300 to 400 sq. ft.), and a compressor and hopper gun. You can buy coarse, medium or fine texture. If you're matching existing ceilings, take a sample of the material with you when you buy the texture and ask for help matching it. Medium is usually the best

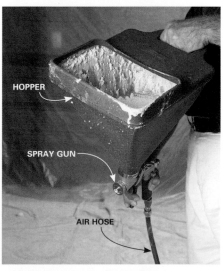

HOPPER

SPRAY GUN

AIR HOSE

Buy a hopper gun like this for about $70 and connect it to any 2.5-cfm or larger air compressor.

choice and will match most ceilings. You can rent a compressor and hopper gun for about $30 for a half day or buy a hopper gun for about $70 and connect it to any average-size or larger compressor. If you use a small compressor, you may occasionally have to stop spraying to let the pressure build up. Minimize rental costs by getting all the prep work done before you pick up the compressor and hopper gun.

Start by removing everything you can from the room. If you must leave large furniture in the room, stack it in the center and cover it with plastic. Cover the floor with sheets or a canvas drop cloth. Then cover the walls with thin (1-mil or less) poly sheeting (Photo 1). Painter's plastic is very thin and works great. Leave an opening with overlapping poly at the doorway so you can get in and out. Turn off the power to the lights and remove any ceiling fixtures. Don't forget to cap the bare wires with wire connectors. Stuff newspaper into the electrical box to keep out the spray texture.

The next step is to scrape off the old texture (Photo 2), but not before you've had it tested for asbestos. If it hasn't been painted, it'll usually come off easily. So try just scraping it first. If that doesn't work (you'll know right away), try wetting the texture with a pump-up garden sprayer. That might make it easier to scrape, but it'll leave a sticky mess on the floor. If you use this method, cover your drop cloths with 4-mil plastic so you can wad it up and dispose of the wet texture and not track it all over the house. Texture that's been painted over can be a lot harder to remove. Just do the best you can. Try to knock off the high spots and flatten it as much as possible. The ceiling doesn't have to be smooth, but it's easier to get a nice-looking job if most of the old texture has been removed.

CAUTION: If you have ceiling texture applied before 1980, it may contain asbestos. Before you remove any ceiling texture, contact your state's department of environmental protection, department of health or a regional asbestos coordinator for information on asbestos testing and removal. For general information on asbestos, go to epa.gov/asbestos.

1 Speed up and simplify your masking job by applying the tape along the ceiling first. Leave the lower edge of the tape loose. Then roll out a length of lightweight poly along the floor, pull one edge up to the ceiling, and stick it to the tape.

2 Suit up with goggles, a dust mask and a hat before you start the messy job of scraping texture. Popcorn spray texture comes off easily if it hasn't been painted.

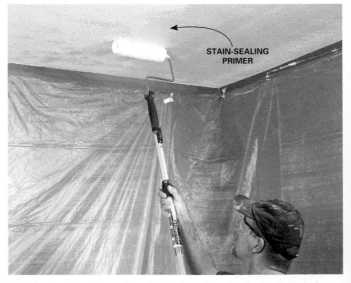

STAIN-SEALING PRIMER

3 Paint the ceiling with a fast-drying primer/sealer. Let it dry before applying the spray texture.

When you're done scraping, paint the ceiling with stain-sealing primer (Photo 3). Use an aerosol can of solvent-based sealer such as white shellac to spot-prime severe stains. Then paint the entire ceiling with a water-based primer/sealer.

The key to a successful spray-texture job is mixing the texture to the right consistency. Don't mix it too thick. Use the amount of water recommended on the bag as a starting point. Then adjust the thickness by adding more water or powder. Mix slowly using a mixing paddle mounted in a 1/2-in. drill (Photo 4). Mix thoroughly, adding water until the material reaches the consistency of runny yogurt—or thick paint—with tiny lumps in it. Let the texture sit for 15 minutes, then remix, adding more water if necessary.

There are a few different versions of hopper guns, but they all have a mechanism at the nose that controls the diameter of the pattern, and a trigger control that helps govern the volume of spray. Start by setting both controls to the middle position. Then load the hopper about half full with texture material and practice on a piece of cardboard or drywall scrap (Photo 5). Adjust the spray pattern and trigger until you can get a nice, even pattern without runs or excess buildup. When you're comfortable with the spraying technique, start on the ceiling.

Start by spraying the perimeter (Photo 6). Hold the gun about 18 to 24 in. from the ceiling and aim so that about two-thirds of the spray hits the ceiling and the rest hits the wall. Move quickly around the room, paying special attention to the inside corners where walls meet. Remember, you can make another pass if it's too light. The goal is to cover the ceiling with an even layer of texture. Don't worry if it looks too smooth. The texture will become more pronounced as it dries. Be careful to avoid puddles. If you mess up and get a puddle or just a thick buildup, stop and scrape off all the texture with a wide putty knife. Then try again. Move the gun back and forth while backing up across the

room. After you've covered the ceiling, turn 90 degrees and apply another light coat at a right angle to the first. Concentrate on filling in light spots to create an even texture.

When you're satisfied with the consistency of the texture, you can clean up the gun, hopper and hose with water and pull down the poly. If your masking job was a little off and there's texture on the wall or flooring, wait for it to dry. Then carefully scrape it off and remove the white residue with a wet sponge.

4 Mix the powdered spray texture and water thoroughly. Lumps will clog the spray tip and could mess up your spray job. Let it rest 15 minutes and remix, adding water if necessary.

JUST RIGHT

TOO MUCH TEXTURE

5 Practice on cardboard or a piece of drywall to get a feel for spraying. Adjust the gun's tip and trigger until you get a consistent spray pattern that's easy to control.

6 Start by spraying the perimeter, then fill in the middle. Avoid heavy buildup—you can always add more.

Paint a wall

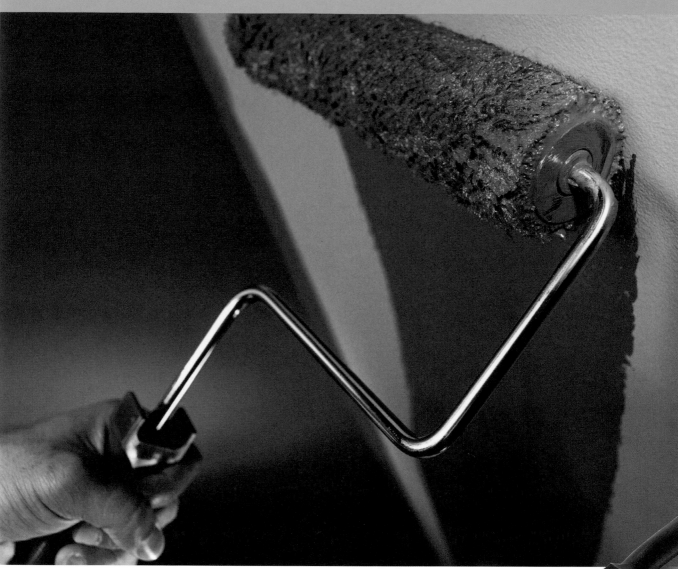

Most people have used paint rollers before, with varying degrees of success. Maybe you just plunged right in and started rolling, developing your own technique as you went. Or maybe you read the instructions telling you to apply the paint in some pattern, usually a "W," before rolling it out. Here you'll learn a slightly different approach: how to simply and quickly spread a smooth, even coat of latex paint on the wall. It's not fancy, but it gets the job done in record time and eliminates common problems like light areas, roller marks and built-up ridges. This technique guarantees pro-quality results.

However, even the best technique won't work with poor-quality equipment. Don't waste your money on those all-in-one throwaway roller setups when you can buy a pro setup that will last a lifetime for less than $20. Start with a good roller frame. Buy one that is sturdy and designed to keep the roller cover from slipping off while you paint (see photo, right). To extend your

STIFF METAL ARM

GRIPPING TEETH

reach and give you better control, screw a 48-in. wood handle onto the end of the roller. You could also use a threaded broom handle.

You'll need a container for the paint. While most homeowners use paint trays, you'll rarely see a pro using one. That's because a 5-gallon bucket with a special bucket screen hung over the edge works a lot better.

1. Lay the paint on the wall with a sweeping stroke. Start about a foot from the bottom and 6 in. from the corner and roll upward at a slight angle using light pressure. Stop a few inches from the ceiling. Now roll up and down, back toward the corner to quickly spread the paint. You can leave paint buildup and roller marks at this step. Don't worry about a perfect job yet.

2. Reload the roller and repeat the process in the adjacent space, working back toward the painted area.

3. Roll back over the entire area you've covered to smooth and blend the paint. Don't reload the roller with paint for this step. Use very light pressure. Roll up and down, from floor to ceiling and move over about three-quarters of a roller width each time so you're always slightly overlapping the previous stroke. When you reach the corner, roll as close as you can to the adjacent wall without touching it. Repeat Steps 1 through 3 until the entire wall is painted.

Here are a few of the advantages of a bucket and screen over a roller pan:

- It's easy to move the bucket without spilling.
- The bucket holds more paint. You won't have to frequently refill a pan.
- You're less likely to trip over or step in a bucket of paint.
- It's quicker and easier to load the roller cover with paint from a bucket.
- It's easy to cover a bucket with a damp cloth to prevent the paint from drying out while you're taking a lunch break.

Use an old drywall compound bucket or buy a clean new bucket. Add a bucket screen and you're ready to go.

Take a wool-blend roller cover for a spin

The most important part of your paint rolling setup is the roller cover, also known as a sleeve. It's tempting to buy the cheapest cover available and throw it away when you're done. But you won't mind the few extra minutes of

Load the roller cover by dipping into the paint about 1/2 in. and then rolling it against the screen. Filling a dry roller cover with paint will require five or six repetitions. After that, two or three dips are all you need. Leave the roller almost dripping with paint.

cleanup time once you experience the difference a good roller cover makes. Cheap roller covers don't hold enough paint to do a good job. It'll take you

four times as long to paint a room. And you'll likely end up with an inconsistent layer of paint, lap marks and built-up ridges of paint.

Instead, buy a 1/2-in. nap, wool-blend roller cover and give it a try. (One good one is a combination of polyester for ease of use and wool for maximum paint capacity.) With proper care, this may be the last roller cover you'll ever buy.

Wool covers do have a few drawbacks, though. They tend to shed fibers when they're first used. To minimize shedding, wrap the new roller cover with masking tape and peel it off to remove loose fibers. Repeat this a few times. Wool covers also tend to become matted down if you apply too much pressure while painting. Rolling demands a light touch. No matter what roller cover you're using, always let the paint do the work. Keep the roller cover loaded with paint and use only enough pressure to release and spread the paint. Pushing on the roller to squeeze out the last drop of paint will only cause problems.

Tips for a perfect paint job

■ **Keep a wet edge.** Keeping a wet edge is crucial to all top-quality finish jobs, whether you're enameling a door, finishing furniture or rolling paint on a wall. The idea is to plan the sequence of work and work fast enough so that you're always lapping newly applied paint onto paint that's still wet. If you stop for a break in the middle of a wall, for example, and then start painting after this section has dried, you'll likely see a lap mark where the two areas join. The rolling technique shown here avoids this problem by allowing you to quickly cover a large area with paint and then return to smooth it out.

■ **Lay it on, smooth it off.** The biggest mistake most beginning painters make, whether they're brushing or rolling, is taking too long to apply the paint. Photo 1 on p. 157 shows how to lay on the paint. Then quickly spread it out and repeat the laying-on process again (Photo 2). This will only work with a good-quality roller cover that holds a lot of paint. Until you're comfortable with the technique and get a feel for how quickly the paint is drying, cover only about 3 or 4 ft. of wall before smoothing off the whole area (Photo 3). If you find the paint is drying slowly, you can cover an entire wall before smoothing it off.

■ **Get as close as you can.** Since rollers can't get tight to edges, the first painting step is to brush along the ceiling, inside corners and moldings. This "cutting in" process leaves brush marks that won't match the roller texture on the rest of the wall. For the best-looking job, you'll want to cover as many brush marks as possible with the roller. Do this by carefully rolling up close to inside corners, moldings and the ceiling. Face the open end of the roller toward the edge and remember

4 Smooth the paint along the ceiling using a long horizontal stroke without reloading the roller with paint.

not to use a roller that's fully loaded with paint. With practice, you'll be able to get within an inch of the ceiling rolling vertically, and can avoid crawling up on a ladder to paint horizontally, as shown in Photo 4.

■ **Pick out the lumps before they dry.** It's inevitable that you'll end up with an occasional lump in your paint. Keep the roller cover away from the floor where it might pick up bits of

Avoid fat edges and roller marks

Ridges of paint left by the edge of the roller, or "fat edges," are a common problem. And if left to dry, they can be difficult to get rid of without heavy sanding or patching. Here are a few ways to avoid the problem:

■ Don't submerge the roller in the paint to load it. Paint can seep inside the roller cover and leak out while you're rolling. Try to dip only the nap. Then spin it against the screen and dip again until it's loaded with paint.

■ Don't press too hard when you're smoothing out the paint.

■ Never start against an edge, like a corner or molding, with a full roller of paint. You'll leave a heavy buildup of paint that can't be spread out. Starting about 6 in. from the edge, unload the paint from the roller. Then work back toward the edge.

■ Unload excess paint from the open end of the roller before you roll back over the wall to smooth it out. Do this by tilting the roller and applying a little extra pressure to the open side of the roller while rolling it up and down in the area you've just painted.

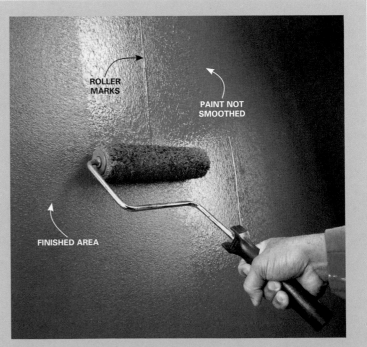

ROLLER MARKS

PAINT NOT SMOOTHED

FINISHED AREA

Smooth walls by rolling back over the wet paint without reloading the roller. Roll lightly without pressing.

5 Lay paint on wall areas above and below windows and doors with a long horizontal stroke. Then smooth it off with short vertical strokes so the texture will match the rest of the wall.

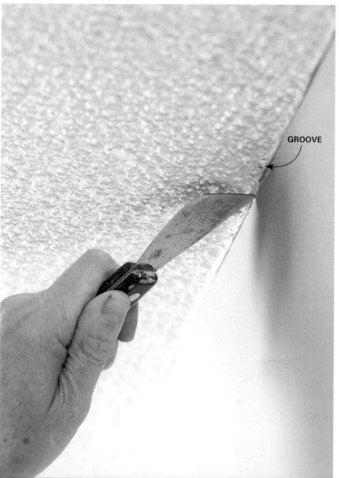

GROOVE

debris that are later spread against the wall. Drying bits of paint from the edge of the bucket or bucket screen can also cause this problem. Cover the bucket with a damp cloth when you're not using it. If partially dried paint is sloughing off the screen, take it out and clean it. Keep a wet rag in your pocket and pick lumps off the wall as you go. Strain used paint through a mesh paint strainer to remove lumps. Five-gallon size strainers are available at paint stores.

■ **Scrape excess paint from the roller before you wash it.** Use your putty knife, or better yet, a special roller scraping tool with a semicircular cutout in the blade. Then rinse the roller cover until the water runs clear. A roller and paint brush spinning tool, available at hardware and paint stores, simplifies the cleaning task. Just slip the roller cover onto the spinner and repeatedly wet and spin out the roller until it's clean.

Paint neatly along textured ceilings

It's almost impossible to paint right next to rough-textured ceilings (cutting in) without getting paint on the ceiling. Taping off the ceiling doesn't work either. The solution? Knock off the texture at the edge with a putty knife. Hold the knife at a 45-degree angle to the wall and run the blade along the edge of the ceiling. The blade scrapes away the texture and leaves a small groove in the ceiling. Clean out the groove with a duster or a dry paintbrush.

Now when you cut in along the top of the wall, the paintbrush bristles will slide into the groove, giving you a crisp paint line without getting paint on the ceiling. And you'll never notice the thin line of missing texture.

Stain concrete

Concrete stain is a fast, simple way to turn your dull gray patio into a lively, colorful surface that will make your outdoor space more inviting. The stain is nearly foolproof to apply—just wet the concrete and spray on the stain. If you're not happy with the result, you can go back and apply a second or third coat to enhance the color.

Here you'll learn how to apply the stain, including ideas for mixing stains to create a unique, multicolored surface that looks like marble. A pro would charge $500 or more to do the work, but you can do it yourself for less than $100. You won't need any special tools—just basic painting tools and rain-free weather. If you're cutting kerfs into the concrete, you'll need a masonry blade for your circular saw.

You can apply the stain over worn concrete, but don't expect a miracle. You'll still be able to see the old appearance through the stain. And avoid staining spalling concrete. The stain will turn a darker color wherever the concrete is pitted.

What is concrete stain?

Concrete stain is a water-based product that coats the concrete and becomes a permanent part of the surface. The stains can fade and wear over time, but sealer helps protect them.

Concrete stains are different from acid (or etching) stains, which chemically react with minerals in the concrete to change the color. Acid stains are available for DIYers, but there are fewer colors to choose from, and applying it involves more steps.

Time and materials

You can do this project in a weekend. Prep the concrete and apply the stain on Saturday, then seal it on Sunday. If you decide to add a second coat of stain, you'll need another day.

The stains are available at home centers in the paint section—the color is added just as with paint. One gallon covers 200 to 400 sq. ft. A gallon of sealer also covers 200 to 400 sq. ft.

KERF

GARDEN
SPRAYER

CHALK
LINE

1 Cut kerfs to separate sections that will be stained different colors. Use a large board as a saw guide to get a perfectly straight cut. Mist the blade with water to contain the dust.

2 Scrub the concrete with TSP substitute using a stiff broom to clean dirt off the surface. Then rinse the entire patio with water.

The color you choose may look slightly different after it's applied. Each patio will accept the stain a little bit differently. However, the color will be close to what you see in the brochure.

The stain is semitransparent. It won't completely cover the surface as paint would. You'll see the concrete through the stain, especially if you're using a light color.

Cut kerfs and clean the concrete

This project is much faster and easier if you stain your whole patio a single color. All you have to do is wet the concrete and apply the stain. Then backroll with a 3/8-in.-nap roller if you want even coverage. That's it—there's no need to block off sections or

Use multiple colors of stain to create a distinct border or design on patios or sidewalks.

QUIKRETE

switch sprayers. If you want a pattern with different colors, start by deciding on a color scheme. Anywhere you want to switch from one color to another, such as for a border or the checkerboard pattern shown here, you'll need a kerf (a shallow cut in the concrete). This gives the colors a crisp separation. Taping off the concrete won't work. The stain will run under the tape.

If you already have expansion joints in the concrete, incorporate them into your design to avoid cutting kerfs. But if you need to cut kerfs, start by snapping a chalk line where you want to cut. It's important for the cuts to be perfectly straight. Crooked cuts will be obvious once you apply the stain. So use a wide board as a saw guide and weight it down with buckets of water (Photo 1).

Install a diamond masonry blade in a circular saw and set it to a depth of 1/4 in. The cuts don't need to be deep—just enough to separate colors. Have a helper spray a water mist on the blade during the cut to contain the dust (Photo 1). Don't use cheap abrasive blades for cutting concrete—you can't spray them with water, and you'll end up with dust all over your siding and windows.

You won't be able to get the saw blade right next to the house, so finish off the kerfs with a masonry chisel and a hammer or a grinder with a diamond blade.

As with any other staining project, surface preparation is critical. Any stains, such as rust, will show through in the finished project. Clean the entire surface with TSP substitute (Photo 2), working in 4 x 4-ft. sections at a time. Rinse the concrete with water until you don't see any more bubbles from the TSP substitute. For tough rust stains, use a stain remover and rinse it off with water. For grease or oil stains, use a product that's designed to remove those stains. Blast dirt and debris out of the kerfs with water.

Prep the area for staining

Now that the concrete is clean, make sure your shoes are, too, before you walk on the patio again. The surrounding ground will be wet from concrete cleaning. It is a good idea to change into a

3 A base coat of stain covers the concrete and makes your topcoat color more vibrant. Spray the first color (the base coat) onto wet concrete, applying just enough stain to cover the surface. Move the sprayer wand in a continuous circular motion.

4 To create a marbleized look, spray on the second color while the first color is still wet. Don't worry about even coverage with the second coat—you want the colors to mix together.

5 To finish creating the marbleized look, blend the first and second colors together with water. Use the water stream to push the stain to bare spots and to produce swirls in the stain.

6 To create a focal point with three colors, follow these steps: Spray on the first color (the base coat). While it's still wet, spray two colors over it at the same time. Let the colors intermix.

pair of clean, dry shoes to work on the patio.

Before cracking open the stain, shield the lower portion of the house and any nearby landscaping materials to protect against drifting spray. Tape plastic film along the siding. You don't have to protect plants and grass if you don't want to (any stain that gets on them will hardly be noticeable). If any dirt gets on the patio after you've cleaned it, brush the concrete lightly with a broom to avoid pushing the dirt into the surface.

Apply the stain

You shouldn't apply the stain in direct sunlight (partial or full shade is best), so wait for a cloudy day or a time of day when the patio is shaded. Also avoid windy days so the stain won't drift. You'll need a few garden sprayers for this project—one for each

stain color you're applying and one for water. Fill the sprayers over tarps on the grass (don't fill them on the patio since spills will stain the concrete). Test the spray pattern on cardboard.

If you're creating a pattern, you'll need shields to place in the kerfs or expansion joints to prevent spraying onto adjoining areas. For this project, fluorescent light lenses were used, but you could use cardboard. Have four or five on hand. Don't use them if they're dripping wet with stain or they'll drip onto (and stain) the concrete.

Work in small sections (4 x 6 ft. or so), starting near the house and working outward. Plan the application so you don't box yourself into a corner.

Start by spraying the concrete section with water. Get it wet but don't leave standing water. To create the marbleized look shown here, have a helper hold the shields in the kerfs (if necessary)

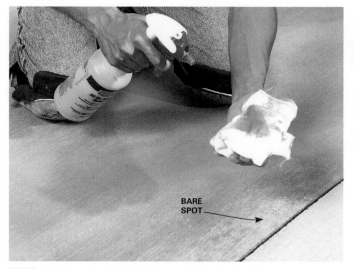

7 Look for bare spots after the surface is dry. Touch them up by spraying stain from a hand-held spray bottle onto a clean cloth, then dabbing the stain onto the spots. Dab the surrounding area so the stain blends naturally.

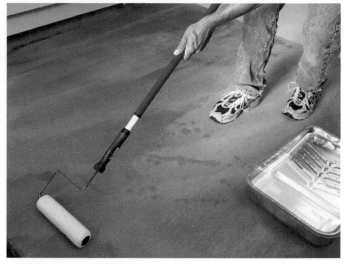

8 Let the stain dry for 24 hours, then apply a sealer to keep the stain from fading. Plan on rolling on a new coat of sealer every three to four years to protect the surface.

and apply the first color (base coat) of stain in a circular pattern (Photo 3). The base coat makes the second color more prominent. Immediately after spraying, mist the section with water and apply the second color (Photo 4). Then spray more water over the top to create swirls or small runs in the second color (Photo 5). The first and second colors will intermix, producing the marbleized effect. Use the water to "push" the color all the way to the edges or onto bare spots. If the water pools in a low spot or starts to run onto an adjacent section, dab it up with a cloth.

When switching to a new stain color, be sure the lens shields are dry, or use new shields so the old color doesn't run onto the section of the patio with the new color. Don't worry if a leaf or debris blows onto the wet stain. After the stain dries, remove the debris and touch up the stain (see the next step).

Add more stain for deeper color

Let the stain dry for 24 hours. If the color isn't as vibrant as you want or the coverage is spotty, go back and add another coat of stain. Wet the concrete and apply the stain using the same steps as

before. Here a second coat was added to the corner squares to give them a deeper, richer color.

You'll probably find bare spots that you missed, especially along the edges. Touch-up is simple. Fill a spray bottle with stain, spray the stain on a cloth and dab it on the bare spot (Photo 7).

Finish with the sealer

The sealing step is recommended because it protects against fading and wear, and it enhances the stain. You'll have to clean the patio with TSP substitute and give the patio a fresh coat of sealer every three to four years.

Give the stain a full day to dry, then apply the high-gloss sealer. Choose a day or time of day when the patio is shaded (don't apply the sealer in direct sunlight). Start by cutting in with sealer along the patio edges with a 3-in. brush. The milky white sealer turns clear as it's applied. Roll sealer on the rest of the patio with a 3/8-in.-nap roller (Photo 8). Let the sealer dry for two hours, then apply a second coat. Roll the second coat perpendicular to the first coat.

Renew a finish

If you're dealing with a finish that has scratches, worn areas and a flat, dull appearance, you can strip it and refinish (big job!) or you can renew the existing finish. Two products make renewal much easier. The first is gel stain, which does a great job of evening out the color and filling the dings. The second is wipe-on polyurethane, which is simplicity itself to apply to wood, especially to existing trim. Wipe-on polyurethane doesn't leave as thick a protective film as a brush-on product, but if you only need to regain a smooth, glossy topcoat, it's a great choice.

Paint a ceiling

Ceilings present some unique painting challenges. For starters, they're usually much larger than any single wall and are often illuminated with raking light that accentuates even the smallest flaw in the paint. Add to that the challenge of working overhead and things can get messy in a hurry. That's why we called in Bill Nunn, one of our favorite painting consultants, to help you out with his best ceiling painting tips.

MEET THE PRO: Bill is the owner of William Nunn Painting, which specializes in classic old home painting. Bill has been painting for more than 35 years.

Sand before you paint

Over time, and as the layers of paint build up, bumps and crud can get stuck to the ceiling. On untextured ceilings, Bill starts with a quick once-over sanding with 100-grit drywall sanding paper. This helps ensure a perfectly smooth paint job and increases paint bonding. The easiest way to do this is with a sanding pole. When you're done sanding, wipe the ceiling with a damp sponge to remove the dust.

Use a stain-blocking primer to cover flaws

Roof leaks, overflowing sinks, tobacco smoke and big spills can all leave ugly ceiling stains or dinginess that is impossible to conceal with plain old paint. But cover the stain with a coat of stain-blocking primer and your troubles are over.

Bill's favorite is white pigmented shellac. You can buy spray cans of pigmented shellac, but Bill prefers brushing it on. Just don't forget to pick up some ammonia or denatured alcohol to clean your brush. If you're painting over a ceiling that's yellow from smoke, roll a coat of shellac over the entire ceiling before painting with latex.

Cut in before you roll

Cutting in before you roll allows you to cover most of the brush marks with the roller. Bill likes to carefully brush paint along the edge of the ceiling a section at a time. He'll cut in about 10 linear ft. and then roll that section. This method has a couple of advantages over cutting in the entire room at once. First, the cut-in section will remain wet until you roll, so it blends in better. Bill says it's also simply less boring to alternate between cutting in and rolling.

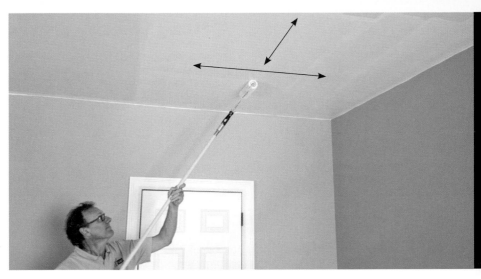

Roll both directions

There are a few tricks to getting a smooth, consistent coat of paint on the ceiling. First, work in sections about 5 or 6 ft. square. Move quickly from one section to the next to make sure the paint along the edge doesn't dry before you roll the adjoining section. This is called "keeping a wet edge" and is the key to avoiding lap marks. Bill says you'll get the best coverage by immediately rerolling each section at a right angle to your first roller direction as you go.

Buy special ceiling paint

While there are exceptions, in general you'll get the best results with paint that's formulated for a ceiling application. For a ceiling, you want paint that doesn't spatter, has a long open time (dries slowly), and is flat instead of glossy. Most ceiling paints are formulated with these qualities. And of course you can have ceiling paint tinted if you want a color other than "ceiling white."

Lap your cut-in onto the walls

If you're planning to paint the walls too, lap the paint onto the walls a little bit. Then when you paint the walls, you can err on the side of leaving a little ceiling color showing when you cut in and it won't be noticeable. Some painters like to skip this cutting-in step and save time by mashing the roller into the corner instead. Bill objects to this method because it's sloppy, builds up excess paint in the corner and can leave runs or a thick paint line on the wall.

Don't be afraid of color

You may not want to paint your ceiling yellow, but don't be afraid to deviate from plain old white. Bill says painting the ceiling a color can make a small room seem bigger, or a room with a high ceiling seem more intimate. Plus, it's just more interesting. Ask at any full-service paint store for help in choosing complementary wall and ceiling colors, or search online for examples of rooms you like.

You don't need an expensive pole

Bill is sort of old-school when it comes to equipment and actually prefers low-tech solutions. You can buy all kinds of fancy extendable paint poles, but Bill prefers a simple wooden broom handle. And his reasons are simple. They're cheap and light and do the job.

Clear the room

Bill prefers to move everything out of the room and cover the floors with drop cloths before painting a ceiling. But if this isn't possible, he groups furniture in the center and covers it with painter's plastic. Sometimes it may be necessary to make two or more small groups so that you can reach over them with the roller.

Use a thick, premium roller cover

Here's a tip that applies to most paint jobs but is even more important for ceilings. You want to get as much paint on the ceiling as you can in the shortest amount of time possible while minimizing spatters. To do this, you need the best roller cover you can buy. Bill prefers a 1/2-in.-nap lambswool cover. If you've never tried a lambswool roller cover, you owe it to yourself to experience the difference. And if you're worried about the cost, keep in mind that lambswool covers are easy to clean and can last a long time if you take good care of them.

LAMBSWOOL ROLLER   INEXPENSIVE ROLLER

Roll gently on textured ceilings

Painting textured ceilings is a bit of a crapshoot. If the texture has been painted over already, it's probably safe to paint again. If the texture has never been painted, there's a risk the water in the paint could loosen the texture, causing it to fall off in sheets. A lot depends on the quality of the texturing job. If you have a closet or other inconspicuous area, do a test by rolling on some paint to see what happens. If the texture loosens, painting over the larger ceiling is risky.

Bill has a few tips for painting over texture. If possible, spray on the paint—it's less likely to loosen the texture than rolling. But spraying in an occupied house is usually impractical. Bill says the best tip for rolling on paint is to avoid overworking the paint. Just roll the paint on and leave it. Don't go back and forth with the roller, as this is likely to pull the texture from

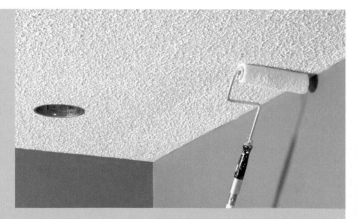

the ceiling. If the ceiling needs another coat of paint, wait for the first coat to dry completely. Then roll another coat perpendicular to the first one using the same careful technique.

Roll on a truck bed liner

You bought a pickup truck because you needed to haul things. But what can you haul in a pickup bed that's not going to destroy the finish and eventually rust out the bed? Pillows? Precisely. That's why you need bed protection. Your choices are a preformed hard plastic drop-in liner, professionally applied epoxy coating or a DIY roll-on coating. The best preformed liners cost about $500. That's about the same cost as for a professionally applied epoxy liner. However, you can roll on a fairly high-quality bed liner yourself for about $150. (See "Other Bed Liner Options," p. 169). That's the path we're going to take you down.

Choosing a roll-on product

Herculiner, Dupli-Color and Rust-Oleum are the most popular retail brands. You can find them at most auto parts stores.

However, you can also find many other brands online. Just search for "roll-on bed liner."

The products come in three types: water-based, solvent-based single-stage and solvent-based two-part formulas. Prices range from $80 to $100 per gallon for water-based and single-stage products, to $150 per gallon for two-stage formulas. One gallon is enough to apply two coats to most truck beds. The preparation work is the same for all three formulas.

All DIY bed liner products contain a gritty material for skid resistance. However, some of the higher-priced versions also include rubberized bits for added impact resistance.

You'll have to brush the product into corners and seams. You may choose to brush it onto the bed itself. But we recommend buying the manufacturer's optional application kit and applying the product with its special roller. If you opt to brush it on, at least back-roll it to achieve a more uniform texture.

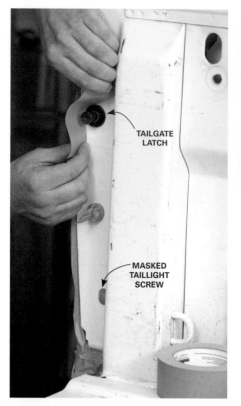

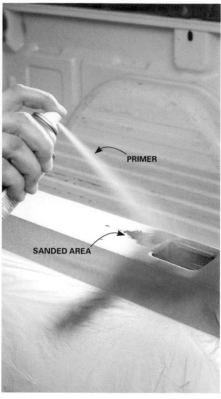

1 **Mask off operational components.** Butt the tape against the painted edge and stretch it around latches and lights. Cover small taillight retaining screws with tape and cut off the excess with a razor blade.

2 **Treat rusty areas.** Spray primer or rust converter over the sanded areas. Allow the first coat to "flash" the recommended time. Then apply a second coat and let it dry.

If cost is your most important consideration, buy the water-based or single-stage product. However, if you want a bed liner that's closest in durability to a professionally sprayed-on product (see "Other Bed Liner Options," p. 169), spend the extra dough and buy a two-part bed liner. We chose the two-part liner kit for this story.

Just like painting, it's all about the prep

No bed liner is going to stick to the factory paint if you haven't done the recommended prep work. It's awful work and there are no shortcuts. First remove any grease stains, dried paint, caulk or adhesive with chemical removers and a scraper. Then wash the entire bed with car wash soap. Rinse and let dry.

Next, remove any remaining car wax using wax remover (from any auto parts store) or acetone. Caution: When you're using these chemicals or applying the bed liner, work in a well-ventilated area and wear a respirator with a charcoal filter. Make sure you're far away from open flames and sparks.

Use the scuff pad provided in the bed liner kit and scuff every square inch of the bed (we told you it was awful work). Sand off any surface rust and feather the edges. Wash the bed a second time with car soap and water and let it dry. Always follow the directions on the product label, especially if they differ from ours.

Mask the truck and tarp the floor

This is an incredibly messy project, and there's no way you can "cut" around lights and latches without getting the goop on them. So mask off any part you don't want covered with bed liner (Photo 1).

If you want to coat the bed rails (the ledges at the top of the bed), mark off the flat portion of the bed rail and mask along it with a painter's tape that prevents paint bleed. Then cover the fenders with a drop cloth. Cover the back and roof of the cab as well. Protect the floor or driveway with drop cloths under the truck and along the sides. Shove a drop cloth under the gaps between the bed and the cab and under the tailgate. Or, remove the tailgate and set it on sawhorses. Once the vehicle is masked and tarped, prime the sanded areas with

3 **Mix the bed liner in a box.** It will contain any mess. Throw the box into the truck bed before you even pop the lid of the bed liner product. Leave the gallon can inside the box and add the activator. Then mix with a drill and a stirring paddle until the product is smooth.

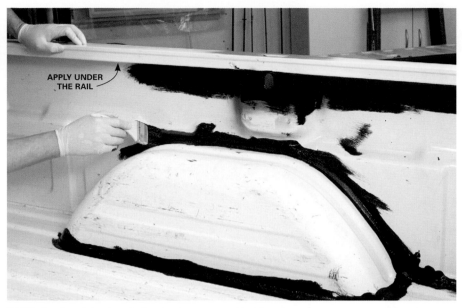

APPLY UNDER THE RAIL

4 **Cut in with a brush.** Brush a heavy coat of bed liner into the corners, around the wheel wells and under the bed rail—all the areas that are hard to reach with a roller.

5 **Brush the tailgate.** Brush an extra-heavy coat of bed liner onto the tailgate. Then use the roller to texture it. Allow additional drying time and then apply a second heavy coat.

6 **Do the floor last.** Working from front to back, roll a liberal coating of the bed liner onto the corrugated flooring. Back-roll to get an even texture, but don't spread the product too thin.

a "rusty metal" primer. If the areas were heavily rusted, use a "rust converter" product instead (Photo 2).

Mix, cut in and apply

You'll find all the traction grit/rubber particles settled into a heavy glob at the bottom of the can, so plan to take the time to mix the product thoroughly. Some kits include a plastic mixing paddle for your drill. The paddle in our kit broke right away. So do yourself a favor and buy a mixing paddle made of metal at the hardware store. Then mix the product (Photo 3). Next, cut in with a brush around the truck bed box (Photo 4).

Coat the front and sides of the box with the roller. Then coat the floor (Photo 6). Allow the first coat to dry the recommended time, then apply a second coat.

Other bed liner options

Custom-molded drop-in bed liners

Prices: $250 to $500, depending on the bed size, material choice and thickness

PROS:
- Best impact protection
- Easiest to clean because the liners don't have sharp corners or seams

CONS:
- Cracks must be repaired immediately to prevent water leaks between the liner and the bed
- The surface will be slippery unless you pay more for a nonskid texture
- Even if the liner stays intact, water and moisture eventually cause the bed to rust prematurely

Professionally installed spray-on two-part bed liners

Prices: $500 to $1,000

PROS:
- Excellent scratch and gouge protection
- More impact protection than roll-on but less than custom-molded liner
- Watertight

CONS:
- Must return to installer to get material match for deep gouges

Restain a wood fence

Shabby to handsome in three easy steps

When did your cedar fence lose its rich, warm glow? Who invited that discolored, shabby-looking impostor into the neighborhood? Don't worry—underneath that thin gray skin, the glow still remains. All you have to do is remove the surface layer of aged wood cells to expose a fresh layer of wood. With a power washer, it's as easy as washing your car. Then apply an exterior wood oil stain to preserve this new layer of wood. It'll prolong the life of your fence to boot.

Power washing makes the huge cleaning task easy

Power washers are aggressive. They'll strip the wood as well as clean off the dirt and grime, but you can also erode the wood too deeply and ruin it. The key is to use the right sprayer tip and technique. In any case, the power washer's spray will slightly raise and roughen the grain on smooth wood. That's actually good—it allows more sealer to soak in and improves the finish.

Rent a power washer that operates at 1,500 or 2,000 psi and avoid more powerful 3,000 or 3,500 psi units. Be sure to get both 15- and 25-degree spray tips. Have the rental people demonstrate the washer's use. It's an easy machine to run.

To avoid damaging the pump, don't run the power washer without first filling the pump and hoses with water. To do this, attach both hoses (Photo 1), snap in a 25-degree tip, turn on the garden hose spigot and hold down the trigger on the wand until water squirts out. Release the wand trigger and start the engine. If it's hard to pull the start cord, pull the wand trigger to release the water pressure.

SPRAYER TIP

Clear the area along the fence by tying back plants that are growing alongside it. Wear water-repellent clothing—you will get wet from the spray.

Start spraying with the wand tip 18 in. from the wood surface. Move in closer as you swing the tip slowly along the length of the board (Photo 2). Keep the width of the fan spray aligned across the boards. The wood's color will brighten as the surface is stripped away. Watch closely and stop stripping when no more color change occurs. You don't have to remove too much surface to expose fresh wood, and continuing to spray won't improve the color.

It takes a little practice to arrive at the proper tip distance and speed of movement, but you'll catch on fast. It's better to make two or three passes than to risk gouging the surface trying to accomplish this job in one pass. As you gain experience, you can switch to a 15-degree tip. This tip cuts more aggressively and works faster than the 25-degree tip.

Simple repairs add years to the life of your fence

With the fence clean, it's time to fix or replace damaged boards, refasten loose boards and countersink any protruding nails. Use waterproof glue (Photo 3) to repair any split and broken boards. Drive corrosion-resistant screws (Photo 4) instead of nails to pull loose pieces tightly together. If a gate is sagging, straighten it with a turnbuckle support (Photo 5). Also coat the posts (Photo 6) where they emerge from the ground or concrete with a wood preservative. This is the area that rots first.

Stain makes the fence look brand new

To preserve the natural color of the wood, use an exterior semi-transparent oil stain. It seals the wood while allowing the grain

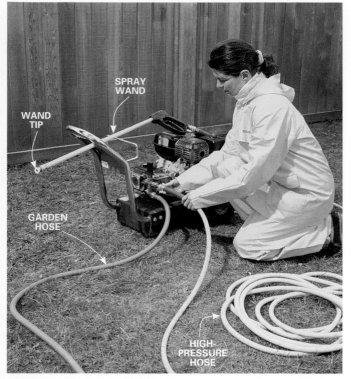

1 Connect a garden hose and the power washer hose to the machine. Snap a 25-degree tip onto the end of the wand. Turn on the water to the garden hose and pull the trigger on the spray wand until water squirts out. Now start up the power washer's engine.

2 Hold the tip of the wand about 18 in. from the fence and move it the length of the boards. Pull the trigger and keep the sprayer tip moving to avoid gouging the wood. Use a variety of attack angles to strip inside corners.

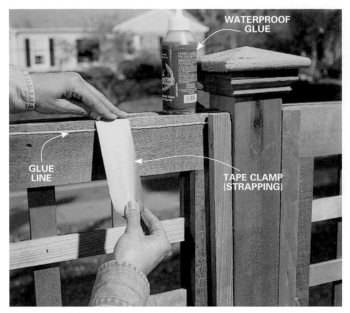

3 Glue split and broken pieces when the wood has dried for at least 24 hours. Apply waterproof glue and clamp or tape the pieces firmly together.

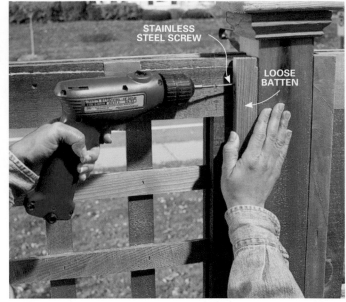

4 Drive weather-resistant or stainless steel screws to tighten loose boards. Recess the head 1/4 in. and fill with a light-colored caulk.

and color variations to show through. And its pigments add an overall color tone. Make sure the stain contains ultraviolet inhibitors, which will slow down bleaching by sunlight, and a mildewcide to slow fungal growth. Look for samples on cedar at the paint store, or bring in your own piece of wood to test. A test sample is the best way to ensure a satisfactory result.

Before applying the stain, be sure the fence is dry. Allow at least 24 hours. If it's cool and humid, allow another 24 hours.

Use a paint roller with a "medium nap" cover (Photo 7) to apply a soaking coat to the wood. Let the wood absorb as much sealer as it can. Roll about a 3-ft. section of fence and then brush (Photo 8) the sealer into the wood. If the wood still appears dry, roll on additional sealer. Work the sealer into all recesses and corners. The roller applies the stain, but you need the brush to work it well into the wood's surface. Coat detailed areas with a trim roller and smaller brush (Photo 9). Keep wet edges to prevent lap marks.

Most semitransparent oil stains are guaranteed to last two to five years. (Solid-color stains last longer but are more difficult to renew.) Fences usually face severe weathering, so expect the finish to last no more than three years. Plan on recoating the fence within this time frame to keep your fence looking fresh. Before recoating, wash the fence with a garden hose sprayer and use a bristle brush on stubborn dirt deposits and stains. Let the fence dry and stain it using the same method.

5 Realign sagging gates with a turnbuckle. We spray-painted the shiny turnbuckle black to make it less conspicuous.

6 Brush a wood preservative into the posts around the base to help prevent rot at this vulnerable area.

7 Roll into the dry wood a soaking coat of semitransparent stain. Coat about 3 ft. of fence, then proceed to the step shown in Photo 8.

8 Brush the stain (backbrush) into the wood grain and all corners and gaps. Brush out any runs or drips.

9 Work the stain into small and tight areas with a trim roller and a 2-in. brush. One generous coat should be enough.

Spray-on paint protection

The paint on the leading edge of car hoods is on the front line for gravel and sand damage. Until recently, you only had two ways to protect the hood: install a "bra" or apply paint protection film. Bras are not only ugly but also lower gas mileage and trap road grit, which damages the paint. Paint protection film looks and works much better, but professional installation costs about $500. Now there's a product that DIYers can apply to protect against paint chips—spray-on/peel-off paint protection film.

Several companies make this paint film, which lasts up to a year. It costs about $25 and contains enough material to coat the bottom third of your hood. Find it at any auto parts store. We asked 3M product expert Todd Mathes to walk us through the prep and application process.

You'll also need car-washing supplies, poly sheeting to cover the entire car and ground, clean-edge masking tape and a microfiber cloth. Or buy the optional installation kit and a spray trigger. The entire job takes less than two hours. Here's how it's done.

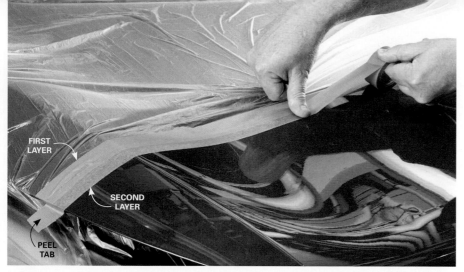

1 **Tape the poly sheeting to the hood.** Carefully apply the first layer and then the second layer directly below it. Make the second tape line as straight as possible, and press down along the edge to seal it to the hood as you apply. Double over one end of the tape to make a peel tab.

FIRST LAYER

SECOND LAYER

PEEL TAB

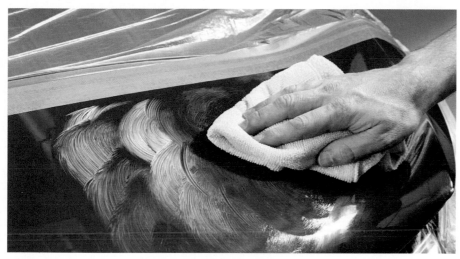

2 **Wax the exposed hood area.** Squirt a dollop of wax onto the hood and work it in with a microfiber towel. Continue wiping until the surface is free of haze.

FIRST COAT (SIDE TO SIDE)
SECOND COAT (UP AND DOWN)
THIRD COAT (SIDE TO SIDE)

3 **Spray the hood with protectant.** Starting at the tape line and spraying down to the bottom edge of the hood, spray the product continuously in alternating left to right rows at the rate of two seconds per foot. Overlap each row slightly. Immediately spray a second layer, moving up and down over the same section. Then apply a third coat in the side-to-side pattern.

Prep the vehicle

The engine and hood must be cool when you apply the product. A hot engine will heat the hood and force-dry the spray between coats, defeating its self-leveling feature. So check the weather report and pick a time when it'll be cool, dry and calm. Park the car in a shaded area the night before. Then start the project by washing the car with car wash soap. Make sure you remove all traces of bug splatter and tar. Then rinse and dry completely.

Next, pop the hood and prop it open about 4 in. with a roll of paper towels or a block of wood.

Tarp, tape and wax

Spread a poly sheet over the entire vehicle. Then spread sheeting on the ground to catch any overspray. Starting at the grille, use a scissors to cut straight up the center of the poly, stopping about 18 in. from the bottom edge of the hood. Then cut right and left out to the fenders until you have formed a "T" cutout. Tuck the flaps under the hood and tape them inside the engine compartment to prevent them from moving while you spray. Secure the rest of the sheeting to the car and floor with tape to prevent it from blowing onto the wet finish.

Next, tape the top of the "T" to the hood. Apply another layer of tape to form the clean edge between the spray film and the rest of the hood (Photo 1). Once the poly is in place, apply the synthetic wax included with the product (Photo 2). Waxing is an important step to make removal easier a year from now. So even if you've recently waxed the car, do it again using the wax packet included with the product.

MEET THE EXPERT: Todd Mathes has 25 years' experience at 3M working with masking, abrasives and vehicle appearance products for both body shops and retail customers. He loves shiny cars but admits his real goal is to build a trail Jeep.

Apply the coating

Shake the can for a full minute before applying. Then hold the nozzle 6 to 8 in. from the hood and apply three coats to one-half of the hood (Photo 3). Spray all three coats in one continuous motion (don't stop and start at the ends of each row or coat). Move the can at the rate of six seconds per pass. Continue spraying onto the fender, over and above the tape line, and below the bottom edge of the hood to get a uniform film thickness at the edges. A proper application should have an "orange peel" texture and a slightly milky look. Don't worry—the product self-levels and dries clear. Then spray the second half of the hood. When you're done, remove the clean-edge tape while the spray is still wet (Photo 4).

Park the car in the sun and let it dry for two to four hours. The film cures fully in one to four days, depending on the air temperature and humidity.

Troubleshooting

- If bugs or leaves land on the wet spray, pluck them off immediately with a pair of tweezers.
- If the spray is solid white, has lumps or develops sags, you've applied too much. Stop spraying and let the product dry. Then peel it off and start over, moving a bit faster and applying less product.
- If the wet spray has a "dry" look or you've missed areas or pinholes, you can apply more product. But do it quickly. You only have a 10-minute window. Wait too long and the product loses its self-leveling quality and you can wind up with a textured look.

A year from now

Our expert says that the film can last a bit longer than one year but may yellow from UV exposure. However, the longer you wait, the harder it is to remove, so don't push your luck. Pop the hood and peel the film loose around all three edges using your fingernail. Then remove all the film (Photo 5).

4 Remove the tape while the spray is wet. Grab the doubled-over peel tab and pull the clean-edge tape up and away from the wet edge.

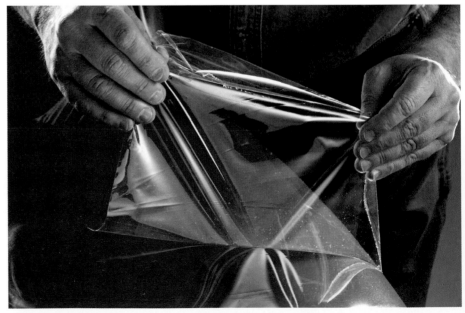

5 After a year, peel off the film. Lift up a top corner and pull the film down toward the bottom of the hood to release as large a piece as possible. Then use both hands to pull the old film up and across the hood. Wipe the excess off the edges with a rag. Apply a fresh layer of protection film following the steps shown.

Avoid painting blunders

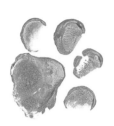

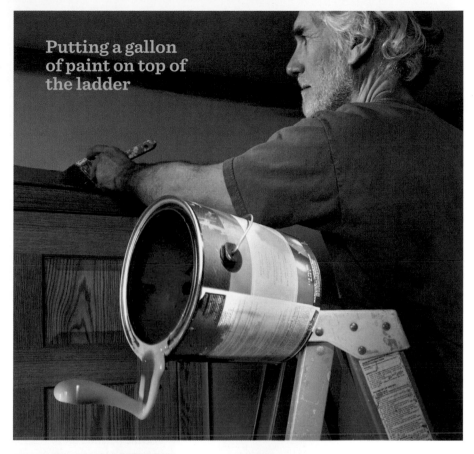

Putting a gallon of paint on top of the ladder

Not locking pets out

"I took a quick break to go to the bathroom and heard pawing at the door. I opened the door and there was my dog Scout with a paintbrush in his mouth. He had carried the dripping brush across the house for me."

Dave Jones, Field Editor

Not putting a rag over the paint can lid when you pound it down!

Leaving the lid off

The most obvious problem with this bad habit is that someone is bound to step on the lid and track paint all over. But there are other reasons to put the lid back on immediately. It'll keep your paint clean and prevent dried-out paint crud from forming in the can or on the lid. Plus, you're less likely to get the lids from two similar colors mixed up, which can cause hassles later.

Chapter Six

ELECTRICAL & PLUMBING

Let there be light! More outlets, too!

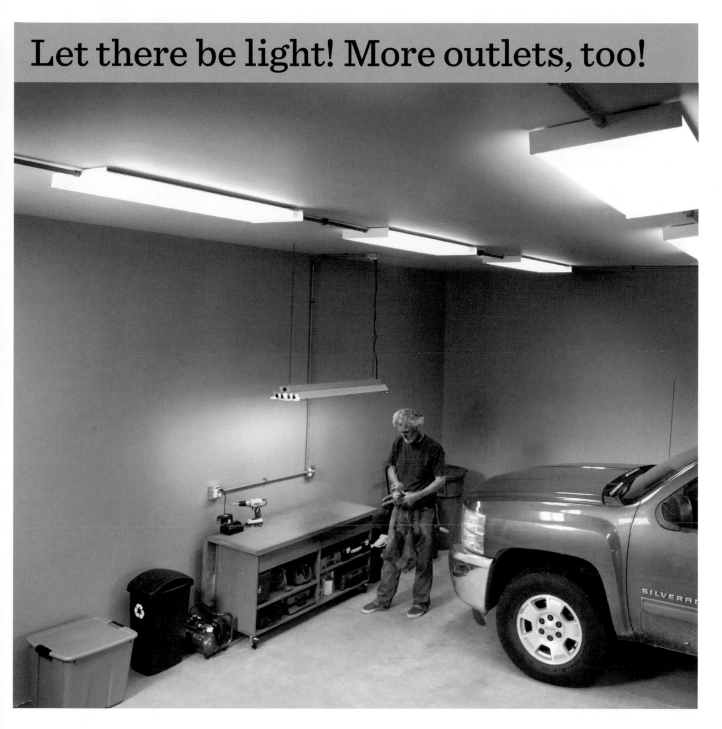

Upgrade wiring the easy way

If your garage doesn't have enough outlets and you're sick of squinting to see what you're working on, then we've got the solution. Using PVC conduit and metal surface-mount electrical boxes, we'll show you how to connect additional outlets to an existing garage outlet and how to add bright, energy-efficient fluorescent lights to an existing ceiling box without cutting into your walls or fishing wires. Our upgrades cost about $600, but most of that went toward the eight fluorescent light fixtures.

WHAT IT TAKES

COST: Varies. About $100 and up depending on the number of light fixtures.

TIME: One weekend

SKILL LEVEL: Intermediate to advanced

TOOLS: Standard hand tools, a noncontact voltage tester, a wire stripper and a drill.

In our garage, we extended conduit from an outlet to add outlets and a hanging fixture over our workbench area. We also removed a ceiling light fixture and extended wiring from it to install eight new fluorescent fixtures. Remember, though, your existing wiring may not be adequate for large power tools like saws or power-hungry appliances like refrigerators or freezers. For these you may have to add a new circuit, a project we won't cover in this story.

First we'll show you how to prepare for installing PVC conduit by adding an extender to your electrical box. Then we'll show you how easy it is to cut and install PVC conduit and push wire through it. Finally we'll show you how to hook up the outlets and lights and make sure everything is properly grounded.

Installing the PVC is simple, but you'll need a basic understanding of electrical wiring to safely connect the wires. We'll show you how we wired our outlets, switch and lights, but if your wiring is different and you're not sure how to make the connections, consult a wiring manual or get advice from an electrician. You can also find dozens of articles at familyhandyman.com. Whatever you do, pull a permit so an inspector can check your work.

Plan the system

The first step is to draw up a simple sketch and figure out how many outlets and lights you plan to add. Keep in mind that there is a limit to how many lights you can add to one circuit. The maximum number of fixtures is determined by the capacity of the circuit, assuming there is nothing else on the circuit that would be turned on at the same time. The maximum wattage of electrical load that can be turned on continuously for three or more hours is 1,440 watts on a 15-amp circuit and 1,920 watts on a 20-amp circuit (which includes a 20 percent reduction for safety).

When your plan is complete, make a list of the materials you'll need. On p. 184 we've included a list of the parts we used for this project. Use this as a guide for making your own list. If you need a single-gang to 4-in. square steel box extender like the one we used (Photo 2), you may have to special-order it or pick it up at an electrical supplier. Also, match the wire gauge to your circuit. Buy 14-gauge wire if your circuit is protected by a 15-amp circuit breaker and 12-gauge wire if it's protected by a 20-amp circuit breaker.

It's easy with PVC conduit

To add lights and outlets, you could spend days crawling around your attic and snaking wire through walls. But running wire through PVC conduit mounted on walls and ceilings makes the job faster and a whole lot less frustrating.

At home centers, you'll find a variety of PVC fittings that let you turn corners and run the conduit exactly where you want it; no need to learn the art of bending conduit as there would be with metal. And unlike metal, PVC plastic is quick and easy to cut. If you goof up, you can cut out your mistake and add new parts using couplings. It couldn't be simpler. And conduit makes your wiring more versatile because you can always add to or reconfigure the wiring later.

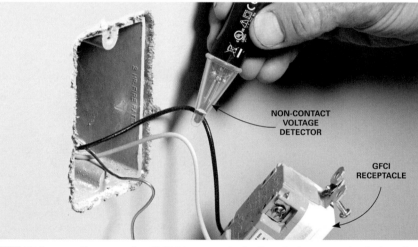

NON-CONTACT VOLTAGE DETECTOR

GFCI RECEPTACLE

1 **Make sure the power is off.** Hold a noncontact voltage tester near each wire to make sure the power is off before you do any work on the wiring.

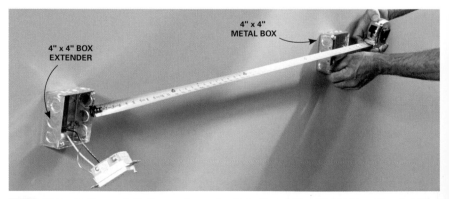

4" x 4" METAL BOX

4" x 4" BOX EXTENDER

2 **Measure for conduit.** Screw a box extender to the existing electrical box. Then hold the next box in position and measure between them. Subtract 1/2 in. for the male adapters to determine the length of conduit needed.

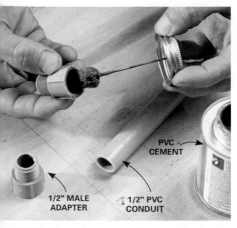

3 Glue adapters to the conduit. Cut the conduit and remove any burrs from the inside of the cut end. Swab PVC cement around the inside of the adapter. Press the adapter onto the pipe, twist it about a quarter turn and hold for a few seconds until the glue sets.

PVC CEMENT

1/2" MALE ADAPTER

1/2" PVC CONDUIT

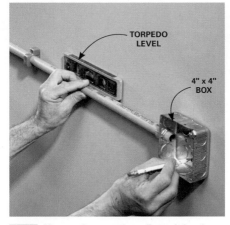

4 Mount the next box. Extend the piece of conduit between the two boxes. Hold it level and mark two holes in the back of the second box. Remove the box and install drywall anchors so you can mount the box to the wall.

TORPEDO LEVEL

4" x 4" BOX

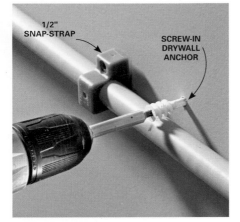

5 Secure the conduit with a strap. Position the anchor and drive a screw through it. If you don't hit a stud, move the strap aside and add a screw-in drywall anchor as shown here. Then screw the strap to the anchor.

1/2" SNAP-STRAP

SCREW-IN DRYWALL ANCHOR

Working with PVC

There are several surface wiring methods, including metal conduit, but we chose PVC conduit because it's inexpensive and easy to work with. You can buy compatible PVC electrical boxes, but at most home centers the selection is limited, so we chose to use metal boxes instead. Combining metal boxes and PVC conduit is fine, but unlike an all-metal system, PVC requires you to run a separate ground wire and bond it to each metal box or light fixture with either a screw or a special grounding clip.

There are a few different techniques for measuring PVC. You can measure between boxes and subtract for the fittings (Photo 2). Or you can install a bend or fitting on one end and mark the other end for cutting (Photos 6 and 12). Then it's simple to cut the pipe. We bought a PVC Conduit Cutter, but you can also use any fine-tooth saw or even a miter saw. After you cut the conduit, ream the inside of the cut edge with a knife or pliers handle to remove any plastic burrs.

Join the conduit to fittings with special PVC cement made for electrical PVC conduit (Photo 3). Use PVC male adapters and metal locknuts to connect the PVC conduit to metal boxes (Photo 7).

You can heat and bend PVC pipe, but we don't show how here. Instead we used 90-degree bend fittings to turn corners. You can also buy offsets that position the PVC flush to the wall surface, but these aren't necessary if you use the type of straps we show in Photo 5.

6 Mark the vertical conduit. Connect a 90-degree bend to the conduit. Hold it against the ceiling and mark the top edge of the electrical box on the conduit. Subtract 1/4 in. and cut the conduit.

90-DEGREE BEND

MARK FOR LENGTH

Straps for 1/2-in. PVC must be within 36 in. of electrical boxes and spaced a maximum of 36 in. between straps. There are at least two types of straps. We like the "snap-strap" shown in Photo 5. Drive a screw through the hole to hold the strap. If you don't hit a stud or something else solid, back out the screw, move the strap aside and drive in a drywall anchor (Photo 5) to secure the strap.

Add outlets and a light over your workbench

First turn off the circuit breaker to the outlet. Use a voltage tester to make sure

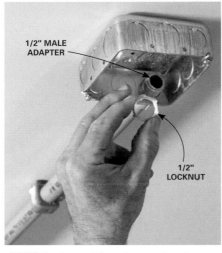

7 Lock conduit to boxes. Once boxes are screwed in place, the conduit will stay put, so it's tempting to skip or forget the locknuts. Don't. Every male fitting needs a nut.

1/2" MALE ADAPTER

1/2" LOCKNUT

the power is off. Then carefully remove the outlet—in our case it's a GFCI outlet—and as a final precaution, test all the wires in the box with a noncontact voltage detector (Photo 1).

If you're planning to hang a plug-in ceiling light like ours over your workbench, first find the center of your workbench. Then measure the fixture you plan to use to determine how far apart the hanging chains are. Plan to position the ceiling outlet directly above where the power cord leaves the light fixture. Then position the outlet and switch on the wall directly under the ceiling box location.

THHN COPPER WIRES

8 Push wires into the conduit. Hang the wire spools on a steel pipe or dowel so they can spin freely. Bend the ends of the wires over so they don't catch on edges inside fittings, and then push them through the conduit.

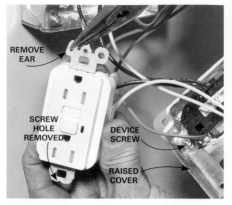

REMOVE EAR

SCREW HOLE REMOVED

DEVICE SCREW

RAISED COVER

9 Attach the outlets to the raised cover. Break off the ears and cut off the screw hole to prepare the outlets for mounting. Attach them to the raised cover with the included device screws.

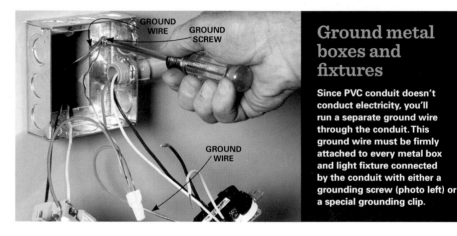

GROUND WIRE

GROUND SCREW

GROUND WIRE

Ground metal boxes and fixtures

Since PVC conduit doesn't conduct electricity, you'll run a separate ground wire through the conduit. This ground wire must be firmly attached to every metal box and light fixture connected by the conduit with either a grounding screw (photo left) or a special grounding clip.

Run the conduit

To get started, screw a metal box extender to the outlet box. We used a single-gang 4-in. square box extender. You'll run conduit from here to the next box. Hold the next outlet box in position and measure between the boxes. Subtract 1/2 in. to get the length of PVC conduit needed (Photo 2). Cut the conduit and glue male adapters to each end (Photo 3).

Remove the round knockouts from the metal boxes by bending them out a little, and then grabbing and twisting them with pliers. Remember to remove the smaller knockouts, not the large ones. Photo 4 shows how to mark for fastening the box. Drive screws at the marks to see if you hit solid wood. If not, remove the screws and install drywall anchors. Connect the two boxes with the PVC conduit and screw the locknuts onto the male adapters in each box. Then screw the second box to the wall. Finally, add

the required clamps (Photo 5). If you want to add more outlet boxes, just repeat this process.

Photo 6 shows how to determine the length of the section of vertical PVC conduit running to the ceiling-mounted box. After marking the conduit, cut it, glue on the male adapter, and connect it to the box. Use a level to plumb this section of conduit and secure it to the wall with straps. Finally, add the last section of conduit on the ceiling and anchor the ceiling box to framing or with drywall anchors (Photo 7).

Run wire and make the connections

All of our conduit runs were fairly short, and we used solid copper rather than stranded wire, so we were able to simply push the wire through the conduit (Photo 8). If you have longer runs, you may have to first push an electrical fish tape through

the conduit and secure the wires to it so you can pull them through.

For a wiring scenario like we show here, you'll need separate hot (black), neutral (white) and ground (green) wires. Leave about a foot of extra wire at each box.

After you've run the wires to each box, you can start making the connections. We're providing ground-fault protection to the outlets and light fixture by connecting them to the "load" side of the GFCI receptacle in the first box. Double-check to make sure the power is still off. Figures A, B and C on p. 184 show the wiring diagrams to add outlets and a switched outlet for a hanging light.

It's important to make sure all the boxes are grounded. Do this by connecting the new (green) ground wire to the existing ground wire at the first box (see "Ground metal boxes and fixtures," above left). Then connect the new ground wire to every metal box with a grounding screw. Photo 9 shows how to mount the outlets and switches to the raised cover using the included device screws. Attach the raised covers to the metal boxes with the included machine screws and you're ready to turn on the power and test your work. Use a plug-in GFCI outlet tester at each outlet to make sure your

CAUTION! If you have aluminum wiring, don't work on it yourself. The connections require special techniques. Call in a licensed electrician who is certified to work with it. For more information, go to cpsc.gov and search for "aluminum wiring."

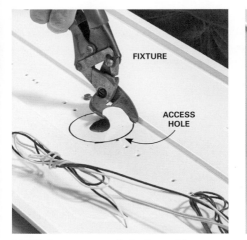

10 Cut an access hole. Start with a hole in the middle to get the snips started. Our fixture had a knockout that we removed. Otherwise, use a small hole saw to drill a starting hole. Snip out to the circle and follow it with the snips.

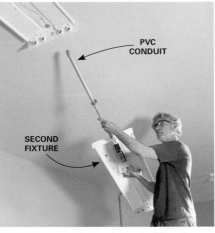

11 Connect in-line fixtures. Hang the second fixture with the conduit already attached. There's no easy way to insert straight runs of conduit between fixtures that are already fastened to the ceiling.

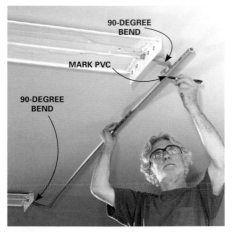

12 Connect parallel fixtures. Connect a 90-degree bend to a length of conduit. Install a 90-degree bend on the second fixture. Hold the conduit with the attached bend in position. Mark the conduit and cut it to length.

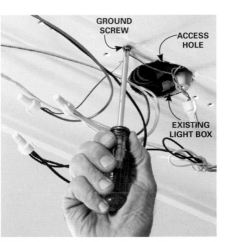

13 Ground the light fixture. Add a ground screw to the light fixture and loop the ground wire around it. Tighten the screw.

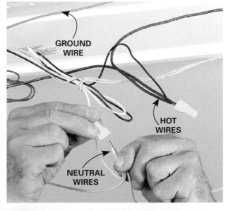

14 Connect the fixture wires. Strip the ends of the new wires and connect them to the wires in the fixture. Connect all neutral white wires together. Connect the colored fixture wire to the black wires.

15 Install the cover. Finish the lighting installation by snapping the cover under the tabs. Then add the fluorescent lamps. Our fixtures also included a prismatic lens that we snapped on to complete the project.

connections are correct.

Add fluorescent lights

Start by making sure the circuit breaker for the existing light is turned off. Then remove the light fixture and check the wires in the box with a noncontact voltage tester. If the electrical box is in the right location, you can start by adding a fluorescent fixture over the box.

Photo 10 shows how to prepare the fixture. The diameter of the hole you cut can be smaller than the electrical box, but should be large enough to reach through to access the wires in the box. After you cut the hole, smooth the edges with a file to remove sharp edges and burrs.

If your preferred location for the lights is not lined up with the ceiling box, then start by adding a box extender to the existing ceiling light box (Photo 2). Then extend conduit to the first fixture.

You can install ceiling fixtures by screwing them directly to the wood framing above or hanging them from toggle bolts. To use toggle bolts, transfer measurements from the mounting holes in the light fixture to the ceiling and drill 1/2-in. holes in the drywall. Then install toggle bolts on the fixture and simply push them into the holes as you hold the fixture next to the ceiling (Photo 11). Measure, use a laser or snap a chalk line (use erasable chalk) to center a row of fixtures and keep them straight.

Photo 11 shows how to connect fixtures end to end. (We already drilled holes in the ceiling for the toggle bolts, but they don't show in the photo.) Photo 12 shows how to connect two rows of fixtures using 90-degree bend fittings. After all the fixtures are mounted and connected with PVC conduit, push wires through the conduit as shown in Photo 8. Photos 13 and 14 show how to connect the ground wire and make the connections to the fixtures.

Finish up by replacing the covers (Photo 15), installing the fluorescent tubes, and snapping on the lenses if your fixtures include them. Turn on the power, flip the switch, and enjoy your brightly lit garage.

Figure A Existing box wiring

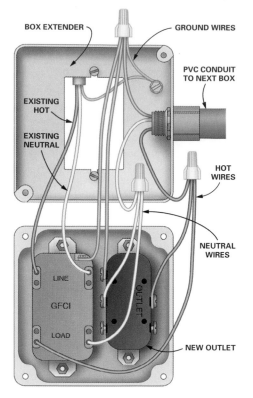

- BOX EXTENDER
- GROUND WIRES
- PVC CONDUIT TO NEXT BOX
- EXISTING HOT
- EXISTING NEUTRAL
- HOT WIRES
- NEUTRAL WIRES
- LINE
- GFCI
- LOAD
- OUTLET
- NEW OUTLET

Figure B Outlet and switch wiring

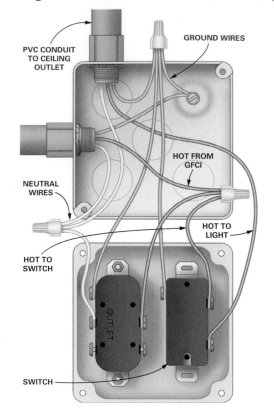

- PVC CONDUIT TO CEILING OUTLET
- GROUND WIRES
- HOT FROM GFCI
- NEUTRAL WIRES
- HOT TO LIGHT
- HOT TO SWITCH
- OUTLET
- SWITCH

Figure C Ceiling outlet wiring

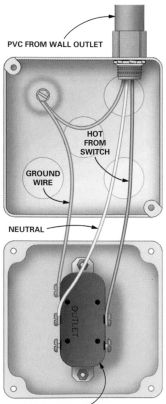

- PVC FROM WALL OUTLET
- HOT FROM SWITCH
- GROUND WIRE
- NEUTRAL
- OUTLET
- CEILING OUTLET

Figure D Light fixture wiring

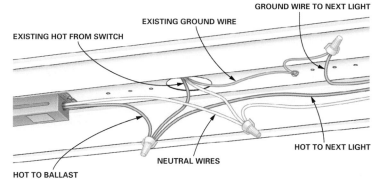

- GROUND WIRE TO NEXT LIGHT
- EXISTING GROUND WIRE
- EXISTING HOT FROM SWITCH
- HOT TO NEXT LIGHT
- NEUTRAL WIRES
- HOT TO BALLAST

Materials you may need:

- Box extender (Raco 187 or similar)
- 4-in. square x 1-1/2-in.-deep metal boxes
- 4-in. square raised covers
- 10-ft. lengths of 1/2-in. PVC conduit
- Container of PVC cement
- 1/2-in. PVC male adapters
- 1/2-in. electrical connector locknuts
- 90-degree PVC bend with hub
- 1/2-in. PVC couplings
- Straps for 1/2-in. PVC

- Green ground screws
- White THHN 14-gauge*
- Black THHN 14-gauge*
- Green THHN 14-gauge*
- 1/4-20 x 3-in. two-piece toggle bolts
- Screw-in drywall anchors
- 15-amp receptacles
- 15-amp single-pole switch
- Light fixtures
- Bulbs or tubes
- Wire connectors

* Use 12-gauge wire for 20-amp circuits.

Upgrade your recessed lights

Dissatisfied with the look of the recessed lights in your kitchen? You can change them in a few minutes just by changing the trim.

Remove the existing trim and bulb and look up inside the metal housing for a sticker with the brand name, the model number and compatible trim styles. If you can't find the information, or the brand isn't available, take the old trim to a lighting store and look for matches. Most manufacturers have several different types and sizes of housing that will accept a variety of trim styles.

Changing old, yellowed trim for new trim is simple—just pull out the old trim and attach the new trim in the same hooks. You can also replace standard trim with an eyeball-style trim that can be aimed in different directions, but it takes an extra step.

First, turn off the switch and circuit breaker and remove the bulb. Unscrew the wing nut that holds the base of the light

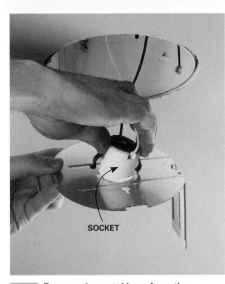

SOCKET

1 Remove the metal base from the housing, then pinch the spring clamps that hold the ceramic light socket in place.

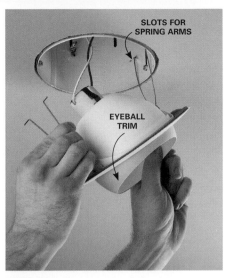

SLOTS FOR SPRING ARMS

EYEBALL TRIM

2 Slide the spring-loaded metal arms up into the slots in the housing, then push the trim up against the ceiling and put the lightbulb in.

in place and remove the socket (Photo 1). Then snap the socket into the top of the eyeball shroud and push the eyeball trim

up into the can (Photo 2). Be sure to use the type of bulb recommended on the label in the housing.

Quicker fixture mounting

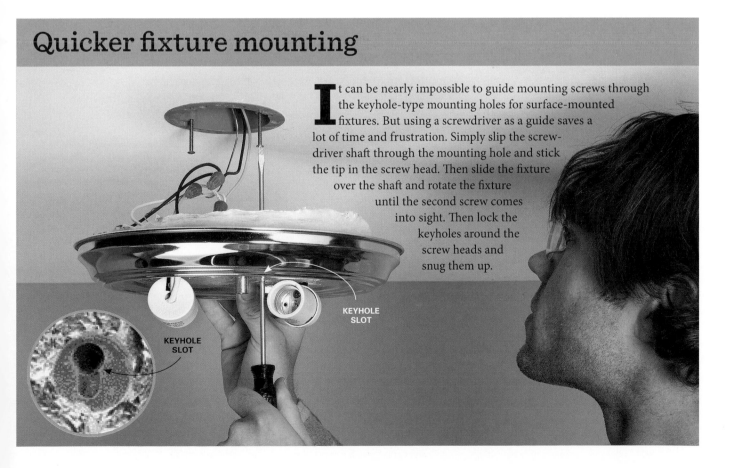

It can be nearly impossible to guide mounting screws through the keyhole-type mounting holes for surface-mounted fixtures. But using a screwdriver as a guide saves a lot of time and frustration. Simply slip the screwdriver shaft through the mounting hole and stick the tip in the screw head. Then slide the fixture over the shaft and rotate the fixture until the second screw comes into sight. Then lock the keyholes around the screw heads and snug them up.

KEYHOLE SLOT

KEYHOLE SLOT

Replace a toilet

*Tips for a fast, trouble-free,
leak-free installation*

Whether you're installing a better-flushing toilet or
resetting the old one after repairs or remodeling,
these tips will help you do it faster and with fewer
problems. The job can take less than an hour, but set aside a
whole morning in case you run into trouble. Everything you'll
need is available at home centers and hardware stores.

Hiring a plumber to replace a
toilet is expensive. If there are
hidden problems, such as a
broken floor flange, the cost
can easily double.

Check the "rough-in"

If you're buying a new toilet, you need to know the "rough-in" measurement of the old one. For the vast majority of toilets, the waste pipe is centered about 12 in. from the wall. But with a few models, that measurement is 10 in. or 14 in. To check the rough-in, just measure from the wall to the toilet's hold-down bolts. If that measurement (plus the thickness of the baseboard) isn't approximately 12 in., toilet shopping will be a bit harder. Most home centers carry only one or two 10-in. models and no 14-in. models. If you have to special-order a toilet, be prepared to spend much more.

If there's a door near the toilet, also measure how far the bowl protrudes from the wall. If you replace a standard bowl with an elongated model, the door may not close.

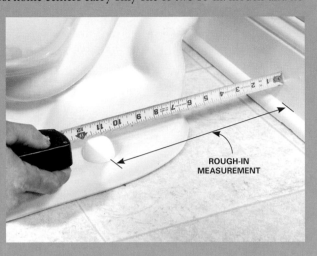

ROUGH-IN MEASUREMENT

Brass bolts are best

Some metal toilet bolts have a yellowish zinc coating that makes them look like brass. So check the label and make sure you're getting brass bolts and nuts. They won't rust away and they're easier to cut off later. If you need to re-anchor the toilet flange (see p. 188), buy stainless steel screws. They won't corrode like steel or break off like brass while you're driving them.

Cut hold-down bolts

Don't be surprised if the old nuts that hold the toilet in place won't budge. Years of corrosion can weld them to their bolts. In that case, a hacksaw blade is the solution. You can buy a "close quarters" blade holder at home centers and hardware stores, or just wrap a bare blade with a rag or duct tape. Most toilet bolts and nuts are brass, so they're easy to cut. If the bolt spins, grab it with locking pliers as you cut.

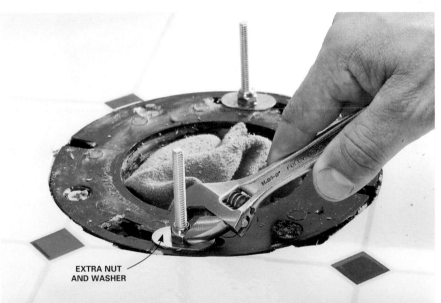

EXTRA NUT AND WASHER

Lock down the bolts

Setting a toilet onto the new bolts can be the most frustrating part of the whole installation. The bolts slip and tip as you're straining to align them with the holes in the toilet. And each time you miss, you risk crushing or shifting the wax ring. The plastic slip-on washers sometimes included with bolts help, but they still allow the bolts to move. The best approach is to buy a second set of nuts and washers so you can lock the bolts in place before you set the toilet. To make sure they're in the correct position, set the toilet and check its height and position. Then lift it off and add the wax ring. To make the bolts easier to find, mark their locations with masking tape.

Flange fixes

A rock-solid toilet flange is the key to a leak-free toilet. The flange is the only thing anchoring the toilet to the floor. If the flange is loose or damaged, the toilet will rock. And a rocking toilet will distort the wax ring and cause leaks. So be sure to scrape off the old wax ring and inspect the flange. Here are some solutions for broken, corroded or loose flanges:

Ear-type ring

Loose flanges are usually the result of wood rot. The flange screws simply won't hold in the soft, decayed subfloor. The best solution depends on the extent of the rot. If the rot is only under the flange, use an ear-type repair ring. The ears let you drive screws into firm wood farther away from the flange. Before you install this kind of ring, hold it up to the drain horn on the underside of the toilet. You may have to cut off a couple of ears to make it work with your toilet. If the rot extends well beyond the flange, you'll have to replace a section of the subfloor.

Repair ring

Plastic flanges often bend or break, but that's an easy fix. Just screw a stainless steel repair ring over the plastic flange with at least four 1-1/2-in. stainless steel screws. Consider doing this even if the plastic flange is in good shape—it's cheap insurance against future trouble. The repair ring raises the flange by about 1/4 in. So before you install the ring, set it on the flange and set your toilet over it to make sure it fits.

Two-part repair ring

Steel flanges attached to plastic hubs can rust away. The easiest solution is a two-part ring that locks onto the plastic just like the old one. To cut away the old flange, use a hacksaw blade or an angle grinder with a metal-cutting wheel. The repair flange is available at some home centers. To buy online, search for "bay flange."

Repair flange

Cast iron flanges can break or corrode. If only the bolt slot is damaged, slip a repair bracket under the flange. If the flange is in bad shape, you can add a brass repair ring similar to the stainless steel ring shown above or install a plastic flange that slips inside. If necessary, break away the cast iron flange with a cold chisel. Home centers carry one or two slip-in flanges. For a wider variety, search online for "replacement toilet flange."

REPAIR BRACKET

Eliminate rocking with shims

A toilet that rocks on an uneven floor will eventually break the wax ring seal and leak. So check for wobbles after you've set the toilet in place and loosely tightened the nuts. For slight wobbles, slip coins or stainless steel washers into the gaps under the toilet. Don't use regular steel washers, which might rust and stain the floor. For larger gaps, use shims. There are plastic shims made especially for toilets, but plastic construction shims like the ones shown here work just as well. When you've eliminated the wobble, tighten the nuts, cut off the shims and caulk around the toilet base. A toilet set on thick vinyl flooring can loosen as the vinyl compresses. In that case, just retighten the nuts a few days after installation.

Squish the wax ring with your own weight

When you set the toilet in place, you have to squish the wax ring until the toilet settles to the floor. DON'T force the toilet down by tightening the nuts on the toilet bolts—that might crack the porcelain base. Instead, sit on the toilet backward with your weight centered over the wax ring. Then wiggle your bottom like a belly dancer until the toilet reaches the floor. But don't overdo it. You want to drive the toilet straight down with minimal twisting or shifting of it from side to side. When the toilet reaches the floor, snug down the toilet bolt nuts.

Don't overtighten the water connections

Do yourself a favor and buy a flexible water supply line. They're a lot easier to install than stiff metal or plastic tubing. Be sure to get one that's covered with stainless steel mesh. For a good seal, hold the hose so it aims straight into the shutoff or fill valve while you're screwing on the connectors. Make them hand-tight, then add another quarter turn with pliers. Connections that are too tight can actually cause leaks or spin the fill valve inside the tank. Check for leaks and tighten them a bit more if needed.

Make life easier with 3-way switches

The simple technique for adding a second switch to that kitchen or stairway light

ired of having to walk up a flight of stairs or across the room to turn on a light? The solution is to add a second switch in a convenient location. No more extra trips across the room or fumbling up a dark stairway.

Controlling a light from two switches is a bit more complicated than first meets the eye, especially if you're dealing with finished walls. The key ingredient is a special type of switch called a "three-way" switch. You'll need two of them, one to replace the existing switch and another for the new switch location. With these, you'll have the convenience of turning a light on and off from two spots.

In this article, we'll show you how to run a new electrical cable and connect the two switches. We'll also tell you how to resolve the most common complication—replacing an undersized electrical box so your work is safe and conforms to the electrical code.

While this project isn't difficult, it does require basic electrical skills: running cable correctly and making solid wiring connections. If you don't have wiring experience or if you get in over your head, don't hesitate to call in a licensed electrician. Apply for an electrical permit at your local inspections department before starting so an electrical inspector can check your work.

If your wall framing is open (an unfinished basement or garage, for example), you can easily run the new cable and

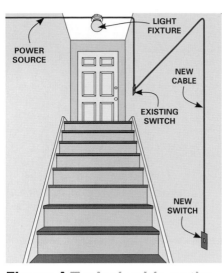

Figure A Typical cable paths

To add a second switch, find the easiest way to run a new cable from the existing switch to the best second switch position.

complete this job in only two hours. However, if the cable has to run through closed walls, allow several more hours. In addition to standard tools, you may need a "fish tape" to pull wire in closed walls. Also, if you don't have a voltage detector, buy one so you can check for live wires and avoid hazardous shocks. You can find them at a home center or hardware store.

Plan the wire path

To start, decide where you want the second switch. You'll run cable from the existing switch to this new switch location, so look for the most accessible path between the two (Figure A).

If possible, start at one switch location, run the cable straight up through the stud cavity in the wall to the attic, then come back down through the wall to the second switch. Or feed the cable down into the basement or crawl space, then come back up. If neither option works for your situation, you may have to run cable horizontally through the walls or through the ceiling. This takes extra effort because you have to cut into, and later repair, finished surfaces. Avoid exterior walls, where you'll run into obstacles such as windows, doors and insulation.

If you can't find an unobstructed path for the cable, move the new switch location.

Once you decide on a path, measure the amount of cable you need, then add 10 ft. so you'll have plenty to work with. It's better to waste a couple of feet than to come up short!

You'll also need a wire stripper, 14-3 or 12-3 cable (match existing wire gauge), two three-way switches and two remodeling boxes.

Prep the switch locations

Shut off power to the existing switch, unscrew it from the electrical box and pull

CAUTION: Turn off power at the main circuit breaker panel before unhooking the existing switch, then check the wires with a voltage detector to verify that the power is off.

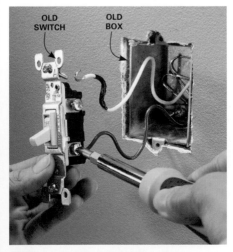

1 Remove the cover plate to the existing switch (the power is off). Then unscrew and remove the switch. Cut the electrical box loose and remove it.

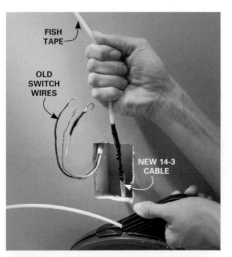

2 Cut a hole for the second switch box. Drill holes as needed in the framing and fish a new cable through the wall back to the old switch position.

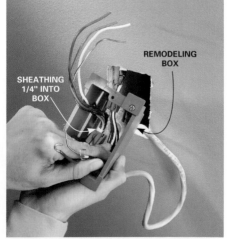

3 Insert the cables into a remodeling box from the back side at each box location. Pull the cables from the front as you push the boxes back into the wall.

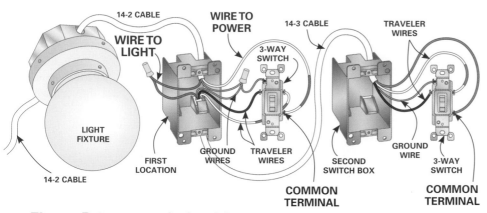

14-2 CABLE · WIRE TO POWER · WIRE TO LIGHT · 14-3 CABLE · TRAVELER WIRES · 3-WAY SWITCH · LIGHT FIXTURE · FIRST LOCATION · GROUND WIRES · TRAVELER WIRES · 14-2 CABLE · SECOND SWITCH BOX · GROUND WIRE · 3-WAY SWITCH · COMMON TERMINAL · COMMON TERMINAL

Figure B 3-way switch wiring

The key to wiring two three-way switches is to run the two wires that were originally connected to the old switch (Photo 1) to the "common" terminals. The "travelers" can go to either terminal.

the switch out of the box. Avoid touching the screw terminals until you confirm that the power is off with your voltage detector. If the detector lights up, then the power is still on. Find the circuit breaker (or fuse) that shuts it off.

Unhook the wires to the switch (Photo 1). In some cases, the existing electrical box will be too small to contain the additional wires and connectors needed for the three-way switch (see "Sizing the Box," at right, to find out). You'll have to replace the old box with a remodeling box anyway so you can pull in the new cable (Photo 3). A remodeling box has clamps that secure the cable to the box. You can mount it solidly in drywall without cutting open the wall.

Label and unhook any wire connections that are inside the existing box (wires that weren't connected to the switch). Then

unscrew the grounding screw and cable clamps (if any) in the box. Slip a hacksaw blade between the old box and the wall stud and cut the nails. (You may have to pry the box away from the stud slightly to create space for the blade.) Saw with short strokes to avoid damaging the drywall on the other side of the wall.

You'll probably have to enlarge the wall opening slightly for the new box. Simply use the new box as a pattern, trace around it on the wall, and enlarge it with a drywall saw. Don't cut the hole too large; you want a tight fit.

Next, fine-tune the position for the second switch. Use a stud finder to find potential obstacles, such as framing. If possible, keep the second switch the same height off the floor as the first switch. Trace an outline of the box on the wall,

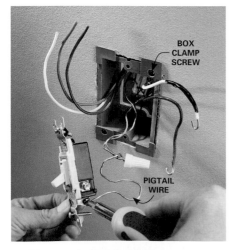

BOX CLAMP SCREW · PIGTAIL WIRE

4 Clamp the first electrical box to the wall. Connect a three-way switch, the ground wires and all other wires following Figure B.

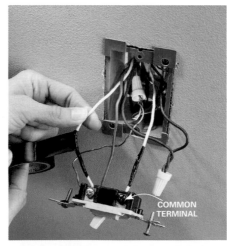

COMMON TERMINAL

5 Wrap the second white wire with black tape to show that it acts as a hot wire. Fold the wires back into the box and screw the switch into place.

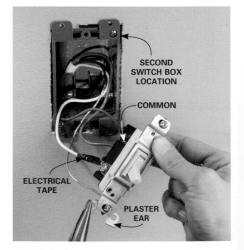

SECOND SWITCH BOX LOCATION · COMMON · ELECTRICAL TAPE · PLASTER EAR

6 Clamp the second electrical box to the wall and wire a three-way switch, following Figure B. Snap off the plaster ears and install the switch.

then cut the opening with a drywall saw. Don't mount the new boxes until you run the new cable.

Run 14-3 cable between the switches

We won't go into the details of running the cable, because each situation is different. But if the walls are open, your job is easy. Drill a 3/4-in. hole into the center of each stud between the box locations and run 14-3 cable from one box opening to the other. If you're going up through an attic or down through an open basement, drill through the center of the wall plates (top and bottom framing members).

If you can't go up or down, you may have to run the cable horizontally through finished walls. If so, cut a 3-1/4-in. by 5-in. slot into the drywall at each stud, notch the studs, fish the cable though the wall, leaving at least 18 in. of cable projecting from each opening, then tuck it into the stud notches. Cover the notch and cable with special nail guards and patch the drywall holes.

Strip 12 in. of sheathing off the ends of the new cable. Insert the cable into the electrical boxes from the back side (Photo 3). It's easier to push cable through the back than to pull it from the front. The first switch location has an existing 14-2 cable running to the light. Wrap the cable with electrical tape where the sheathing ends to help it slide into the box.

Pull the cables from the front as you slide the box into the wall opening. Pull the cable at an angle that minimizes pressure on the plastic cable clamp in the box. Otherwise, the sheathing could snag or the clamp could break. The cable sheathing should extend 1/4 in. into the box (the clamps should push against the sheathing and not the wire; see Photo 6) and make sure the wires extend at least 3 in. past the outside edge of the box when the box flanges are snug against the wall.

Tighten the screws at the top and bottom of the box to clamp it into place.

Wire the switches

Strip 3/4 in. of insulation from the end of each wire, then connect the wires following Figure B and Photo 5. The black electrical tape on the white wire indicates that it's a hot rather than a neutral. For secure connections, hook the ends with needle-nose pliers before placing them under the screw terminals (Photo 4). Make sure the wire ends face clockwise around the screw for better clamping strength.

Clip the plaster ears off the switches so they'll fit tight on the remodeling box (Photo 6). Gently fold any excess wire into the boxes, then screw the switches into place. Be careful not to apply so much pressure that you loosen the box.

Install the cover plates, then turn on the power. Ideally, both toggles should be in the up or down position when the light is off. If necessary, remove the second switch, rotate it 180 degrees in the box, then reattach it so the two toggle positions are coordinated.

Extra wires in the box

You might find two 14-2 cables in the existing electrical box instead of the one we show in Photo 1. There may also be other cables present. Don't worry. Regardless of what you find in the existing box, the wiring for the three-way switches will not change.

You only need to focus on the two wires connected to the existing switch. Keep the other connections the same, even if you have to disconnect them when you change to a larger box.

The two wires you unhook from the old switch and the three wires you'll add from the new 14-3 cable are the only wires you need to work with.

Key wiring components: 3-way switches and 14-3 cable

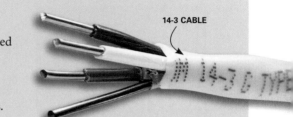

Three-way switches are always installed in pairs to control a light from two locations. The switches have three hot screw terminals—one "common" and two "travelers"—and a grounding terminal. The position of the screws varies by manufacturer, but the common terminal is always a different color than the other two hot terminals. Unlike other switches, you won't see "On" and "Off" markings on the toggle, since either switch can control the light.

You'll find 14-3 cable at any home center or hardware store. If the circuit breaker is 20 amps rather than 15 or the existing wire is 12 gauge, use size 12-3 cable.

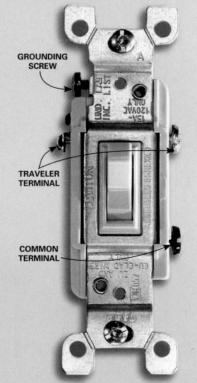

Add a faucet anywhere in your yard

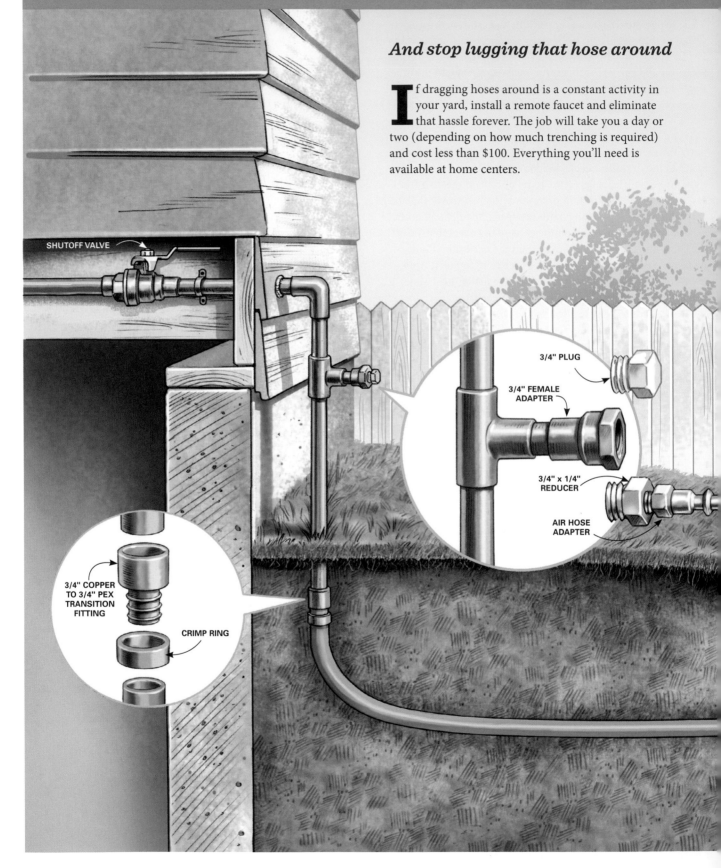

And stop lugging that hose around

If dragging hoses around is a constant activity in your yard, install a remote faucet and eliminate that hassle forever. The job will take you a day or two (depending on how much trenching is required) and cost less than $100. Everything you'll need is available at home centers.

SHUTOFF VALVE

3/4" PLUG

3/4" FEMALE ADAPTER

3/4" x 1/4" REDUCER

AIR HOSE ADAPTER

3/4" COPPER TO 3/4" PEX TRANSITION FITTING

CRIMP RING

The inside connection

To get the best flow rate at the garden, tap into an interior 3/4-in. cold water line. If you can't find one that's convenient, tap into a 1/2-in. line instead (you'll just get a slightly lower flow rate). If you have a water softener, tap into a water line before the softener.

The trench

Call 811 a few days before you dig so the utility companies can locate buried pipes and cables in your yard. You only have to bury the water line about 6 in. deep. If you're trenching in hard clay or rocky soil, that's about as deep as you'll want to go. If you're working in soft soil, it's smart to go at least 12 in. deep to reduce the risk of future damage. At any depth, you can easily protect the water line from shovel attacks: Cover the tubing with a couple of inches of soil, then pour in about 2 in. of dry concrete mix before backfilling the trench. Soil moisture will harden the concrete.

The pipeline

Copper pipe is best for the exposed plumbing at the house, but PEX tubing is best for underground. It's a lot cheaper than copper and it's easier to install than CPVC plastic. With PEX, you can make a continuous run from your house and make turns without installing a single fitting. Plus, PEX tolerates mild freezing better than either CPVC or copper (in case you're late blowing out the line). However, you'll have to invest about $50 in a 3/4-in. PEX crimping tool. If you don't want to shell out the cash, use CPVC.

The blow-out system

If you live in a freeze zone, you'll have to blow out the system before the first hard freeze. It's easy to do with a home air compressor, but you'll have to install the components now (instead of during a snowstorm).

At the house, splice in a tee and a threaded female 3/4-in. adapter, and cap it with a plug. That's where you'll connect your compressed-air line.

At the garden, install a blow-out valve (a ball valve is best) below grade in a gravel pit. Use a sprinkler system

valve box to cover it. Before the first freeze, close the shutoff valve and unscrew the plug. Next, screw in a standard air hose fitting and a reducer and connect your air hose. Out at the faucet, open both the faucet and the blow-out valve and let the water drain. Then, close just the faucet and blow out any remaining water with your compressor. Finally, close the blow-out valve and replug the blow-out fitting back at the house.

The post and faucet

We cut a length of hollow PVC fence post to mount the faucet, but you can build your own post out of any material. Make sure the PEX runs inside it to protect it from sunlight—UV rays reduce its life. Set the post at least 18 in. deep. Screw the sill cock flange to the post and install a screw-on backflow preventer. Note: Check with your local plumbing inspector for backflow prevention requirements in your area.

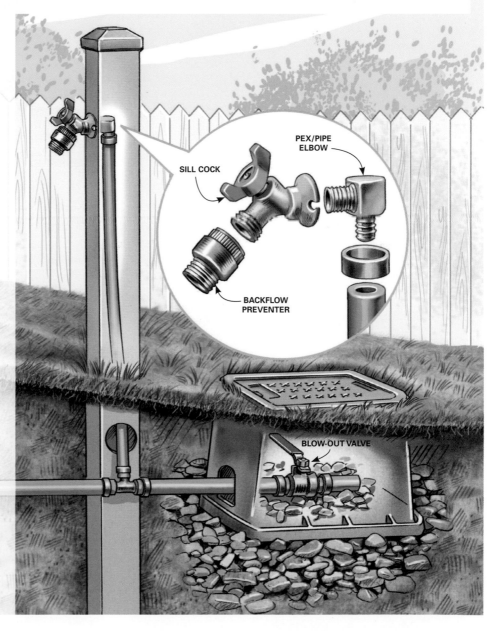

SILL COCK

PEX/PIPE ELBOW

BACKFLOW PREVENTER

BLOW-OUT VALVE

Add an outdoor outlet

5 ways to get power where you need it

Wiring a new outdoor outlet isn't complicated. But getting wire to the right spot—without tearing into walls—can be a huge challenge. In this article, we'll help you choose the best strategies for locating and powering your new outlet. We'll show you some of the different wiring techniques you can use to provide power to your new outlet and tell you the pros and cons of each. As with any electrical project, before starting, make sure to talk to your local electrical inspector to find out what permits and inspections are required.

Run cable from the basement or crawl space

The rim joist is the wide board that rests on the foundation and supports the exterior walls. If your basement ceiling is unfinished, installing an outlet on the rim joist is a simple project. But there are a few things to watch out for.

If you want to put the outlet on the rim joist that runs parallel to the floor joists, make sure you can reach into the space from the basement. Sometimes the joists are too close together to allow easy access. If you want to add the outlet to the rim joist that runs perpendicular to the floor joists, make sure the outlet is near the center of a joist space so you aren't drilling into the end of a floor joist. Use a long 1/8-in. drill bit or a section of stiff clothes hanger to drill a locator hole in your desired spot. Then you can see from inside whether the spot you've chosen is easily accessible. You'll probably have to remove insulation, and in older houses even pry out concrete or rubble, to get good access to the rim joist near the new outlet.

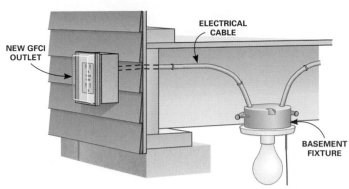

Through the rim joist. If you have a crawl space or an unfinished basement, this is the best way to go. It's easy and your choice of power source and outlet location is unlimited.

From the rim joist, it's usually easy to run the new cable to the circuit breaker panel or to an existing basement lighting circuit. If the circuit is in an unfinished basement or crawl space, you don't have to add AFCI protection (arc fault circuit interruptor—see p.199).

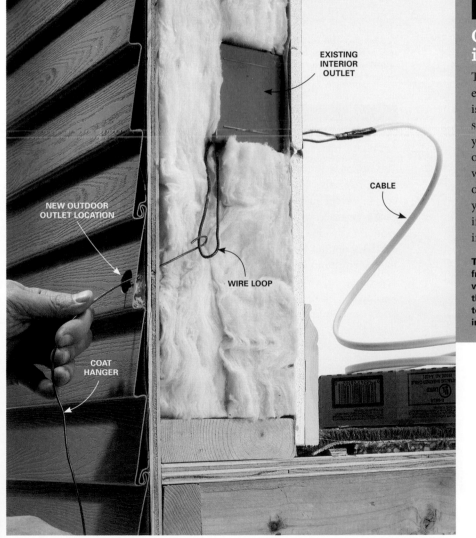

Connect to an interior outlet

This option is one of the easiest, especially if you don't have an unfinished basement or crawl space. You simply find a spot on the outside of your house that lines up with an outlet on the inside. Then you can fish new wires from the interior outlet to the one outside. But keep in mind that you may have to add AFCI protection if it doesn't exist. Ask your electrical inspector to be sure.

Through the wall. You can run wiring from an interior outlet without tearing up walls. But your options are limited with this approach: Your exterior outlet has to be within a few inches of an existing interior outlet.

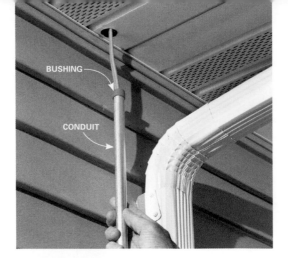

Strategy 3

Run a cable from the attic

If you don't have a basement or crawl space, this is a good option for getting power to an exterior outlet without fishing wires through the wall. Basically, you run UF cable through a hole in the soffit and through the attic to your power source, leaving enough cable to reach the new outdoor outlet plus an extra foot. Then you slide the conduit, with bushing, over the cable until the conduit extends a few inches into the soffit. To finish, connect the box to the conduit, add straps and wire the new outlet. Insulation and the cramped space can make getting wire through the attic a nasty job. Consider this option as a last resort.

Here are a few tips for running the cable:

- Choose a spot for the outlet that's alongside a downspout or exterior trim where the vertical conduit will be less conspicuous.
- Use UF (underground feeder) cable, not regular NM (nonmetallic).
- Connect the conduit to the Bell box with a weatherproof compression fitting, not a setscrew-type conduit connector.
- Install a bushing on the top of the conduit sleeve to protect the cable from the sharp edge of the conduit.

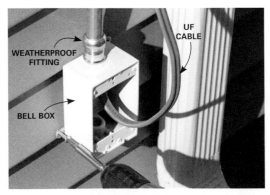

Down from the attic. If other options aren't available, you can run UF cable through the attic and down through a sleeve on the wall to your new outlet.

Strategy 4

Run conduit from an existing outlet

If you have an existing exterior outlet and don't mind the look of surface-mounted conduit, this is a good option for adding an outlet. If your existing outlet is surface mounted, you can simply remove one of the knockouts in the weatherproof box and connect your conduit with a weatherproof fitting. But if your outlet is recessed, you'll have to add a weatherproof box extension to allow for a conduit connection. Use an LB fitting to turn a corner with conduit.

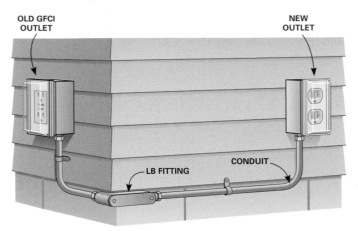

Tap into another outlet. Extending conduit from an existing outlet is a great way to add another outlet without running new cable through walls, basements or attics. You can run the conduit under a course of siding or near the ground to make it less conspicuous.

Strategy 5

Run underground cable from an existing outlet

This option is similar to No. 4 above, but rather than run the conduit on the surface of your house, you can run it underground to the new outlet. You also have options for handling the underground wiring, depending on how deep you want to dig. The easiest method doesn't require running conduit underground. Instead it uses UF cable buried 12 in. deep.

There are a few caveats, though. The cable must be protected by a GFCI. If the existing outlet isn't GFCI protected, simply replace it with a GFCI outlet. Also, you must protect the cable with a plastic or metal conduit sleeve from the outlet boxes to a depth of 12 in. below the surface of the ground. You can use this same method to run wiring to a post in your yard.

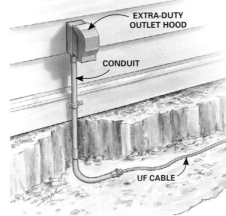

Run power underground. If you don't want to run exposed conduit, you can run power underground instead. A 12-in.-deep trench is all you need for UF cable.

Consider a new circuit

It may seem like overkill to run a whole new circuit to power just one outlet, but a new circuit has several advantages. First, you can be sure that the entire capacity of the circuit is available at the outlet. If you're planning to operate power tools or lawn equipment, this is a big advantage. In fact, for the additional cost of 12-gauge wire, you can run a 20-amp circuit with plenty of power for practically any tool you want to use. With a new circuit, you don't need to calculate the load on the circuit or worry about overcrowding an existing box.

Of course, a new circuit requires running a new cable all the way from your outdoor outlet to the electrical panel, which may be difficult in some situations. And when you get to the main electrical panel, you'll have to connect the wires for the new circuit to a new circuit breaker in the box, a job best left to a licensed electrician unless you're an experienced DIYer.

NEW CIRCUIT BREAKER

Add a circuit. Running a cable from your new outlet to the circuit breaker box and connecting it to a new circuit breaker is a good alternative to connecting to an existing circuit.

Connecting to an existing circuit

Using an existing circuit to provide power to your new outlet is a logical choice, but there are several things to consider. First, the National Electrical Code requires that any new outlets in living areas be protected by an AFCI (arc fault circuit interrupter). Interpretation and enforcement of this code is largely up to the local electrical inspector or code authority, so check with your inspector before connecting to any existing circuits. You may be able to simply add an AFCI-protected outlet, or you may have to add an AFCI circuit breaker.

Second, to avoid overloading the circuit, you should calculate the load on the circuit before adding an outlet to it. And finally, make sure to calculate the capacity of the box you intend to connect to. You may have to add a larger electrical box to accommodate all the wires.

Buy the right outlet

When you shop for an exterior outlet, first make sure it's a GFCI protected outlet like the one shown here. Then look for the labels WR (weather resistant) and TR (tamper resistant).

Three types of boxes

Standard outlet boxes

A standard plastic or metal box cut into the wall is a good option if you want to avoid a surface-mounted box. Finish the job by installing an in-use cover to protect receptacles from water while cords are plugged in.

Boxes with built-in covers

For a sleeker look, install a box with the in-use cover built in, like this InBox by Arlington Industries. There are many variations of this box to fit different situations. If your home center doesn't have them, you can buy one online.

Weatherproof surface-mount boxes

One advantage of a surface-mount box like this is that you only need to drill a hole for the cable or conduit to enter through the back. Plus, this type of box easily accommodates surface-mount conduit.

Install a sink and faucet

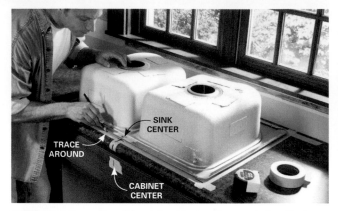

1 Mark the center of the sink cabinet on the countertop. Center the sink (or sink template) on the mark and set the front edge far enough back to fit inside the cabinet frame. Trace around the sink or template, then add an inner cutting line.

2 Drill a 1/2-in. starting hole in each corner and cut out the sink opening with a jigsaw and fine wood-cutting blade. Screw a strip of wood to the cutout to prevent it from falling in when you complete the cut.

Installing a new sink and faucet is one of the easiest things you can do to make a big impact on the way your kitchen looks and functions. With the wide selection of sinks and faucets available from home centers and on-line plumbing suppliers, you can choose features that match your cooking style (such as a deep sink for extra-large pots) and colors that complement your countertop and appliances. And most are designed for easy installation, even for a novice.

We chose a stainless steel sink for its classic looks and durability. The 8-in. deep bowls along with the arching faucet spout make it easily accommodate large pans. Both the sink and faucet were in stock at a local home center.

The most critical step in the sink installation is cutting an accurate hole in the countertop (if you don't have one already). Some basic carpentry and plumbing experience would be helpful, but by following our instructions, you'll be able to successfully complete the job in a day.

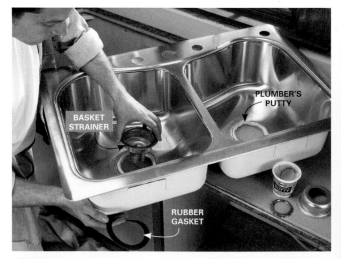

3 Roll plumber's putty into a pencil's-width rope and press it around each drain opening. Set the basket strainer into the opening and press it down.

4 Install the rubber washer, then the cardboard washer (if included). Assemble the remaining parts. Tighten the nuts with large slip-joint pliers.

LARGE SLIP-JOINT PLIERS

TIGHTEN NUT

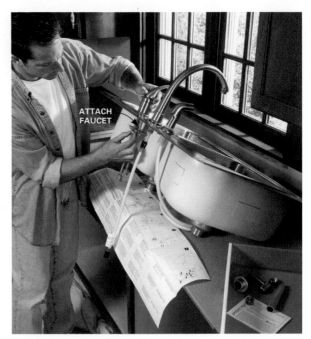

5 Install the faucet handles, spout and spray attachment before you set the sink. Follow the faucet manufacturer's instructions.

ATTACH FAUCET

6 Apply a bead of mildew-resistant tub-and-tile caulk to the countertop perimeter and lower the fully assembled sink into the opening.

CAULK DRIES CLEAR

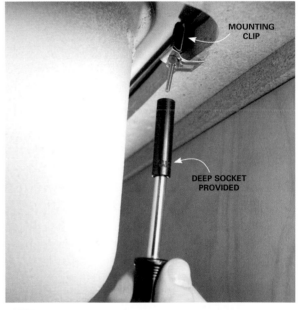

7 Snug up the sink clips according to the instructions. Be careful. Overtightening can dent the sink. Then wipe off excess caulk around the sink.

MOUNTING CLIP

DEEP SOCKET PROVIDED

In addition to basic hand tools, you'll need a drill and jigsaw to cut the hole, and wrenches and large slip-joint pliers to connect the plumbing. Any fine-tooth saw will work to cut the plastic pipe.

If you have chrome drain parts, we recommend replacing them with new plastic drains. Plastic is much easier to work with, seals better and doesn't corrode like metal. Buy the drain parts you need to fit your situation, including parts for a garbage disposer or dishwasher if you have them.

Use a template or the sink itself to mark the counter for cutting

Some sinks include a paper template that you cut out and use as a pattern. Others, like ours, instruct you to use the sink as a template, and then draw a second cutting line 1/2 in. inside the outline. The key is to locate the sink cutout just far enough back from the front of the countertop to fit inside the cabinet frame (usually about 2 in. back). This will then leave room behind the sink. In Photo 1, we show how to center the sink on the sink

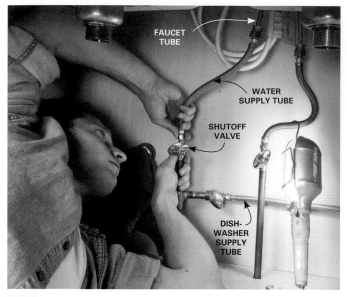

8 Connect the faucet to the shutoff valves with braided stainless steel supply tubes. Hold the valve with one wrench while tightening the nut with a second wrench.

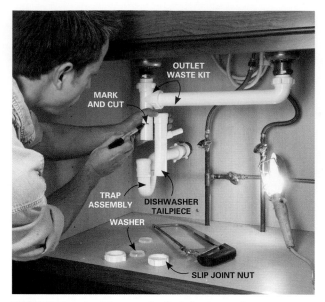

9 Mark and cut the new plastic drain parts and connect them with plastic nuts and washers. Hand-tighten the nuts. Run water in the sink and check for leaks. Tighten the connections if necessary.

cabinet. We put down masking tape to make the pencil lines more visible on the dark laminate and to protect the top from scratches (Photo 2).

Mark the cutout line according to the instructions and then saw out the hole. Drill 1/2-in. starting holes in each corner to make turning the corner easier. A jigsaw works well for cutting the hole. Just be sure to use a top-quality wood cutting blade and cover the bottom of the saw bed with tape to avoid marring the counter. Screw a scrap of wood to the cutout (Photo 2) to keep it from falling through as you complete the cut. Use a handsaw or oscillating saw to cut the back line if your jigsaw doesn't fit.

Install the basket strainers and faucet before setting the sink

The less time you spend on your back under the sink, the better, so install as much of the hardware as possible before setting the sink. Photos 3 – 5 show how. Follow the instructions included with your faucet. If you use the countertop as a workbench, protect the surface with a sheet of cardboard or a dropcloth.

The next step is to caulk around the opening and set the sink (Photo 6). Stainless steel sinks like ours are held in place by clips. These are included with the sink along with instructions on how they work. Tighten the clips from underneath (Photo 7). Cast iron sinks usually rest on the counter and are held in place by the caulk. Cast iron is heavy. You'll need a helper to set a cast iron sink in the hole. Clean up the caulk with a wet rag after you tighten the sink clips.

Complete the job by connecting the supply lines and hooking up the drains (Photos 8 and 9). Turn on the water and check for leaks. Most leaks are easy to fix by slightly tightening the supply line connections or slip-joint nut on the drain lines.

Parts and supplies

- Plumber's putty
- Tub-and-tile caulk
- Two basket strainer assemblies (only one if you're installing a disposer)

You'll need the following 1-1/2-in. plastic drain parts:

- One P-trap assembly
- One "end" or "center" outlet waste kit
- Two sink tailpieces—only one if you're installing a disposer. If you have a dishwasher and no disposer, get a special "dishwasher" tailpiece that has a tube to connect the dishwasher drain hose.
- One "disposer" waste arm if you have a disposer.
- Two flexible water supply tubes for kitchen sinks. Match the nuts on the ends to the threads on your faucet and shutoff valves. Also measure to determine the right lengths.

Light up a dark room

NONCONTACT VOLTAGE DETECTOR

WHITE NEUTRAL WIRES

1 **Test for power.** With the power turned off at the main electrical panel, unscrew the switch and pull it out. Turn the power back on and use a noncontact voltage detector to locate the hot wire.

I s your bathroom dimly lit? Do you have a hallway that could use more light? Here's how to add a wall-mounted light directly above a light switch.

This project requires an understanding of how a switch is wired and a few basic tools. You'll need a noncontact voltage detector, a wire-stripping tool, a screwdriver and a drywall saw. Then, with our instructions and a few hours' work, you'll be able to add a sconce to any room that has an appropriate switch.

Not all electrical boxes with a light switch in them contain the necessary ground, hot and neutral conductors. To find out, first shut off the power to the switch at the main electrical panel. Then remove the switch cover, and hold the noncontact voltage detector against the wires attached to the switch. This is to ensure the power is off before you remove the screws and pull the switch from the box.

To locate the required neutral, look for two or more white wires joined with a wire connector. If the only white wire entering the box is connected to the switch, then there's no neutral and you can't power a sconce from this box. If your switch wiring looks different

You can add a sconce above nearly any light switch in about three hours.

from what we show here and you don't understand how it's connected, put everything back together and abandon the project or call a licensed electrician.

There's one more important test you must complete while the power is still turned on. With the light switch turned off, hold the noncontact voltage detector against each of the wires connected to the switch. Take note of which wire causes the tester to light up. This is the hot wire and the one you'll connect to the "hot" side of the new double switch. If you're adding a separate single switch, this is the wire you'll use to power both switches. Now

CUTOUT FOR REMODELING BOX

2 **Cut the hole.** Trace around the box. Then draw a second line inside the first to indicate the cutout. Cut notches for clamps and other protrusions.

turn off the power to the switch at the main electrical panel. Back at the switch box, test once again to make sure the power is off and mark the hot wire with a wrap of black electrical tape.

Finally, make sure the existing switch box is large enough to accept more wires.

After you've determined that the existing switch box will work to power the new light, it's time to shop for the sconce and pick up the remodeling box, cable and electrical connectors you'll need. Choose the fixture first. Then pick a rectangular or round remodeling box that is small enough to be covered by the light fixture canopy. You'll need enough cable to reach from the switch to the box plus about 3 ft. Match the cable, either 14-2 or 12-2, to the existing wire gauge. Fourteen-gauge wire is as thick as a dime and 12-gauge wire is as thick as a nickel.

Cut the hole and run the cable

Locate the studs. Then hold the fixture against the wall somewhere between the studs to determine the best location and lightly mark the top and bottom of the canopy with a pencil. Center the remodeling box on the marks and mark the box cutout carefully, taking note of notches needed for the clamps and other protrusions. Cut out the hole (Photo 2). Next, punch out one of the knockouts in the top of the switch box and push the cable up to the hole (Photos 3 and 4). Prepare the remodeling box for mounting by stripping about 12 in. of sheathing from the cable and pushing it into the box through one of the cable entry points on the back. Make sure at least 1/4 in. of sheathing is visible inside the box. Leave some slack cable

inside the wall to allow some leeway when you connect the switch (Photo 5). Then fit the remodeling box into the hole and tighten the clamps.

Connect the fixture and switch

Photo 6 and Figure A show how to connect the light fixture. Start by mounting the fixture strap to the box. Strip the ends of the wires and connect them to the fixture.

At the switch, cut the cable about 12 in. beyond the box. Strip 8 in. of sheathing from the wires and push the cable through the knockout, leaving 1/4 in. or more sheathing visible inside the box. Trim the black and white wires to the same length as the wires they will connect to. Then strip the ends of the wires. Connect the white neutral wires with a wire connector. Connect the wires as shown in Figure A. Connect the hot wire to the side of the double switch that has the "jumper tab" between the terminals (Photo 7). Complete the project by mounting the light fixture, screwing the switch to the box, and installing the cover plate.

What if you have to go fish?

We're showing how to run a cable through the same stud space that contains the switch. Positioning the light in an adjacent stud space is more difficult. You may need to cut a channel in the wall, or run the wire up into the attic or down to the basement.

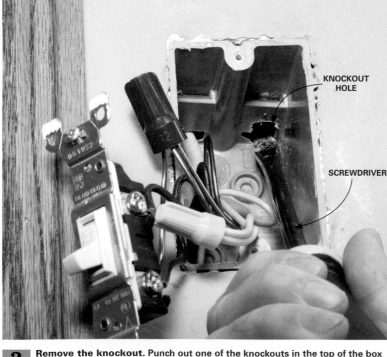

3 Remove the knockout. Punch out one of the knockouts in the top of the box with a screwdriver. You'll push the cable through this hole.

KNOCKOUT HOLE

SCREWDRIVER

4 Push in the cable. Push the cable through the knockout and up toward the hole. If you're lucky, it'll come into sight. Otherwise, reach through the hole to grab it.

NEW CABLE

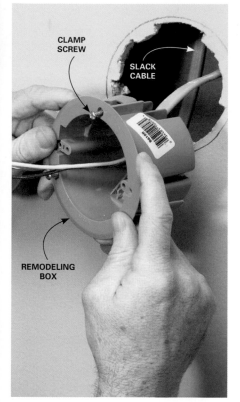

CLAMP SCREW

SLACK CABLE

REMODELING BOX

5 **Mount the box.** Strip the sheathing from about 12 in. of cable. Push the wires through the built-in wire clamp at the back of the box. Make sure at least 1/4 in. of sheathing is visible inside the box. Push the box into the hole and tighten the clamp screws.

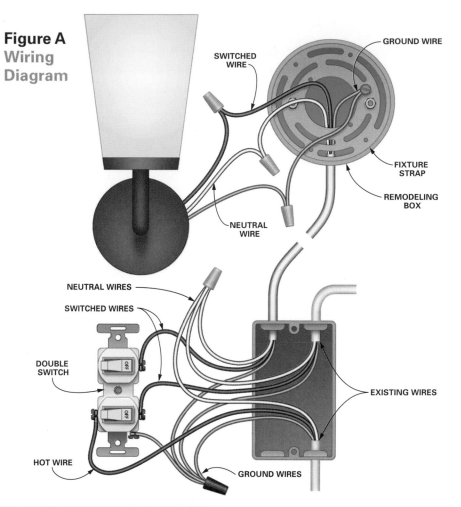

Figure A
Wiring Diagram

GROUND WIRE

SWITCHED WIRE

FIXTURE STRAP

REMODELING BOX

NEUTRAL WIRE

NEUTRAL WIRES

SWITCHED WIRES

DOUBLE SWITCH

OFF

OFF

HOT WIRE

EXISTING WIRES

GROUND WIRES

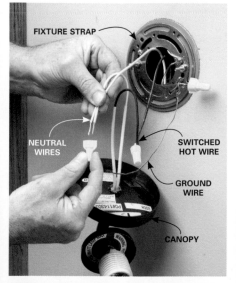

FIXTURE STRAP

NEUTRAL WIRES

SWITCHED HOT WIRE

GROUND WIRE

CANOPY

6 **Install the fixture.** Trim the black and white wires to 8 in., leaving the ground wire long. Strip the ends of the wires. Connect white to white, black to black and bare copper to bare copper. Loop the bare copper wire clockwise around the grounding screw on the fixture strap before connecting it to the fixture ground wire.

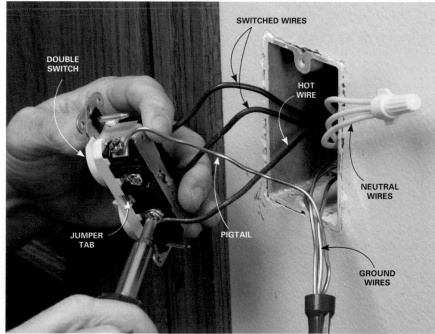

SWITCHED WIRES

DOUBLE SWITCH

HOT WIRE

NEUTRAL WIRES

JUMPER TAB

PIGTAIL

GROUND WIRES

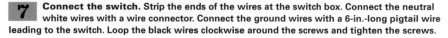

7 **Connect the switch.** Strip the ends of the wires at the switch box. Connect the neutral white wires with a wire connector. Connect the ground wires with a 6-in.-long pigtail wire leading to the switch. Loop the black wires clockwise around the screws and tighten the screws.

Reverse-osmosis water filter system

If you buy lots of bottled or filtered water or you're worried about your tap water, a reverse-osmosis water filter can be a good investment. For $150 to $300, it can provide 10 or more gallons of drinking water a day. Replacement filters will cost $100 to $200 annually.

Reverse-osmosis filters remove many pollutants and chemicals, separating them from the water and then flushing them into the drain line. The purified water is then fed to the storage tank or the spout on the sink. However, reverse-osmosis filters remove the minerals like calcium and magnesium that give water its taste, so try a gallon of filtered water (available at most supermarkets) and make sure you like it before buying a system.

First, hang the filter assembly on the back or side wall of the sink base (or in the basement close to the sink location) at the height specified in the instructions. Turn off both the cold and the hot water shutoffs, and then install (after the cold water shutoff) the tee or saddle valve included with the unit.

Cut the color-coded water supply line so that it's above the cabinet base and won't get kinked. Fasten the plastic tubing to the supply valve (Photo 1).

Shorten the supply and waste lines to the faucet to eliminate excess tubing, but don't cut the larger black waste line yet. Attach the lines to the fittings on the base of the faucet (Photo 2). The black waste lines feed through the base of the faucet to keep them above possible sink backups, but they have no connection to the supply.

Fasten the faucet to the sink, then install the drain-line adapter under the sink basket. Cut the waste line so that it flows downhill with no loops, then push it into the adapter (Photo 3).

Set the storage tank into place and install the final water line. Sterilize and fill the system according to the manufacturer's instructions (Photo 4).

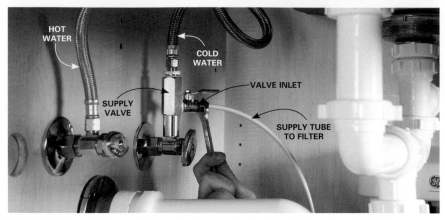

1 Push the plastic supply tube onto the supply valve, then tighten the nut a half turn past hand-tight.

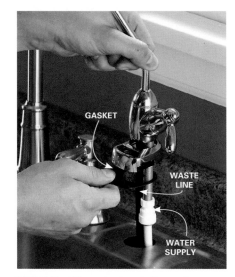

2 Feed the water supply line and the two waste lines up through the hole in the sink and through the gasket and faucet base, then attach them.

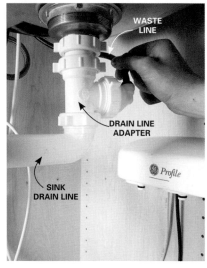

3 Install the drain line adapter just below the sink and above the discharge from the disposer and/or dishwasher.

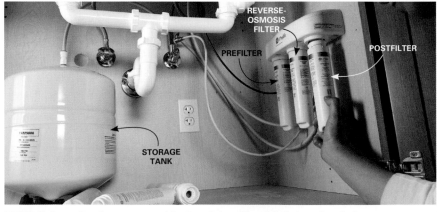

4 Before using the system, sanitize it and then fill and drain it to rinse it clean. Check all the fittings for leaks.

Light up your closet

CABLE FROM
POWER SOURCE

SWITCH
BOX

MOTION
SENSOR
SWITCH

24" FIXTURES

CABLE TO
LIGHTS

CABLE
CLAMP

The best way to add light to a dark closet is to mount a pair of fluorescent fixtures as low as possible on the wall over the door. This lights your clothes and shelving well and casts light into those shadowy areas along the floor.

Linear fluorescents have several advantages over conventional lightbulbs. The long tubes cast light more evenly over the length of the closet. The slim profile lets you position them more easily in tight places, like over the door. The plastic cover on the "under-cabinet" or "closet" style shown protects them from bumps. They don't require an electrical box, so installation is easier. And the National Electrical Code allows more flexibility for their placement. NEC rules prohibit any fluorescent fixture mounted within 6 in. of the front edge of a shelf (measure from an invisible vertical line extended directly above the shelf lip). Incandescent fixtures must be at least 12 in. away. That much clearance isn't possible in most closets.

TIP: Look for a light fixture that has several "knock-outs" (prepunched holes) to give you more options for connecting the new cable.

We recommend an under-cabinet–type fixture that uses a T-8 (1-in.-diameter) bulb. Buy the longest fixture that meets the electrical code and fits over the door. You can usually find the fixtures in 18-, 24- and 36-in. lengths at home centers. For maximum light, simply join two fixtures end to end or even stack them on top of each other if your space is especially narrow.

The best (and coolest!) way to control the light is with a motion detector mounted in the ceiling. The light will come on when you open the door or reach into the closet. And it will automatically switch off. Most under-cabinet fixtures have electronic ballasts, so buy a motion switch that works with electronic ballasts.

Otherwise, you can mount a standard switch in a box on the wall outside the closet, or easier yet, mount a pull chain switch on the fixture itself. To center a pull chain switch in the closet opening, join two fixtures with a short length of conduit when mounting them. You may have to drill a hole in the fixture to mount the switch. You can also order fixtures with pull chain switches online.

The biggest challenges are finding a power source and pulling a cable to the new fixture position. If you have an open area above the ceiling (attic shown here) or below the floor (basement, crawl space), you're in luck. You can generally find a nearby junction box with power and can run the

new cable from there. Then either drill down through the top plates or up through the bottom plate and "fish" in the new cable. If you don't have open access from below or above, you'll probably have to cut open a wall to reach a junction box with power. If possible, make that cut inside the closet; say, opposite the junction box to an outlet in another room. Then run the cable, making as few wall cutouts as possible to get the cable to the switch and fixture. If you keep all cutouts inside the closet, you can more easily hide the wall repairs.

The rules for closet lights are stringent. Be sure to apply for an electrical permit so an inspector will check your plan and your work.

Install a nonclogging dryer vent hood

Our appliance expert, Costas Stavrou, gets lots of service calls for dryers that take too long to dry a load of clothes. He always starts his diagnosis by checking for a clogged vent hood. If it's a flapper style, the lint builds up on the critter guard screen under the flap. On the louver style, lint builds up on the inside edge of the flaps. And, once airflow falls off, the lint settles in the

dryer vent pipe. The restricted airflow dramatically increases drying time.

Costas cleans the screens and louvers and then the vent pipe. But he recommends replacing a flapper- or louver-style vent with a hood that doesn't capture lint (search "dryer vent closure" or check at home centers). Here's how to replace your existing vent hood with that style.

Start by disconnecting the dryer vent

from the vent hood stub pipe. Then go outside and remove any siding trim pieces from around the vent hood. Next, remove the vent hood retaining screws and pull the vent hood and stub pipe out of the wall. Disconnect the hood from the stub pipe and toss the hood. Insert the old stub pipe into the new vent hood base and seal the connection with caulk. Then install the new vent hood base (Photo 1).

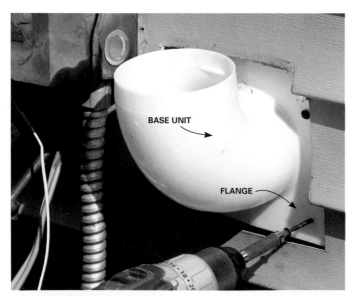

1 **Connect the base to the vent.** Lay a bead of outdoor caulk around the perimeter of the base flange. Slide the stub pipe through the hole in the wall until the base is flush with the house. Level and secure the base flange loosely with screws.

2 **Add the diverter.** Slide the diverter onto the base and secure to the house with screws. Then tighten the base screws and secure the trim.

Upgrade your laundry sink

OLD LAUNDRY SINK
SHUTOFF VALVE
OLD CHROME TRAP

1 Disconnect the plumbing and remove the screws that hold the sink to the wall.

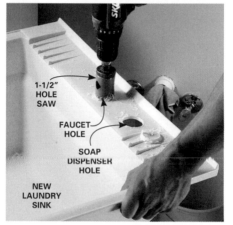

1-1/2" HOLE SAW
FAUCET HOLE
SOAP DISPENSER HOLE
NEW LAUNDRY SINK

2 Drill holes in the sink for the new faucet and soap dispenser.

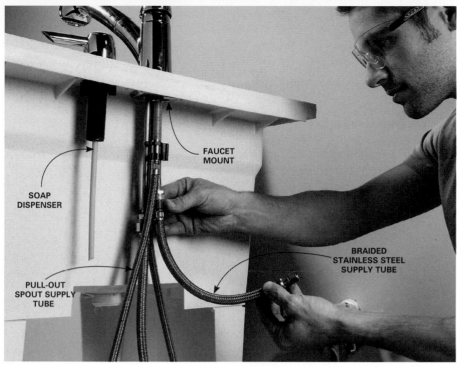

SOAP DISPENSER
FAUCET MOUNT
PULL-OUT SPOUT SUPPLY TUBE
BRAIDED STAINLESS STEEL SUPPLY TUBE

3 Mount the faucet and soap dispenser to the laundry sink according to the instructions with the faucet. Connect the braided supply tubes to the faucet.

Replacing a grungy old laundry sink is a simple Saturday morning project that will dramatically improve the look of your laundry room. And you can make your sink more functional too by upgrading from a typical laundry faucet to a kitchen sink faucet with a convenient sprayer and soap dispenser.

You'll find a selection of laundry sinks and kitchen faucets at home centers. Inspect your sink plumbing before you shop and make a list of the parts you'll need. If your old trap assembly is chrome plated, consider replacing it with plastic. Plastic traps are easier to install and maintain. Also, buy flexible braided stainless steel supply tubes. They simplify the task of connecting the

faucet to the water supply. We spent $175 for the sink, faucet, and new supply tubes and drain parts.

Start by closing the water valves that lead to the faucet and disconnecting the supply tubes. Put a small pail under the trap to catch the water, then remove the trap by unscrewing the large slip nuts (Photo 1). Finally, remove screws that may secure the laundry sink to the wall and then remove the sink.

Your new laundry sink may have punch-outs for a laundry faucet, but if you'll be installing a kitchen faucet, don't use them. Drill holes instead. Check your new faucet to determine the hole locations and mark them on the sink. Drill the holes with a 1-1/2-in. hole saw (Photo 2). To enlarge an existing hole, clamp a scrap of wood to the bottom of the sink deck, under the existing hole. Then mark the center of the new hole on the wood and drill the hole with a hole saw as you normally would. The wood scrap will keep the hole saw centered.

Mount the faucet and soap dispenser on the sink according to the manufacturer's

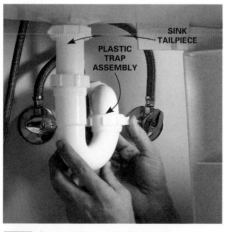

SINK TAILPIECE
PLASTIC TRAP ASSEMBLY

4 Connect the supply lines to the shutoff valves. Cut and install the new drain parts.

instructions (Photo 3). Then move the laundry sink into position (Photo 4). Hand-tighten the braided stainless supply tube nuts onto the valves and then tighten one more revolution to create a good seal. If you're using new plastic drain parts, use a hacksaw to cut the trap arm and tailpiece to fit. Secure the sink to the wall with adhesive caulk or screws.

Chapter Seven

YARD & GARDEN

Cheap and simple paths

Most books and articles on paths—including ours—show you how to build paths the hard way, by digging out tons of soil and bringing in tons of gravel to create a sturdy path that will last almost forever. And this backbreaking, costly method is definitely the best way to build a front walkway or other primary path.

But there are easier alternatives. If you want a more casual path and don't mind if it needs occasional upkeep or eventually becomes a bit uneven, consider these labor- and money-saving approaches. We'll cover the pros and cons of mulch and gravel, stepping-stone and planted paths and give you some building tips for each.

Mulch and gravel paths

Mulch and gravel are the cheapest path materials you can buy, and they make construction simple too. All you have to do is remove the sod, roll out landscape fabric and spread the mulch or gravel.

Mulch and gravel paths can be meandering, wood chip–covered trails or carefully planned designs, and range from casual to formal depending on the design and edging material. You can choose from a wide variety of loose materials including coarse bark, decorative mulch, washed stones and crushed gravel or shells.

Mulch

Bark, wood chips and other types of organic mulch make soft paths that blend well with natural settings. Since these path materials are lighter than stone, they're easier to haul and spread. Mulch is also a bit cheaper than gravel or stone pebbles. Remember, though, that organic paths decompose over time, so you'll have to rejuvenate them every two to five years with new material. Also, don't use bark, wood chips or mulch for paths that run through areas with poor drainage or that are wet. It'll lead to a soggy path.

You'll find bags of mulch at home centers, but for the best selection of organic materials for a path, check your local nursery or landscape supplier. Depending on how big your path is, it may be cheaper to have bulk material delivered than to buy bags. A 3-in.-deep layer of mulch for a 3-ft.-wide path will cost about $1.50 per linear foot. Call the public works department at your city hall or check with local tree trimming services. They often have piles of wood chips or mulch that are free for the hauling.

Gravel

For a path that's more formal or longer lasting than a mulch path, consider washed gravel, crushed stone or crushed shells. These materials last indefinitely and only need occasional weeding to look their best. If you want to run a wheelbarrow or lawn mower along the path, choose crushed stone rather than smooth pebbles. The jagged edges of crushed stone lock together to form a firm surface. Crushed stone is also less likely to get kicked out into the yard.

Gravel for paths is sold by type and size. Smaller stones, averaging under 1/2 in., are best for paths because they offer more comfort underfoot and pack together better. Visit your local nursery or landscape supply specialist to see what's available in your area. Gravel is usually sold by the ton. Measure the length and width of the path. Take these measurements to the supplier and ask for help

WOOD CHIPS

COCOA BEAN

CYPRESS BARK

CRUSHED, WASHED GRAVEL

CRUSHED LIMESTONE

PEA ROCK

figuring out the quantity of gravel you need. Unless your path is very short, it usually makes sense to have the material delivered. Gravel for a path 3 in. deep and 3 ft. wide will cost about $1.50 per linear foot.

Gravel paths do have a few limitations, though. The stones can get tracked into the house, so don't use them near entries. And gravel paths are a bad choice in areas where you have to shovel snow. The gravel can end up in your lawn or flower beds.

Borders and edging

Gravel or mulch paths require edging to keep the material from spreading out onto your lawn or flower bed. You can also add a border or an edge as a design element. Here are some common types of edging you can use:

- Plastic landscape edging (50¢ to $1 per linear foot) is cheap. And it's fast and easy to install. If you object to the look of the rounded top edge, hide it with a border of plants.
- Steel or aluminum edging ($2.50 to $3.50 per linear foot) forms a crisp edge that gives the path a neat appearance. It costs more than plastic, though, and is less forgiving on sloped terrain.
- Brick and stone borders ($3.50 to $5 per linear foot) are attractive and versatile, but they're more expensive and a lot more work to install.
- Concrete edging ($2.50 to $3.50) is less expensive than brick or stone but has the same advantages. Newer types that look like random pieces of tumbled stone are a great lower-cost alternative to a real stone border.
- Landscape timbers are an economical alternative to stone or brick borders. They're especially useful for building shallow steps on gradually sloping terrain.

METAL EDGING

BRICK

Stepping-stone paths

Stepping-stones are the fastest, easiest way to build a path. There's very little digging involved. And although the stone is heavy, a little goes a long way. Since there's distance between the stones, you don't have to worry about leveling them with one another. Stepping-stone paths also cost less because you'll cover more distance with less stone. Stones that are flat and about 18 in. across and 2 in. thick are ideal. Check your local landscape supplier or quarry to see what's available. If you're building a short stepping-stone path, you can usually pick the stones you want from the pallet or pile of stones on hand at the supplier. For longer paths, ask for help figuring the quantity and have the stone delivered. If you're lucky enough to live in an area with naturally occurring outcroppings of stone, you may find stepping-stones free for the hauling. Otherwise, expect to pay $3 to $6 per linear foot of path, plus delivery charges.

You can also make attractive stepping-stone paths using 12-in. square or round concrete patio blocks ($3 to $5 per linear foot of path). These are available in a wide selection of colors and textures from home centers, landscape suppliers and masonry dealers. Search online for "patio blocks" to see the variety.

Tips for building a stepping-stone path

- Arrange stones so the distance from the center of one to the center of the next one is 20 to 24 in.
- Set the stones in place and cut around them with a spade or rock saw. Then lift the stone and dig out the grass and a little soil.
- Spread a 1/2- to 1-in.-thick layer of sand under the stone if you want to make leveling the stones easier. Sand is easier to work with than soil. A 60-lb. bag of sand is enough for about four to six stones.
- Set the top of the stepping-stones about 1 in. above the soil level. This will give you a dry place to step while still allowing you to run a lawn mower over the path.

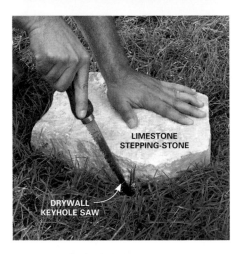

LIMESTONE
STEPPING-STONE

DRYWALL
KEYHOLE SAW

TROWEL

Planted paths

Including ground cover plants in your path makes a stone walkway easier in two ways: First, you can skip the thick, compacted gravel base underneath. That eliminates the back-breaking digging, plus the hauling and compacting of gravel. Without the solid base, the stones will shift and become uneven, but the plants will hide that. The second advantage is that you don't have to spend extra time laying the stones perfectly. The plants will hide wide gaps.

There are quite a few perennial plants that can withstand foot traffic and will grow between stones. Check with your local nursery to see what's available that will grow in your area. Here are some ground cover plants that can tolerate some foot traffic: Creeping Thyme, Blue Star Creeper, Brass Buttons, Creeping Mazus and Sedum.

Tips for building a planted path

- Arrange the stones along the walkway, leaving at least 4 in. between them for plants. Then cut along the edge of the stones with a flat spade to outline the path.
- Slice off a layer of sod and soil about 1-1/2 in. deep.
- Spread a 1/2-in. layer of sand. This will allow the stones to settle in slightly and keep them from rocking.
- Choose plants that will stand up to traffic and grow in the available light and soil type.
- Water the new plants frequently for the first few months until the plants are well established.
- Pull weeds and grass from between the stones every few weeks to prevent them from overrunning the plants.

Remote garden storage

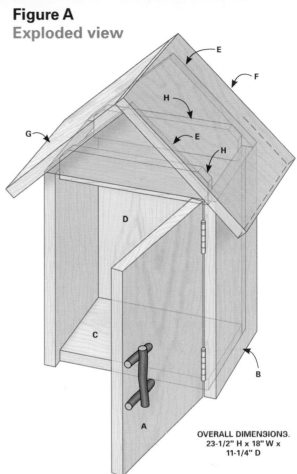

Figure A
Exploded view

OVERALL DIMENSIONS.
23-1/2" H x 18" W x
11-1/4" D

Keep tools and supplies right next to your garden with this small storage house. It only takes a few hours to build, and can be made with pine or rough-sawn cedar as shown here.

Cut flat, dry 1x12s to the sizes in the Cutting list. Nail and glue the sides, base and back together, then attach the rafters and gables.

Fasten the shorter roof panel on one side, leaving 7/8-in. overhangs in the front and back. Caulk the top edge, then nail the long panel on.

Cut the hinge mortises into the door and side, and hang the door. Stain or paint the wood inside and out to seal it. Use green branches for the handle, nailing them in place.

Make a rustic door handle from a tree branch. Nail the crosspieces to the door with brad nails, then notch the back of the handle so it sits flat on the crosspieces and nail it in place.

Cutting list

KEY	QTY.	SIZE & DESCRIPTION
A	1	11" x 15-3/4" door
B	2	9-1/2" x 15-7/8" sides
C	1	11-1/4" x 8" bottom
D	1	11-1/4" x 15-7/8" back
E	2	12-3/4" x 6-1/2" gables
F	1	11-1/4" x 12-3/4" long roof panel
G	1	11-1/4" x 12" short roof panel
H	2	11-1/4" x 2-1/2" rafters

Note: All dimensions are for 3/4"-thick wood.

Materials list

QTY.	ITEM
2	1x12 x 8' cedar or pine
1	4x4 x 8' post
1 pr.	2" x 2" mortise hinges
1	Magnetic catch
1 lb.	1-1/2" galvanized finish nails

Concrete garden bench

Make two simple forms, add three bags of concrete and you'll have a bench in two weekends!

In the mood to create something timeless and beautiful for your garden? Build this fun three-piece concrete bench a little at a time over the course of a week or so. You can give it a unique personal design and then sit and enjoy it for a lifetime.

All you have to do is build simple plywood forms, mix and pour your own concrete to fill them, and then install the bench in your favorite garden spot. You can build the plywood and hardboard forms over the weekend, buy three 80-lb. bags of dry concrete mix, pour the forms after a few days and wait for the magic. You can follow the plan exactly as shown to learn the process and then experiment with your own shapes and designs.

The concrete forms for this bench are not only cheap but also reusable. You'll spend about $40 for form material and hardware. You can make about five benches from a single set of forms before

they start to deteriorate. And with concrete at $4 per bag, this is one inexpensive project.

The bench details come from panels built into the forms that appear as recesses once the form is poured. You can leave the recesses empty to create lines and shadow or fill them with tile or stone to add color and texture. Note, however, that you can raise the cost substantially if you buy fancy tile or stone. We spent about $50 for the cut stone mortared into the top recess, but you can achieve similar results using bulk flat river stones, which are available from landscape suppliers for a fraction of the cost. You can also use ceramic tile, even broken tile, to create a unique personal design.

You can complete the project with ordinary carpentry tools, including a circular saw and a jigsaw. But a table saw is helpful to cut the thin 1-in.-wide strips of hardboard for the details in the form. Also, a wheelbarrow is handy for mixing the concrete, but if you don't have one, you can buy a tough plastic bin at a home center.

Figure A
Seat details

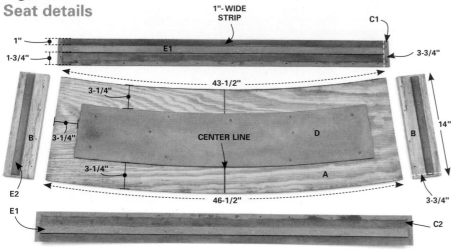

Figure B: Leg details

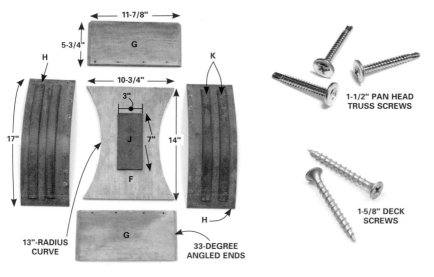

1-1/2" PAN HEAD TRUSS SCREWS

1-5/8" DECK SCREWS

11-7/8"

5-3/4"

10-3/4"

3"

7"

14"

17"

13"-RADIUS CURVE

33-DEGREE ANGLED ENDS

1"-WIDE STRIP

1"

1-3/4"

3-3/4"

43-1/2"

3-1/4"

3-1/4"

3-1/4"

CENTER LINE

14"

46-1/2"

3-3/4"

Materials list

ITEM	QTY.
3/4" plywood (2' x 4')	2
1/4" standard hardboard (2' x 4')	2
1-5/8" deck screws	2 lbs.
3/4" drywall screws	1 lb.
84" No. 4 rebar	1
80-lb. bags of 5,000-lb. concrete mix	3
Polyurethane varnish	1 qt.
Silicone spray	1 can
2" paint brush	1
Wood glue	1 pt.
1-1/2" truss screws	1 pkg.
1/2" wire nails	1 pkg.
PL Landscape Block Adhesive	1 tube

Cutting list

KEY	PCS.	SIZE & DESCRIPTION
A	1	3/4" x 24" x 48" plywood seat form base (scribe to size)
B	2	3/4" x 3-3/4" x 14" plywood seat (ends of the form)
C1	1	1/4" x 3-3/4" x 45" hardboard seat (side of the form)
C2	1	1/4" x 3-3/4" x 48" hardboard seat (side of the form)
D	1	1/4" x 10" x 42" hardboard inset (trim to size)
E1	2	1/4" x 1" x 46-1/2" hardboard strips (trim to size)
E2	2	1/4" x 1" x 14" hardboard strips (trim to size)
F	2	3/4" x 10-3/4" x 14" plywood leg (base of the form)
G	4	3/4" x 5-3/4" x 11-7/8" plywood leg (ends of the form)
H	4	1/4" x 5-3/4" x 17" hardboard leg (sides of the form)
J	2	1/4" x 3" x 7" hardboard inset
K	8	1/4" x 1" x 16" hardboard strips (trim to size)

Get the right stuff

Home centers sell 2 x 4-ft. panels of plywood and hardboard along with the full-size sheet goods (plywood and paneling). These small, easy-to-handle sheets are all you need for this project. Make sure to get standard hardboard, not tempered, for this project. Tempered hardboard has a very hard, slick

surface that won't make the tight bends you'll need for the curved pieces on the two leg forms.

Not all concrete mixes are the same. For this project, use only Quikrete or Sakrete 5,000-lb. concrete. If you can't find it at your home center or hardware store, check online for a dealer near you.

Ordinary twine works great for marking the curves

Find a large, wide-open space like a garage floor or a flat driveway to mark the curve onto the base of the seat form. Tape to your floor a large washer (Photo 1) with a length of twine tied to it. Draw a center line on the 2 x 4-ft. piece of 3/4-in.

plywood as shown. Align the plywood so the taut twine falls right over the center line. Be sure the far edge of the plywood is 12 ft. 6 in. from the washer. Tie the pencil to the twine at this distance and scribe a curve along the whole length of plywood, keeping the twine taut. Next, scribe another arc 14 in. shorter than this onto the plywood. Now look at the dimensions on Figure A, above, and mark the outer sides of the plywood. Cut out the shape with your jigsaw and sand any irregularities along the curve with your belt sander.

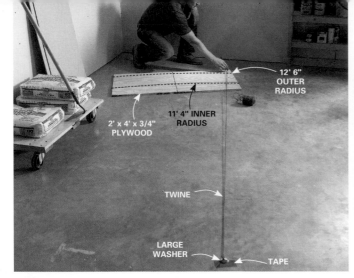

1 Using a pencil and twine, scribe the two concentric arcs onto a sheet of 2 x 4-ft. plywood to form the basic shape of the bench. The two arcs should be 14 in. apart.

Labels on image: 12' 6" OUTER RADIUS; 11' 4" INNER RADIUS; 2' x 4' x 3/4" PLYWOOD; TWINE; LARGE WASHER; TAPE

2 Screw 3/4-in. plywood ends (B) to the form base with 1-5/8-in. deck screws. Then cut strips of 1/4-in. standard hardboard, predrill pilot holes and screw them to the sides of the form base (A) and to the form ends (B). Use 1-1/2-in. truss screws.

Labels on image: B; A; C1; 3-3/4"; B; C2; 1/4" STANDARD HARDBOARD

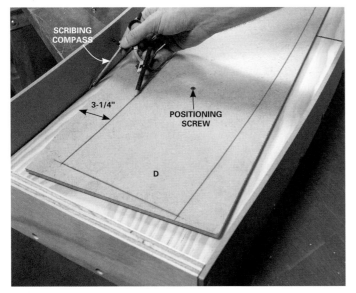

3 Cut a piece of 1/4-in. hardboard and screw it to the seat form with a pair of 3/4-in. screws. Then scribe the panel with a compass to mark an equal reveal on each side. Remove the panel, cut it to the line, then glue and screw it to the seat form base (A).

Labels on image: SCRIBING COMPASS; 3-1/4"; POSITIONING SCREW; D

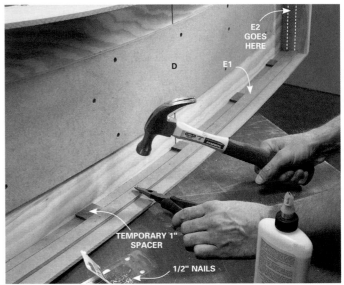

4 Rip 1-in.-wide strips of hardboard and glue and nail them to the middle of the form sides to form the edge recesses in the bench top. Use water-resistant glue.

Labels on image: E2 GOES HERE; D; E1; TEMPORARY 1" SPACER; 1/2" NAILS

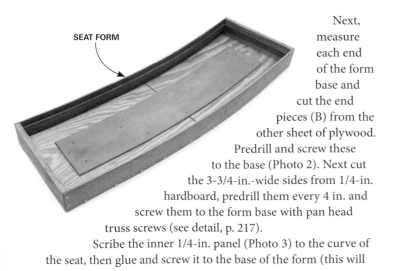

SEAT FORM

Next, measure each end of the form base and cut the end pieces (B) from the other sheet of plywood. Predrill and screw these to the base (Photo 2). Next cut the 3-3/4-in.-wide sides from 1/4-in. hardboard, predrill them every 4 in. and screw them to the form base with pan head truss screws (see detail, p. 217).

Scribe the inner 1/4-in. panel (Photo 3) to the curve of the seat, then glue and screw it to the base of the form (this will form a recess in the top of the bench once you pour the concrete). If you plan to make a deeper recess, use 3/8-in. plywood instead. This may work out better if you plan to use thicker tile or stone for your inlay. Be aware, however, that any panel thicker than 3/8 in. will make it tougher to remove the form from the concrete.

To finish the seat form, rip strips from 1/4-in. hardboard and then glue and nail them to the form sides with 1/2-in. wire nails, which are available at any hardware store (Photo 4).

Soak the hardboard for the leg forms in water overnight

Cut the pieces of 1/4-in. hardboard for the sides to the dimensions in the Cutting list. The lengths for the sides (H) are about 1 in. longer than needed, so it'll be easier to fasten them to the curved base bottom and the sides. You can trim them after assembly.

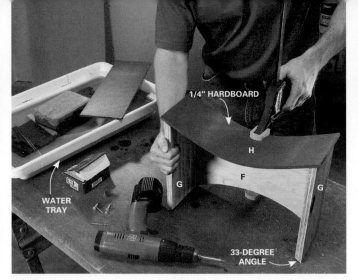

1/4" HARDBOARD

H

G   F   G

WATER
TRAY

33-DEGREE
ANGLE

5 Soak the leg form sides (H) and the strips (K) overnight. The next day, assemble a pair of leg forms. Clamp the center of the hardboard side and gently squeeze it to the curved base of the leg form. Then screw it into place with truss screws.

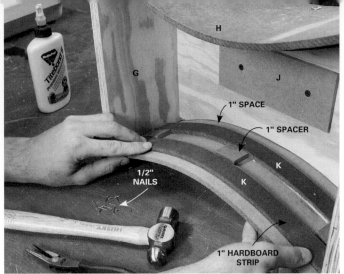

H

G

J

1" SPACE

1" SPACER

K

K

1/2"
NAILS

1" HARDBOARD
STRIP

6 Fit 1-in.-wide hardboard strips to the inside of the leg form to make recesses in the leg fronts and backs. Let the curved side pieces dry for two hours for better glue adhesion before installing strips. Tack them in place with 1/2-in. nails. Let the form and strips dry overnight, then disassemble.

POLYURETHANE

MINWAX
Polycr

7 Brush on two coats of polyurethane varnish or shellac to protect the insides of all the forms. It's best to take apart the form to get the entire surface.

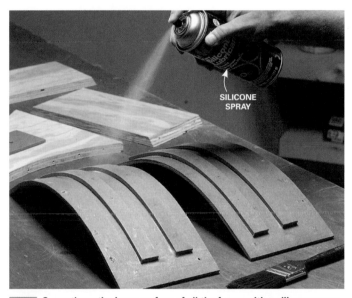

SILICONE
SPRAY

8 Spray the entire inner surface of all the forms with a silicone spray lubricant. When the lubricant beads up, brush it into an even layer with a paintbrush.

Soaking makes them flexible enough to conform to the 13-in.-radius arc in the leg form.

Before you assemble the form, cut the base (F) and ends (G) to the dimensions in Figure B, p. 217. Predrill and screw the sides to the base using 1-5/8-in. deck screws. You'll notice the angle cut on each end of G is about 33 degrees. You can cut this by setting your circular saw at a 33-degree bevel and then using a square as a guide against the foot of the saw to end-cut it square. Don't fuss about the 33-degree angle. If it's off by a couple of degrees either way, it'll still work out.

Grab the wet hardboard out of the soaking tank (a laundry tub works great) and set it onto the form (Photo 5). Gently squeeze the clamp onto the form until it bends into position. Then predrill and screw it every 1-1/2 in. along the curve. Work one screw at a time from the center out to keep the bottoms flush. Once you've fastened the long edge, screw the sides to the end pieces

(G). Check the end pieces with a framing square to make sure they're square to the base (F). Complete the other side and then the second leg form using the same method. Let the hardboard air-dry for about three hours before gluing and nailing the hardboard strips (K), as shown in Photo 6.

Remove the thin 1-in. hardboard strips (K) from the soaking tank. Cut them to length so they fit snugly into the corners against the ends (G). Next, glue the bottom and nail them into place as shown in Photo 6. Use the 1-in. spacers as shown to get the strips positioned properly. Let the strips and glue dry for several hours before the next step.

LEG
FORM

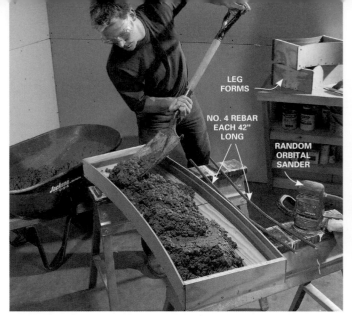

9 Mix the special concrete mix to the consistency of oatmeal. It should clump and settle a bit as you dump it into the form.

LEG FORMS

NO. 4 REBAR EACH 42" LONG

RANDOM ORBITAL SANDER

10 Bounce the forms a few times onto the tops of the sawhorses at each end to settle the concrete. Then hold a vibrating sander firmly along the entire perimeter of the forms and vibrate until you get air bubbles to appear (about two minutes).

AIR BUBBLES

SANDER USED AS VIBRATOR

11 Pound the rebar into the concrete as soon as you're finished vibrating it. Push it about 1-1/2 in. below the surface. You'll notice this fast-setting concrete getting stiff already.

NO. 4 REBAR

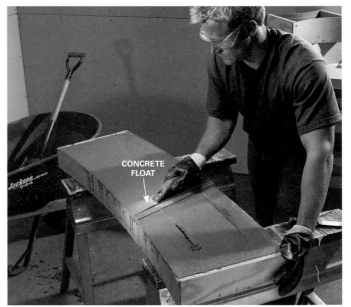

12 Float an even surface to the tops of the forms. Add a little concrete if necessary. Now wet the concrete left in the wheelbarrow and add the other bag, mix and pour the leg forms. Let it harden for two days.

CONCRETE FLOAT

Seal the forms before pouring concrete

When the forms are completely dry, label each piece and disassemble them. To help your forms release better later, ease the sharp inside edges with 100-grit sandpaper. Lay the pieces out on a workbench and brush two coats of waterborne polyurethane on the inside of all the forms. Let them dry for two hours.

Now you'll need to apply a lubricant to help release the forms from the hardened concrete. You can use silicone spray, vegetable oil or paste wax. Silicone spray was used here with good results. When you spray the silicone, it'll have a tendency to bead up on the polyurethane. To break the surface tension of the liquid, brush it after spraying until it smooths out into a uniform coat. Let the surface dry to the touch and then screw the forms together. Next cut two lengths of rebar to 42 in. and prebend them to follow the curve of the form. Set them aside.

Mix the concrete to a stiff consistency

Set your forms onto sawhorses as shown in Photo 9. This special concrete sets up a bit faster than normal, so cancel all appointments and avoid distractions. Mix two bags of concrete to a firm but fluid consistency. Shovel the concrete into the large seat form to about two-thirds full, then grab one end of the form and lift it

13 Lay the seat onto a pair of blocks, unscrew the sides and remove the forms piece by piece. The top is tricky to get off. To loosen it, gently pry it up, working your way around the form. Pull the top free and clean the forms for your next bench.

TOP OF BENCH

4" SCRAPER AS PRY BAR

14 Position the legs onto a solid patio or slab. Turn them in slightly to a pigeon-toed look and set the top onto the legs. Adjust the legs so the seat overhangs the legs about 6 in. on each side. Glue the legs to the top with landscape block adhesive.

STONE TILE

a few inches and drop it onto the sawhorse. Do this several times on each end to settle the concrete and work it into the form. Now fill the form and then use a float to level the top. Next load your vibrating sander or random orbital sander with 100-grit sandpaper and place it firmly on each side for about 30 seconds each. The vibration from the sander will bring all the trapped air bubbles to the top. Now, grab your rebar lengths and insert them into the form as shown in Photo 11. Tap the rebar into the mix about 1-1/2 in. deep with a stiff-blade scraper. When both rebar pieces are submerged, smooth the top again even with the top edge of the forms (Photo 12) and let the mix harden.

You'll have a bit of concrete left in your wheelbarrow. Dump the next bag right in with it, add water and mix it again. Fill the leg forms to the top in the same way, vibrate them with your sander and level the tops. Let the concrete set for two days before you continue.

Remove the forms

The concrete seat top inside the form is heavy. Carefully lift the seat form and place it on your workbench upside down with some scraps of wood beneath it to elevate it above the work top. Remove all the screws that hold the form pieces together. Remove the long hardboard sides first and then gently pry the ends away from the concrete.

The top piece of the seat form is the most challenging. Tap the stiff-blade scraper in between the top of the form and the concrete. Wiggle the blade back and forth, moving from corner to corner to coax the form free. Once the form is removed, use a concrete-sanding block to ease the edges (Photo 15).

To remove the forms on the leg pieces, start with the 3/4-in. plywood ends, then move to the flexible hardboard sides and gently pry, being careful not to force the form from the concrete. You may need to slide a screwdriver into the grooves of the recesses to pry out the strips.

15 Ease any sharp edges with an abrasive block, which is sold at tile stores and concrete suppliers. Work slowly and use a light touch.

ABRASIVE BLOCK

Finishing touches

You can now add tile or stone to your bench or leave it as is. To set up your bench, set the legs onto a level, stable base. The legs should be arranged about 6 in. in from the edge of the seat top and pigeon-toed slightly to follow the curve. Use landscape block adhesive to fasten the legs to the patio stones or other stable base. Then apply it to the tops of the legs to fasten the seat (Photo 14). Let it set up for a day before you use your bench.

Easy garden arch

A small project that makes a big impression in your backyard

Building an arch is one of the easiest ways to give your landscape a striking centerpiece. And this arch is easier than most. Made from just six parts, it can be built in less than a day—even if you're a rookie carpenter. The design is versatile, too: The arch can become a gateway in a fence, frame a walkway through a hedge or stand alone in your yard or garden. You can stain it for a rustic look or paint it for a more formal look.

Figure A
Garden arch

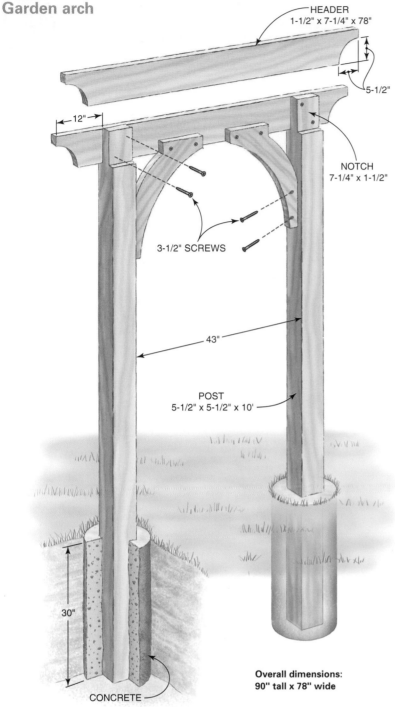

HEADER
1-1/2" x 7-1/4" x 78"

5-1/2"

12"

NOTCH
7-1/4" x 1-1/2"

3-1/2" SCREWS

43"

POST
5-1/2" x 5-1/2" x 10'

30"

CONCRETE

**Overall dimensions:
90" tall x 78" wide**

Materials list

ITEM	QTY.	
6x6 x 10' (posts)	2	Note: All measurements given on Figure A are for standard "surfaced" lumber. If you choose "rough-sawn" lumber, some measurements will change slightly because rough-sawn lumber dimensions vary.
2x8 x 8' (headers)	2	
2x10 x 8' (brackets)	1	
2x4 x 8' (stretcher, stakes, braces)	3	
Concrete mix (60-lb. bags)	3	
3" and 3-1/2" screws		

Money and materials

The total materials bill for our cedar arch was about $200. Built from pressure-treated lumber, it would cost about $100. Depending on where you live, you may have other choices of rot-resistant lumber available, such as cypress or redwood. If you choose treated lumber, you'll find everything you need for this project at home centers. If you choose another wood species, you may have to special-order lumber or visit a traditional lumberyard.

You'll need only standard tools like a drill, a circular saw and a jigsaw. Make sure your framing square is a standard model (16 x 24 in., with a longer leg that's 2 in. wide). If yours is an oddball, buy a standard version so you can easily mark out the brackets (see Photo 2). A few days before you dig the postholes, call 811 to have underground utility lines marked.

Cut the parts

To get started, cut notches in the tops of the beams (Photo 1). If you're using "rough-sawn" lumber, as shown here, you may have to change the length and depth of these notches to suit your 2x8 headers. (The dimensions of rough-sawn lumber vary.) Set the cutting depth of your circular saw to 1-1/2 in. to make the crosscuts for the notches. Then set your saw to full depth to make the other cuts.

Next cut the 2x8 headers to length and mark arcs at the ends as shown in Figure B. To mark the curves, use the bottom of a 5-gallon bucket or any circle that's 10 to 11 in. in diameter. Cut the curves with a jigsaw.

The curved brackets may look complicated, but they're easy to mark out since they're based on a standard framing square. After marking with the square (Photo 2), set a nail in your sawhorse 20 in. from the edge of the board. Carefully adjust the position of the board until both corner marks of the bracket are 24 in. from the nail. Then, holding

1 Notch the tops of the beams. Cut as deep as you can from both sides with a circular saw, then finish the cuts with a handsaw.

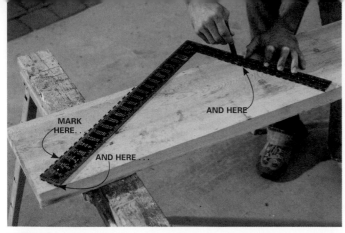

2 Mark out the brackets without fussy measurements or geometry—just align a framing square with the edges of a 2x10 and make three marks.

3 Draw perfect curves fast using a tape measure to guide your pencil. Cut out the bracket and use it as a pattern for the other bracket.

4 Screw through the posts and brackets into the header. That way, one header will have no visible screws. Screw through the second header into the posts.

5 Set the arch level and plumb before you pour concrete into the postholes. Wedge shims under the stretcher until the header is level, then plumb and brace the posts.

your pencil at the 24-in. mark on the tape, draw an arc. To draw the second arc, move your pencil to the 29-in. mark on the tape (Photo 3). Cut the straight edges of the brackets with a circular saw and the arcs with a jigsaw. If the curves turn out a bit wavy, smooth them with an orbital or belt sander. Don't be too fussy, though. Nobody will notice small imperfections.

Put it all together

Mark one header 12 in. from both ends and lay out the posts, aligned with the marks. Take measurements at the other end to make sure the posts are perfectly parallel. Drive 3-1/2-in. screws through the posts and into the header. At the tops of the brackets, drive 3-in. screws at a slight angle so they won't poke through the face of the header (Photo 4). Set 1-1/2-in.-thick blocks under the other ends of the

Figure B
Bracket detail

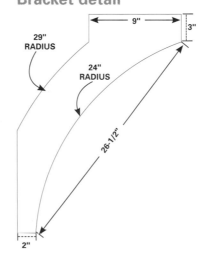

brackets. Then drive screws at an angle through the sides of the brackets and into the posts. Be sure to drill 1/8-in. pilot holes

so you don't split the brackets. Set the second header in place and screw it to the posts. Note: The brackets are not centered on the posts, so there's a 1-in. gap between the second header and the brackets.

Set it up

You'll set the arch posts into 10-in.-diameter holes 30 in. deep. But before you move the arch into place, screw on a temporary 2x4 "stretcher" 30 in. from the post bottoms. Then round up a helper or two and set the posts into the holes. Patiently level and plumb the arch, using stakes and 2x4s to brace it (Photo 5). Be careful not to nudge the posts out of position as you fill the holes with concrete. Let the concrete harden for at least four hours before you finish the wood. Brush on two coats of clear penetrating wood finish to deepen the color of the wood and repel moisture.

Mix-and-match planters

Build planters in a variety of styles—from one simple design

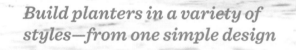

Building an attractive planter is easy with the method shown here. Each starts with a simple plywood box. Then you add a beveled cap, legs and siding to match your house, deck or patio. For extra durability and longevity, these planters are designed to accept standard size plastic liners to contain the moist soil.

The cost of the materials for the planters ranges from $50 to $80, depending on what you choose for siding. You can complete each one in a day. Two power tools—a table saw and a power miter saw—make this project much easier. Use the table saw to cut the bevel on the top cap and to rip the leg pieces to width. A power miter saw simplifies the task of getting tight-fitting miters on the top cap. You can also use it to make all the square cuts on the ends of legs and trim. Shop for the plastic liners first; if you can't find the exact size shown here, simply modify the planter dimensions to fit the ones you find. You'll find a wide variety at any home or garden center.

The core of each planter is a box of 3/4-in. CDX or BC plywood. Most home centers and lumberyards will sell you a partial sheet of plywood and cut it into easily manageable sizes for you to haul home. Cut plywood pieces to final size with a table saw, or clamp a straightedge to the plywood and cut it with your circular saw. Assemble the box with water-resistant wood glue and

Lap siding planter (see p. 228)

Cedar shingle planter (see p. 229)

6d galvanized nails (Photo 1). Add plywood braces inside the long planter to square the box and hold the long sides straight. The braces shown here are centered, but you can shift them down if they obstruct the liner (Photo 2). The other two planters don't need braces if you make sure they're square after you assemble them. Check with a framing square and add braces if they're needed.

Shown here is 5/4x6 (1 in. x 5-1/2 in. actual dimensions) cedar decking for the legs, but you can substitute other 5/4 decking if cedar isn't available.

First rip the deck boards to 5-1/4 in. to remove the rounded corners on one edge. Then run the squared edge against the table saw fence when you rip the 3-in.- and 2-in.-wide leg pieces. Cut the pieces to length and glue and nail them together with 8d galvanized casing nails (Photo 3). Sand the saw

Buy your liners first and adjust the planter dimensions if necessary.

marks from the board edges before you screw the assembled legs to the box.

Ripping the bevel on the 2x4 top cap may require you to remove the blade guard. If so, use extreme caution to keep your fingers well away from the blade. Make sure the blade is tilted away from the fence as shown in the photo. Mount a feather-board and use push sticks to complete the cut (Photo 5). Start the cut by pushing with your back hand while holding the board down with a push stick in your front hand. Keep a second push stick within easy reach. When your back hand gets to the rear edge of the table saw, pick up the second push stick and use it along with the front push stick to push the board clear past the saw blade. Keep your attention focused on the saw blade at all times. Shut off the saw and wait for the blade to stop before retrieving the beveled board.

Photo 6 shows how to assemble the top cap pieces into a frame that's easy to attach to the box. Start by gluing the miters and clamping one long side as shown. Then drill 1/8-in. pilot holes for the nails. Drive a pair of 8d galvanized casing nails from opposite sides at each corner to pin the miters together. Offset the nails slightly so they don't hit each other.

Cutting list

KEY	QTY.	SIZE & DESCRIPTION		KEY	QTY.	SIZE & DESCRIPTION
A	2	3/4" x 8" x 11-7/8" plywood ends		F	2	1-1/2" x 3-1/2" x 13-1/2" beveled cap
B	2	3/4" x 32" x 11-7/8" plywood sides		G	2	1-1/2" x 3-1/2" x 36" beveled cap
C	2	3/4" x 8" x 7-3/4" plywood braces		H	4	3/4" x 2-1/2" x 28-1/2" trim (cut to fit)
D	4	1" x 3" x 15" legs		J	4	3/4" x 2-1/2" x 6" trim (cut to fit)
E	4	1" x 2" x 15" legs		K	22	5/8" x 3-1/4" x 6-7/8" beaded boards

Figure A
Beaded board planter

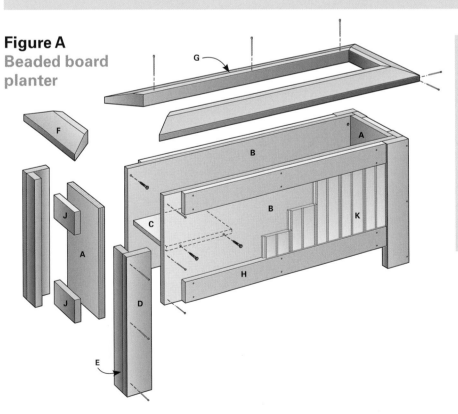

Materials list

QTY	ITEM
1	2' x 4' 3/4" CDX plywood
1	5/4x6 x 6' deck board
2	2x4 x 6' cedar or pine
2	1x3 x 6' cedar or pine
14'	5/8" x 3-1/2" beaded tongue-and-groove
	Water-resistant glue
	4d, 8d and 12d galvanized casing nails
	6d galvanized box nails
	1-1/4" deck screws
	Plastic liner (to fit 6-1/2" x 29" opening)

1 Cut the plywood sides to size and glue and nail the sides together. Use clamps to hold the sides upright.

6d GALVANIZED BOX NAILS

WATER-RESISTANT GLUE

2 Predrill screw clearance holes through the planter sides and screw in a plywood brace at each end. Center the brace.

1-1/4" DECK SCREWS

PLYWOOD BRACE

6"

3 Rip 5/4 decking material and cut it to length for the legs. Glue and nail a 3-in. piece to a 2-in. piece.

8d GALVANIZED CASING NAILS

D
E

PLANTER LEG

4 Set the plywood box on a flat surface and screw the leg assemblies to it. Make sure the legs are flush with the top of the planter box.

1-1/4" DECK SCREWS

BOTTOM OF PLANTER

TOP OF PLANTER

CAUTION: You may have to remove the blade guard for this cut. Saw carefully.

PUSH STICK

FEATHERBOARD

20° BEVEL

5 Rip a 20-degree bevel on the 2x4 tops with a table saw. Use a featherboard and push stick for extra safety.

Mount the frame to the box by centering it with an even overhang all around and nailing it down with 12d galvanized casing nails (Photo 7). Measure and drill 5/32-in. pilot holes for the nails, making sure they're centered on the top edges of the plywood.

Add siding to complete the planter

Beaded board is great for a traditional-looking painted planter. For the best-looking planter, plan ahead and cut an equal amount from the first and last boards. Start by nailing the top trim (H) to the plywood box with 4d galvanized casing nails. Use a precut beaded board as a spacer to position the bottom board precisely. When you glue in the beaded boards, make sure to leave a 1/8-in. space at each end to allow room for expansion (Photo 8). Fill the space with caulk before painting.

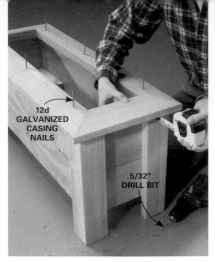

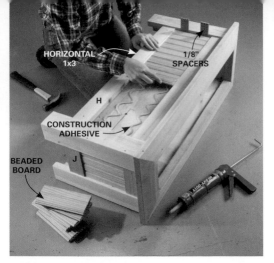

6 Cut the cap pieces to length with 45-degree miters on the ends. Drill pilot holes for the nails. Then glue and nail the miters together.

7 Drill pilot holes and glue and nail the cap to the planter box. Measure to make sure the overhang is even on all sides.

8 Cut the trim pieces H and J to length and nail them to the top and bottom edges of the box. Cut beaded board to fit and glue the pieces onto the plywood with construction adhesive.

In image 2: 1/8" DRILL BIT; 8d GALVANIZED CASING NAILS

In image 1: 12d GALVANIZED CASING NAILS; 5/32" DRILL BIT

In image 5: HORIZONTAL 1x3; 1/8" SPACERS; H; CONSTRUCTION ADHESIVE; BEADED BOARD; J

Lap siding planter

The tall box shown in the lower left corner on p. 225 is sided with 1/2-in. x 3-1/2-in. cedar lap siding. Simply cut the siding to fit between the legs. Rip a 1-in. strip off the thin edge of a siding piece for a starter. (Rip the leftover to fit at the top later.) Then nail the starter strips along the bottom of the plywood (under the first row of siding) to hold the first piece of siding at the correct angle. Predrill 1/16-in. holes 3/4 in. from the end and 5/8 in. from the bottom of each piece to prevent splitting. Then nail on the siding with 4d galvanized box nails. The top cap on this planter fits flush to the inside edge of the plywood box, which may cause the nails protruding through the inside to interfere with the plastic liner. If so, bend them flat or clip them off using end-cutting pliers. You'll save measuring time by making a simple spacing jig as shown. This planter was finished with a clear exterior finish.

Figure A

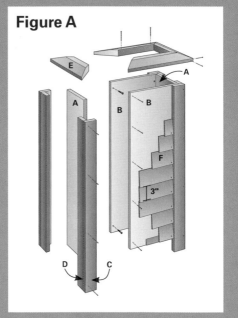

In figure A: E; A; A; B; B; B; F; 3"; D; C

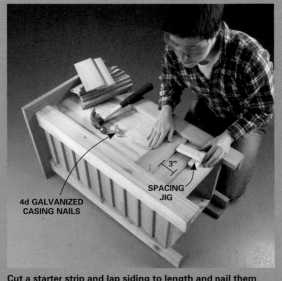

In image 4: 4d GALVANIZED CASING NAILS; 3"; SPACING JIG

Cut a starter strip and lap siding to length and nail them to the plywood starting at the bottom and working up. Lap each row 1/2 in. over the siding below.

Materials list

1	4' x 8' x 3/4" CDX plywood
2	5/4x6 x 6' deck board
1	2x4 x 8' cedar or pine
36'	1/2" x 3-1/2" lap siding
	Water-resistant glue
	4d, 8d and 12d galvanized casing nails
	6d galvanized box nails
	1-1/4" deck screws
	Plastic planter (to fit 12" x 12" opening)

Cutting list

KEY	QTY.	SIZE & DESCRIPTION
A	2	3/4" x 12" x 29" plywood ends
B	2	3/4" x 13-1/2" x 29" plywood sides
C	4	1" x 3" x 32" legs
D	4	1" x 2" x 32" legs
E	4	1-1/2" x 3-1/2" x 19" beveled cap
F	40	1/2" x 3-1/2" x 9-3/4" siding (cut to fit)

Cedar shingle planter

Wood shingles are perfect for a rustic, natural-looking box. And finishing the planter is a snap if you use stain. The only drawback to shingles is that you may have to buy a whole bundle, many more than you'll need to side one planter.

The butt end of shingles is a little too thick for the proportions of this planter. So before cutting the shingles to their final length, trim off about 4 in. from the thick end (assuming your shingles are about 16 in. long). Then cut and install them as shown. Start with a double thickness of shingles on the first row. Then offset the joints by at least 1-1/2 in. from one row to the next. Also stagger the shingles up and down if you like the "shaggy" look. Nail the shingles to the plywood box with 3d galvanized box nails. Position the nails so the next row will cover them. The nails will stick through the inside of the box but won't interfere with the plastic liner.

Choosing a finish

Cedar shingles can be stained to extend their life, but they shouldn't be painted. Cedar shingles need to breathe. When the exterior surface is painted, the backs still absorb moisture, which "pushes" the paint off the shingles.

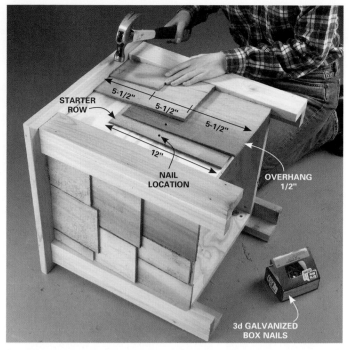

Cut 4 in. off the thick end of all 16-in. shingles to reduce their length to 12 in. Then cut them to fit and nail them to the plywood, starting at the bottom. Stagger the slots between shingles.

Figure B
Cedar shingle planter

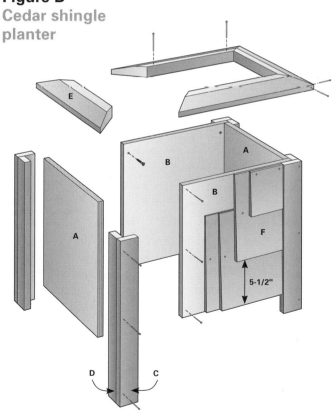

Materials list

1	16" x 62" x 3/4" CDX plywood
1	5/4x6 x 8' deck board
1	2x4 x 8' cedar or pine
1	Bundle of cedar shingles (50 or 60)
	Water-resistant glue
	8d and 12d galvanized casing nails
	3d and 6d galvanized box nails
	1-1/4" deck screws
	Plastic planter (to fit 13" x 13" opening)

Cutting list

KEY	QTY.	SIZE & DESCRIPTION
A	2	3/4" x 16" x 14-1/2" plywood ends
B	2	3/4" x 16" x 16" plywood sides
C	4	1" x 3" x 19" legs
D	4	1" x 2" x 19" legs
E	4	1-1/2" x 3-1/2" x 20" beveled cap
F	50-60	12" cedar shingles cut to fit

Pebble mosaic stepping-stones

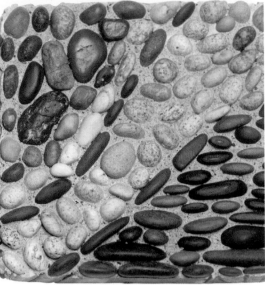

*Collect some river rock and make
your own unique stepping-stone path*

Alice Medley loves to create works of art from the
pebbles she collects. And she was generous enough
to share her garage workshop to explain how to
make these beautiful pebble mosaic stepping-stones. She
uses a "dry-set" technique that makes it easy to change or
adjust the pattern as you go without having to dig the stones
out of wet mortar.

In addition to showing how to make these stepping-stones,
check out the plans for an ingenious reusable wooden mold
that Alice purchased from a North Woods carpenter. The initial
investment for this project—about $50—gets you the plywood, a
bag of mortar, pigment and muriatic acid. It's enough material to
make about seven or eight stepping-stones. After that, each one
will cost you less than a dollar.

Build the mold

A small sheet of 3/4-in. plywood and some 1-1/4-in. screws are
all you'll need to build the mold. Cut out the pieces according to
the Cutting list. Figure A shows how the parts go together. When
you're done, brush linseed or vegetable oil on the mold to protect
it from moisture.

Start by collecting the stones

Alice collects her stones on the north shore of Lake Superior.
You'll find similar stones in most parts of the country. Look for
them in river and creek beds or along lakeshores. Wherever you
find them, make sure you have permission and that it's legal to
collect them. Another possible source is your local landscape

Meet Alice Medley

Alice started out using more traditional mosaic materials like
tile and glass for her outdoor art projects. Then she discovered she could marry her love of stones with her love of
mosaics. Alice learned this dry-mortar technique from Laura
Stone, a stone mosaic artist from Minnesota.

supplier or wherever landscaping stone is sold.

Alice likes to sort them by color. She's got buckets and cans
full of red, gray, white, brown and speckled stones. Keeping them
sorted makes it a lot easier for her to find the right one as she
creates a pattern.

Assemble the stepping-stone

Photos 1 – 4 show the assembly steps. Alice likes to add a little
brown pigment to the dry Type S mortar mix to give the stepping-
stones a mellower look. You'll find cement pigments and Type S
mortar at home centers and masonry suppliers. Or you can cheat
like Alice does and just mix in a little colored ceramic tile grout.
Make sure to wear rubber gloves to protect your skin from the
mortar, which can cause skin burns.

You don't have to plan your pattern ahead of time. Alice says
she has a design in mind and just starts arranging the stones. It's
easier to start along the edges or in a corner and work toward
the center, though. You'll have less fitting to do as you fill in the
last few stones. Keep the stones close together and oriented with
the long axis up and down. While it's tempting, Alice cautions
against laying a stone flat. She says it doesn't look as good as you
think it will and is more likely to pop out later. When you're done
tamping the stones into the dry mortar, inspect the space between

Figure A
Stepping-stone mold
(forms 12" square steppers)

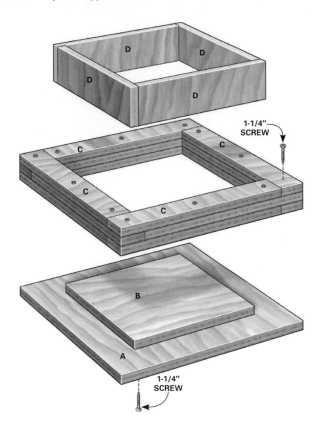

1-1/4"
SCREW

1-1/4"
SCREW

Materials list

Collection of small stones

One bag of Type S mortar mix

2' x 2' square piece of 6-mil poly

48" x 48" x ¾" plywood

Forty 1-1/4" corrosion-resistant screws

Optional items: mortar pigment or colored grout, muriatic acid and stone sealer

Cutting list

KEY	QTY.	SIZE & DESCRIPTION
A	1	18" x 18" x 3/4" subbase
B	1	12" x 12" x 3/4" base
C	12	2-1/4" x 15-3/4" x 3/4" frame
D	4	3-1/4" x 12-3/4" x 3/4" sides

1 **Assemble the mold.** This plywood mold goes together quickly and comes apart easily after the mortar hardens. And you can use it again and again.

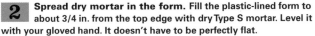

2 **Spread dry mortar in the form.** Fill the plastic-lined form to about 3/4 in. from the top edge with dry Type S mortar. Level it with your gloved hand. It doesn't have to be perfectly flat.

the stones to see if there are spots that require more mortar. They should be buried at least halfway. Fill sparse areas with more mortar. Dust any dry mortar off the stones with a small brush.

The trickiest part of the process is wetting the mortar (Photo 5). It's impossible to say exactly how much water to add, but it's better to sprinkle on several small doses than to get impatient and risk adding too much. Alice says the key is to alternate between wetting the top and tapping on the mold with the rubber

mallet until it seems like not all of the water is being absorbed and bubbles quit appearing (Photo 6). Expect to spend about 45 minutes sprinkling and tapping.

When the mortar is thoroughly dampened, set the completed stepping-stone in a shady spot and cover it with a damp cloth and plastic. Wait at least 48 hours before removing the mold.

After you remove the mold from the stepping-stone (Photo 7), brush the stone off to remove any loose mortar and rinse it with clear water. If, after drying, the embedded stones have a film of mortar on them, clean it off with muriatic acid diluted according to the instructions on the container. Remember, always add acid to water, not the other way around, and wear rubber gloves and safety glasses.

To enhance the color of the stones, coat them with stone sealer. You'll find stone sealers at home centers and masonry, landscape and tile suppliers and online.

3 Arrange stones in a pattern. The only rule is to keep the stones close together so they touch and stand up and are not laid flat.

4 Tamp the stones to level the tops. Lay a board across the stones and pound on it with a rubber mallet to embed the stones in the dry mortar and set the tops level with each other.

5 Sprinkle the stone. Adjust your spray wand or sprayer to the finest spray setting and sprinkle water over the completed stepping-stone to wet the mortar.

6 Tap on the form. Tap on the form with the mallet to remove air and help the water penetrate. Continue sprinkling and tapping until is seems like no more water will be absorbed by the mortar.

7 Pull off the mold. Allow the stepping-stone to harden and cure for at least two days. Then carefully flip it over and remove the mold. Clean it with water and then acid if needed.

Brick fire pit

Backyard fire pits are still all the rage, and for good reason. There's nothing like a crackling fire to draw friends and family together. Sure, you could set some stones around a hole or spend hundreds of bucks on a steel fire ring. But for about $200 you can build a handsome brick fire pit that's maintenance free, easy to clean out, and it will last forever.

If you've ever wanted to learn to lay brick, a backyard fire pit is an excellent project to start with. Even if your brickwork isn't perfect, the fire pit will still look great. Set aside several days to complete your fire pit: First you'll pour the footing and let it set up. Then you'll mortar the bricks into place.

Keys to a better fire pit

DRAW HOLES ALLOW OXYGEN TO REACH THE FIRE

HIGH SIDES CONTAIN SPARKS AND PREVENT KIDS AND PETS FROM FALLING IN

FIREBRICK AND REFRACTORY CEMENT WON'T DETERIORATE UNDER INTENSE HEAT

1" OVERHANG SHIELDS MORTARED JOINTS FROM DRIPS

FACE BRICKS BROKEN IN HALF MAKE A GENTLE CURVE

THICK FOOTING PREVENTS WALLS FROM CRACKING AS GROUND MOVES OVER TIME

3/8" REBAR RING REINFORCES FOOTING

4" OF GRAVEL ALLOWS RAIN AND SNOWMELT TO DRAIN

1 **Mark out the pit.** Set the larger form in position and spray paint around it. Dig a hole about 8 in. deep and 3 in. larger in diameter than the form.

2 **Level the pit.** Check the bottom of the hole with a level. Remove high spots by scraping off soil rather than digging. That way, you won't loosen the underlying soil. Compact the soil with a hand tamper or a 4x4 post.

3 **Stake the forms.** If the forms aren't quite level, raise one end and drive a screw through the stake. If the forms aren't completely round, reposition the stakes.

4 **Add the rebar.** Bend rebar into half circles and tie them together with wire to make a ring. Fill the forms halfway. Press the ring into the concrete, making sure it doesn't touch the sides of the forms.

Dig the pit

Before digging, dial 811 or visit call811.com to confirm the location of buried utility lines. Also check the fire pit code in your area. Most require a fire pit to be 25 ft. away from any structures and overhanging trees. Think about how the prevailing winds blow through your backyard. Don't locate your pit upwind of your patio or where the smoke will blow into your windows or those of your neighbors.

A 3-ft.-diameter fire pit creates enough room for a good fire, yet keeps everyone close enough to chat (and complies with most codes). To make measuring the pit and pouring the concrete footing easy, use two cardboard concrete form tubes ($45 for the two from a concrete supply company). You could also make your own forms by screwing together 1/8-in. hardboard. Rip a 4 x 8-ft. sheet into four 8-in.-wide strips. Carefully bend and screw two

5 **Finish the footing.** Shovel in the remaining concrete until the forms are filled. Recheck level, hammering the forms down if necessary, and smooth the top of the footer. Let the concrete set overnight.

6 **Dry-set the firebrick.** Adjust the spacing between bricks so you won't have to cut the last brick to fit (cutting firebrick ain't easy). Mark the position of every brick on the footing.

7 **Mortar the firebrick.** Butter a thin layer of cement on the footer and position your first brick. Butter the second brick and butt it against the first. Continue around the circle checking level side-to-side and back-to-front as you go.

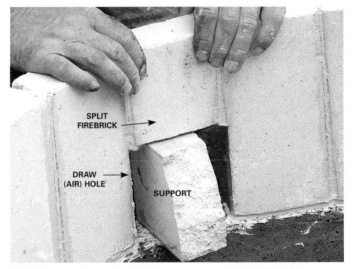

8 **Create draw (air) holes.** Leave gaps in the firebrick in four spots and then fill them with half bricks. These gaps are "draw holes" that feed air to the fire. Prop up the half bricks until the mortar sets.

strips together to create a 36-in.-diameter circle, and use the other two to make a 48-in.-diameter circle.

Mark the outside edge of the pit (Photo 1). Then shovel out the soil to a depth of 8 in. (Photo 2). Don't disturb the underlying soil.

Pour a sturdy footing

The concrete footing will create a stable base for the pit walls and keep the sides of your pit from cracking as the ground moves over time. Stake the forms (Photo 3) and mix up ten 80-lb. bags of concrete mix according to the manufacturer's directions. If you're using hardboard forms, stake them so they're nice and round. Fill the forms halfway and press a rebar ring into the concrete for strength (Photo 4). Finish filling the

forms to the top and tap the tubes gently with a sledgehammer until the concrete mix is level. Smooth the top of the footing (Photo 5). Let the concrete completely set up overnight and then remove the forms.

Dry-set the firebrick liner

Because regular clay brick can crack at high temperatures, use firebrick (also called "refractory" brick) to line the inside of the pit walls. Firebrick is a dense brick that's kilned to withstand high temperatures. It's larger, thicker and wider than regular brick, and you can find it at most brickyards. Firebrick is more expensive, but it will stand up to nightly fires for years to come. You'll need 25 firebricks for a 3-ft.diameter pit.

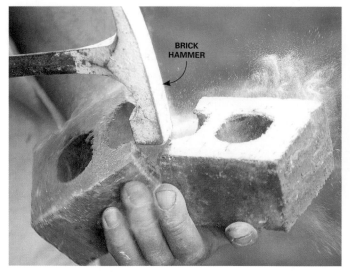

9 **Split 80 bricks in half.** Cup the brick in your hand, keeping your fingers below the top edge of the brick. (This mason doesn't use gloves, but you should!) Give the brick a solid tap (a very solid tap for firebrick) on the outside edge near the center hole. Avoid hitting your hand. Repeat 79 times.

10 **Set the face brick.** Lay a thick bed of mortar and let it harden for 15 minutes. Then lay 3/8 in. of fresh mortar and begin setting brick. Butter one side of each brick before you set it in place.

11 **Work in sections.** Working on one-third of the pit at a time, check the level of each course and tap down the bricks as necessary. Stagger the joints between courses for strength.

12 **Strike the joints.** After you finish each section of face brick, use a jointer to smooth ("strike" or "tool") the joints before the mortar dries too much. The mortar is ready to strike if you press your finger into it and the indentation remains. Striking gives the wall a uniform, polished look.

Because firebrick is so dense, it's tougher to split than regular brick. "Soldiering" the brick (standing it on end) minimizes the amount of splitting and lets you easily accommodate the curve of the pit. You'll only need to split four firebricks (use the technique shown in Photo 9), which you'll place across from one another around the pit to create draw (air) holes for oxygen for your fire. After you split your firebricks, dry-set them in place on top of the footing (Photo 6).

Mortar the firebrick

Firebrick is mortared with refractory cement, which, unlike regular masonry mortar, can withstand high heat. Refractory cement comes premixed in a bucket and has the consistency of peanut butter.

A margin trowel makes it easier to scoop cement out of the bucket and butter the bricks. A tuck pointer is useful for cleaning up the joints.

Work with four bricks at a time. The secret is to trowel the cement on thin, like you're spreading peanut butter on toast, and use the tightest joints you can (Photo 7). Continue mortaring the firebrick around the pit, placing the half bricks for the draw (air) holes at four opposite points around the ring (Photo 8). Check for level across the pit and the vertical level of the bricks as you go.

Complete the outside walls with face brick

For this project, SW ("severe weathering") face brick (also called "common" or "building" brick) was used to line the outside walls.

FLUSH WITH FIREBRICK

3/8" MORTAR BED

TUCK POINTER

1" OVERHANG

13 **Mortar the cap bricks.** Lay a 3/8-in. bed of mortar across 10 to 12 bricks at a time. Lay the bricks on edge and butter the face of each brick on the outside edge as you go.

14 **Fill gaps.** Add a small amount of mortar to the joints to fill any gaps. Check level frequently and tap gently with a brick hammer to adjust the spacing. Leave a 1-in. overhang on the outside to allow for rain to drip off. Once all the bricks have been mortared in place, strike the joints for a smooth, finished look.

Materials list

QTY.	ITEM
36"	Cardboard concrete form (from a concrete supply company)
48"	Cardboard concrete form (from a concrete supply company) or use a 4' x 8' sheet of hardboard to make both forms
10	80-lb. bags of concrete mix
2	10' lengths of 3/8" rebar (from a concrete supply company)
25	Firebricks (from a brickyard)
1	Half-gallon bucket of refractory cement (from a brickyard)
120	Face bricks
5	80-lb. bags of Type N mortar mix
	Margin trowel
	Tuck pointer
	Mason's trowel
	Concave jointer
	Concrete float
	Brick hammer
	Spray paint (for marking grass)
	Stakes

If your climate doesn't include freeze/thaw cycles, you can use MW ("moderate weathering") building brick. Home centers and brickyards carry a large variety of brick. You'll need 80 face bricks for a 3-ft.-diameter pit. Face brick with holes ("cored") is easy to split with a brick hammer (Photo 9). It's easier to form the curve of the pit walls with half bricks. You'll lay three courses of face brick and mortar them together with Type N mortar mix (sold in 80-lb. bags at home centers, and you'll need about five bags).

Because face brick is smaller than firebrick, you'll need to make up the size difference as you lay your three courses of face

brick. The difference between the height of your firebrick and the total height of three stacked face bricks will determine the width of your mortar beds between courses. Dry-set the face brick, marking where each course of face brick has to hit the firebrick to make the third course of face brick level with the firebrick.

To keep your mortar joints between courses a reasonable width, first lay a 2- to 3-in.-thick bed of mortar right on top of the footing. Let it set up slightly (15 minutes) and smooth out the top. Then, working on one-third of the pit at a time, mortar each course of face brick into place, leaving a 1/4 in. gap between the firebrick and the face brick (Photo 10). Level the brick between courses, tapping the bricks down when necessary (Photo 11). Remember to leave the draft holes open as you mortar each section of face brick and smooth out the finished joints (Photo 12).

Finish off the top lip

Finish the pit with a matching "row-lock" cap using regular face brick set on edge. You'll need about 40 face bricks for this cap, which will help protect the wall joints from rain, keep sparks contained and give you a nice ledge to warm your feet on. Shown here is brick, but you could use natural stone for a different look. Work with 10 to 12 bricks at a time. Lay a 3/8-in. bed of mortar, then butter each brick and press it into place (Photo 13). Work your way around the circle, filling any gaps with mortar and checking level and placement frequently (Photo 14). Smooth the finished joints with a concave jointer.

Give the cement and mortar a week to cure completely before lighting a fire in your pit. Pour a few inches of gravel on the pit's floor for drainage and you're ready for your first wienie roast.

Cast concrete table

The look and durability of natural stone— the cost and simplicity of concrete

If you want a tabletop that's elegant enough for any indoor setting and tough enough to withstand outdoor weather, you've found it. Tables similar to this one sell for hundreds at garden centers and outdoor furniture stores. But you can make one yourself for $50 to $100.

The total materials cost for the table shown here was about $100. Your cost will depend mostly on the wood you choose for the base and the concrete mix you use. You don't need any special skills or tools, though a table saw and an air-powered brad nailer will speed up building the form. Give yourself half a day to build the form and pour the concrete and an hour to build the table base. A few days after casting the top, you'll spend a couple of hours removing the form, chipping the edges and applying a sealer.

Build the form

Melamine-coated particleboard is the perfect form material for this project because it's smooth, water-resistant and inexpensive. Cut the form parts as shown in Figure A. The two long sides overhang the form for easier removal later. A brad nailer is the fastest way to assemble the form (Photo 1). If you use screws or drive nails by hand, be sure to drill pilot holes to avoid splitting the particleboard. Whatever fastening method you use, space fasteners about 6 in. apart and make sure they don't create humps inside the form.

Next, caulk the inside corners to seal the form and create rounded edges on the tabletop (Photo 2). Do this even if you plan to chip off the edges later. Use colored silicone caulk, which will show up well against the white Melamine. That way, you can easily spot and clean off smudges. Keep in mind that every tiny imperfection on the form will show up on the finished tabletop.

For neat caulk lines, run masking tape about 3/16 in. from the corners. Apply the caulk one side at a time, smooth it with your finger and remove the tape quickly before the caulk skins over (Photo 2). The tape ridges along the caulk lines will show on the finished top and make

Endless possibilities

Most of us think of concrete as a practical material, but it's also one of the most versatile decorative materials around. It can take on just about any color or shape. And surface treatment options are endless. You can cast "fossil" imprints using leaves, ferns or seashells. For a completely different look, you can cast inlays like glass or tile permanently in the surface.

STAINED GLASS

GLASS TILE

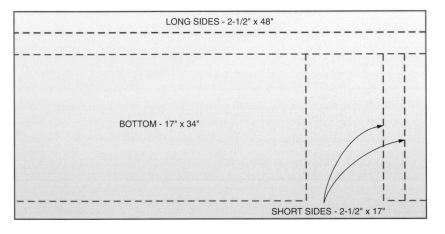

1 Build the form from Melamine-coated particleboard to give the concrete a smooth finish and make the form easy to remove.

Figure A
Cutting diagram for the concrete form

LONG SIDES - 2-1/2" x 48"

BOTTOM - 17" x 34"

SHORT SIDES - 2-1/2" x 17"

Figure B
Table base

Cut the parts to the dimensions shown and join them with metal brackets. We spent $30 on cedar lumber, but any rot-resistant wood in 2x4 and 4x4 dimensions is a good choice. Pressure-treated lumber will cost about $12. Fasten the top to the base with a few dabs of hot-melt glue.

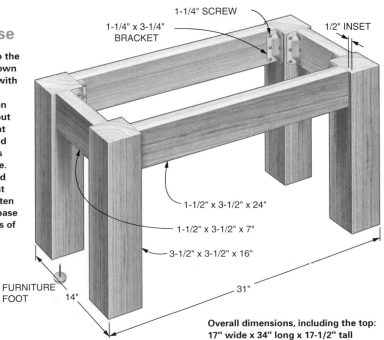

1-1/4" SCREW

1-1/4" x 3-1/4" BRACKET

1/2" INSET

1-1/2" x 3-1/2" x 24"

1-1/2" x 3-1/2" x 7"

3-1/2" x 3-1/2" x 16"

FURNITURE FOOT

14"

31"

Overall dimensions, including the top: 17" wide x 34" long x 17-1/2" tall

a perfect chisel guide for chipping the edges later (Photo 8).

If you want to cast leaf or fern "fossils" in the top, first press them for a day or two in a book or between scraps of cardboard. Then lay them out on newspaper and coat them with spray adhesive. Press them onto the form so they lie perfectly flat (Photo 3). Thick stems may not lie flat and can leave imprints that are too deep. To avoid this, we shaved some of our fern stems down with a razor blade.

Mix and pour

You can mix concrete in a bucket, using a drill and a large paint mixer attachment. This method is fast, but it requires a powerful 1/2-in. drill and won't work well with thicker mixes. Instead, you can use a garden hoe and a plastic cement tub. Be patient and mix thoroughly so you completely wet all the powdered ingredients. Pay attention to the product's mixing instructions, especially the recommended amount of water. An extra cup of water can make the mix too thin.

Set your form on a solid surface and level it both front to back and side to side. Otherwise one side of your top will be thicker than the other. Then pour in the mix around the edges to get an even distribution of material (Photo 4). Pouring the entire mix in the middle might concentrate the heavier particles there and weaken the edges. Wear plastic gloves as you work the material into all corners and edges (Photo 5). Use a gentle touch, however, if you have fragile objects glued to the bottom. If the mix you use requires wire reinforcement, pour and work in about two-thirds of the mix. Then add the

Materials list

Everything you need—except the concrete mix—is available at home centers.

2' x 4' sheet of 3/4"-thick Melamine

4x4 x 8'

2x4 x 8'

Plastic furniture feet

Silicone caulk

Spray adhesive

Cement colorant

1-1/4" screws

8 metal brackets

Acrylic grout and tile sealer

Countertop mix

wire and the remaining mix.

All pours contain trapped air, which will leave holes in the finished top unless you work them out. To drive out bubbles, tap the sides and bottom of the form with a hammer and continue rapping until you don't see any more bubbles coming up. However, if you have pea gravel or other "aggregate" in your mix, limit your tapping. Otherwise, the aggregate will settle to the bottom and weaken or perhaps ruin the appearance of your table. And keep in mind that the tabletop doesn't have to be perfectly smooth. A few holes or imperfections in the surface may simply add more natural character.

When you're finished, cover the top with plastic and let the concrete harden and cure anywhere from four hours to two days, depending on the brand.

Release the form and finish

To remove the form, pry off the long sides and then the short sides. Pry against the form base rather than the concrete. If you have to pry off the form base, use a plastic putty knife; metal will mar the surface (Photo 6). If your top has

Easy inlays

It's easy to embed small decorative objects in the concrete top. Unlike the casts of ferns and leaves, which leave only the imprint behind, an inlay stays in place permanently. You can inlay anything that's durable and has crisp edges. Tiles and colored glass are the most common inlays, but you can also use coins or other metal objects. Simply spread a thin coat of silicone caulk over the face you want exposed and press it down on the Melamine base. After the concrete mix hardens, carefully scrape away the silicone film left on the inlay with a razor blade.

Glue inlays face down to the form with silicone caulk. Be sure to remove excess caulk that squeezes out around the inlay.

SMOOTH CAULK BEAD

2 Caulk the corners of the form. Any imperfections in the caulk will show up on the tabletop. So use masking tape to create neat, even edges.

3 Glue down leaves with spray adhesive to cast "fossils" in the tabletop. Press the leaves completely flat so concrete can't seep under them.

LEVELING SHIM

4 Pour the mix evenly around the perimeter of the form. The form must be level—set a level across it and slip shims under the low end.

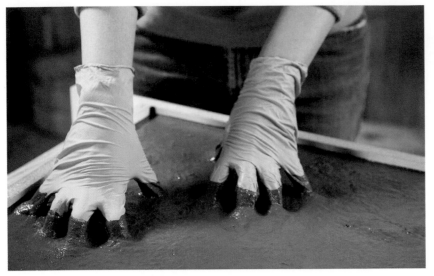

5 Work the mix into corners and around objects cast into the tabletop. Then lightly tap the sides of the form with a hammer to drive out air bubbles.

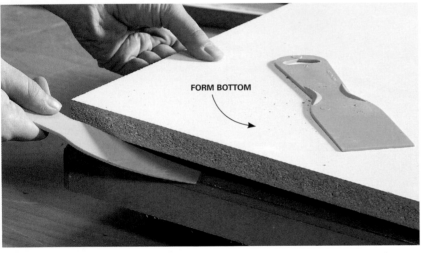

FORM BOTTOM

6 Remove the form, starting with the sides. Then flip the tabletop over and pry off the bottom panel with a plastic putty knife.

7 Scrub the leaves out of their imprints with a stiff plastic brush. Scour the whole surface to remove excess colorant and Melamine residue.

Choosing a mix

The best concrete mix for this project is a countertop mix. You'll need about 50 lbs. of mix to make the 17-in. x 34-in. x 1-1/2-in. top shown. Countertop mix has one key factor—special additives called "super-plasticizers," which allow you to add less water. Less water means a denser, stronger top. Some mixes contain fibers to help prevent cracking. Others require wire reinforcement.

We added 5 ozs. of Quikrete Liquid Cement Color ("Charcoal") to our 50-lb. sack of mix to get a gray, slate-like color.

imprints with fine detail, cover it with plastic and let it harden for an extra day. Then scrub with water (Photo 7). Use a plastic putty knife to scrape off Melamine residue that won't scrub off.

The mix used here chips off neatly for a rough edge look (Photo 8). Be sure to set the top on plywood on a solid surface. Shown is a 3/4-in.-wide cold chisel, but you can use whatever width best produces the effect you want. For safety, hone down any sharp edges with a file or sandpaper.

Your top will withstand outdoor weather, but it's susceptible to stains. To prevent them, and to bring out more color, seal it with an acrylic sealer (in the tile aisle at home centers). The first coat will sink in and the surface will remain dull. After it dries, apply a second coat, and perhaps a third, until the surface retains a shine.

Well done! Chances are that once you complete one top, you'll want to make another.

8 Create a natural stone look by chipping the edges with a cold chisel. Chip around all four edges, then flip the top over and chip from the other side.

Mud-busting boot scraper

O rdinary doormats simply can't handle serious muck, but you can clean out packed dirt from even the deepest boot treads with this boot scraper made from 2x4s.

1. Screw the base pieces (A and B) together upside down so that the screw heads are hidden.
2. Fasten the uprights (C) to the sides (D), then screw the side brushes on with 2-in. screws.
3. Screw the bottom brushes to the base with 2-in. screws.
4. Space the side pieces so that the bristles are roughly 4-1/2 in. apart.
5. Add a piece of aluminum angle to the front edge so you can scrape boots before brushing them.

Use stiff-bristle brushes—either "bilevel" brushes or deck scrub brushes. You may need to cut off part of the handle so the brush will lie flat.

Figure A
Exploded view

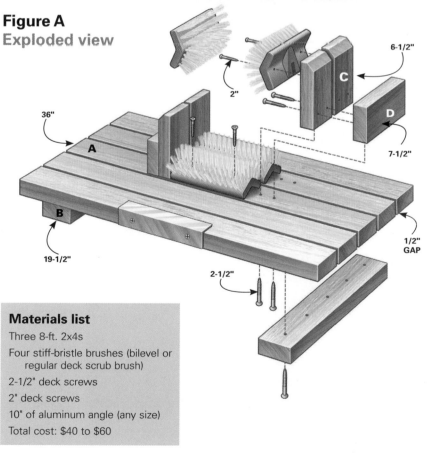

6-1/2"

C

D

7-1/2"

36"

A

1/2"
GAP

B

19-1/2"

2"

2-1/2"

Materials list

Three 8-ft. 2x4s

Four stiff-bristle brushes (bilevel or regular deck scrub brush)

2-1/2" deck screws

2" deck screws

10" of aluminum angle (any size)

Total cost: $40 to $60

Scout bench

Simple enough for kids, tough enough for camp, perfect for your yard!

Photographer Tom Fenenga (he's the one with the striped shirt and big grin), is very involved with his son Adam's Boy Scout troop. Tom wanted to teach the scouts about construction, and they needed benches around the fire pit at the scout camp they visit each year. This bench is simple enough for teenage boys to build, tough enough to handle their roughhousing and economical, at less than $100 each. You could build one in a Saturday.

WHAT IT TAKES

TIME: 4 hours for the bench, plus an hour of shovel work

COST: Less than $100 per bench

TOOLS: Circular saw and screw gun

FLUSH WITH PLYWOOD

SEAT SUPPORT

10° ANGLE

FRONT LEG

BACK LEG

BASE PIECE

GUIDELINE

GUIDELINE

90°

10° ANGLE

23-1/2"

6-3/4"

1 Screw together the leg units. Screw the parts together with two 3-in. deck screws at each joint. Draw guidelines alongside the 4x4s to use for the other set of legs. Center the base piece and make the seat support flush with the top of the front 4x4 and square to the back one. Flip the assembly over and screw the second base piece and seat support onto the other side of the legs.

Treated wood is a must—along with exterior 3-in. deck screws rated for treated wood. And the benches have to be embedded in concrete in the ground to keep them from being "relocated."

Assemble the legs

Start by cutting all the parts to length, following Figure A and Photos 1 and 2. Then pre-assemble the legs with screws. You can do this in your shop or garage where you have a flat surface. Place a plywood scrap under the first set of legs and position the 4x4s following the measurements in

8" x 1/2" CARRIAGE BOLT

SEAT SUPPORT

2 Bolt the seat supports to the 4x4s. Bore through both seat supports and the 4x4s with a 3/8-in. spade bit. Connect the parts with 8-in. carriage bolts.

Figure A
Scout bench

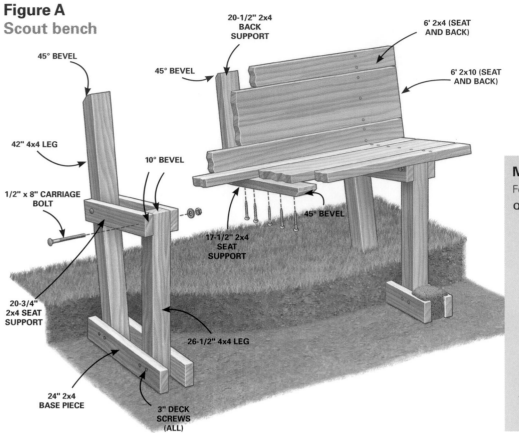

45° BEVEL

42" 4x4 LEG

10° BEVEL

1/2" x 8" CARRIAGE BOLT

20-1/2" 2x4 BACK SUPPORT

45° BEVEL

6' 2x4 (SEAT AND BACK)

6' 2x10 (SEAT AND BACK)

45° BEVEL

17-1/2" 2x4 SEAT SUPPORT

20-3/4" 2x4 SEAT SUPPORT

26-1/2" 4x4 LEG

24" 2x4 BASE PIECE

3" DECK SCREWS (ALL)

Materials list

For each bench you'll need:

QTY.	ITEM
2	8' treated 4x4s (legs)
2	10' treated 2x4s (base pieces, seat, seat supports and back support)
2	6' treated 2x10s (seat and backrest)
4	6' treated 2x4s (seat and backrest)
3	4' untreated 2x4s (temporary spacer boards)
4	1/2" x 8" carriage bolts with nuts and washers
74	3" deck screws
3	60-lb. bags of concrete mix

TEMPORARY BRACE

3 **Brace the legs.** Cut the three untreated 2x4s to 4 ft. and screw them to both ends of the feet and the front of the seat supports. They'll serve as temporary braces while you attach the bench seat and backrest boards.

PENCIL

4 **Add the seat and back.** Cut the seat boards to 72 in. Evenly space the ends of the seat boards from the edges of the legs. Screw the boards to the seat supports with 3-in. deck screws: two in each 2x4 and three in each 2x10. Space the boards with a carpenter's pencil.

Photo 1. Outline those positions so you can use them as a pattern for the other set of legs to be sure they match perfectly. Keep the screws away from the center of the 4x4 so you don't hit them when you drill holes for the carriage bolts. Drill and bolt together the seat supports and 4x4s. You can buy a special 1/2-in.-dia. x 12-in.-long spade bit or extend a standard-length spade bit with a magnetic bit holder (Photo 2).

Brace it temporarily

Set the legs on a level surface, spacing them 4 ft. apart, and temporarily brace both ends of the base pieces and the front of the seat supports with 2x4s (Photo 3). That'll hold everything together with the proper spacing while you attach the seat and back boards. Once they're screwed on, remove the braces.

Attach the seat and back

Evenly space the seat boards from the edges of the seat supports and screw them to both seat supports with 3-in. deck screws: two screws into each support for the 2x4s and three for the 2x10s. Place a carpenter's pencil between the boards to space them (Photo 4). Flip the bench upside down, center the back supports and attach them with 3-in. screws (Photo 5). Run those in at an angle so the tips won't penetrate the seat and back (or your seat or back).

Dig the trenches and add the concrete

Set the bench exactly where you want it and outline the trenches around each base. Then set the bench aside and start digging (Photo 6). Your goal is to have a level bench with the seat about 15 in. above the ground at the front—the typical height for benches. But once you achieve that, just sit on the bench. You might want it lower, higher or reclined a bit more. Get it just the way you like it. Then mix up three bags of concrete mix and pour half over each base, filling the space between and alongside. Throw any extra over the top. Then backfill the holes, wait a few hours, start the campfire and roast some hot dogs and marshmallows.

BACK
SUPPORT

BEVELED
ENDS

5 Screw on the seat supports. Screw the seat supports to the middle of the seat and back, then remove the temporary braces.

6 Dig the trenches and install your bench. Position and mark the trenches and dig them about 8 in. deep. Rest the bench in the trenches. Check the bench for level and height, then remove it and adjust the soil levels as necessary. Pour 1-1/2 bags of concrete mix beside, between and over each base and cover with soil.

One-day pond and fountain

Add life to your backyard with this easy and affordable fountain

The idea behind this project was fairly simple: we wanted a small pond with running water in the backyard, something that would attract birds, frogs and other local critters—but not cost much money.

We accomplished this goal by using an inexpensive preformed pond shell and a ceramic flower pot. The materials for this project cost about $125, not including stone, and it took only a day to finish. You can get carried away with the stonework, but the basic project is easy—dig a hole, drop in the pond, run a tube from the pump into the bowl and fill the pond with water.

Dig the hole

The pond will take up a roughly circular 5 x 5-ft. area after flagstones are laid around it and will need a GFCI outlet nearby for the pump. Plastic circular ponds are strong enough to be freestanding, so if rocks or tree roots are a problem, your pond can be partly or entirely above ground, or set into a hillside, as ours was. Just hide the exposed sides by building up the rock wall. Interlocking retaining wall blocks can also be used.

Set the pond upside down on the ground and outline it with spray paint or flour—or just start cutting the sod around the rim. Set the pond aside and cut out the sod (you may need to reuse it later), then start digging a few inches in from the circular outline. Dig the hole the depth of the pond plus 2 in., and remove any protruding roots or stones that might puncture the pond. Check to make sure the pond fits, then pour in 2 to 3 in. of sand.

Level and backfill

Push the pond down into the sand base, then walk in it to compact the sand. The rim of the pond should be roughly even with the highest point on the surrounding ground. Level the pond as you work it down by moving the sand under it.

Hold the pond in place and backfill around the edges with sand, tamping and filling up to ground level (Photo 1).

CAUTION: Before you do any digging, call 811 to have your electrical, gas, phone and cable lines marked. Schedule this at least three working days in advance.

1 Set the plastic pond in a hole with a few inches of tamped-down sand underneath. Backfill around the edges with additional sand.

2 Partially fill the pond and set blocks in place to hold the pot. Check them with a level and shim with galvanized washers if necessary.

SAND LEVEL WITH RIM

DECK PIER

CHANNEL FOR TUBING

SHIMS

SAND FOLLOWS SLOPE

Set up the fountain

The fountain is made by running a tube from a submersible pump up through the drainage hole of the ceramic pot. The pot can sit below or above the water surface, but it will be heavy when it's full of water and needs a level, stable base. Start with a 6 x 8 x 12-in. block or two 3-in.-thick x 12-in.-diameter concrete pads, then set an 8-in. deck pier (which has a slot for the tubing) on top.

Fill the pond partway with water so that it fully settles into the sand, then level the pier (Photo 2).

Cut a 3-ft. length of tubing and push 1 ft. of it through the hole in the bottom of the pot. Seal the hole with silicone caulk or plumber's epoxy and set it aside until it cures. Use black tubing to cut down on algae growth.

Install a shutoff between the pump and the pot to stop water in the pot from siphoning back into the pond and over-flowing it when the pump is turned off (Photo 3). (You can also install a coupling instead of a shutoff, then just add more water when the pot drains.) To pump water out of the pond for cleaning, just

pull off the tubing from the shutoff and hang it over the side of the pond.

Set the pot on the pier and put the pump in the water, then turn it on and make sure everything works and that the water flows evenly over the pot rim. Leave enough tubing from the pump to the shutoff to pump out the pond, but be careful not to twist or kink it.

Lay the flagstones

We surrounded the pond with flagstones, laying them on a bed of sand and lapping them over the black plastic rim (Photo 4). Fitting the stone is like working on a jigsaw puzzle, so buy a few extra pieces. Cut the stone to fit with a circular saw or grinder equipped with a dry-cutting diamond blade (or inexpensive but short-lived masonry blade), or score and break it with a cold chisel. Wear eye protection when you work with stone.

Use stone chips or a few hidden squirts of urethane foam to keep flagstones steady and in position if you build up the wall. Use conventional mortar if the wall is larger than shown here or if kids will be walking on it.

Landscaping and final touches

Cut the tube inside the pot to half the depth of the pot, then prop it up with rocks so it points straight toward the center. Leave the tube long if you want the water to spout higher.

Lay a few large rocks in the bottom of the pond for decoration and to hide the pump. Use bricks as needed to elevate water plants.

Most garden supply stores carry a large selection of accessories, chemical additives and aquatic plants, and small fish can be added if you install a special filter. Other creatures will discover the pond on their own.

Keep the pond clean by pumping out half the water once or twice a month and refilling it with clean water. Remove the pump and clean off leaves when you change the water or anytime the water flow seems slow. Empty the pond and pot completely in the fall, and keep the plants in buckets in the house until the weather warms up again.

COUPLINGS

SILICONE CAULK

SHUTOFF

PUMP

3 Run black tubing from the pump to the pot. Add a shutoff valve to keep water in the pot when the pump is off.

Materials list

3'-diameter preformed pond (other shapes and sizes are available at home and garden centers)

Large ceramic pot with drainage hole (3- to 6-gallon capacity)

Four bags of sand

A 200-gallon-per-hour submersible pond pump

6' of black tubing (check pond pump to determine size—usually 1/2" inside diameter)

1/2" threaded PVC shutoff

Two plastic 3/8" (outside diameter) barbed x 1/2" threaded coupling (lawn irrigation system fitting)

8" concrete deck pier

6" x 8" x 12" concrete block (or two 12"-diameter concrete pads)

Flagstones (at least 12) to ring pond

Pond equipment is available at home centers, garden supply stores and pet stores.

FOAM FOR LEVELING

1/2" TUBING

SAND BASE

4 Lay flagstones around the pond to cover the edge. Place plants in the water, using bricks to elevate them as needed.

Butterfly house

Butterflies like the protection of dark, sheltered areas—whether it's for months at a time (during long, cold winters), or for just a few moments (when dodging hungry predators). Here's a simple refuge you can build for them for under $20.

Use smooth or rough-sawn cedar; it's rot-resistant and weathers to a mellow gray. For durability, assemble the house using moisture-proof glue and galvanized nails. Make sure to hinge and latch one side so you can insert and maintain the long twigs and tree bark the butterflies roost on (Figure A, p. 253).

A jigsaw, drill and common hand tools are all you need, although a table saw (to cut angles and the wood to size) speeds up the work greatly.

To attract butterflies, locate the house in an area with lots of flowering plants, and mount it 2 to 3 ft. off the ground.

Build the butterfly house

Cut the parts to the sizes and angles listed in the Cutting list, p. 253, and shown in the photos.

Lay out the entry slots on the front (Figure A), drill the ends with a 3/8-in.-dia. bit, then cut the slots the rest of the way with a jigsaw (Photo 1). Smooth the sides of the slots with sandpaper.

Use a 7/8-in. spade bit to drill the holes for the support pipe in the bottom, and in one of the pipe stops.

Glue and nail the back to the side. Glue and clamp the two support pipe stops together, then glue and clamp them to the back. Glue and nail the bottom to the assembled back and side.

Glue and nail the false front roof pieces to the front, then glue and nail the front in place, and attach the roof boards. Use the door as a spacer between the front and back when you attach the roof.

Trim the door, if necessary, so it fits loosely between the front and back. Align the door, and hammer in the two hinge pivot nails (Photo 2).

Use two pliers to bend a nail in half. Drill a pilot hole, then tap in this latch.

Insert the support pipe through the bottom and into the pipe stop. Drill pilot holes for the pipe strap screws, attach the strap (Photo 3), then loosen it and remove the support pipe.

Determine the best location and height for the house (keep it low). Hammer the pipe into the ground (protect the end of the pipe with a scrap piece of wood), then slide the house on the pipe, tighten the pipe strap, and watch for your first fluttering house guests.

1 Create the entry slots. Drill 3/8-in. holes for the top and bottom of each slot, then connect the holes using a jigsaw.

JIGSAW

3/8"-DIA. STARTER HOLES

2 Assemble the house. Use straight nails for the door hinges and a bent one for the latch. (Note: Here the door is open so you can see the inside, but it's easier to align everything with the door closed.)

HINGE NAIL

SUPPORT PIPE STOP

BOTTOM

DOOR

3 Loosely screw the pipe strap to the back, using the support pipe as a guide. Remove the pipe, pound it into the ground, then permanently tighten the strap around the pipe to prevent the house from spinning.

BENT NAIL DOOR LATCH

3/4"-DIA. COPPER PIPE

3/4" PIPE STRAP

Figure A
Butterfly house

B

45° BEVELS

90°

24"

C

BARK OR TWIGS

HINGE NAIL

3-1/2"

F

3/8"

6"

3/4"

E

3/4" HOLES

D

5/8"

LATCH NAIL

A

13"

3/4" COPPER PIPE

3/4" PIPE STRAP

Materials list

QTY	ITEM
1	1x6 x 10' cedar
25	4d galvanized casing nails
1	3/4"-dia. type L copper pipe*
1	3/4" copper pipe strap*
2	No. 8 x 1/2" pan head screws
Small bottle	Titebond III moisture-proof glue
	*Available at home centers

Cutting list

KEY	PCS.	SIZE & DESCRIPTION
A	2	3/4" x 5" x 24" cedar (front and back)
B	2	3/4" x 5" x 6-1/4" cedar (roof boards)
C	2	3/4" x 3-3/4" x 22-1/4" cedar (side and door)
D	1	3/4" x 3-3/4" x 3-1/2" cedar (bottom)
E	2	3/4" x 1-1/4" x 3-1/2" cedar (support pipe stop)
F	2	1/2" x 3/4" x 3-1/2" cedar (false front roof)

Low-upkeep mailbox

The strength of wood and the convenience of PVC!

I f your old wooden mailbox is falling apart—or if it was run over by your teenage driver—this low-maintenance mailbox made from treated wood and PVC is the perfect replacement.

All the materials are available at any home center. The PVC post sleeves can be a little tricky to work with, but PVC boards are easy to cut and fasten with regular woodworking tools. And PVC doesn't tear out, split or splinter.

The whole project costs under $120. Building it takes about a day, including shopping and digging the post hole.

Start with a trip to the post office

Don't assume the dimensions used here will work for you. The height, distance from the curb and newspaper box requirements may be different in your area. The dimensions for this box are based on a pamphlet from the local post office. The USPS recommends that a post be buried no more than 24 in. It's safer if the post gives way if someone runs into it.

Cutting the parts

A 6-ft. fence post sleeve leaves virtually no extra length for cutting mistakes. Start your 45-degree cut as close to the end as possible; a 20-in. angle bracket will leave you a 52-in. post sleeve. Cut into the sleeve slowly; thinner plastic can shatter if you cut too aggressively, especially when it's cold. After cutting the angle bracket sleeve, use it as a template to mark the wood angle bracket. Once again, start your cut as close to the end as possible. An 8-ft. post with 20 in. cut off will leave you with 2 ft. of post to bury in the ground.

The two newspaper box sides (J) only need to be cut to length, but don't assume the factory ends are square—they're usually not. Trim just as much as necessary to make a true 90-degree end. After cutting the top (H) and bottom (G) to length, you'll need to cut them to width. Start by removing 1/4 in. from one side of each board to remove the rounded edges. The leftover scrap from the top should be about 1-1/8 in. wide. Save that piece to make the mailbox base.

Materials list

QTY.	ITEM
1	Mailbox
1	8' x 4x4 treated post
1	6' x 4x4 PVC/vinyl fence post sleeve
1	10' x 1x6 PVC trim
1	Vinyl fence post cap
1	Tube of PVC-vinyl-fence cement
1	Tube of white exterior-grade silicone
1	Box of 1-5/8" screws approved for treated lumber
1	Box of 3" screws approved for treated lumber
4	White hinged screw cover
4	Black hinged screw cover

Cutting list

KEY	QTY.	SIZE & DESCRIPTION
A	1	52" x 4" x 4" post sleeve
B	1	20" x 4" x 4" angle bracket sleeve
C	1	76" x 3-1/2" x 3-1/2" wood post
D	1	20" (long side) x 4" x 4" wood angle bracket
E	1	17-1/2" x 3/4" x 1-1/8" mailbox base
F	1	17-1/2" x 3/4" x 5" mailbox base (glue to part E)
G	1	14" x 3/4" x 4" newspaper box bottom (with kerf cuts)
H	1	20" x 3/4" x 4" newspaper box top
J	2	30" x 3/4" x 5-1/2" newspaper box sides

Any circle with an 8- to 9-in. diameter will work as a template to mark the curves on the sides (Figure B). Once all the curves are cut, clamp the two sides together and sand the curves smooth so the pieces are identical.

The mailbox we used required a 17-1/2-in. x 6-1/8-in. base. Your mailbox might be different. The total length of the base is not the same as the length of the mailbox—it has to be about 1 in. shorter to allow the door to open. Cement the scraps (E and F) together to form a base board that fits your mailbox.

Cut kerfs in the bottom of the newspaper box (G) to allow water to drain. Set your table saw blade at a height of 1/4 in. and set your fence 1/2 in. from the blade. Run the board through, then flip it around and do the same on the other side. Then run both sides of the board through at 1 in. and then again at

Figure A
Mailbox post

Figure B
Newspaper box sides

1 **Cut the side curves.** A dull blade actually works better than a sharp blade, which tends to grab and shake the PVC as it cuts. Cut one side of the newspaper box, then use it as a template to mark the other side.

1-1/2 in. The middle kerf should be centered at 2 in., but you may want to double-check and line the last kerf up manually. Practice on a sacrificial board.

Assemble the newspaper box

Use PVC-vinyl-fence cement to assemble the newspaper box. The cement is a little runny, so be prepared to wipe off the excess after clamping.

Clamp the box together, bottom side up. Hold both the top (H) and the bottom (G) out flush with the curves on the front of the sides (J), as shown in Photo 2. The bottom is shorter than the top at the back of the box. This gap allows water to escape.

Putting it all together

If your 4x4 post is twisted on one end, use the straight portion above ground. Slide the PVC sleeve over the post, leaving it flush at the top. Attach the wood angle bracket. Slide on the angle bracket sleeve (Photo 3).

Once the newspaper box is in place, clamp a framing square onto the post to ensure a true 90 degrees (Photo 4). Don't worry about splitting the small areas between the kerfs—PVC is much more forgiving than wood.

Screw the mailbox base to the newspaper box flush with the front edge of the box. Use 1-5/8-in. screws, and be sure to screw down into the sides or your screws will poke through into the box. Attach the mailbox to the base. Slide it all the way forward to allow room for the door to open (Photo 5).

Apply the cement to the cap, not the post—it's less messy. We used a pretty basic fence post cap, but feel free to decorate your post with a fancier cap, or one with a built-in solar light.

There will be a little play in the vinyl angle bracket sleeve. Use a putty knife to slip a bit of cement underneath each end of the sleeve in order to seal it to the newspaper box and post. Caulk both sides of the angle bracket with white exterior-grade caulk. Silicone is the easiest to work with. You're done!

2 Assemble the box, bottom side up. Dry-fit the entire newspaper box before you apply any cement. Cut a couple of 4-in. blocks to hold the bottom (G) at the right height. Tape along the joints to catch excess cement. Work fast—the cement won't wait.

3 Screw on the wood angle bracket. Most post sleeves aren't perfectly square, but slightly rectangular with one side a hair wider than the other. Attach the bracket to the narrow side. The newspaper box will slide on easier that way.

4 Fasten the newspaper box. Bore two 3/4-in. access holes in the top of the box. You will need a magnetic bit holder at least 4 in. long to reach the screws that attach the box to the angle bracket.

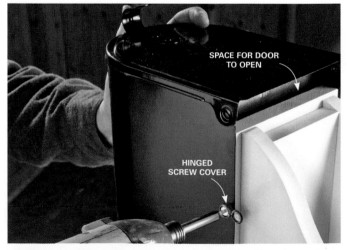

5 Mount the mailbox. Leave a gap under the mailbox door so it can open without binding against the base (E). Hinged screw covers snap shut and hide the screw heads for a clean look.

Spike's wonder cart

Better than a wheelbarrow and easy to build

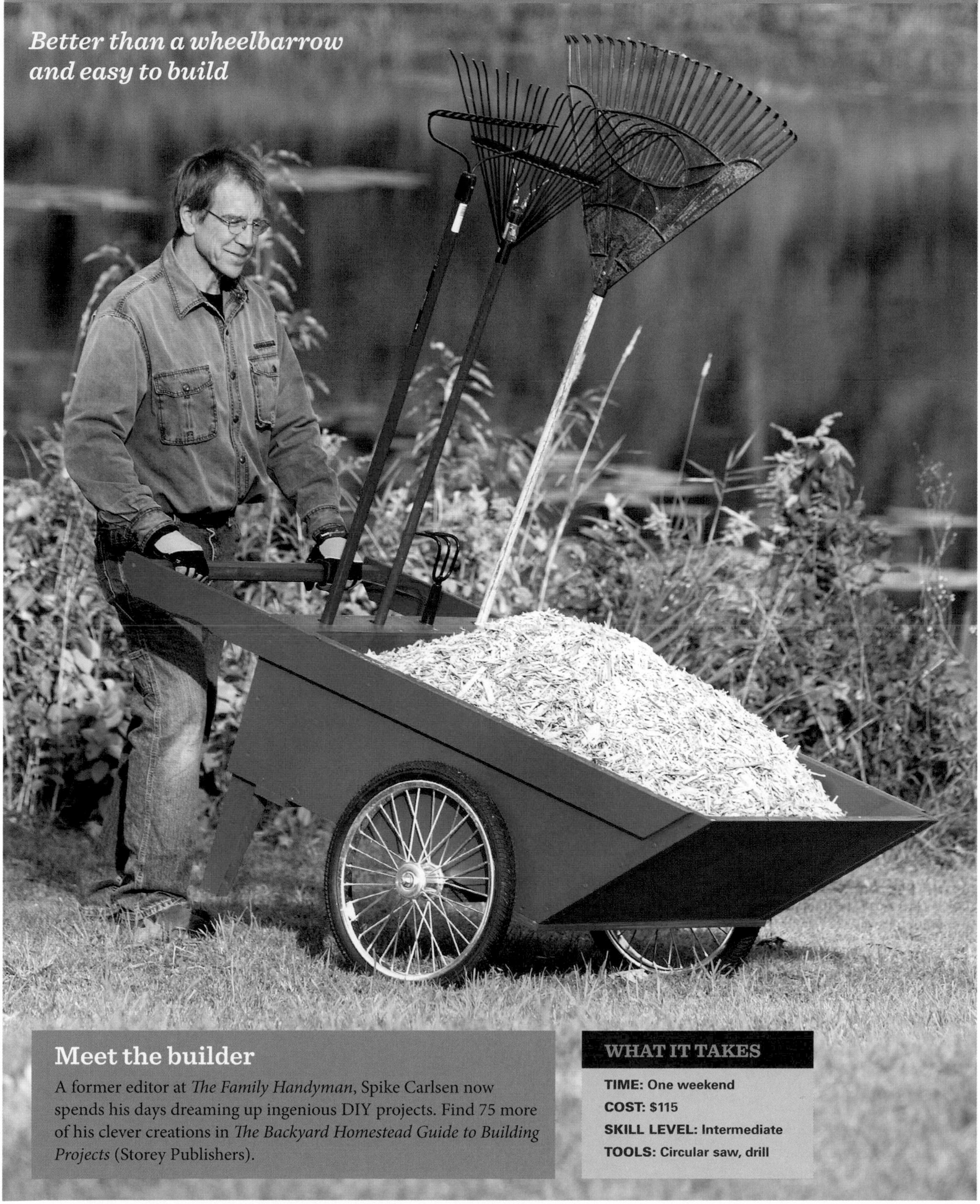

Meet the builder

A former editor at *The Family Handyman*, Spike Carlsen now spends his days dreaming up ingenious DIY projects. Find 75 more of his clever creations in *The Backyard Homestead Guide to Building Projects* (Storey Publishers).

WHAT IT TAKES

TIME: One weekend
COST: $115
SKILL LEVEL: Intermediate
TOOLS: Circular saw, drill

Wheelbarrows are great for hauling stuff around the yard—unless you're working on a hill ... or trying to negotiate steps and rough terrain ... or moving a lot of bulky material like leaves and branch trimmings ... or trying to load something big into them.

Since I added this garden cart to my outdoor arsenal of tools, life has gotten way easier. Two wheels means it doesn't tip; large pneumatic tires means it's easy to push; a big box lets me haul 10 bags of mulch in one load; and because the front tilts down for loading, my aching back doesn't ache as much. I'll still use my trusty wheelbarrow for mixing concrete and hauling the super-heavy stuff, but these days I "cart" nearly everything else.

I designed this cart to be as rugged and durable as any cart you can buy at any price, yet the materials cost less than $115. It's one of the wisest landscaping investments you can make.

Round up materials

You'll need a straight-cutting jig to cut the plywood. I used exterior plywood and standard pine boards for the structure. You can use treated plywood and lumber, but it may be hard to find treated material that's dry and flat.

I bought wheels online. The threaded rod, washers and nuts are available at home centers and hardware stores.

Assemble the box

Lay out the plywood as shown in Figure B. Start by cutting the sheet lengthwise into 14-in., 30-in. and 3-1/2-in. strips (Photo 1). After positioning the jig for each cut, clamp or screw it into place. Cut the angled sides (A) from the 14-in. strip and the bottom braces (E) from the 3-1/2-in. strip. Cut the front (C), bottom (D) and back (B) from the 30-in. strip.

If you use your straight-cutting jig, as is, for cutting the 45-degree bevels, you'll cut a bevel on the jig itself, making it unusable for future square cuts. Temporarily modify your jig by screwing a 3/4-in. strip of wood to the jig's fence (Photo 2), positioning the edge of the guide on the cutting line (like you would for a square cut), then make your 45-degree cut.

Drill 1/8-in. holes about 3/8 in. away from the edges of the sides (A), spaced about 4 in. apart. Then secure the front with 2-in. exterior screws through the predrilled holes

Easy to load

Onboard tool storage

Huge load? No problem

1 Cut the plywood parts. A homemade straight-cutting jig turns your circular saw into a precision plywood slicer.

STRAIGHT-CUTTING JIG

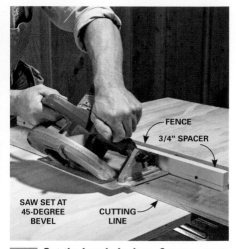

2 Cut the beveled edges. Screw a spacer to the fence of your jig and line up the edge with your cutting line just like you would for a standard cut. Then make the long 45-degree cuts.

FENCE
3/4" SPACER
SAW SET AT 45-DEGREE BEVEL
CUTTING LINE

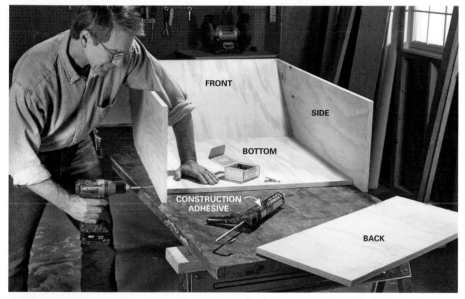

3 Build the box. Secure the panels to one another using construction adhesive and 2-in. screws. Drill pilot holes to avoid splintering the edges of the plywood. Flip the cart upside down and install the three bottom braces (E).

FRONT
SIDE
BOTTOM
CONSTRUCTION ADHESIVE
BACK

4 Install the wheel assembly. Install a washer, a wheel, another washer and a locknut on one end of the threaded rod. Measure the overhang required by the wheel assembly, add that length to the other end, then cut the rod to length. Install the axle braces and cover.

FENDER WASHER
LOCKNUT
AXLE BRACES

5 Install the legs. Apply two beads of construction adhesive, clamp the legs into place and secure them with screws. The spacer block positions the leg, leaving room for the tool rack.

LEG (H)
3/4" SPACER BLOCK

in the sides. Note: To ensure maximum sturdiness, use construction adhesive for all the connections—even for the metal corners.

Install the bottom (Photo 3) flush with the edges of the sides (A). Make sure the front beveled edge of the bottom makes solid contact with the bottom edge of the front (C). To complete the box, add the back (B). If you've cut and assembled everything correctly, there will be a 3-1/2-in. cavity at the back of the box to accommodate the tool rack. If it's a little larger or smaller, no big deal.

Install the wheels

Turn the cart box upside down. Secure the bottom braces (E). Secure the middle bottom brace so the center of it is exactly 20-3/4 in. away from the back of the back bottom brace (E). If you don't get this positioned right, it will affect the balance of the cart.

Position this assembly (Photo 4) snugly against one side of the cart and measure the amount of space it takes up. Transfer that measurement to the other end of the rod and mark the rod. Cut the rod and install the other wheel assembly.

Figure A
Garden cart

Overall Dimensions:
66" long x 24-1/2" tall x 41" wide (including wheels)

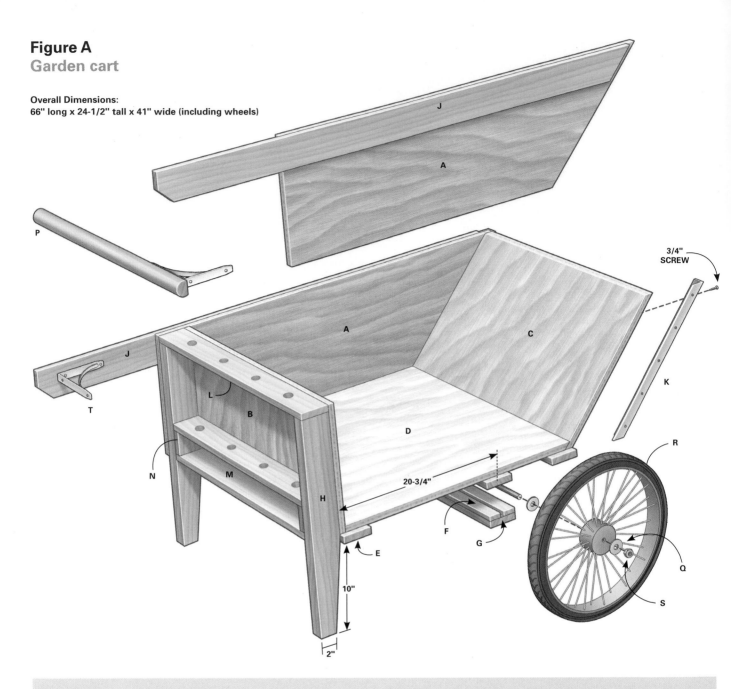

Cutting list

PART	QTY.	SIZE
A - Sides	2	3/4" x 14" x 50" *
B - Back	1	3/4" x 14" x 30"
C - Front	1	3/4" x 19-3/4" x 30" ‡
D - Bottom	1	3/4" x 31-5/8" x 30" §
E - Bottom braces	3	3/4" x 3-1/2" x 31-1/2"
F - Axle braces	2	1/2" x 1-1/2" x 31-1/2"
G - Axle cover	1	3/4" x 3-1/2" x 31-1/2" pine
H - Legs	2	1-1/2" x 3-1/2" x 23-3/4" pine
J - Handles	2	3/4" x 3 1/2" x 64-1/2" pine #
K - Corner braces	2	Cut to fit #
L - Long tool rack slat	1	3/4" x 3-1/2" x 30"
M - Short tool rack slats	2	3/4" x 3-1/2" x 27"

PART	QTY.	SIZE
N - Tool rack blocks	2	3/4" x 3-1/2" x 3"
P - Handle bar	1	1-1/4" handrail
Q - Washers	4	1/2" fender washer
R - Wheels	2	20" w/pneumatic tire
S - Locknut	2	1/2" locknut
T - L-brackets	2	6" shelf brackets (or similar)

NOTES:

* Angled cut

‡ 45-degree bevel cut, both ends

§ 45-degree bevel cut, one end

45-degree cuts, both ends

Materials list

ITEM	QTY.
4' x 8' x 3/4" exterior plywood	1
2x4 x 48" pine	1
1x4 x 96" pine	3
1-1/4" x 30" handrail	1
1/2" x 3" x 31-1/2" plywood or solid wood	1
20"-diameter wheels	2
1/2" x 48" threaded rod	1
1/2" washers	4
1/2" locknuts	2
6" L-shaped shelf brackets	2
1" x 1" x 2' aluminum angle	2
3/4" exterior screws	20
1-1/4" exterior screws	1 lb.
2" exterior screws	2 lbs.
Heavy-duty construction adhesive (pint tubes)	2

Figure B
Plywood diagram

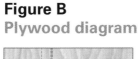

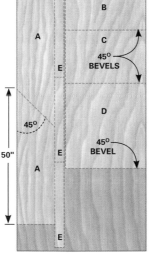

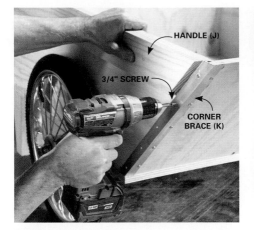

6 Strengthen the corners. Cut aluminum angle stock to length, then drill holes and countersink "dimples" for the screw heads. Install the corner braces using construction adhesive and screws.

7 Install the handle bar. Secure the handle bar by driving screws through each handle into the end of the rail. Add the L-brackets to beef up the connection.

8 Add a tool rack. Cut three tool rack slats and drill holes for tool handles. Adjust the size and spacing of the holes to suit your tools. Use adhesive and screws to install the slats.

Tip: Before cutting the rod to length, twist a regular nut onto it beyond the cut mark. After making the cut, twist the nut off; it will "recut" any damaged threads so the locknut will go on easier.

Apply glue to the axle braces (F), snug them tightly against the axle, then secure them to the middle bottom brace (E) with 2-in. screws. Finally, install the axle cover (G). Note: If you want to strengthen the wheel assembly for hauling heavier loads, use oak for the middle bottom brace, two axle braces and cover.

Install the legs, handles and tool rack

Cut the legs and screw them to the protruding sides (Photo 5). Use the spacer block as shown so the legs can accommodate the upper tool rack slat. Cut and install the handles (J), leaving space at the front for the aluminum angle.

Cut two lengths of aluminum angle. Don't try to measure them; just hold them in place and mark them for cutting. Drill holes and drill countersink "dimples" for the heads of the screws to nest into. Install the aluminum using adhesive and 3/4-in. screws (Photo 6).

Position the handle bar (P) and add the L-brackets (Photo 7) to reinforce the handle. Finally, install the three tool rack slats (Photo 8).

Remove the wheels and apply a coat of high-quality exterior primer, followed by two coats of exterior paint. To keep your cart in good condition, store it inside; if it will be outside, flip it upside down on a couple of scrap 4x4s.

Backyard spring

Build this bubbling fountain in 4 hours

If you've ever been to Yellowstone, you probably remember the magic of the natural springs. In less than half a day, you can build your own small spring to enjoy at home. Here's what you need:

- A large sturdy tub or bucket (about a 15-gallon size).
- A piece of pond liner large enough to line the bucket plus an additional foot on each side. The liner shown here is 5 ft. square.
- A small fountain pump (this one moves 210 gallons per hour).
- A piece of flexible braided plastic tubing the diameter of the pump outlet and cut to the length of the bucket height.
- A hose clamp to connect the tubing to the pump.
- A brick to rest the pump on.
- A square piece of heavy-gauge, galvanized hardware cloth with a 1/4-in. grid, cut 6 to 8 in. larger than the diameter of the bucket.
- About 40 lbs. of round rocks 1-1/2 to 3 in. in diameter. Mexican beach pebbles from a local nursery were used here.

You can tuck this spring fountain in the corner of a patio where you can easily see and hear the water. It can go anywhere in your yard or garden, but you'll need an outdoor outlet nearby.

Dig it in

- Dig a hole the size of your bucket, but slightly deeper. Place the top lip of the bucket 2-1/2 in. below the surface of the patio or ground.
- Place the bucket in the hole and backfill around it.
- Line the inside of the bucket with your pond liner. Extend the liner out at least 8 in. beyond the diameter of the bucket, more if you want your spring to shoot up higher. You want the liner to catch any water splashing on the rocks and direct the runoff back into the bucket. Curl up the edge of the liner to create a ledge for that purpose. Create a ledge by wedging the liner between two bricks.
- Place the brick and the pump in the center of the bucket. Connect the tubing to the pump outlet with a hose clamp.
- Follow the manufacturer's instructions for running the cord. Don't bury it. Caution: Plug the cord into a GFCI-protected outlet.
- Place the hardware cloth over the bucket and snip a small hole in the center to allow the tubing through. The hardware cloth should be larger than the diameter of the bucket.
- Place the stones and brick on top of the hardware cloth and fill the bucket with water.
- Turn the pump on and adjust the tubing, wedging it between the rocks to get the desired effect. You can restrict the flow of the water by pinching the pipe with wire or buying a flow restrictor from your pump supplier. The diameter of the pipe will determine how high the water bubbles up.

Figure A
Spring details

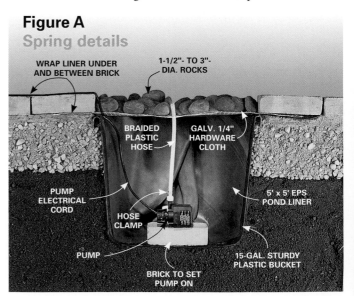

WRAP LINER UNDER AND BETWEEN BRICK

1-1/2"- TO 3"-DIA. ROCKS

BRAIDED PLASTIC HOSE

GALV. 1/4" HARDWARE CLOTH

PUMP ELECTRICAL CORD

HOSE CLAMP

PUMP

5' x 5' EPS POND LINER

15-GAL. STURDY PLASTIC BUCKET

BRICK TO SET PUMP ON

Second-story bird feeder

Here's a great way to look out a second-floor window and watch the birds at your feeder. To make refilling the feeder easy, attach a small pulley to the soffit of the overhang, thread some thin nylon rope through it and attach one end of the rope to the bird feeder using an S-hook. After refilling the feeder, hoist it back up to its spot so it's ready for the birds' next meal. Secure the rope down below by wrapping the end around a cleat attached to the siding.

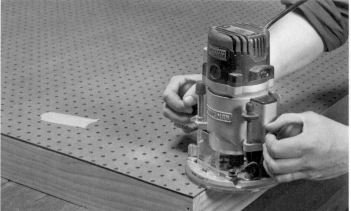

Chapter Eight

WORKSHOP PROJECTS

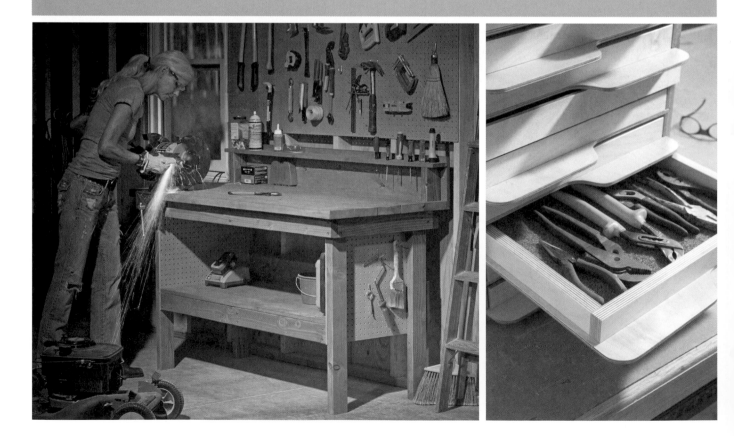

Mobile tool chest

MAGNETIC CABINET CATCH

SHELF FOR SANDPAPER

BUTT HINGE

9-1/4"

8

36"   VELCRO TOOL HOLSTER

9-1/4"

18-1/2"

2"-WIDE CLEATS

Build this mobile tool chest and take all your tools to the job in just one trip. All you need is a new dolly and some pine boards. If you use 1x10 pine boards, you won't need to cut any boards to width.

Screw the cabinet together with 1-5/8-in. drywall screws after drilling pilot holes. Clamp on the plywood back, check for square, then screw it to the sides, top and floor with 1-5/8-in. drywall screws. Attach the doors with 2-1/2-in. butt hinges.

Pine boards tend to warp, so to keep the doors flat, screw several 2-in.-wide cleats across the inside. The cleats can be drilled to double as great drill and driver bit holders.

To raise the cabinet to a more comfortable height, screw four scrap boards into a frame and attach this base to the dolly's base with lag screws. Next, drill holes in the base, then rest the cabinet on the base and attach it with 1-5/8-in. drywall screws through the floor into the base. To attach the upper part of the cabinet to the dolly, drive two 5/16-in.-diameter bolts through a board positioned behind the dolly's frame and into two 5/16-in. tee nuts set in the cabinet back. If this won't work for your dolly or design, use metal strapping or drill a couple of bolt holes through the dolly.

The cabinet's 9-1/4 in. depth provides plenty of space for power and hand tools plus full sheets of sandpaper. Have fun engineering convenient holders for your tools using pegboard, magnets, hooks and shop-fashioned holsters. Be sure to securely store tools so they won't fall or roll around as you cruise to and from the job.

Materials list

QTY.	ITEM
4	36-in.-long 1x10 pine boards (actually 3/4 in. x 9-1/4 in.) for the doors and sides
2	18-1/2-in.-long 1x10 pine boards for the cabinet top and floor
1	18-1/2-in. x 36-in. piece of 1/2-in.- thick plywood for the back
	Scrap boards for a base
	Assorted fasteners

BARREL BOLT LATCH

BASE

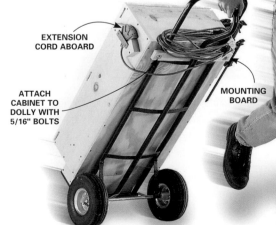

EXTENSION CORD ABOARD

ATTACH CABINET TO DOLLY WITH 5/16" BOLTS

MOUNTING BOARD

Hardware organizer

DIY isn't just about building and fixing things. It's also about inventory management: maintaining a supply of the stuff you need and knowing where to find it. This simple bin system is the perfect project to get you organized. It's modeled on the systems used in cabinet shops, plumbers' vans and mechanics' garages.

French cleats make it neat

This simple hanging system—made from a 1x4 cut at a 45-degree bevel—lets you grab a bin and take it to the job, or rearrange bins instantly as your needs change.

WHAT IT TAKES

TIME: 4 hours

COST: $55 or less

TOOLS: Table saw, miter saw, brad nailer

SKILL LEVEL: Beginner

The materials cost for the bins shown here is $30 to $55, depending on the type of plywood you choose. A store-bought light-duty system would cost just a few bucks more, but these homemade bins offer two big advantages: They're far tougher than plastic bins, and you can customize them to suit your stuff. Plus, they make the perfect scrap-wood project because all the parts are small. We built these bins from leftovers and didn't spend a dime.

Mass-produce parts

Begin by measuring the items you want to store. We found that the basic bin (see Figure A on p. 268) was just right for most stuff: nuts and bolts, construction screws,

1 **Cut the parts.** Rip strips of plywood to width on a table saw, then cut them to length with a miter saw. Clamp a scrap of plywood to the saw's fence to act as a stop block. That lets you cut identical lengths from several strips with one chop.

2 **Cut divider slots.** Mount a fence on your saw's miter gauge and position a stop block on the fence. Run the bin side across the blade. Then rotate the side 180 degrees and make a second pass to widen the slot. Caution: You have to remove the guard for this step. Be extra careful!

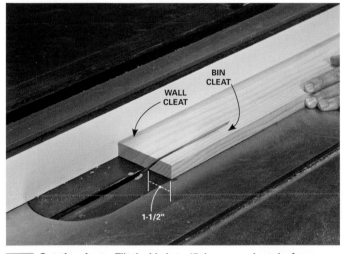

3 **Cut the cleats.** Tilt the blade to 45 degrees and set the fence so that the bin cleat is 1-1/2 in. wide. Getting the fence positioned may take some trial and error, so cut a test scrap first. Our guard was removed for photo clarity. Use yours!

4 **Assemble the bins.** Join the parts with glue and brads. The glue will provide plenty of strength, so drive only as many brads as needed to hold the parts together while the glue sets.

plumbing and electrical parts. For larger items, we made a few bins wider, but didn't change the bin sides (A). That approach is the most efficient because the sides are the most complex parts and changing them requires more fuss.

Once you've determined the sizes you want, fire up your table saw and rip plywood into strips. If you're following our plan, you'll need strips 1-3/4, 3-1/2 and 6 in. wide. Then cut the strips to length, making parts for one box only. Test-assemble the box to check the fit of the parts. Note: "Half-inch" plywood is slightly less than 1/2 in. thick, so the bin bottom (B) needs to be slightly longer than 6 in. Start at 6-1/8 in., then trim as needed.

When you've confirmed that all the parts are the right size, mass-produce them by chopping the strips to length (Photo 1).

If you want dividers (E) in any of the bins, your next step is to cut the divider slots. Set your table saw blade to a height of 3/16 in. Screw a long fence to your miter gauge and run the fence across the blade to cut a notch on the fence. Position a stop block 3-1/4 in. from the center of the notch. Place a side (A) against the block, run it across the blade, rotate it and cut again (Photo 2). Check the fit of a divider in the slot and reposition the block slightly to adjust the width of the slot. It may take two or three tries before you get the width right.

Materials list

To build an organizer similar to the one shown on p. 266, you'll need:

ITEM	QTY.
4' x 8' x 1/2" plywood	1
2' x 4' x 1/8" hardboard	1
1x4 x 8' pine	3
1" brads, 2-1/2" screws, wood glue and Watco natural Danish Oil	

When you're done cutting slots, it's time to clip off one corner of each side. Set your miter saw 45 degrees to the right. Clamp on a stop block and "gang-cut" sides just as you did when cutting parts to length (similar to Photo 1). Remember this:

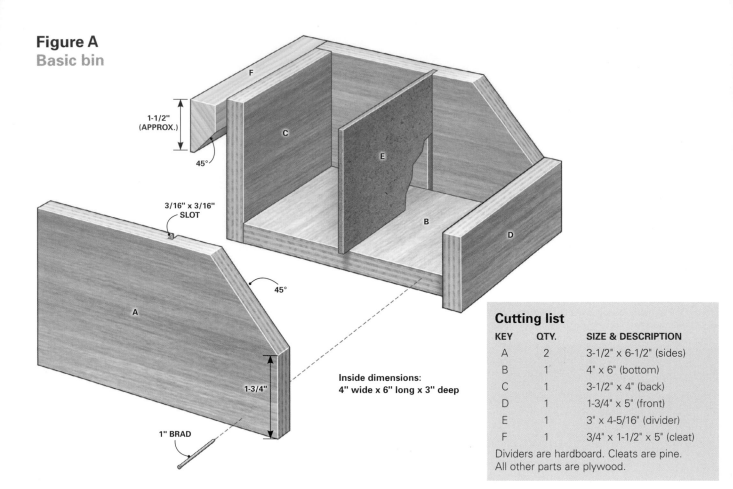

Figure A
Basic bin

1-1/2"
(APPROX.)

45°

F

C

E

B

D

3/16" x 3/16"
SLOT

45°

A

1-3/4"

Inside dimensions:
4" wide x 6" long x 3" deep

1" BRAD

Cutting list

KEY	QTY.	SIZE & DESCRIPTION
A	2	3-1/2" x 6-1/2" (sides)
B	1	4" x 6" (bottom)
C	1	3-1/2" x 4" (back)
D	1	1-3/4" x 5" (front)
E	1	3" x 4-5/16" (divider)
F	1	3/4" x 1-1/2" x 5" (cleat)

Dividers are hardboard. Cleats are pine.
All other parts are plywood.

Slotted sides require left/right pairs. For every side that you cut with the slot facing up, cut another with the slot down.

Next, cut the cleats (Photo 3). The 45-degree bevel cuts will leave sharp, splintery edges, so crank the table saw blade back to zero degrees and shave 1/8 in. off each cleat before cutting them to length.

Assemble them and hang them up

Assembly is fast and easy with glue and an 18-gauge brad nailer. First, tack the back (C) to the bottom (B), then add the sides (A), the front (D) and finally the cleat (F). After assembly, we wiped on two coats of Watco Danish Oil to keep the wood from absorbing greasy fingerprints and oils from hardware.

When mounting the wall cleats, start at the bottom. Make sure the bottom cleat is level and straight. Then cut spacers at least 1-3/4 in. tall and use them to position the remaining wall cleats (Photo 5). Larger cleats will create more space between rows of bins, making it easier to reach in and grab stuff. Bins filled with hardware put a heavy load on the cleats, so drive a screw into every wall stud.

SPACER

5 **Mount the wall cleats.** Mark the stud locations with tape and screw on the lowest cleat. Then work your way up the wall, using spacers to position each cleat.

Tool tote

Keep all your hand tools within easy reach in a portable 16-in. pine carton. Build one from a 1x8 x 12-ft. pine board, 1/4-in. plywood and a 3/4-in. oak dowel, and you'll never run back to the garage for a bit, blade, wrench or nail. Here's how:

- Cut and screw together the sides and ends with the ends protruding 1 in. beyond the sides. Drill holes in the top of the ends for a 3/4-in. dowel handle and tap it in the holes before assembling the ends and sides. Drill the 3/8-in. storage holes in the top edges of the sides before assembly.
- Saw 1/4-in. x 1-1/2-in. pine strips for the side slats and screw them to the protruding ends.
- Cut and screw on the 1/4-in. plywood floor.
- Cut 3/8-in. pine partitions and screw them behind the side slats to create custom-width pockets for the tools.

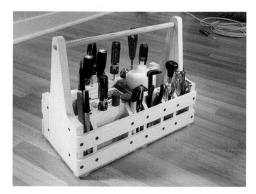

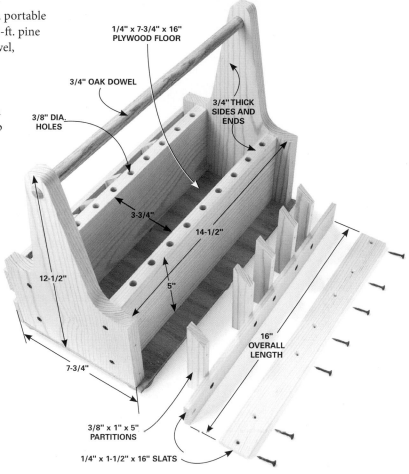

1/4" x 7-3/4" x 16" PLYWOOD FLOOR

3/4" OAK DOWEL

3/8" DIA. HOLES

3/4" THICK SIDES AND ENDS

3-3/4"

14-1/2"

12-1/2"

5"

7-3/4"

16" OVERALL LENGTH

3/8" x 1" x 5" PARTITIONS

1/4" x 1-1/2" x 16" SLATS

Drill bit rack

Here's the Cadillac of drill bit racks. It comes with a sizing index to check round work pieces and the bits themselves for drilling the exact corresponding hole. The length of the rack is up to you—build it to hold all your bits in order of size. You can either build it freestanding for tabletop use or without the base pieces for wall mounting.

To build one, lay your bits—spade and/or twist bits—on a table with 1/2-in. spacing. Cut two 3/4-in. x 3/4-in. strips of hardwood, then mark, clamp and drill according to the bit spacing you determined. (Drill through both strips for spade bits but only halfway through the second strip for twist bits.) Position two 2-3/4-in. blocks between the strips and screw them together. Use the bits you laid out to drill holes in a piece of 1/4-in. plywood for the sizing index. Screw it to the rectangle and get those bits in order!

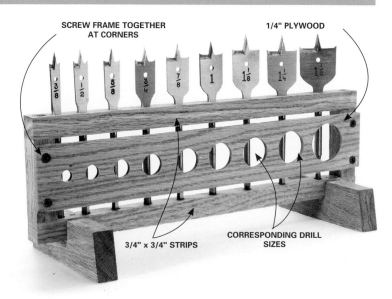

SCREW FRAME TOGETHER AT CORNERS

1/4" PLYWOOD

3/4" x 3/4" STRIPS

CORRESPONDING DRILL SIZES

A classic workbench

A timeless design that's simple and strong

WHAT IT TAKES

TIME: One day

COST: $85

SKILL LEVEL: Beginner

TOOLS: Circular saw, drill,
No. 6 countersink bit

If this workbench looks familiar, it's probably because you've seen one a lot like it in your father's or grandfather's shop. Variations of this design have been around for decades, and for good reason: The bench is strong, practical and super easy to build. You can run to the lumberyard in the morning, grab a few boards, and by noon you'll have a perfectly functional workbench.

The workbench isn't fancy—it's built from standard construction lumber. But you can easily customize it with drawers or other features now or later.

If you can cut a board, you can build this bench. And you don't need any fancy tools either. In addition to a small square and a tape measure, you'll need a circular saw to cut the parts and a drill to drive the screws.

Getting started

You'll find all the materials at a lumberyard or home center (see Materials list on p. 273). Choose lumber that's straight and flat, and that doesn't have too many gouges, slivers or cracks. We used Torx-head screws with self-drilling tips. But you can substitute any construction screw. If you're not using screws with self-drilling tips, drill pilot holes to avoid splitting the wood.

> **Tip:** If your car is too small for the long boards, you can ask to have the boards cut to length. Just remember to take the Cutting list with you to the store.

Cut the parts according to the Cutting list on p. 273. We used a miter saw, but a circular saw will work fine. Mark the 2x4s with a Speed square or combination square. Then carefully cut the boards to length. If you plan to stain or paint the bench, now is the time to sand the parts. And to really simplify your job, you could also stain or paint the parts before you assemble the bench.

Start by building the top and shelf frames

We used an old door propped up on sawhorses as a work surface, but the floor

1 **Build the frames.** Use 3-in. screws to assemble the frames that support the top and the shelf. To avoid splitting the 2x4s, either drill pilot holes or use self-drilling screws. Build both frames and set the top frame aside.

2 **Attach the shelf boards.** Attach the outside boards first. Then position the two remaining boards to create equal spaces between them and screw them to the frame. Before driving screws, drill pilot holes with a countersink bit.

3 **Assemble the legs.** Drill five holes about 2 in. from the edge of the pegboard with the countersinking bit. Spread a bead of construction adhesive on the legs and attach the pegboard with 1-1/4-in. screws. If glue oozes through the holes, wait for it to dry. Then shave it off with a sharp chisel.

4 Screw the legs to the top frame. Apply construction adhesive where the legs contact the top frame. Then attach the legs with screws.

TOP FRAME

SHELF

BOTTOM OF PEGBOARD

5 Add the shelf. Rest the bench on one end. Slide the shelf between the legs and line it up with the bottom of the pegboard. Screw through the shelf into the legs.

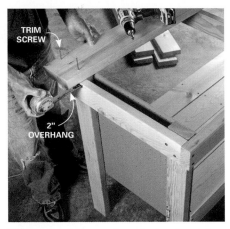

TRIM SCREW

2" OVERHANG

6 Mount the top boards. Starting at the back, align the first 2x6 flush to the back and measure for the 2-in. overhang on the side. Attach the 2x6 with trim screws. Attach the rest of the boards the same way. The front 2x6 will overhang the frame about 2 in.

7 Install the backboard. Attach the 1x4 shelf to the 1x10 backboard. Then add a 2x4 block at each end. Rest the backboard assembly on the workbench and drive screws through the back to hold it in place.

will work too. Lay the 2x4s for the front and back of the top and shelf on the work surface and mark the centers. Remember, if you're not using self-drilling screws, drill pilot holes for the screws. Photo 1 shows how to assemble the frames. Set the top frame aside and screw the shelf boards to the shelf frame (Photo 2).

Build and attach the leg assemblies

Photo 3 shows how to build the leg assemblies. You'll notice that the leg assemblies are 1/8 in. narrower than the inside dimension of the top. That's so you can install the legs without binding, which would cause the pegboard to bow. Also, if the only pegboard you can find is thinner than the 1/4-in. pegboard specified, add the difference to the front and back of the shelf frame (C). For example, if you buy 1/8-in. pegboard, add 1/4 in. to parts C.

The pegboard is useful for hanging tools, but its real function is to stabilize the workbench as a brace. We added the construction adhesive to make sure the assemblies stayed strong and rigid. Be aware, though, that some of the adhesive will be visible through the holes.

The pegboard holes are a little too big to use as screw holes, so use a No. 6 countersink bit to drill pilot holes and make countersinks for the screws. Secure five evenly spaced 1-1/4-in. screws into each leg.

The next step is to attach the legs to the top frame. Apply construction adhesive to the top 3 in. of the legs. Then attach the leg assemblies with 3-in. screws (Photo 4).

Add the shelf and top

Stand the workbench on one end. Then it's simple to slide the shelf into place and line it up with the pegboard (Photo 5). Drive 3-in. screws through the shelf frame into the legs to support the shelf.

The top of this bench is 2x6s, placed tight together. The boards overhang the frame 2 in. on the sides and front. The overhang makes it easier to use clamps on the edges of the workbench. Photo 6 shows how to get started. We attached the 2x6s with trim screws, but you could substitute 16d casing nails.

Figure A
Exploded View

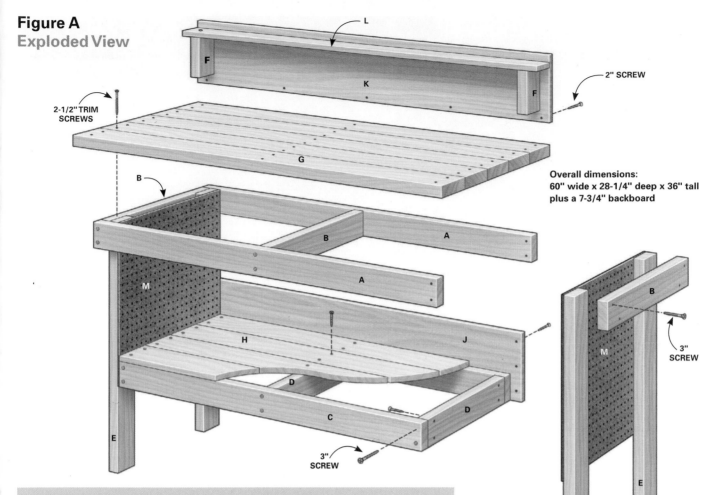

2-1/2" TRIM SCREWS

L

F

K

F

2" SCREW

B

**Overall dimensions:
60" wide x 28-1/4" deep x 36" tall
plus a 7-3/4" backboard**

G

B

A

A

M

J

B

H

M

D

3" SCREW

E

C

D

3" SCREW

E

E

Materials list

ITEM	QTY.	ITEM	QTY.
2x4 x 8' pine	6	2' x 4' x 1/4" pegboard	1
2x6 x 10' pine	2	3" self-drilling screws	42
2x6 x 8' pine	1	2" self-drilling screws	50
1x10 x 10' pine	1	1-1/4" self-drilling screws	20
1x6 x 10' pine	2	2-1/2" trim screws	30
1x4 x 6' pine	1	Tube of construction adhesive	1

Attach the back brace and backboard

The 1x10 back brace keeps things from falling off the back of the shelf, but it also stiffens the bench to prevent side-to-side rocking. Apply construction adhesive before attaching the brace with 2-in. screws.

The backboard is a 1x10 with a 1x4 shelf attached. On the side of the 1x10 you want facing out, draw a line the length of the board, 1-3/4 in. down from the top. This is where you'll align the bottom of the 1x4. Draw a second line 1-3/8 in. from the top. Drill pilot holes with the countersink bit every

8 in. along this line. Now ask a helper to hold the 1x4 on the line while you drive 2-in. screws into the shelf through the pilot holes. After the shelf and 2x4 blocks at each end are attached, screw the backboard to the workbench (Photo 7).

You can modify your bench to fit your space and work style. We mounted an inexpensive woodworking vise on the front of the workbench and drilled holes in the 1x4 shelf to hold screwdrivers. If you've got a pint-size carpenter in the family, check out the mini version of the bench on p. 274. It would make a great project to build with your kids or grandkids.

Cutting list

KEY	QTY.	SIZE & DESCRIPTION
A	2	1-1/2" x 3-1/2" x 56" top frame front and back
B	3	1-1/2" x 3-1/2" x 22-1/2" top frame crosspieces
C	2	1-1/2" x 3-1/2" x 49-1/2" shelf frame front and back
D	3	1-1/2" x 3-1/2" x 19-1/2" shelf crosspieces
E	4	1-1/2" x 3-1/2" x 34-1/2" legs
F	2	1-1/2" x 3-1/2" x 6" back shelf supports
G	5	1-1/2" x 5-1/2" x 60" top boards
H	4	3/4" x 5-1/2" x 49-1/2" shelf boards
J	1	3/4" x 9-1/4" x 53" back brace
K	1	3/4" x 9-1/4" x 60" backboard
L	1	3/4" x 3-1/2" x 60" backboard shelf
M	2	22-3/8" x 22-3/8" x 1/4" pegboard leg braces

Mini-classic for mini DIYers

Here's a plan for a downsized version of the workbench. All of the construction steps are the same; it's just smaller to fit the young carpenter in your family. The height is about right for a 42- to 48-in.-tall DIYer, but you can easily increase the height just by making the legs longer.

Figure B
Small bench

Overall dimensions: 48" wide x 22-3/4" deep x 24" tall plus a 5-3/4" backboard

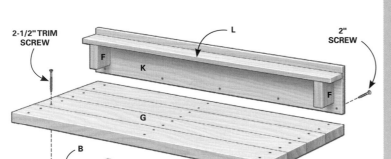

2-1/2" TRIM SCREW

2" SCREW

3" SCREW

3" SCREW

Cutting list (small workbench)

KEY	QTY.	SIZE & DESCRIPTION
A	2	1-1/2" x 3-1/2" x 45" top frame front and back
B	3	1-1/2" x 3-1/2" x 17-1/2" top frame crosspieces
C	2	1-1/2" x 3-1/2" x 38-1/2" shelf frame front and back
D	3	1-1/2" x 3-1/2" x 14-1/2" shelf crosspieces
E	4	1-1/2" x 3-1/2" x 22-1/2" legs
F	2	1-1/2" x 3-1/2" x 4" back shelf supports
G	4	1-1/2" x 5-1/2" x 48" top boards
H	3	3/4" x 5-1/2" x 38-1/2" shelf boards
J	1	3/4" x 7-1/4" x 42" back brace
K	1	3/4" x 7-1/4" x 48" backboard
L	1	3/4" x 3-1/2" x 48" backboard shelf
M	2	17-3/8" x 17-3/8" x 1/4" pegboard leg braces

Materials list (small workbench)

ITEM	QTY.
2x4 x 8' pine	4
2x6 x 8' pine	2
1x8 x 8' pine	1
1x6 x 10' pine	1
1x4 x 4' pine	1
2' x 4' x 1/4" pegboard	1
3" self-drilling screws	42
2" self-drilling screws	40
1-1/4" self-drilling screws	16
2-1/2" trim screws	24
Tube of construction adhesive	1

Roll-around tool caddy

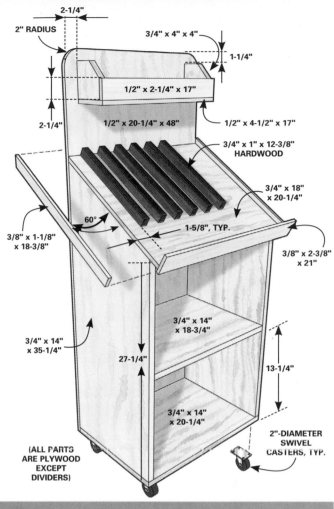

2-1/4"

2" RADIUS

3/4" x 4" x 4"

1-1/4"

1/2" x 2-1/4" x 17"

1/2" x 20-1/4" x 48"

2-1/4"

1/2" x 4-1/2" x 17"

3/4" x 1" x 12-3/8" HARDWOOD

3/4" x 18" x 20-1/4"

60°

1-5/8", TYP.

3/8" x 1-1/8" x 18-3/8"

3/8" x 2-3/8" x 21"

3/4" x 14" x 35-1/4"

3/4" x 14" x 18-3/4"

27-1/4"

13-1/4"

3/4" x 14" x 20-1/4"

2"-DIAMETER SWIVEL CASTERS, TYP.

(ALL PARTS ARE PLYWOOD EXCEPT DIVIDERS)

This simple workstation rolls right up to the job—anywhere in your work area. With your specialty tools organized and at your fingertips, you can concentrate on the project at hand. No more wandering around the shop trying to find tools.

The caddy shown here is configured for woodturning and ready to roll up to the lathe. If you're a gearhead, you could build it with a flat top with bins for sockets and wrenches, and shelves below for car supplies. If you're a woodworker, outfit it with planes, mallets and chisels. Whatever you use it for, when you're done for the day, you can just roll it out of the way.

Tape caddy

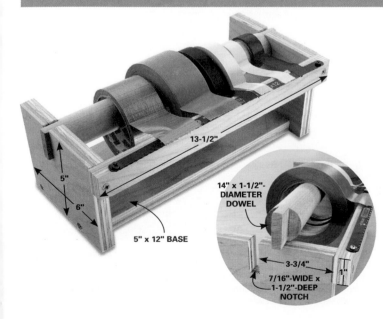

13-1/2"

5"

6"

5" x 12" BASE

14" x 1-1/2"-DIAMETER DOWEL

3-3/4"

7/16"-WIDE x 1-1/2"-DEEP NOTCH

1"

Keep your tape rolls in one place and easy to use with this plywood dispenser. When you run out of tape, just lift the dowel out of the notches, reload and slide it back in the notches. You'll need:

- Two 5-in. x 6-in. side pieces of 3/4-in. plywood
- One 5-in. x 12-in. plywood base
- One 1-in. x 13-1/2-in. hacksaw blade support
- One 14-in. x 1-1/2-in.-diameter dowel rod
- An 18-tooth, 12-in. hacksaw blade

Notch the sides to the dimensions shown and screw them to the base along with the hacksaw blade support.

Saw the dowel ends to fit in the notched sides and screw the hacksaw blade on the support, positioning it so the saw teeth extend a little beyond the edge of the plywood. That's it. Load up with tape and you'll never go hunting for stray rolls again.

P.S. You may want to screw the dispenser to your workbench to aid in pulling tape (especially duct tape) off the roll.

Compact tool cabinet

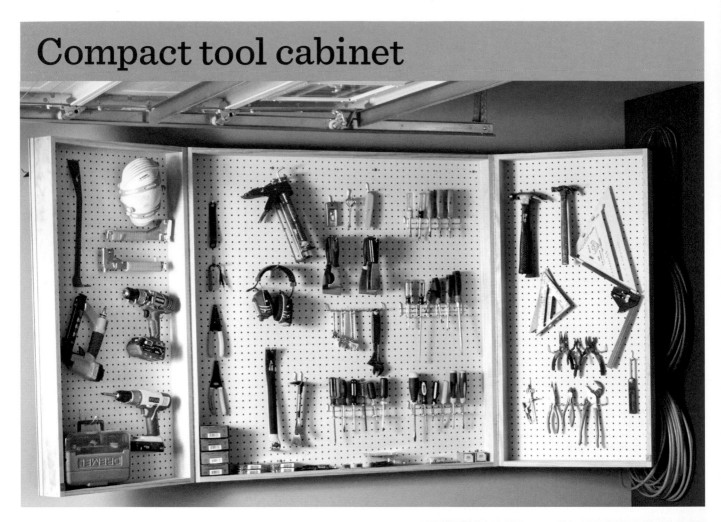

Build an easy-access pegboard storage unit

Curtis Petersen is a building maintenance guy, so he knows a thing or two about tools and how to store them. We recently visited his workshop and were instantly drawn to the pegboard cabinet he'd built. Pegboard is his favorite way to store tools. He loves the easy access, and an empty peg always lets him know that a tool has gone AWOL. What he doesn't like about pegboard is that it takes up wall space, which is scarce in any shop. So he built a pegboard cabinet that delivers the best of both worlds. His design provides almost 48 sq. ft. of pegboard while taking up only 16 sq. ft. of wall space.

Build the base frame

Cut your 1x4 frame boards to size. We used a higher-grade pine. It was worth the extra money to be able to work with straight, knot-free wood. Sand all the boards with 100-grit sandpaper before assembling the frames. Glue the joints and nail them with 1-1/2-in. brads, just to hold them together. When the base is fully assembled, go back and drive in two 2-in. trim head screws. If you don't have a brad nailer, no problem; the screws are plenty strong on their own.

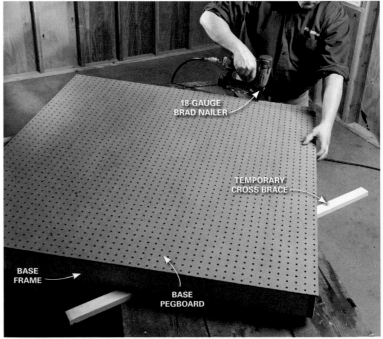

1 **Fasten pegboard to the base frame. Attach temporary braces to hold the base frame perfectly square. Lay a 4 x 4-ft. sheet of pegboard over the frame. The oversize sheet lets you position the holes so they won't be along the outer edge of the cabinet. Note: If you don't have a router to trim off the excess pegboard (see Photo 2), position the pegboard, mark it with a pencil and cut it to size before nailing it in place.**

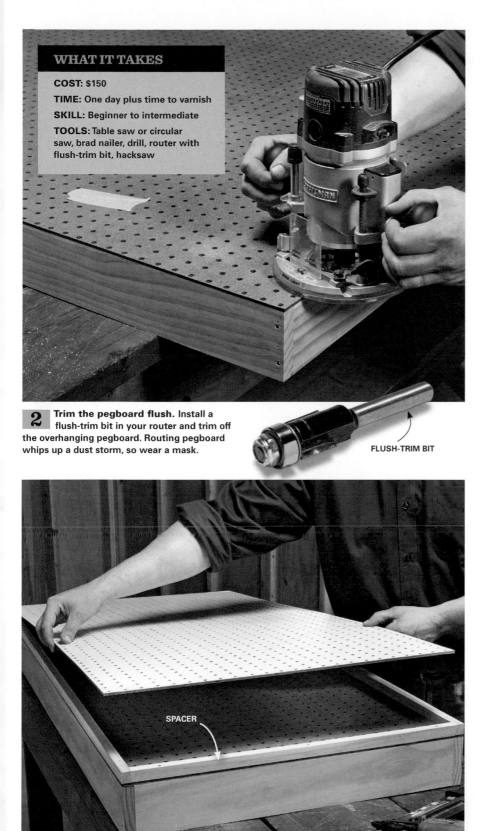

Attach the pegboard to the base frame

We wanted solid material along all the edges, which meant we couldn't just measure 47-3/4 in. from the end of the sheet and assume the holes wouldn't be exposed. Not all sheets of pegboard are the same size, and sometimes the holes aren't perfectly centered on the sheet. Square up the frame and hold it in place with a couple of temporary cross braces and brads. Lay a half sheet of pegboard on top of the frame so all the rows of holes are inset at least 1/4 in. before fastening it down. Fasten the sheet with 1-in. brads every 8 in. or so (Photo 1), and use glue on all the unfinished sides of the pegboard.

Once the pegboard is secure, trim off the excess material with a router equipped with a flush-trim bit (Photo 2). If you don't own a flush-trim bit, this is an excellent opportunity to buy a tool you'll definitely use again. Trimming down pegboard creates clouds of very fine dust, which seems to get into everything. Don't even think about doing this without wearing a dust mask. If you don't have a router to trim off the excess, just mark the outline of the base frame onto the half sheet of pegboard and trim it with a saw.

Build the doors

Use the same process to build the door frames and install the pegboard as you did on the base. Again, pay special attention to the spacing of the holes before you attach the pegboard and rout it flush. The only difference this time is that the first layer of pegboard should be facing down.

Once the first layer of pegboard is in place, rip down 3/4-in. strips of wood to act as a spacer between the first and the second layers (Photo 3). This will allow clearance for the peg hardware on both sides of the door. Align the spacers the same way you did with the frame, so the end grain cannot be seen from the sides. Tack them in place with 1-1/2-in. brads.

Tack on the outer layer of pegboard or dry-erase board (white/gloss hardboard panel board) with 1-in. brads, and then drive in 2-in. trim head screws about every 8 in. or so. Pegboard and other hardboard materials tend to pucker when you screw into them, so predrill the holes with a

2 **Trim the pegboard flush.** Install a flush-trim bit in your router and trim off the overhanging pegboard. Routing pegboard whips up a dust storm, so wear a mask.

FLUSH-TRIM BIT

3 **Complete the doors.** A 3/4-in. spacer between the two layers of pegboard creates space for the hooks.

WHAT IT TAKES

COST: $150

TIME: One day plus time to varnish

SKILL: Beginner to intermediate

TOOLS: Table saw or circular saw, brad nailer, drill, router with flush-trim bit, hacksaw

SPACER

small countersink drill bit. Don't attach the screen mold on the outside of the doors until the doors are hung onto the base.

Finish the back side of the base

There needs to be space for the peg hardware on the back of the base, so install 3/4-in. strips of pine on the back two sides of the base. Fasten them with glue and 1-1/2-in. brads. Next, install a full pine 1x4 on the top and bottom of the back side of the base. These are the boards you'll screw through when you hang the cabinet on the wall. Glue and tack these boards into place, and then drive 2-in. trim head screws through the boards into the base frame.

Use another 3/4-in. strip of pine to brace up the center of the pegboard. Install this center brace between the holes. Secure it with glue and a few 1-in. brads from the front side of the base. This will prevent the 4 x 4-ft. sheet of pegboard from getting too floppy.

The doors will be thicker than the base once you add the screen molding. This means they'll make contact with the walls before they fully open. If you add filler strips of pegboard on the back side of the pine boards you just installed, the doors will open farther, and you'll get another cool-looking dark strip resembling a walnut inlay (Photo 4). Even with the filler strips, the cabinet doors will make contact with the wall about 4 in. before they fully open. If you really, really want the doors to open all the way, you can add another 1/4 in. of filler to the back. But if you hang tools on the front of the cabinet or on the walls on either side, it shouldn't matter at all.

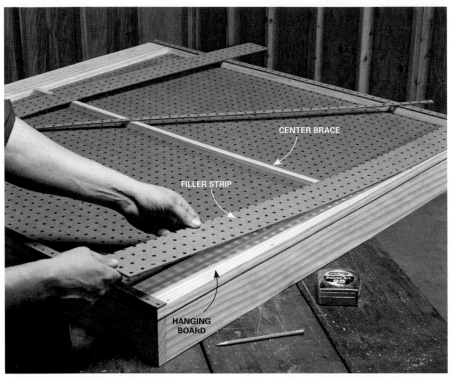

4 Add filler strips. Installing filler strips on the back of the base will allow the doors to open a little wider.

CENTER BRACE

FILLER STRIP

HANGING BOARD

Attach the doors

The cabinet is a little shorter than the hinges; use a hacksaw to trim them down. Install the hinges to the base first. Fold it over the front edge of the base at a 90-degree angle and install the screws. Clamp the doors into place before you screw the other half of the hinge. Use a self-centering screw hole punch to make sure the screws are perfectly aligned (Photo 5). Make sure the doors stay shut by installing a magnet catch on the top and bottom.

If the gap between the doors isn't perfectly even, adjust the screen mold on the front of the doors as you install them until it is. Fasten the screen mold with 1-in. brads.

Finish it up

After filling the holes with putty, you can cover the wood with clear polyurethane. It keeps the wood color light and really darkened up the edges of the pegboard. Don't use an aggressively sticky tape when you tape off the hardboard/dry-erase board or you may pull the finish right off them. Screw the cabinet to the wall with screws that penetrate the studs at least 1-1/4 in., and try to hit at least three studs on the top and three on the bottom. You can install handles on the bottom if you like.

Now that you're done, it's time to shop for the hardware you'll need to hang all your tools. Here's a suggestion for you: Avoid 1/8-in. hooks. They fit in the 1/4-in. holes but tend to pull out when you remove a tool.

SCREW HOLE PUNCH

PIANO HINGE

5 Install the doors. Clamp the doors to the cabinet and install the piano hinges. A self-centering screw hole punch helps you center the screws in the hinge holes.

Figure A
Pegboard cabinet

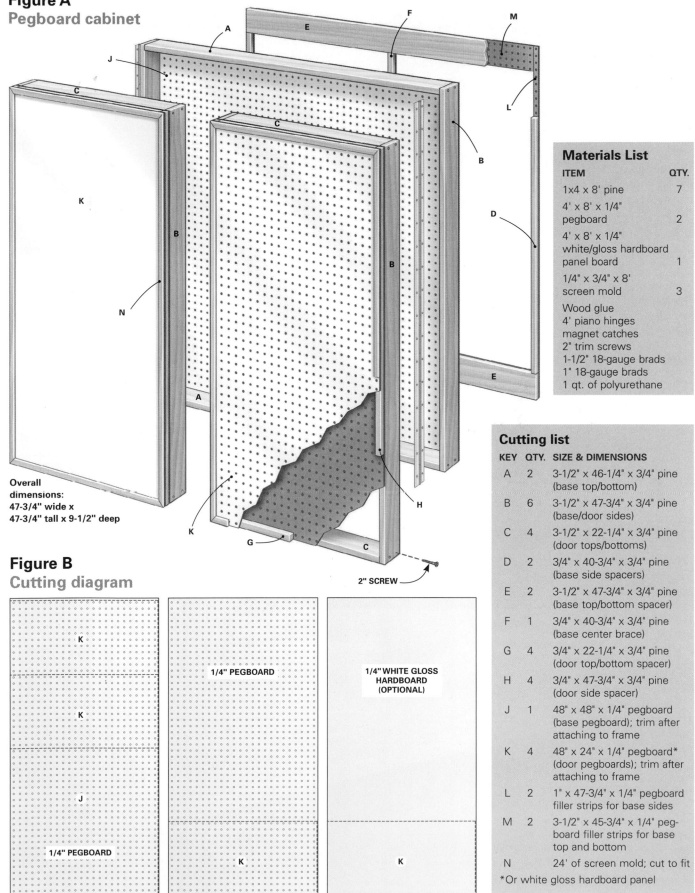

Overall dimensions:
47-3/4" wide x
47-3/4" tall x 9-1/2" deep

2" SCREW

Materials List

ITEM	QTY.
1x4 x 8' pine	7
4' x 8' x 1/4" pegboard	2
4' x 8' x 1/4" white/gloss hardboard panel board	1
1/4" x 3/4" x 8' screen mold	3

Wood glue
4' piano hinges
magnet catches
2" trim screws
1-1/2" 18-gauge brads
1" 18-gauge brads
1 qt. of polyurethane

Cutting list

KEY	QTY.	SIZE & DIMENSIONS
A	2	3-1/2" x 46-1/4" x 3/4" pine (base top/bottom)
B	6	3-1/2" x 47-3/4" x 3/4" pine (base/door sides)
C	4	3-1/2" x 22-1/4" x 3/4" pine (door tops/bottoms)
D	2	3/4" x 40-3/4" x 3/4" pine (base side spacers)
E	2	3-1/2" x 47-3/4" x 3/4" pine (base top/bottom spacer)
F	1	3/4" x 40-3/4" x 3/4" pine (base center brace)
G	4	3/4" x 22-1/4" x 3/4" pine (door top/bottom spacer)
H	4	3/4" x 47-3/4" x 3/4" pine (door side spacer)
J	1	48" x 48" x 1/4" pegboard (base pegboard); trim after attaching to frame
K	4	48" x 24" x 1/4" pegboard* (door pegboards); trim after attaching to frame
L	2	1" x 47-3/4" x 1/4" pegboard filler strips for base sides
M	2	3-1/2" x 45-3/4" x 1/4" pegboard filler strips for base top and bottom
N		24' of screen mold; cut to fit

*Or white gloss hardboard panel

Figure B
Cutting diagram

1/4" PEGBOARD

1/4" PEGBOARD

1/4" PEGBOARD

1/4" WHITE GLOSS HARDBOARD (OPTIONAL)

Build a rolling shop cart

MEET THE EXPERT

Tom Caspar has been rolling around his workshop for more than 40 years. He recently retired as editor of American Woodworker magazine.

Figure A
Rolling shop cart
Overall dimensions: 20" wide x 32" long x 34-1/4" tall
All materials are 3/4" thick

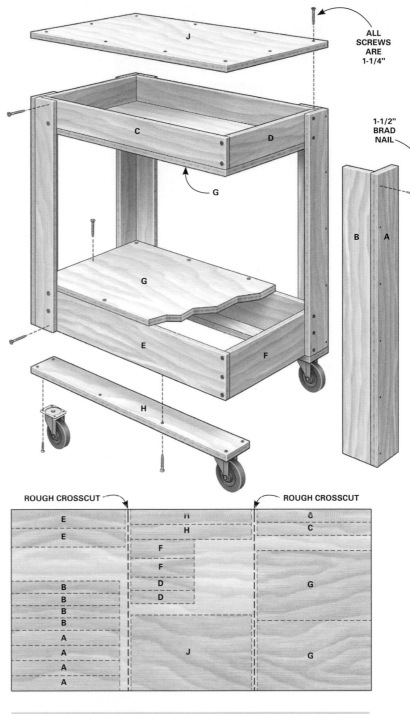

ALL SCREWS ARE 1-1/4"

1-1/2" BRAD NAIL

ROUGH CROSSCUT — ROUGH CROSSCUT

Whether your shop is big or small, it's sure handy to have a cart or two for moving stacks of parts from one machine to another. My carts make an endless journey around my shop, from planer to table saw to drill press to sander, and on and on. They're never empty!

Constructing this cart is simple—all the parts are just glued and screwed or nailed together. You'll need one full sheet of 3/4-in. plywood and a box of 1-1/4-in. screws.

Sometimes I use a cart to support my table saw work, so I built my carts the same height as my saw. If you want to do the same, buy the casters for your cart before cutting any parts to size. (I recommend using casters that are at least 2-1/2 in. in diameter.) Then measure the total height of one caster and alter the lengths of the cart's legs as needed.

I've laid out the parts so you can crosscut your plywood into three 32-in. pieces before having to cut anything to exact size. It's OK if these crosscuts are rough; a jigsaw or circular saw would work fine. After this, it's best to use a table saw for ripping the parts and a miter saw or table saw for cutting them to length.

After breaking down the plywood into manageable sizes, cut all the leg pieces (A and B). Glue them together, using nails or screws to hold them together while the glue dries. Make sure their ends are even.

Cut the parts for the upper and lower boxes (C, D, E and F) and glue and screw them together. Next, cut the shelf and bottom (G) to fit the boxes and glue and screw these pieces into place. (Adding a bottom to the upper box makes it easier to clamp things to the top of the cart. Without a bottom, you'd only have a narrow 3/4-in. edge to clamp to.) Make sure the shelf and bottom don't overhang each box or the legs won't fit correctly. To avoid any overhang, you could cut the shelf and bottom 1/16 in. smaller all around.

Fasten the legs to the boxes, using three screws at each corner. Finally, cut the caster supports (H) and top (J) to size and add them to the cart. Fasten the casters using 3/4-in. No. 14 sheet metal screws.

Cutting list

KEY	QTY.	DIMENSIONS	NAME
A	4	3/4" x 4" x 29"	Wide leg pieces
B	4	3/4" x 3-1/4" x 29"	Narrow leg pieces
C	2	3/4" x 3-1/2" x 30-1/2"	Upper box, long sides
D	2	3/4" x 3-1/2" x 17"	Upper box, short sides
E	2	3/4" x 5" x 30-1/2"	Lower box, long sides
F	2	3/4" x 5" x 17"	Lower box, short sides
G	2	3/4" x 18-1/2" x 30-1/2"	Shelf and bottom
H	2	3/4" x 4" x 32"	Caster supports
J	1	3/4" x 20" x 32"	Top

Tool tray tower

BUILT-IN PULL

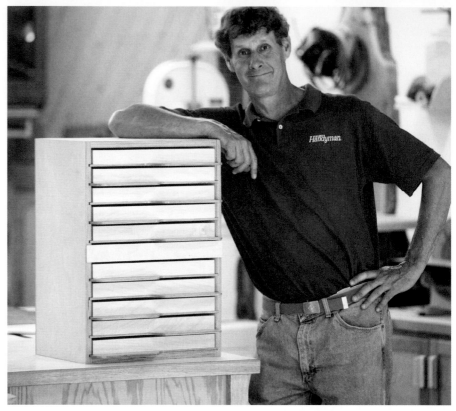

Because most hand tools are relatively flat, piling them in deep drawers wastes a lot of space and makes them hard to find and dig out. This rather fetching cabinet separates and organizes all those tools. Best of all, you can remove the tray containing, say, the open-end wrenches, and take the whole collection to wherever you're wrenching.

There are several plain versions of this design: a few drawers made from MDF with utilitarian handles. We decided to bump it up a notch and build a 10-tray unit out of cabinet-grade birch plywood. And rather than use handles, we made the tray bases with built-in "paddle pulls."

Shaping the paddle pulls is the trickiest part of the whole project. You'll get the best results by clamping the tray bottoms together and "gang-cutting" the paddle pulls all at once with a band saw. Sanding them all at once also saves lots of time and ensures that the parts are identical (Photo 5). (Then get the alternating paddle pulls by flipping over half of the tray bottoms.)

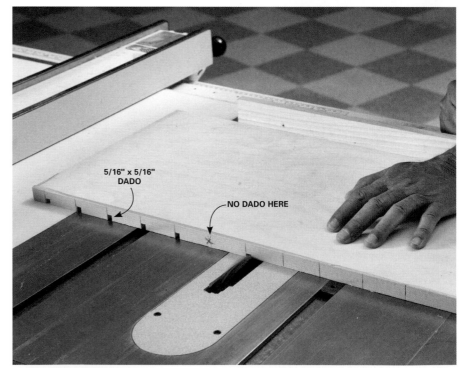

5/16" x 5/16" DADO

NO DADO HERE

1 **Mark and cut the dadoes for the drawers.** Mark the dado bottoms on the edges beginning at 13/16 in. up from the bottom and then every 2 in. Don't cut a dado in the center—that's where the stretcher goes. After cutting all 10 dadoes, cut off the top, 2-3/4 in. above the last dado bottom.

If you don't have a band saw, a jigsaw will do. If you're jigsawing, mark one paddle pull on a tray bottom and use it to scribe and gang-cut five at a time. You can also just skip the paddle pulls and add the drawer pulls of your choice. To do that, cut the tray bottoms to 15-1/2 x 12 in., but "gang-sand" them all as shown in Photo 5.

This project calls for a table saw and a dado blade. The good news is that absolutely no hardware is needed, including fussy, expensive drawer slides to mess around with.

This project is a real plywood eater. You'll need a full sheet of both 1/4-in. and 3/4-in. plywood to build one. Build it with more or fewer trays; it's up to you. If you choose to make a wider or taller cabinet with more trays, fine. But it'll take more than two sheets of plywood!

Cut the back and sides a little oversize

Cut the 1/4-in. back first. Take a notch out of a corner of the sheet rather than ripping a whole strip or you won't have enough leftover plywood to make the drawer bases. Cut the back 1/8 in. larger than the illustration calls for. After the cabinet is assembled, you can get extremely accurate measurements and either cut the back to fit or use a flush-trim router bit after it's attached. Cut the sides a full 24 in. tall and cut them to length after the dadoes

2 Prefinish the interior surfaces. Protect the gluing areas with masking tape and varnish surfaces on the cabinet interior. It's much easier to do now than later. For smooth tray operation, be sure to brush out any varnish pools or drips inside the dadoes.

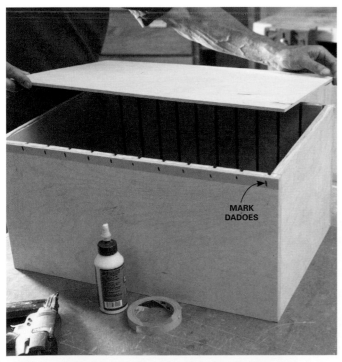

3 Assemble the box. Glue and nail the box together with 1-1/2-in. brads. Then mark the dadoes to avoid misses when you nail on the back with 1-in. brads. Glue the perimeter, then nail one edge flush with the box side. Square up the box with the back to nail the second side. Then finish nailing the remaining two sides.

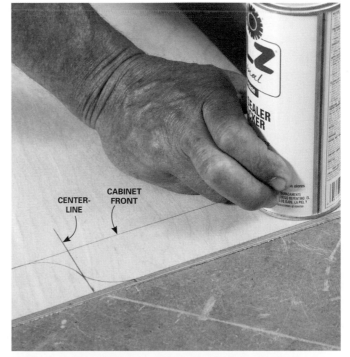

4 Mark the paddle pulls. Cut the tray bottoms into 15-1/2 x 13-3/4-in. rectangles. Draw a line 12 in. from the back edge of the trays and mark a centerline. Use the centerline and one of the corners as a guide while you trace around a spray paint can to mark the curves. Then cut the shapes with a band saw or jigsaw.

are cut. (You don't need to cut a dado in the center where the stretcher goes. We forgot and cut one there, but it's hidden anyway.)

Gang-sand the exposed tops of the tray sides before assembly. After you get the cabinet box and trays assembled, finish sanding and apply the clear coat. A nice finishing touch is to line the tray bottoms with squares of indoor/outdoor carpeting.

12"

15"

16-1/2" x 23-1/2"

DADOES: 5/16" x 5/16" DEEP

23-1/2"

12"

1-3/4" x 16-1/2" STRETCHER

LEAVE OUT THIS DADO

10-1/2" x 1-1/2"

14-3/4" x 1-1/2"

2"

2"

13/16"

13-3/4"

15-1/2"

5 Gang-sand the tray bottoms. Clamp the tray bottoms together and sand the fronts of them all at once. Get them roughed out and then finish up with a random orbital sander. (If you have a dedicated drum sander or drum sander accessory for your drill press, use that for the inside curves.)

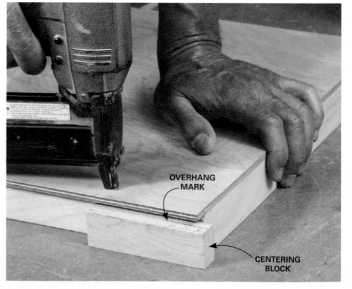

OVERHANG MARK

CENTERING BLOCK

6 Build the trays. Glue and nail the tray sides together. Center one of the bottoms with equal overhangs, then mark a centering block to guide you while you glue and nail on the bottoms. You'll need to use the block on just one side for each tray.

Table saw sled

To get dead-on square cuts every time!

If you own a table saw, you know it works great for ripping long pieces. But did you know that you can crosscut wide pieces with the same ease and accuracy? All it takes is a table saw sled. A table saw sled rides in the miter gauge slots and has a fence that's mounted exactly 90 degrees to the blade, enabling accurate square cuts. We'll show you how to build a sled using a 42-in. square sheet of 1/2-in. plywood.

We used top-quality nine-ply birch, but any flat plywood with smooth faces will work. The tricky parts of the construction are cutting runners that slide smoothly in the tracks, and getting the fence perfectly square to the blade. We'll show you how to accomplish both as you construct the sled.

Start by cutting strips of plywood for the stiffener, front fence and blade cover (Figure A). Cut them 1/4 in. wider and 1/2 in.

longer than the finished size to allow for trimming. Then spread wood glue on the mating faces and clamp them together. Clamp them onto a perfectly flat surface like the top of your table saw. Try to keep the layers lined up as you clamp them. After about 20 minutes, scrape off the partially hardened glue. Then run the pieces through the table saw, removing about 1/4 in. Using Figure A as a guide, mark the shapes onto the pieces and saw them out with a jigsaw. Smooth the curves with a belt sander.

The next step is to cut the runners from strips of hardwood. If you have standard 3/4-in.-wide miter gauge slots, sand or plane a 1x3 hardwood board until it slides easily in the slots (Photo 1). (For narrower slots, you'll have to plane or cut the 1x3 to reduce its thickness.) Then rip strips from the 1x3 that are about 1/16 in. thinner than the depth of the slot. Photos 2 and 3 show how to

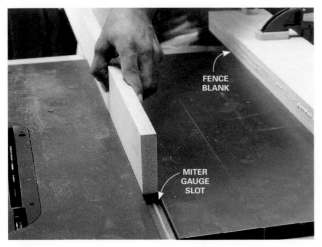

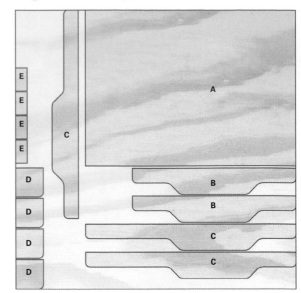

Figure A Sled pieces

1 Slide a hardwood board in the miter gauge slot on your table saw to check the fit. If it's too tight, sand and plane it until it slides easily with no slop. Work on this while you're waiting for the glue to set up on the fence blank (about a half hour).

attach the strips to the sled base. Let the glue set for about 20 minutes. Then remove the assembly from the table saw and scrape off excess glue from the edges of the runners and bottom of the base. You'll also have to clean out any glue that has gotten into the slots on the table saw. Slide the sled back and forth in the slots. If the sled doesn't slide easily, inspect the runners for darkened areas where the metal has rubbed on the wood. Use spray adhesive to attach a piece of 80-grit sandpaper to a square-edged block of wood and sand the darkened areas to remove a little wood (Photo 4). Repeat this process until the sled slides freely.

Glue and screw the stiffener to the front edge of the base, being careful to keep screws away from the path of the table saw blade. Then set the table saw blade to about 3/4 in. high and slide the base into the blade. Stop cutting when you get within 3 in. of the back of the base. Turn off the saw and let it come to a stop before removing the sled. Align the fence with the back edge of the base and drive a screw into the right end. Photo 5 shows how to square the fence to the saw blade and clamp it in place. Screw the blade cover to the back of the fence, being careful to keep the screws well away from the path of the blade.

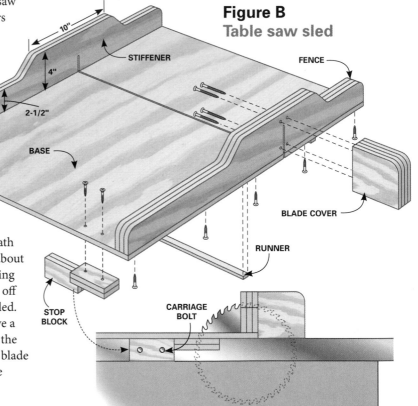

Figure B
Table saw sled

Caution

You must remove the blade guard on your table saw to use the sled. To prevent accidents:

- Adjust the blade so that no more than 1/4 in. is exposed above the board you're sawing.
- Keep your hands well away from the path of the blade.
- After completing a cut, turn off the saw and let the blade come to a complete stop before moving the sled.

Materials list

42" x 42" x 1/2" plywood
3/4" x 2-1/2" x 3'
  hardwood board
Eleven 1-1/2" screws
Four 3" screws
Two 2" carriage bolts and
  nuts (for stop block)
Wood glue

Cutting list

KEY	QTY.	SIZE & DESCRIPTION
A	1	32" x 24" x 1/2" base
B	2	24" x 4" x 1/2" stiffener
C	3	32" x 4" x 1/2" fence
D	4	4" x 4" x 1/2" blade guard
E	4	1-1/2" x 3-1/2" stop block

2 Rest the runners on pennies to elevate the top edge above the surface of the saw. Apply a thin bead of wood glue down the center of the top of the runners.

RUNNER

3 Glue the base to the runner, using the table saw fence to position it. Make sure the edge farthest from the fence overhangs the table saw at least 2 in. Set weights on the base until the glue dries.

BUTT AGAINST FENCE

4 Sand the edges of the runners where they rub on the sides of the miter gauge slots. Dark spots indicate areas that need sanding.

80-GRIT SANDPAPER

OAK RUNNER

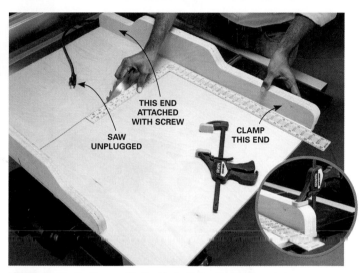

5 Square the fence with the blade. Raise the blade and press a framing square against it. Swivel the fence on a single screw in one end, and clamp the opposite end when the fence is square to the blade.

THIS END ATTACHED WITH SCREW

CLAMP THIS END

SAW UNPLUGGED

Test the cut

With the clamp firmly in place, set a 12-in. or wider scrap of plywood on the sled and cut it in two. Test the accuracy of the sled by flipping one side of the cut scrap over and pushing the freshly cut edge against the other half (Photo 6). If the two pieces fit perfectly with no gap, the sled is cutting squarely and you can drive three additional screws into the fence to hold it in place. Otherwise, tap the clamped end of the fence with a hammer to nudge the fence a bit. Then make another test cut. Repeat this process until the cut is perfect. Then add the screws.

Complete the sled by adding the stop blocks. With the blade half covered by the fence and blade cover, screw a block to the bottom of the sled. Use carriage bolts to attach another stop block to the table saw bed (Photo 7).

6 Check the position of the fence by cutting a scrap of plywood. Flip one side over and butt the two pieces together. A gap means the fence isn't square.

GAP

FLIPPED-OVER CUTOFF

7 Install stops to prevent the blade from cutting through the blade cover.

STOP BLOCK

STOP BLOCK BOLTED TO SAW

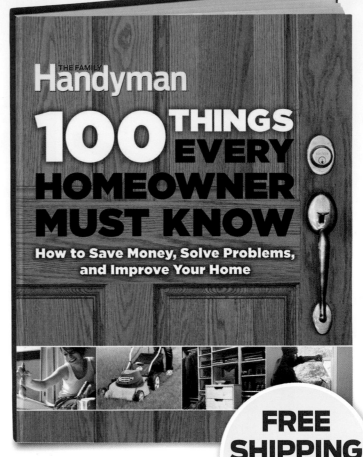